Virtue That Matters

HARVARD EAST ASIAN MONOGRAPH SERIES 477

Virtue That Matters

*Chastity Culture and Social Power
in Chosŏn Korea (1392–1910)*

Jungwon Kim

Published by the Harvard University Asia Center
Distributed by Harvard University Press
Cambridge (Massachusetts) and London 2025

Published by the Harvard University Asia Center, Cambridge, MA 02138

The Harvard University Asia Center publishes a monograph series and, in coordination with the Fairbank Center for Chinese Studies, the Korea Institute, the Reischauer Institute of Japanese Studies, and other facilities and institutes, administers research projects designed to further scholarly understanding of China, Japan, Korea, Vietnam, and other Asian countries. The Center also sponsors projects addressing multidisciplinary, transnational, and regional issues in Asia.

Library of Congress Cataloging-in-Publication Data

Names: Kim, Jungwon, author.
Title: Virtue that matters : chastity culture and social power in Chosŏn Korea
    (1392-1910) / Jungwon Kim.
Other titles: Harvard East Asian monographs ; 477.
Identifiers: LCCN 2024035523 | ISBN 9780674298644 (cloth)
Subjects: LCSH: Sex role—Korea—History. | Chastity. | Sexual ethics for women. |
    Sexual ethics—Korea—History. | Women—Korea—Attitudes. | Koreans—Attitudes. |
    Korea—Social life and customs—1392-1910. | Korea—Civilization--1392-1910.
Classification: LCC HQ1075.5.K6 V57 2025 | DDC 305.3095195—dc23/eng/20240920
LC record available at https://lccn.loc.gov/2024035523

Index by Steven Moore

⊛ Printed on acid-free paper
Printed in the United States of America

In memory of my grandmother,
Cho Magdalene

Contents

Illustrations and Tables

Illustrations

Tables

Acknowledgments

Completing this book took much longer than I ever imagined. Life is full of surprises, and a number of significant, unexpected events and transitions in my life caused the publication of this work to be exceptionally delayed. This journey has resulted in a long ledger of intellectual debts to people and communities alike. I have eagerly awaited this moment, and it is a tremendous relief to finally be able express my sincere gratitude.

From the moment I began to step into the field of premodern Korean history, I have owed so much to many incredible people from whom I learned enormously—whether I encountered them through their scholarly works or met them in person. It was English-language scholarship by senior scholars and pioneers in the study of premodern Korea that, when I was a shy graduate student, first sparked my intellectual curiosity about Chosŏn Korea and eventually led me to pursue an academic career in America. I owe more than I can say to their groundbreaking scholarship and the foundations they laid for future research. To my teachers and mentors, I am eternally grateful. First and foremost, I am indebted to Sun Joo Kim, who not only trained me as a Chosŏn historian but instilled in me the highest scholarly integrity, shaping me into a meticulous researcher and writer. Even during my most challenging times, she has never failed to maintain her firm belief in the value of my scholarship, to offer me timely advice, and to push me forward. It is thanks to her dedicated guidance and encouragement that this book has been finally brought to light, and I hope only to be able to offer my students half of what she has devoted to hers. I am also deeply grateful to Carter Eckert both for his unwavering support and for his challenging seminars, which reoriented me as a historian and critical thinker. My profound thanks go to David McCann and Michael Szonyi for their intellectual generosity and encouragement. I would also like to express my sincere gratitude to Peter Bol for introducing me to the Chinese legal materials that ultimately inspired me to uncover the lives of Korean women concealed within the Chosŏn legal and local archives. The late Irene Bloom taught me to find genuine happiness in writing, and her words have always resonated deeply within my heart.

As the writing of this book accompanied me step by step along my academic path, I received consistent support from many esteemed institutions and individuals. At Columbia, I have been nurtured by brilliant colleagues who have also been incredibly generous. My heartfelt thanks go to Ted Hughes for his tireless support and confidence in my work, to Dorothy Ko for being an endless source of intellectual inspiration, to Haruo Shirane for his invaluable mentorship and wisdom, and to Gray Tuttle for his precious advice and care. I would also like to especially thank Eugenia Lean, Madeleine Zelin, Shang Wei, David Lurie, Robert Hymes, Michael Como, Greg Pflugfelder, Tomi Suzuki, and Paul Anderer for their indispensable and warm guidance. I have been truly fortunate as well to have such a supportive group of junior colleagues, particularly Guo Jue, Ying Qian, Zhaohua Yang, and Seong Uk Kim, who have brightened my life in New York City with their intellectual vigor, laughter, and conversation. I would also like to extend my thanks to Joowon Suh, Hee-sook Shin, and Jooyeon Kim for their assistance and friendship.

During my time at the Institute for Advanced Study at Princeton, I had the privilege of broadening the intellectual horizons of my scholarly path. I learned and benefited immensely from the company of the East Asian Studies Group directed by Nicola Di Cosmo. Having Yonglin Jiang as my neighbor was a great joy, as he patiently answered my numerous questions about the *Great Ming Code* and Chinese legal history. Hyun Ok Park nurtured me intellectually, emotionally, and even in terms of food; her scholarly passion and generosity continue to inspire me beyond words. At the University of Illinois, Urbana-Champaign, I was lucky to be surrounded by exceptional scholars in both the East Asian Languages and Cultures Department and the History Department. I am forever grateful to the late Nancy Abelmann, my dearest colleague and mentor, who was my hero and role model as a scholar and a human being. I miss her every day and still long to hear her cheerful voice calling my name. I will always cherish her memory and hold her wishes in my heart. I am humbly indebted to Ronald Toby for his unfailing guidance and faith in my scholarship. Dana Rabin, Craig Koslofsky, Elizabeth Oyler, Bob Tierney, Brian Ruppert, Adrienne Lo, and Poshek Fu showered me with boundless support and encouragement, and the arrivals of Elizabeth LaCouture, Jason Petrulis, and Erica Vogel made my days in Urbana-Champaign even more delightful.

Throughout various stages of working on this book, I have been enriched by valuable insights, feedback, and support from colleagues and friends. While it is impossible to name everyone in this limited space, I would like to extend special thanks to Donald Baker, Yumi Moon, Hwasook Nam, Hyaeweol Choi, Jisoo Kim, Michael Pettid, Eugene Park, George Kallander, Jennifer Jung-Kim, Sonja Kim, Yuson Jung, Seung-kyung Kim, Ellie Choi, Ksenia Chizhova, Sixiang Wang, Frank Rausch, Andre Schmid, Charles Kim, Jinhee Lee, Joy Kim, Sue Jean Cho, Joe Wicentowski, Yoonjeong Shim, Yeojoo Kim, Ho Kim, Sun-hui Yi, So-hyun Park, Kuen-tae Kim, and Jae-woo Shim. Marion Eggert and Janet Theiss read an earlier draft of the manuscript, and I am extremely grateful for their critical comments, which greatly helped me sharpen my argument when revising and rewriting the manuscript. I also thank Maya Stiller for introducing me to the women's board game that is now included in chapter 2. The diverse perspectives and thoughtful critiques I received from discussants and audiences at various workshops, conferences, and talks were instrumental in refining my ideas and enhancing the overall quality of my work. I thank them all. My appreciation goes as well to Kristen Wanner and Daniel Lee of the Harvard University Asia Center for their careful and professional assistance in preparing the manuscript. I was fortunate to work with Akiko Yamagata, whose keen eye and meticulous editing brought clarity to the final stage of the editing process. I am also grateful to the anonymous readers for their inspiring reviews, encouraging comments, and thoughtful suggestions. To Victoria Scott, who always made time for me in her busy schedule as I polished numerous manuscript drafts, words cannot adequately convey my profound gratitude for her thorough work and patience. Any remaining errors and shortcomings are solely my responsibility.

My special gratitude also goes to institutions and organizations that generously provided research funding for this project: the Northeast Asia Council Research Grant from AAS; the ACLS Collaborative Research Fellowship; the William and Flora Hewlett International Research Fellowship; the Humanities Time Release Award and Scholars' Travel Fund Award from UIUC; the Academy of Korean Studies Grant (AKS-2010-DZZ-2101); the Andrew W. Mellon Fellowship for Assistant Professors at IAS; the Junior Faculty Summer Research Support, Hettleman Junior Faulty Summer Research Grants, Lenfest Junior Faculty Development Grant, and funding from the Weatherhead East Asia Institute at Columbia University. I would also like to thank those archives, libraries, museums, and local cultural heritage departments for kindly granting me photographic permissions.

My family deserves the final, but certainly not the least, mention. My beloved grandmother Cho Magdalene raised me with utmost affection and was the epitome of a strong and intelligent woman, whose teachings and example have been a guiding light in my life. The steadfast prayers of my parents have been my anchor, keeping me grounded and secure throughout this journey, and my remarkable mother has never doubted my intellectual pursuits, consistently embracing me with unlimited support and positive energy. My dear niece Regina was by my side during countless nights of struggle while I worked to finalize the manuscript, and I look forward to many more nights with her in the future. Last, to my husband, Kiwhan. Thank you for believing in me and for your unflagging support through every challenge. Your patience, understanding, and love have been a source of immense strength and have made all difference.

Note to the Reader

This book uses the McCune-Reischauer system for the romanization of Korean, pinyin for Chinese, and the modified Hepburn system for Japanese. Unless otherwise noted, dates are given according to the traditional lunar calendar, and *yun* is added to indicate an extra inter-calary month (year/*yun* month/day). Following the East Asian convention for personal names, family name precedes given name in the text and notes (and no comma is used after East Asian surnames in the bibliography, except in cases of works published in English).

In the biographical genres and legal records cited in this volume, most women are referred to only by a family name because a woman's given name was rarely used in public. An upper-class *yangban* woman was generally referred with *ssi* right after her natal surname, and I translate *ssi* as "Madam" (e.g., Madam Ha). For a non-*yangban* commoner woman, the term *choi*, which is the colloquial reading of *sosa*, was used, and I translate *choi* as "Ms." (e.g., Ms. Kim). However, when a woman's given name was supplied (mostly for a woman who was a slave and sometimes for a commoner woman), I refer to her by her given name (e.g., the commoner widow Yŏngdae in chapter 5). Koreans in the traditional period followed the Chinese system of counting ages (*nyŏn*), which I translate as "years old." A person was considered to already be one year old at birth and turned a year older on the following New Year's Day. Therefore, a person's recorded age could be one or two years older than it would be when counting strictly from the date of his or her birth. Life dates of people, including some women and lower-ranking individuals, are provided whenever available.

In premodern Korean sources, a *ch'aek* 冊 refers to a volume and a *kwŏn* 卷 refers to a chapter, which differs from today's terminology. Therefore, "vol(s)." indicates *ch'aek* numbers in the bibliography. For citations of literary collections in the notes, I provide the title of the specific piece, the title of the original collection, and then *kwŏn*: page number(s) (e.g., Kim Yangnyŏn, "Kim yŏllyŏ chŏn," *Tuam chip*, 5:35a–36b). In the bibliography, I also include the reference for *Han'guk munjip ch'onggan* (*HMC*; Comprehensive Publication of Korean Literary Collections) if the original collection is included in *HMC*. Chinese characters and Korean scripts for author names and titles are provided for the primary sources, but not for the secondary sources.

Citations from the *Veritable Records of the Kings of the Chosŏn Dynasty* (*Chosŏn wangjo sillok*), including references to the *Yŏnsan'gun ilgi* and the *Kwanghaegun ilgi*, are drawn from the National Institute of History (Kuksa p'yŏnch'an wiwŏnhoe) database at http://sillok.history.go.kr/ and take the following form: the title of the specific *sillok* followed by *kwŏn*:page number(s), with the date in square brackets (e.g., *Chungjong sillok* 64:12a [1528/yun10/19]). For *Record of Daily Reflections* (*Ilsŏngnok*) and *Records of the Royal Secretariat* (*Sŭng jŏngwŏn ilgi*), I used the online databases provided by Kyujanggak Institute for Korean Studies (Kyujanggak Han'guhak Yŏn'guwŏn) at https://kyudb.snu.ac.kr/series/main.do?item_cd=ILS and https://kyudb.snu.ac.kr/series/main.do?item_cd=SJW#none, respectively. I cite them as follows: *kwŏn*:page number, followed by date in brackets (e.g., 94:145 [1780/12/23]). For translated sources or reprint original sources, I use the volume number for citations.

Chinese characters for some proper nouns, terms, and phrases appear in the body of the text for clearer understanding. Although Chinese characters for authors' names are provided in the glossary, there are two authors named Yi Chae with different Chinese characters (李縡 and 李栽), which I specify in the text to prevent confusion. Unless otherwise specified, all translations are mine.

Reigns of the Chosŏn Dynasty Kings

T'aejo	太祖	1392-1398
Chŏngjong	定宗	1398-1400
T'aejong	太宗	1400-1418
Sejong	世宗	1418-1450
Munjong	文宗	1450-1452
Tanjong	端宗	1452-1455
Sejo	世祖	1455-1468
Yejong	睿宗	1468-1469
Sŏngjong	成宗	1469-1494
Yŏnsan'gun	燕山君	1494-1506
Chungjong	中宗	1506-1544
Injong	仁宗	1544-1545
Myŏngjong	明宗	1545-1567
Sŏnjo	宣祖	1567-1608
Kwanghaegun	光海君	1608-1623
Injo	仁祖	1623-1649
Hyojong	孝宗	1649-1659
Hyŏnjong	顯宗	1659-1674
Sukchong	肅宗	1674-1720
Kyŏngjong	景宗	1720-1724
Yŏngjo	英祖	1724-1776

Chŏngjo	正祖	1776–1800
Sunjo	純祖	1800–1834
Hŏnjong	憲宗	1834–1849
Ch'ŏlchong	哲宗	1849–1863
Kojong	高宗	1863–1907
Sunjong	純宗	1907–1910

Introduction

A CHASTE WOMAN (*YŎLLYŎ*) CUTS HER FLESH TO FEED
A HUSBAND: AIMS TO CURE HER HUSBAND'S ILLNESS
BY FEEDING HIM HER LEG FLESH.

Chang Chuhwan of Talsŏ-dong, Ch'ilgok-kun, of North
Kyŏngsang Province, has been crippled with palsy since
several years ago. His wife, Ms. Pak, at the age of twenty-
three, always exerted herself to the utmost to heal his
illness, yet was concerned that there was no visible prog-
ress at all. Hearing about the immediate effectiveness of
human flesh to cure the symptoms of palsy, she secretly
entered her room and took out half of her leg flesh, which
was sliced and presented to her husband by deceiving
him that it was *suyuk* [boiled meat slices]. The husband,
perhaps thanks to eating [the flesh], gradually recovered.
Ms. Pak is now hospitalized for treatment at Nasu Hospital
in Taegu.
—*Maeil sinbo* (Daily News), August 23, 1921

This early twentieth-century account of a devoted wife is not unlike
numerous stories celebrated in moral texts and women's biographies throughout the Chosŏn dynasty (1392–1910). Although Korean
society had undergone dramatic political, ideological, and cultural
transformation beginning in the late 1870s, Ms. Pak is still described

as a *yŏllyŏ* (chaste woman) in this 1921 newspaper headline. More-over, the article itself not only fails to recognize the violence of her action but also underscores her wifely virtue in sacrificing her own flesh to save her ill husband. Ms. Pak's action is rather familiar in Confucian terms, exemplifying the notion of unconditional wifely devotion, as richly illustrated in works ranging from Chosŏn moral textbooks to biographies of chaste women. Yet it is nevertheless striking, consider-ing that by the 1920s, Confucian ideals had been severely criticized by new intellectuals who saw the solution of the "woman question" as a crucial link in strengthening Korea.[1] What, then, would be Ms. Pak's real motivation in sacrificing her body for her husband? Was her in-tention solely to follow the "wifely way" that presumably dominated the hearts of Korean women in Chosŏn society, or did she act sponta-neously, out of a deep, natural wish to try anything to rescue her ill husband, even if it meant harming her body?

I start with this early twentieth-century account even though the central focus of this book is the culture of chastity during the long-lasting Chosŏn era. Certainly, female chastity was never a virtue or a practice that was restricted to Chosŏn Korea. Existing sources, both textual and visual, abundantly describe chastity as a subject of ongo-ing debate in the history of Korea, whether under (or even prior to) the Chosŏn state, the Japanese colonial regime, or the contemporary South Korean government, and its lingering historical implications for women in Korean society are undeniable. Yet there is no question that it was during the Chosŏn dynasty that the ideal of chastity was most ardently pronounced, promoted, documented, and visualized. As one of the most fascinating topics addressed in a vast range of writings, women's exemplary actions and heroic deeds fill page after page in the official histories, literati works, and local gazetteers with descrip-tions of how faithfully they displayed the chastity ideal. Even a glimpse into the extensive official and unofficial documents on chaste women produced throughout the dynasty attests to the society's fetishism of

---

1. On this topic, see Theodore Jun Yoo, *Politics of Gender in Colonial Korea*; Hyaeweol Choi, *Gender and Mission Encounters*; and Hyaeweol Choi, *New Women in Colonial Korea*.

female chastity, and almost all the contributors to this immense collection of sources were men—from elites of the central state and scholar-officials to literate men in the remote countryside. Of course, male literati were the ones formally trained in writing, and with access to writing tools, in Chosŏn society. Yet questions still remain: Why were these male members of the society preoccupied with this seemingly "women-exclusive" virtue of chastity, fashioning and refashioning their own interpretations of the chastity discourse? And what does this imply for our understanding of chastity as the dominant culture that was distinctive to Chosŏn Korea in relation to shifting political and historical conditions throughout the dynasty?

Certain notions have long accompanied the image of female chastity in the minds of Koreans—ideas of Confucian principle and its rigidness, of women's repression and victimization, and of violence and backwardness. Any study of chastity in Korean historiography is linked immediately and exclusively to the female body or to women's sexuality. I do not reject all these characterizations, and indeed, this book emphasizes the significance and the evolution of such depictions. Of the three pillars of Confucian doctrine—loyalty, filiality, and chastity—none went through more contentious and subversive negotiations than female chastity within the cultural, intellectual, legal, social, and political realms of Chosŏn Korea. Interestingly, no study has considered men of loyalty as passive inheritors of Confucian ideology, whereas women of chastity have conventionally been portrayed as victims of the same moralization process. Moreover, because numerous chaste women—from elite *yangban* to female slaves and unmarried girls to widowed wives, whether alive or dead—left a profound imprint on Korea's shifting historical realities, the study of chastity cannot be complete without properly reflecting women's own views on and voices about their experiences. In other words, chastity did not remain merely a gender-specific virtue imposed on women and their private lives; rather it evolved as a cultural phenomenon that was a focal point of communication among the state, local communities, individual families, and people on multiple levels of their interactions.

Examining the perception and practice of chastity in Chosŏn society therefore not only offers the broad historical context in which the "culture" of chastity was (re)produced, consumed, and shaped throughout the dynasty but provides a crucial intellectual vantage point from which to observe how the concept of chastity has continued to be understood, contested, and retrieved into modern times. Deliberating on such intertwined relations, this book considers two major facets of chastity culture as an essential part of historical changes in Chosŏn Korea. First, it investigates the official and local process of the institutionalization, inculcation, and familiarization of the chastity ideal in Chosŏn society; and second, it delves into women's participation in—or reaction to—evolving chastity discourse, and the eventual driving force that emerged for women to shape their identities and lives in such ways as they chose. In mapping out the meaning of the chastity ideal and its practice, neither of these two issues should be neglected, nor should they be examined separately because they are equally fundamental to understanding how chastity culture evolved and endured in the multifaceted landscape of Chosŏn Korea. In this book, I take the copious stories of chaste women—in writings by male elites and by women themselves, as well as in records of oral testimonies at local courts—as compelling evidence of how women interacted with the ideals and systems that bound their lives; I contend that the implications of chastity as an extreme cultural phenomenon in Chosŏn society ultimately complicate the very marginality of women's place in forging the history of the period.

Contested Virtue: Chastity, Women, and Troubling Tradition

Despite the growing consciousness of women's changing position in modern Korean society, much of gender relations remains in the shadow of the Confucian legacy that dominated the country during its final dynasty, the Chosŏn, up to the Japanese annexation in 1910. Although what is termed the Confucian transformation of Chosŏn society was uneven and gradual, there is no doubt that the steady penetration of Confucian patriarchy and patrilineality influenced and molded the familial, social, and legal patterns of women's lives—a claim that has also had enormous historiographical implications for the study of modern Korean women's history and life.[2] Any discussion of female chastity during Chosŏn Korea can hardly bypass the pervasive Confucian transformation that Chosŏn legislators embarked upon as early as the late fourteenth century. Although it remains a matter of debate whether the inculcation of Confucian norms reached all levels of society, it is indeed clear that Chosŏn officials deemed the Confucian instructions fundamental for establishing social order. The burgeoning ideal of female chastity, too, reflects the entrenched anxiety of the Chosŏn state and of male elites about the preservation of Confucian principles, which gradually reinforced a strict patriarchal and patrilineal system.[3] If we view Confucianism as a hegemonic power that governed the lives of men and women, it is not surprising that Chosŏn women and female chastity have been examined predominantly within the context of Confucianization's extensive impact on women's position in Chosŏn society.

Moreover, with Chosŏn Korea's internal and external challenges, as well as the influx of new Western ideas at the turn of the twentieth century, the earlier practice of chastity began to be deemed "a socially and culturally constructed device of the patriarchal system to control women's bodies and minds."[4] Often manifested in the bleak performance of women's "chaste suicide," the practice of chastity came to be seen as a troubled, shameful tradition that had become ingrained in Chosŏn society. This perspective—which was upheld by the new group of educated, enlightened intellectuals in the early twentieth century and later continued to occupy the historiography of modern Korea as a dominant narrative—saw the chastity ideal as a powerful apparatus that suppressed a woman's body and soul to fit the patriarchal model of the past. Assuming that male-dominated society did not allow women to foster their own culture, mainstream Korean scholarship has tended to historicize Chosŏn women by highlighting some of their outstanding accomplishments in fields such as literature and

2. The term "Confucian transformation" was coined in Martina Deuchler's influential work *The Confucian Transformation of Korea*, which sees the Confucianization of Chosŏn society as a gradual process through the seventeenth century.

3. Deuchler, "Propagating Female Virtues," 146.

4. Hyaeweol Choi, *New Women in Colonial Korea*, 140.

the arts, since recognizing the small number of talented women whose triumphs could match those of men was more feasible than offering an overview of women's lives in a wider social context.[5]

For the past decade, however, there has been considerable effort by scholars of Korean women and gender across time periods and disciplines to propose a new outlook on the lives of women. A growing number of studies has problematized the conventional view of the history of women and gender relations in Korean historiography, and these works have introduced new questions, source materials, and research methodologies. The field of Chosŏn history, too, has probed the received picture of women's lives in Korean history, which has painted women as submissive under the Confucian patriarchy as a result of its adoption of the discourse of female victimhood—the perspective manifested during the early twentieth-century reform movement. In particular, scholarship in English examining women's status and roles in the Korean past from various angles began in the late 1970s to challenge the oppressive image of women, noting that existing scholarship at the time had completely omitted women from the historiography of Korea.[6] The 1990s saw two masterpieces— Martina Deuchler's *The Confucian Transformation of Korea* and Mark Peterson's *Korean Adoption and Inheritance*—both of which offered a comprehensive historical, ideological, and cultural context for the Confucian transformation of Korean society that ultimately affected the lives of women. Though small in number, a stream of publications with a focus on women's agency has followed, aiming to move away from a uniform or timeless category of "women" or idea

5. For an overview of Korean scholarship on Chosŏn women, see Chŏng Haeŭn, "Chosŏn sidae yŏsŏngsa yŏn'gu," 317–38.

6. Sandra Mattielli's 1977 *Virtues in Conflict* was the first such volume, including studies from disciplines such as anthropology, history, sociology, psychology, and linguistics; this was followed by Laurel Kendall and Mark Peterson's 1983 *Korean Women: View from the Inner Room*. *Virtues in Conflict* includes Deuchler's preliminary research on Chosŏn women, investigated through the tension between Confucian norms and native elements in Korean society, and Mark Peterson's earlier work on adoption and inheritance practice was introduced in *Korean Women*. For an overview of English-language scholarship on Chosŏn women, see Jungwon Kim, "Pungmi esŏ ŭi Chosŏn yŏsŏngsa," 339–56.

of "Confucian tradition."[7] These studies emphasize "the agency of women" in creating women's own lives and in balancing life's conflicting demands, or focus on women's ability to express powerful identity through their literary works. Inspired by such scholarship, other scholars have continued to question whether gender can be an effective category for deliberating either the lives of Chosŏn women or Chosŏn society in general, and have tried to employ the analytical framework of gender to illuminate male-female relations, on both the individual and institutional levels, as gendered relations evolved through various negotiations.[8] Moreover, realizing that textual materials generally touch only on the lives of upper-class women, a few recent studies have tried to present the broader scope of women's lives by employing a variety of sources containing voices from all walks of life.[9] Yet on the subject of chastity alone, exhaustive investigation in English is meager and scattered. The few shorter studies to date either identify chastity culture as an outcome of the elite female population's indoctrination by the state and by Neo-Confucian scholar-officials, or link the later Chosŏn intensification of chastity culture to restoration projects after the Imjin War (1592–1598) and Manchu Invasions (1627 and 1636).[10]

7. Two representative volumes are Ko, Haboush, and Piggott, *Women and Confucian Cultures in Premodern China, Korea, and Japan*, and Kim-Renaud, *Creative Women of Korea*. The most recent edited volume on Chosŏn women proposes this approach: Kim and Pettid, *Women and Confucianism in Chosŏn Korea*. Also, the pioneering role by scholars of Chinese women and gender has critically interrogated the received notion about women's victimization under Confucian patriarchy in late imperial China (contemporaneous with Chosŏn Korea). Outstanding works include Dorothy Ko, *Teachers of the Inner Chambers*; Mann, *Precious Records*; Judge, *Precious Raft of History*; and Bossler, *Gender and Chinese History*. For a review of this scholarship, see Siyen Fei, "Virtue, Talent and Her-Story," 458–67.

8. On the issue of gender as a category of historical analysis, see Scott, *Gender and Politics of History*, 30–31.

9. Especially on the use of legal archives for locating women's voices, see Jungwon Kim, "Finding Korean Women's Voices"; Jungwon Kim, "Deeper than the Death"; Jungwon Kim, "'You Must Avenge'"; Jisoo M. Kim, *Emotions of Justice*; Jisoo M. Kim, "From Jealousy to Violence"; and Jungwon Kim, "Between Morality and Crime."

10. There is no book-length study in English to date on the subject of chastity in Chosŏn Korea. The few important book chapters and articles on the subject include Deuchler, "Propagating Female Virtues," 142–69; Pettid, "Fashioning Womanly

In contrast, scholars in Korea have widely researched female chastity during the Chosŏn dynasty. Acknowledging chastity as a vital value of Chosŏn society, which upheld Confucianism as the state ideology, Korean historical scholarship has presented chastity as a crucial marker of the Confucianization of Korean society. According to this view, female chastity was something that every woman was able to embody, and as a virtue it was linearly developed through social norms exclusive to women. Examining the development of chastity discourse by drawing upon the dynasty's wide-ranging materials, Korean scholarship confirms the two dominant views on female chastity during Chosŏn Korea: (1) chastity as a political mechanism devised to control women's bodies and sexualities, and (2) chastity as the absolute law and moral convention that women had to blindly follow. Illustrating how women's indoctrination into the chastity ideal successfully governed their souls and behaviors, most studies highlight women's internalization of Confucian norms in explaining the overwhelming practice of widow suicide in the late Chosŏn period, depicting women as either sufferers of the dominant Confucian patriarchy or mere compliant adopters of the prescribed female virtues.[11] Although some recent studies examine female suicide from late Chosŏn court cases as having been driven by sexual assaults or insults, their arguments

---

Confucian Virtue," 357–77; and Lee Sook-in, "Imjin War and the Official Discourse," 137–56.

11. Historical examination of female chastity was done by the historian Pak Chu primarily as part of the state-reward system for moral subjects (chŏngnyŏ). Pak's pioneering studies, based on official records as well as numerous local gazetteers mostly from the southern regions, are indispensable for gaining a general picture of the reward system during the Chosŏn dynasty. See Pak Chu, Chosŏn sidae ŭi chŏngp'yo chŏngch'aek; Pak Chu, Chosŏn sidae ŭi hyo wa yŏsŏng; and Pak Chu, Chosŏn sidae ŭi yŏsŏng kwa yugyo munhwa. It was not until 2009 that Kang Myŏnggwan, a scholar of premodern literature, published the first book-length study on the subject of female chastity during the Chosŏn dynasty. Meticulously analyzing copious works by male literati as well as moral handbooks, Kang's subtitle, "A Brutal History of Patriarchy and Chosŏn Women," connotes his approach to this subject. For him, chaste women were victimized products of the state's systematic agenda and mechanisms, such as the publication and control of moral texts. See Kang Myŏnggwan, Yŏllyŏ ŭi t'ansaeng. In 2012, Yi Sugin published a monograph presenting a more nuanced discussion of how female chastity was developed through male intellectuals' anxiety to control women's sexuality. Yi Sugin, Chŏngjŏl ŭi yŏksa.

remain the same, asserting that the women's various reactions to external challenges only support the collective social phenomenon that celebrated women's sacrifice under the banner of chastity and women's reception of it.[12] These studies tend to reflect the gaze of the state and of male scholars, silencing women's subjectivity with respect to whether they internalized the official discourse or confronted it and granting them a marginalized place in the course of historical changes, despite the fact that women's experiences are at the very core of their discussions.[13]

None of the current scholarship adequately presents a fuller and complex picture of chastity as an integral culture of Chosŏn Korea. If the chastity ideal sprang from the loam of the Confucian state, how were the norms valued before the Chosŏn dynasty incorporated them into its new ideological soil? What was the state orthodoxy that legitimated and sustained the ideal of chastity, which persisted for more than five hundred years? If the country's late sixteenth-century war experiences transformed the chastity discourse in the immediate postwar era of the seventeenth century, what were the long-term effects on the practice of chastity in the next two centuries, up to the close of the dynasty? Also, how can we make sense of the escalation of chaste suicide in the eighteenth and nineteenth centuries in light of

12. Kim Hyŏnjin, "*Simnirok* ŭl t'onghae pon 18-segi yŏsŏng," 197–230; Yi Sugin, *Chŏngjŏl ŭi yŏksa*; Paek Okkyŏng, "Chosŏn sidae ŭi yŏsŏng p'ongnyŏk," 93–126.

13. Thanks to the large number of biographies dedicated to virtuous women included in the individual collections of male literati (*munjip*), premodern Korean literature scholars have been at the forefront of the study of female chastity, examining images of virtuous women as depicted by Confucian scholars from multiple angles. Taking the "discourse of chaste women" (*yŏllyŏ tamnon*) as the product of male literati seeking to articulate their own definition of the ideal, these studies argue that the development of chastity was closely related to the Confucian scholars' historical, ideological backgrounds. Presenting the fictive elements of chaste women embedded in oral literature such as songs and tales—the literary genres mostly enjoyed by the non-elite population—they also highlight hidden perceptions about chastity by people of different societal groups, suggesting an alternative window providing a view of chastity culture in a wider social setting. Some representative studies on chaste women by scholars in Korean literature include Im Yugyŏng, "Yi Ok ŭi *Yŏllyŏjŏn*," 397–418; Hong Insuk, "17-segi yŏllyŏjŏn yŏn'gu," 95–117; Han'guk Kojŏn Yŏsŏng Munhakhoe, *Chosŏn sidae yŏllyŏ tamnon*; Chŏng Chaesŏ, *Tongasia yŏsŏng ŭi kiwŏn*; and Hong Insuk, *Yŏllyŏ* 列女 X *Yŏllyŏ* 烈女.

its potential tension with the fundamental Confucian value of filiality? How did Confucian literati reconcile the unfilial act of a chaste woman ending her own life with the core human impulse of filial piety? To what extent was chastity perceived as the ultimate expression of women's emotion and passion, rather than simply as the product of moral indoctrination? How was the official ideal of chastity interwoven with and determined by a woman's sense of identity and her socioeconomic situation?

This book delves into these questions. Building on the claims of existing scholarship, yet departing from the conventional approach to female chastity, I challenge the unidirectional interpretation of the practice of chastity during the Chosŏn dynasty. Rather than confining it to the upshot of Chosŏn society's Confucianization, I contextualize female chastity in diverse historical settings and expand it to encompass the larger cultural functions of the state's moralization (*kyohwa*) vision, sociopolitical agendas, and gender relations. If we see female chastity solely within the ideological logic of Korean society's Confucianization, we cannot observe how its fluid discourse was integrated into people's behaviors and practices in response to the state's changing policies and directions. The ideal of chastity was a cultural code that informed individual behavior, particularly behavior related to women. This book examines the diverse ways the culture of chastity thrived in Chosŏn society as it was absorbed by women and men of different classes, ages, and marital statuses.

Rethinking the Paradigm and Discourse of Chastity

For modern Koreans, the term *yŏllyŏ* immediately evokes the image of a traditional woman who either devotes her life to her husband or kills herself to follow her deceased husband into death. Within this understanding, the foremost concern of a *yŏllyŏ* is her sexual integrity (*sujŏl*) toward her husband—and this was also the most imperative criterion for becoming a *yŏllyŏ* in Chosŏn society. An exact definition of *yŏllyŏ*, however, is not as simple as a modern reader may think. Although I translate *yŏllyŏ* as "a chaste woman" in this book, no single English word or phrase can convey all the compound cultural connotations that the term came to embody over the centuries and in many historical contexts. Even a cursory examination of primary sources reveals a wide array of terms used to indicate women displaying the virtue of chastity. They are called *chŏlbu* (principled wife), *yŏlbu* (chaste wife), and sometimes *chŏngnyŏ* 貞女 (faithful maiden), while *yŏllyŏ* seems to embrace all these women in a broader sense, at least in the Korean context.[14] Since these terms were used interchangeably, there were no clear distinctions for what precisely constituted each category. The sixteenth-century Chosŏn scholar Ŏ Sukkwŏn, for instance, remarked that the absence of a concrete definition for each term perplexed the state's reward-selection process when it had to judge the integrity of a chaste deed for official recognition.[15]

The *History of Koryŏ* (*Koryŏsa*), compiled in the mid-fifteenth century by the early Chosŏn state, includes eight women under the "*yŏllyŏ*" category in its "Biographies" section, most of whom were either killed or killed themselves in the wake of losing their sexual integrity during the wars.[16] The selection of these particular cases

14. In China, too, these same terms were used to categorize virtuous women. According to Chia-Lin Pao Tao's study, a married woman who observed sexual abstinence in widowhood was recognized as a *jiefu* (chaste widow); a *zhennu* (faithful maiden) was a betrothed (not yet wed) young girl remaining a lifelong widow; *lienü* (chaste woman) referred to both an unmarried maiden who had died resisting assault and one who had committed suicide after her fiancé's death; and *liefu* (chaste wife) meant a married woman fitting the same criteria of resistance or sacrifice. Age requirements for these definitions varied in different periods in Chinese history; for example, early in the Ming dynasty (1368–1644), *jiefu* was restricted to women over sixty years of age who had become widows before the age of thirty. See Tao, "Chaste Widows and Institutions," 102. Siyen Fei notes that "the age requirement for chaste widows was not invented in the Ming, but originated in the Yuan dynasty." Fei, "Writing for Justice," 993. On the subject of *zhennu*, see Weijing Lu, *True to Her Word*.

15. Ŏ Sukkwŏn even suggested that the Chosŏn should learn from the Chinese model when it came to articulating these terms. Ŏ Sukkwŏn, *P'aegwan chapki*, 2:468.

16. Kim Pusik's *Historical Records of the Three Kingdoms* (*Samguk sagi*), compiled in 1145, during the Koryŏ period (918–1392), contains some stories of exemplary women in the "Collected Biographies" section labeled "Yŏlchŏn," but this section also includes stories of notable men.

In China, there was a shift from use of the character 列 (a listing, a series) to the character 烈 (chaste, fierce) in referring to collected biographies of (exemplary) women reflects the state's understanding of the foremost female virtue, which was linked directly to a woman's sexual loyalty to her husband. The notion of female chastity was consistently revisited throughout the dynasty, creating an ideal of womanhood that evolved to meet the values of the specific historical moment and event. During the first part of the dynasty, the state normally recognized and rewarded the devotion of a widow who never remarried but committed herself to lifelong service to the lineage of her late husband. In the wake of the devastating wars with Japan and the Manchus from the late sixteenth to early seventeenth century, however, the meaning and practice of chastity changed in a visible way, as women's sexual purity was strictly enforced at a time when it clashed most tragically with social realities such as foreign invasions. Countless men and women met heroic deaths in defending their political, moral, or personal integrity, and postwar Korean society entered an age of commemoration and martyrdom. Loyalty was considered the primary quality required to restore the state's authority and moral vision, and female chastity, as the counterpart of male loyalty, was equally extolled. Women's bodily sacrifice in resisting foreign outsiders and their willingness to die to protect their sexual integrity were praised as identical to men's loyal deaths on the battlefield. As the state publicly commemorated such loyal suicide, the act of killing oneself rapidly became the ultimate expression

---

(going from 列女傳 to 烈女傳). *Categorized Biographies of Women* (*Lienü zhuan* 列女傳) by the Han dynasty (206 BCE–220 CE) scholar Liu Xiang (77 BCE–6 CE), whose authorship is much debated, was the first classified collection of biographies of women, compiled in the first century BCE in China. As the character 列 implies, it listed or categorized life stories of women from these periods but did not confine the biographies exclusively to women of extraordinary sexual virtue. According to Yuet Keung Lo, women categorized under the virtues of the "Rectitude and Compliance" ("Zhen shun") section in the *Categorized Biographies of Women* were not what the early Chinese conceptualized as "chaste women," although they are mistakenly cited by modern scholars as exemplars of Confucian female chastity; see Yuet Keung Lo, "Conversion to Chastity," 24–26. Also, on the issue of Liu's authorship, see Raphals, *Sharing the Light*, 109–12. As the criteria for the official recognition of female virtue increasingly focused on cases of self-sacrificing women from the Ming dynasty (1368–1644) on, the character 烈 became widely adopted to denote woman's fidelity. See Chŏng Chiyŏng, "Yŏllyŏ mandŭlgi ŭi yŏksa," 135–36; Chŏng Chaesŏ, *Tongasia yŏsŏng ŭi kiwŏn*, 29; and Hong Insuk, *Yŏllyŏ* 列女 X *Yŏllyŏ* 烈女, 18–19.

of moral commitment, furthering the late Chosŏn societal obsession with chaste death. The concept of women's fidelity then became enmeshed with the most violent form of its corporeal practice—suicide, which was taken as the definitive vindication and criterion of chaste womanhood. Numerous writings on virtuous women published after the seventeenth century highlight death as the apogee of chastity, both elucidating the consciousness of a woman's absolute commitment to self-sacrifice and painting women as incomparable moral paragons who epitomized familial and community rectitude.[17]

As the value of chastity—an ideal commemorated in exceptional cases—came to be fervently acclaimed by both the state and the literati in late Chosŏn society, only women who fulfilled this moral expectation through excessive bodily performance captured the most glowing public attention. This change is echoed in the eighteenth-century scholar Song Hwangi's (1728–1807) account that "the state no longer acknowledges faithful women in general, but honors only those women who kill themselves to die with their husbands."[18] Song stressed the "narrowed" definition of female chastity by distinguishing chaste women (yŏllyŏ) from principled women (chŏlbu) in the way they "performed and completed" the ideal. Another scholar of the time, Yi Tŏngmu (1741–1793), also drew a clear distinction between a widow who did not remarry (chŏlbu) and a widow who committed suicide of her own free will (yŏlbu).[19] In the meantime, the radical act of destroying the body bequeathed by one's parents had to be justified according to the rhetoric of Confucian morality—according to which "righteousness" was ranked higher than life itself. This point was advocated by Mencius in his famous epigraph—a dictum that officials and scholars quoted more frequently than any other Confucian phrases in the chaste-suicide debates of the late Chosŏn.[20]

17. Yi Hyesun, "Chosŏnjo yŏllyŏjŏn yŏn'gu," 95–152.
18. Song Hwangi, "Yŏlbu Yunssi chŏn," Sŏngdam chip, 30:41b–43b.
19. Yi Tŏngmu, "Sasojŏl," 196.
20. Mencius said, "I like fish, and I also like bear's paws. If I cannot have the two together, I will let the fish go, and take the bear's paws. So, I like life, and I also like righteousness. If I cannot keep the two together, I will let life go, and choose righteousness." Mencius 6A:10.

The term *yŏllyŏ*, or "chaste woman" in an extensive sense, was thus a historically perceived one. Whenever a woman was honored for her virtuous act—whether by being nominated for a reward, being a subject of biographical and eulogistic writings, or having her name engraved on a memorial arch (*chŏngmun*)—the government and Confucian literati had to agree on a certain terminology, or title, that encapsulated her internalization of the chastity ideal. Both a woman's marital status and the type or intensity of her action played an important role in the determination—for instance, she could be titled either a principled or a chaste woman. The reasoning and politics behind the choice of a specific term reveal how the society of that time perceived the meaning and performance of women's chastity, attesting both to a shift of emphasis in the definition of chastity and to the diverging paths women took in fulfilling their moral integrity.

Examining chastity culture therefore requires us to consider the interplay of ideas, actions, and experiences associated with the changing discourse of chastity along the wider socio-cultural-historical spectrum. In Chosŏn society, female chastity was indeed a powerful value; however, it was neither a rigid ideology nor a unilateral agenda implemented by the state. Rather, it was an ideal often used in diverse ways—and formulated by diverse means—in everyday power struggles involving virtually everyone in society.[21] Ideas about chastity were not only the concern of women but affected the multidirectional relationships between men and women, individuals and families, and communities and the state. Although the politics of female chastity naturally involve the notion of sexuality and power, this idea may have been "a dispersed and decentered force that was hard to grasp and possess fully."[22] As I demonstrate, the shape and content of chastity culture constantly shifted to meet the social realities, the interests of various groups, and the negotiations of each historical era, complicating the state orthodoxy, the normative gender structure, and state-society relations. Stories woven by the dense social grid and by individual struggles that culminated in chastity offer an alternative window through which to see Chosŏn society, by moving the actual

21. Brownell and Wasserstrom, "Gender and the Law," 45.
22. Walkowitz, *City of Dreadful Delight*, 8–10.

culture of chastity beyond the politics of chastity—that is, beyond both the conventional view of women's exclusive experiences and the male gaze itself.

The Making of Chosŏn Chastity Culture

Women's sexual integrity was central to gender relations in premodern societies across the world, albeit to variable degrees. In premodern East Asia, it constituted the heart of female virtue, which was one of the core principles of Confucian doctrine. In China, the Song dynasty (960–1279) Neo-Confucian scholar Cheng Yi's (1033–1107) famous admonition that a woman ought to starve to death rather than fail to preserve her chastity encouraged the massive production of records on chastity in succeeding dynasties, with late imperial China witnessing an unprecedented surge in the cult of chastity.[23] In Chosŏn Korea, where Cheng Yi's adage was repeatedly cited and almost worshipped by scholar-officials engaged in chastity debates, the culture of chastity thrived. A similar fascination with female chastity rendered it the most visible cultural phenomenon in Chosŏn's history. The late Chosŏn scholar Pak Chiwŏn's (1737–1805) note on his conversation with two Chinese officials about chastity practice reinforces the fanatical cele-bration of female chastity in both societies.[24] During his trip to Qing

23. Scholars in Chinese history have long examined the cult of chastity. Some of the most representative studies are Elvin, "Female Virtue and the State," 11–52; Mann, "Kinship, Class, and Community Structure," 37–56; Ju-K'ang T'ien, *Male Anxiety and Female Chastity*; Chia-Lin Pao Tao, "Chaste Widows and Institutions," 101–19; Carlitz, "Social Uses of Female Virtue," 117–48; Angela K. Leung, "To Chasten Society," 1–32; Elliott, "Manchu Widows and Ethnicity," 33–71; Sommer, "Uses of Chastity," 77–130; Carlitz, "Shrines, Governing-Class Identity," 612–40; Fangqin Du and Mann, "Competing Claims on Womanly Virtue," 219–50; Theiss, *Disgraceful Matters*; Weijing Lu, *True to Her Word*; and Siyen Fei, "Writing for Justice."

24. A detailed comparison of how the Chinese viewed the Korean (or vice versa) attitude toward chastity is beyond the scope of this book, and it is difficult to locate pertinent sources. A statement by Qing soldiers during the Manchu Invasion of 1636, however, notes Korean women's extreme adherence to chastity. In Wang Xiuchu's well-known 1645 account of the Yangzhou massacre, he recounts, "The [Qing] soldiers said to people, 'When we conquered Korea, we captured tens of thousands of women, and

China (1636–1912) as part of a Korean embassy in 1780, Pak, asked about some of the beautiful aspects of Chosŏn culture, pointed out four things—one of which was "a woman not serving two husbands."[25] He further explained how elite women's upholding of widow chastity even under conditions of extreme poverty or childlessness had inspired the non-elite female populace for the past four hundred years. In response, one of the Chinese officials remarked that the chastity cult in China had become a deep-seated evil practice, to the extent that extreme cases of faithful-maiden suicide persisted.[26] Interestingly, Pak and the two Chinese officials ended their conversation by rather sarcastically citing some episodes of women's radical performance of self-sacrifice, as well as magical incidents that the state had honored as cases of exceptional morality, laughing hollowly at how difficult it was to become a sufficiently virtuous subject nowadays.[27]

Pak's discussion with the two Chinese officials reveals that the practice of chastity had peaked in China and Korea by the eighteenth century and that the two countries certainly shared overarching stories of moral heroines and obsessive praise of the chastity ideal. Despite

---

yet not one of them lost her chastity [because they killed themselves before this could befall them]. How can there be so little shame in a great country like China?' Alas, this is why China is in chaos." Of course, Wang's comment reflects the chaotic situation in China of that time, rather than offering any concrete comparative view on chastity practices between China and Korea. Wang Xiuchu, "Yangzhou shiri ji," 1:5a.

25. The Chosŏn state sent the congratulatory Korean embassy to China for the seventieth birthday of Emperor Qianlong, who was staying at the summer palace in Yŏrha (Ch. Rehe) at that time.

One of the Chinese officials, Wang Minhao, asked Pak Chiwŏn about Chosŏn civil service examination practices and marriage rituals, and Pak replied that Chosŏn followed Zhu Xi's (1130–1200) family rituals for the four ceremonial occasions of coming of age, weddings, funerals, and ancestral rites. Responding to Pak, Wang stated that China did not strictly adhere to the rituals because Zhu Xi's book was incomplete.

26. The Chinese official Wang Minhao also noted that the faithful-maiden cult was even more serious in the southeastern regions of China, despite legislation punishing the parents of faithful maidens. Unlike in China, where the problem of faithful maidens was debated as vigorously as the issue of chaste widows, faithful-maiden cases are scarcely found in Korean historical records or scholarly works and were regarded as indistinguishable from the general category of women's fidelity in Chosŏn society.

27. Pak Chiwŏn, Yŏrha ilgi, 621.

many political and societal differences between late imperial China and Chosŏn Korea, several common institutional factors behind the prevalence of chastity practice—the state-reward system (Kr. *chŏng-nyŏ* 旌閭; Ch. *jingbiao*), tradition of civil service examinations, law and lineage associations, and circulation of local gazetteers—explain the diffusion of the influential language of chastity in both countries.[28] Starting in the fifteenth century, both began to see an escalating passion for the chastity ideal (under the Ming dynasty and the early Chosŏn state), then witnessed a deepening chastity discourse and practice from the mid-seventeenth century on (in the Qing dynasty and in postwar Chosŏn society). In bolstering and disseminating the ideal, in particular, the two societies strove to implement reward programs honoring women of exceptional virtue as an integral part of a moralizing campaign.

Depicting such chastity fanaticism, scholars of late imperial China have used the word "cult" to indicate the social fever of immense admiration for female chastity. The English word "cult" does not have a counterpart in Chinese, as noted by Joan Judge, yet it is used to connote the quasi-religious aspects of the chastity performances that dominated the sexual and gender relations in Chinese society of that time.[29] It is difficult to gauge whether or not the term "cult" is applicable to the level of appreciation of and preoccupation with chastity practice in Chosŏn Korea. Notwithstanding China and Korea's similar pattern of fascination with female chastity, backed by the state's dedication to popularizing the ideal, the shifting sociohistorical impetus that produced a matrix of state agendas and human responses prevented the discourses and actions of chastity in the two countries from taking the exact same path. Though rooted in the very essence of the

28. According to Katherine Carlitz, the long history of civil service examinations generated a tradition of male loyalty to Confucian principles that outlined the various qualities of women's virtuous conduct: "The four [factors of state rewards, civil service exams, gazetteers, and law and lineage associations] are interrelated, with the examination culture perhaps the most pervasive: a system of education and socialization that made examination aspirants throughout the empire far more like one another in their patterns of thought than like anyone outside the system." Carlitz, "Desire, Danger, and the Body," 106.

29. Judge, *Precious Raft of History*, 33–34.

Confucian value, divergent motivations behind the emergence, production, and promotion of the chastity ideal in China and Korea
prompted varying degrees of contestation, negotiation, and popularity
in these contexts. The culture of chastity therefore provides an engaging site for investigating how the very same ideal, embedded in the core
Confucian principles, was integrated into two different societies—
in particular, for investigating the case of Chosŏn Korea examined in
this book.

Late imperial China and Chosŏn Korea each underwent unique
historical experiences: for China, the fall of the Ming dynasty and the
rise of the Qing dynasty under the Manchus; for Chosŏn, traumatic
wars with Japan and the Manchus, followed by the eventual collapse
of Ming China in 1644. These changes led the two countries in different directions vis-à-vis people's perceptions and practice of chastity.
Facing the complication of ethnic differences, the Manchu rulers of
China had to transform the cult of chastity central to Qing political
culture into an instrument of their "civilizing project," in an effort to
legitimize their Confucian rulership.[30] For Chosŏn Korea, in contrast,
the fall of the Ming served as a critical epistemological opportunity
to reconfigure a chastity culture of its own. Korean Confucian scholars
saw the Ming's humiliating defeat as the loss of the center of Confucian civilization to the barbarian Manchus, and hence as a threat to
the very basis of Korean cultural and ideological identity; and they
began to foster the conviction that Chosŏn was now the sole guardian
of Confucian civilization.[31] As much as the Ming–Qing transition had
tremendous impact on the conflation of chastity and loyalty in Chinese
society, the new East Asian world order demanded that the Chosŏn
state seek ways to preserve its political and cultural identity by

---

30. Janet Theiss states that chastity practice during the Ming dynasty remained a
local community phenomenon, and it was indeed not until the reigns of the Qing emperors Yongzheng (r. 1723–1736) and Qianlong (r. 1736–1796) that the state institutionalized veneration of chaste widows and chastity martyrs, which shaped the chastity
cult into an integral component of the "civilizing project" of their Confucian rulership.
Theiss, *Disgraceful Matters*.

31. Chŏng Okcha, *Chosŏn hugi Chosŏn chunghwa*; Haboush and Deuchler, *Culture and the State*, 1–14.

amplifying loyalty—the foremost quality needed to stabilize the society.[32] Injo's (r. 1623–1649) coup in 1623, in which he accused King Kwanghae (r. 1608–1623) of being disloyal, unfilial, and immoral (in his dealings with domestic politics and also in his diplomatic relations between the declining Ming and rising Qing), not only eventually dethroned Kwanghae but deepened the concepts of loyalty and filiality, which then served to acquit the political insurrection and King Injo's government. With unprecedented weight being given to loyalty and filiality, female chastity was equally emphasized. The state praised women's willingness to die to preserve their sexual integrity as equivalent to men's loyal actions on the front lines for the sake of the state.

It was the state-reward system that served as the core of the official production of numerous chaste women following the Chosŏn state's postwar restoration efforts. Although the practice of rewarding moral paragons had existed during the Koryŏ dynasty, early Chosŏn Confucian statecraft mobilized the reward systems as a vital means to effect the state's dynastic moralization mission. One of the most remarkable aspects of Chosŏn chastity culture was its resilience vis-à-vis the reward process. Although Chosŏn society was structured on a deeply hereditary social hierarchy, chastity reward procedures were inclusive both in principle and in actual practice. The system was open from the outset to women of every social class (including that of slaves), age, region, and marital status; there were no laws outlining prerequisites for chastity candidates based on their legal status; and the state did not prescribe specific definitions of a chaste subject or criteria for nominating one, as was done in China.[33] Any woman who, embracing the state's vision of moralizing the populace, displayed outstanding virtue could attain official recognition, and the reward program proved to be the

32. On the topic of Ming loyalism and its popularity beyond the realm of the court and scholar-officials in late Chosŏn society, see Bohnet, "Subversive Ming Loyalist Narratives," 1–29.

33. In China, legal qualifications for chaste women were set and revised by a Board of Rites as early as the Yuan dynasty (1271–1368) and were then further sophisticated by the Qing. They specified, for example, the number of years a woman had preserved fidelity and her social status. Sommer, "Uses of Chastity," 80. Siyen Fei notes that the government set detailed criteria only for the chastity reward, not in other categories such as filiality; Fei, "Writing for Justice," 995.

most critical and visible tool for stabilizing the postwar social order. A 1739 royal order sent down to the local magistrate's office inviting nominees for chastity rewards still stressed that women of exceptional virtue be considered for the nomination, regardless of their "social status (high or low; *kwich'ŏn* 貴賤), age (old or young; *nyŏnse kugŭn* 年歲久近), and aliveness (living or dead; *chonsein hasein* 存世人下世人)."[34] This absence of precise prerequisites for reward eligibility and screening procedures occasionally raised the thorny question of the veracity of recommendations during court discussions (as examined in chapter 2), yet the Chosŏn state continued to sustain a flexible approach to the reward policy throughout the dynasty.

Despite this openness in honoring chaste subjects, however, Chosŏn society sternly operated on the basis of social status when it came to the violation of female chastity. Status distinction was evident in the judicial process for sexual crimes, and the obvious discrepancy in treatment between members of the *yangban* elite class versus the non-*yangban* populace was gradually integrated into the late Chosŏn penal code. In adjudicating crimes against female sexual integrity, the Chosŏn state followed the *Great Ming Code* (Kr. *Taeyŏngnyul*; Ch. *Da Ming lü*), the mother of the Chosŏn penal code. The Ming Code remained instrumental throughout the dynasty, but the increasing complexity posed by the war experiences of the late sixteenth and early seventeenth centuries, as well as subsequent economic and social changes, compelled the state to enact additional statutes to deal with different kinds of challenges. The most conspicuous facet of the newly added statutes in the mid- to late Chosŏn was the reinforcement of elite status. Although the Ming penal code incorporated status distinction and discriminatory punishment pertinent to one's social class, the Chosŏn notion of elites such as the *sajok* (distinguished aristocrat families) was not precisely demarcated in the category of *yangin* (commoners, or good people) under Ming law.[35] With the enactment of

---

34. *Karim poch'o*, 675–76. I used a reprinted copy included in *Han'guk chibangsa charyo ch'ongsŏ*.

35. *Yangin* is translated literally as "good people." The terms *yangin* and *sangmin* (commoners, or ordinary people) were both used to refer to ordinary people (excluding the debased categorized of *ch'ŏnmin*) during the Chosŏn dynasty.

supplementary statutes targeting elite status, the *yangban* gained more privileges at the late Chosŏn court: for instance, the punishment for a non-*yangban* man violating any woman of a *yangban* man (even his concubine or his daughter by a concubine) became far more severe than the punishment for a non-*yangban* man assaulting a non-*yangban* woman. Such enforcements addressed discrepancies in socio-economic-political areas that could not be explicated by the Ming Code, and resulted in a series of edicts complementing existing laws on crimes dealing with female chastity. In reviewing sexual crimes, the late Chosŏn state thus did not indiscriminately adopt the Ming penal code; rather it urged that Chosŏn statutes and edicts be prioritized in cases where they competed with the Ming Code, while also taking into account factors in legal reasoning that ranged from a person's intention to, most critically, his or her class status. The final disposition of the punishment for crimes against female chastity depended not merely on one's gender and sexuality but, more importantly, on the social stratum to which one belonged; indeed, the codification and adjudication of transgressions against chastity signify an integral relationship between gender and social status in Chosŏn society.

Nevertheless, the state's efforts to make legal distinctions based on social status did not simply strengthen the *yangban* elites' rights in the legal sphere but led to higher moral responsibility being expected from members of the elite groups. The reward program acclaimed any exemplary woman, but did so more enthusiastically in the case of a non-elite woman's achievement, since those of lower status were presumed to lack an inherent capacity for moral refinement. These differing socio-ethical expectations according to women's social status meant that elite women shouldered augmented moral obligation: the new supplementary statutes prescribed that a *yangban* woman who lost her sexual integrity receive a harsher sentence than a non-*yangban* woman.[36] Although the added laws protected elite women's sexual integrity more than that of non-elite women, this also implied heavier blame and punishment when an elite woman failed to uphold her chastity.

36. See table 4.2 in chapter 4 for the added statutes on punishing elite women's immoral behavior.

It was within this dual context that the Chosŏn state's initial ethos of moralizing the larger female populace remained both resilient and effective through the end of the dynasty. While designating the moral and legal perimeters of women's chastity in an acutely hierarchical structure, the strikingly flexible and all-embracing reward policy on female chastity—molded in hopes of achieving the state's moral vision—functioned in a complex relationship to social status, making the culture of chastity evolve in a distinct way in Chosŏn Korea.[37]

Tales of Chastity: Sources and an Overview

Because this book seeks not only to offer the historical evolution and the cultural, intellectual, institutional, and legal settings of the shifting chastity discourse but also to retrieve people's perceptions and practice of chastity, it is necessary to engage with a plethora of archival materials containing countless stories of chastity. To explicate the historical contexts in which the discourse of chastity was produced and debated at the state level, I examine a rich array of governmental publications and official records, such as moral handbooks, royal edicts, and legal codes, as well as major histories. The discussion based on these materials is enriched by the numerous accounts of chastity that were drafted at both local and individual levels. Biographies, epitaphs, eulogies, anecdotes in local gazetteers, and miscellaneous stories passed down among people provide multilayered views on the subject of female chastity—and, more significantly, on the collective mode and episteme that enabled that culture of chastity to prevail. Circular letters and joint petitions, composed through the communal efforts of families

---

37. Unlike Chosŏn society, which increasingly emphasized social status in normative prescriptions of female sexuality, Qing society witnessed "a fundamental shift in the organizing principle for the regulation of sexuality: from *status performance*, whereby different status groups had been held to distinct standards of familial and sexual morality, to *gender performance*, in which a uniform standard of sexual morality and criminal liability was extended across old status boundaries and all people were expected to conform to gender roles strictly defined in terms of marriage." Sommer, *Sex, Law, and Society*, 5–12.

and/or communities of Confucian scholars to request official recognition for chaste women, also offer insights into how Chosŏn society accepted and justified the violent actions taken by women who chose death, whether for the sake of virtue or to vindicate their moral integrity. These textual documents are supplemented by visual sources, such as memorial arches, illustrations, and paintings that illuminate a previously unexamined aspect of the state's chastity agenda and its reception in the society. Although the first part of the book uses sources found mostly in traditional archives—documents that may be considered the products of male-dominant perspectives and institutions "inimical to women's interests or agency"[38]—these materials, produced with a specific function and purpose, also "sustain, resist, contest, or seek to transform [social and discursive formations] depending on the individual cases."[39] Chaste-woman biographies written by men, for example, cannot be read solely as typical narratives that stress a chaste widow's self-denial and sacrifice as markers of female virtue. Rather, they should also be linked to Confucian scholars' reconfiguration of political spaces that embodied chaste suicide as their own moral conviction at that particular historical moment.

To recapture perceptions and practices of chastity from people of diverse socioeconomic backgrounds—and especially to include women's voices and experiences—I analyze a number of untapped sources, including women's own writings, such as testaments they wrote before taking their lives, and their own accounts contained in legal cases and trial records. For the latter, in particular, I focus on how the values, priorities, and attitudes of the people in the community where a given trial took place were manifested in the very processes by which trials of crimes or disputes related to women's chastity were conducted as well as in the outcomes of such trials. Careful reading of detailed legal testimonies recorded at the local courts delivers voices of people from all social classes, regardless of their literacy. Unlike legal documents such as petitions, which could be carefully prepared beforehand, often with others' assistance if the protagonist was illiterate, trial

---

38. Chaudhuri, Katz, and Perry, *Contesting Archives*, xiv–xv.
39. Spiegel, *Romancing the Past*, 10.

records provided everyone with an equal opportunity to give oral testimony, whether one was an elite male literatus, a woman, or a non-elite illiterate.[40] Documented in colloquial language, testimonies in the trial records leave the almost audible impression of hearing ordinary people's voices in their interactions with the investigators, whether in narrating the circumstances of the incident in which they were involved or in defending their position. As historians using legal and court records have noted, however, the judicial context in which the documents were produced needs to be scrutinized with due diligence, precisely because legal testimonies "cannot be read transparently" without taking into consideration that they were documented by and possibly also edited by local officials.[41] Nevertheless, trial records are multi-perspective sources that contain the viewpoints both of the legal authorities and of ordinary people at court. As such, these records disclose various cracks within the lives of spouses, families, and communities, not to mention aspects of the normative

40. Although people of all social statuses could use legal channels to voice their grievances in Chosŏn society, women and non-elite illiterates often had to rely on someone with literacy to draft petitions, which had to adhere to strict document formats prescribed by the state. Without deliberating on the nature and background of document production in detail, it may be precarious to assume that everyone was able to prepare his or her own documents and that those documents reflect the authentic voices of the petitioners themselves. On the complexity of legal document preparation and ordinary people's dependence on scribes, see Kim Kyŏngsuk, "Chosŏn hugi sansong," 253–80; Chŏn Kyŏngmok, Komunsŏ, Chosŏn; Jungwon Kim, "Inscribing Grievances," 293–97; and Pak Chunho, "Chosŏn hugi p'yŏngmin yŏsŏng," 427–28.

41. Peirce, Morality Tales, 8–9. For criticism on the "neutrality" of trial records and social hierarchy possibly embedded in transcribing oral testimony into written form, see Clark, History, Theory, Text, 77–79. Natalie Davis's pioneering work based on sixteenth-century letters of remission for crimes shows the importance of distinguishing between fact and fiction in the judicial archives; see Davis, Fiction in the Archives. On the production of written legal records from oral testimony, see Karasawa, "From Oral Testimony," 101–22. In general, it can be challenging to assess the intensity in people's descriptions of sexual assault, domestic violence, and homicide arising out of crimes of passion. Also, since most people who appear in the legal cases got into trouble, trial records are indications of atypical and antisocial behavior. Nevertheless, the participants in these legal cases were ordinary people who had to confront everyday negotiation and conflicts. On the complex nature of the Chosŏn trial records or inquest reports, see Sun Joo Kim and Jungwon Kim, Wrongful Deaths, 6–10.

order and gender relations that have come into conflict through their daily negotiation.[42]

In the numerous legal cases dealing with a range of sexual crimes, we see women, most of whom were socioeconomically marginalized, taking on roles not only as victims but as defendants, litigants, witnesses, and relatives or neighbors. These women turned to strategies of sexual accommodation for survival, utilizing the legal norms and rhetoric of chastity to vindicate their position when they were caught in an unfavorable situation. Analyses of their court testimonies on sexual crimes unveil many responses that belie the possible attribution of any single fixed behavioral mode to the entire female populace. Women told their versions of the contested events at the trial, and for most ordinary illiterate women, it was the only time their words were documented with proper attention. This legal process enabled them to testify to the events in dispute in their own voices, focusing on their part in their own words and describing their extended relationships to people beyond the sphere of their family circles.

Although in this book I interweave stories of chastity as comprehensively as possible, it is almost impossible to avoid a sampling approach for the archival sources, which are extensive but uneven in terms of their availability. Especially in part 2, the majority of the legal cases and detailed testimonies that I analyze come from the second half of the dynasty, concentrated on the eighteenth to mid-nineteenth century. Though I trace the changing laws on and legal implications

42. Theiss, *Disgraceful Matters*, 5–6. Historians have actively used various legal archives to access the stories of people from all walks of life in premodern societies. In Chinese history, Matthew Sommer and Janet Theiss utilize Qing legal archives, providing us with an unprecedented lens through which to see the lower strata of society and changing gender relations. Theiss, *Disgraceful Matters*; Sommer, *Sex, Law, and Society*; Sommer, *Polyandry and Wife-Selling*. In the field of Chosŏn history, a number of scholars have already used legal documents in examining the socio-legal aspects of the society through petitions and litigations: Han Sanggwŏn, *Chosŏn hugi sahoe wa sowŏn chedo*; Cho Yunsŏn, *Chosŏn hugi sosong yŏn'gu*; Kim Kyŏngsuk, "Chosŏn hugi yŏsŏng ŭi chŏngso hwaltong," 89–123; Kim Kyŏngsuk, "Chosŏn hugi kyŏlsongiban," 325–57; Jisoo M. Kim, *Emotions of Justice*; and Kim Sŏnggap, *Sosong kwa punjaeng*. A few recent studies examine trial records (inquest reports), such as Jungwon Kim, "'You Must Avenge'"; Sun Joo Kim and Jungwon Kim, *Wrongful Deaths*; Sim Chaeu, *Kŏman kwa kŭndae hanguk sahoe*; and Ho Kim, *Paengnyŏn chŏn sarin sagŏn*.

of crimes against women's chastity from the early Chosŏn on, one might wonder whether these much later selected cases can truly represent the discourses on and practices of chastity practice over the entire course of the long dynasty. However, it was this later Chosŏn period that saw compilation of important judicial revisions brought about by the state's burgeoning efforts to amend legal codes and publish legal texts, the result of which the majority of legal cases and testimonies extant today are accessible to us. Given that legal transformation never fails to reflect a range of people's attitudes and reactions to existing laws and subsequent modifications, analyzing later cases (often in comparison with those of earlier times) offers significant insights into shifting perceptions about female sexuality and chastity that had been shaped through sociohistorical experiences for centuries.

This book is composed of several interconnected themes and is divided into two parts: "History and Evolution" and "Social Power and Negotiation." The three chapters in part 1 present the formation of chastity culture within the broader historical context of the state and local discourses on its idealization, implementation, and mediation throughout the dynasty. To delineate the evolution of the chastity ideal over several centuries, chapter 1 traces the concept of chastity prior to Confucianism being firmly grounded in Korean soil. In examining earlier accounts, it revisits the conventional notion of the "birth of chastity" that is viewed to have radically taken place with the foundation of the new Chosŏn dynasty.

Chapter 2 investigates the political and social contexts in which the culture of chastity was fostered by the Confucian reformers and discusses why the early Chosŏn state attempted to formalize the chastity ideal. Probing the four aspects of institutionalizing, inscribing, visualizing, and commemorating chastity as a vital part of the state-led moralizing project, chapter 2 shows that the implementation of and discourse on female chastity were neither promulgated unidirectionally by the state nor promoted indiscriminately by scholar-officials. As the chapter details, chastity discourse turned into a most contested site, and continued to generate a wide array of debates and tensions in the political and intellectual spheres and beyond.

Chapter 3 asks how chastity culture came to thrive so vigorously in the second half of the dynasty. War experiences in the late sixteenth and early seventeenth centuries certainly intensified the Chosŏn state's attitude toward Confucian norms as part of the reordering of postwar society, which included active commemoration of virtuous deaths. The traumas of these wars and the collapse of the Ming dynasty also had a profound impact on Chosŏn people's epistemological and emotional mores, as the entire society navigated the postwar turmoil. Reflecting sociocultural alterations, the massive corpus of chastity accounts written from this period did not merely fulfill Confucian literati's duty of instilling moral norms in the minds of the populace; rather, male literati's participation in the drafting, editing, rewriting, and transmitting of chaste-woman stories became an important part of their sense of membership in the scholarly community, forging their collective actions and deepening the culture of chastity at the local level.

Shifting focus from historical and institutional settings to the sites where incidents related to chastity actually unfolded on the judicial level, the three chapters in part 2 look at the diverging choices women made when their sexual integrity was threatened. These chapters are particularly concerned with questions of moral agency and illuminate the friction between dominant values and lived experiences as people navigated the lawful boundaries on sexual crimes. Chapter 4 analyzes legal codes and legal testimonies in cases of sex crimes, divulging the range of attitudes of women trapped in various marital and familial circumstances. Despite the state's moral campaign—which was bolstered by an official reward program both to tighten women's behavior concerning chastity and to standardize virtue in the realm of women's private experiences—both men and women adeptly used female chastity to maintain their power and defend their situations. Closely reading crimes against female chastity, this chapter uncovers rare voices of women facing charges of unchaste acts as they appear in legal testimonies, and shows how women as energetic complainants carved out their position in the legal terrain of the changing discourse on chastity practice.

Chapter 5 brings widow identity and sexuality into reconsideration. Although chastity was expected of every woman in Chosŏn society, widows were subject to the heaviest pressure to enact the abstract ideal in practice. As putative heroines of marital fidelity, widows became female figures of public extolment; in their lived experiences, however, they had to constantly face the specter of being accused of promiscuous rather than virtuous widowhood. Investigating the ways ordinary widows related to normative structures and societal realities, I argue that no matter how much Chosŏn society applauded chaste widowhood as the epitome of morality, it still viewed widows of all social statuses as sexual beings, so that a widow's real position in her family and community was often complicated and contradictory.

Chapter 6 probes the linkage between female chastity and female suicide, as reflected in the distinct but overlapping collective and individual modes of fulfilling the chastity ideal. For the former, I investigate how the shift not only to emphasizing the corporeal manifestation of the chastity ideal but also to excessively honoring chaste suicide endorsed the discursive construction of the gendered notion of suicide in Chosŏn society. For the latter, I focus on the voices of chaste women who killed themselves, as inscribed in sources that range from their own final testaments to the legal testimonies of others. Questioning the genuine intentions behind women's chaste suicides and the significance of their acts of self-inscription at the moment of suicide (aspects that have not been a focus in studies of chastity to date), this chapter delves into the extremely intricate relations between and among Confucian prescriptive codes, women's moral agency, and the great fortitude that a woman resorted to in the act of chaste suicide. In contrast to the impassive, ideal-ridden portrayal of chaste women in male writings— which writers at the turn of the twentieth century criticized as indicative of Chosŏn women's lack of passionate love for their husbands—I show that women's own voices, inscribed prior to taking their lives, often reveal the emotional toll of maintaining the chastity ideal as well as their spousal affection.

Finally, the epilogue takes the issue of women's chastity beyond the Chosŏn context. Because the discourse of chastity, neither monolithic nor static, had long occupied a deeply contested site that constantly complicated power dynamics among the state, the elites, local communities, and men and women throughout the Chosŏn dynasty, an influx of new perspectives on the position of women could not suddenly terminate its long-standing impact on Korean society. Although our view of women after the arrival of the so-called modern era, with the advent of imperialism and colonialism, has been heavily influenced by the construction of the "New Woman" in the early twentieth century, the epilogue reminds us that the issue of women's chastity continued to have an enduring effect on Korean society a century later, at the turn of the millennium.

PART I

HISTORY AND
EVOLUTION

Part I investigates the cultural, historical, political, and local impetuses that critically shaped the formation and evolution of chastity culture in Korean society. The core question it addresses is why and how chastity practice was sustained throughout the long-lasting Chosŏn dynasty, making it the distinct culture of the dynasty, as acclaimed by Confucian literati. Delving into this question requires placing the discourse of chastity within broader historical contexts and engaging with multiple institutions and factors. Part I therefore begins by examining the virtue of chastity engrained in Korean society prior to the arrival of Neo-Confucian ideology and rituals, and reconsiders how radical the birth of chastity in Chosŏn society was.

As the chapters in part I demonstrate, the culture of chastity during the long Chosŏn dynasty was continuously molded by shifting political climates, intellectual debates, and socio-legal changes at both the central and local levels. Although the chastity ideal was appreciated as a pillar of Confucian morality prior to the Chosŏn era, there is no doubt that it was the establishment of the Chosŏn dynasty that marked a turning point in the attitude toward female chastity. The culture of chastity was also affected by external circumstances such as the war experiences with Japan and China in the late sixteenth and early seventeenth centuries. Constantly engaging with changing political and intellectual debates throughout the dynasty, the discourse of chastity was neither monolithic nor static but emerged to occupy a most contested site in Chosŏn society. Exploring the historical development of chastity discourse also reveals it to have been the core orthodoxy that the Chosŏn state never failed to cherish. There were continuing problems, of course, both in disseminating the chastity ideal and in honoring chaste subjects as the state initially envisioned while navigating the persistent chasm generated by people's normative virtue, social realities, and lived experiences. Chastity culture nevertheless remained the moral foundation of the dynasty and upheld the state's resilient stance toward these problems, which in turn supported the culture of chastity to the end of the dynasty.

CHAPTER ONE

Chastity Culture before the Confucian State

Being unfortunate, I lost my wife early.
Concerned about my young children being unhappy,
I did not remarry and have been widowed for twenty-
  one years.
Relieved that my sons and daughters are all married
  now,
I write a poem for myself:
"Facing motherless children,
I endured more than twenty years of poverty and knew
  my place.
With a thousand books stacked in [my] library,
I did not mind not having a penny in my pocket.
Though aged,
I never had a plan for a new [married] life,
only thinking of the conjugal tie [with my late wife].
With all my children married now,
I have no regrets and can die at peace."
　　　　　　　　　—Wŏn Ch'ŏnsŏk‡

‡ The epigraph is from Wŏn Ch'ŏnsŏk, *Un'gok haengnok*, 3:2b–3a.

Wŏn Ch'ŏnsŏk (1330–?), a scholar who lived through the last phase of the Koryŏ dynasty and the foundation of the new Chosŏn state, left the note and poem above in his biographical record.[1] Whereas many of Wŏn's pieces epitomize his loyalty to the Koryŏ dynasty, this particular piece, dedicated to Wŏn himself, divulges a devotion quite rare in male literary works. Though widowed, Wŏn decided not to remarry; in the poem, he celebrates his accomplishment of raising his children by himself and seeing them all successfully wed. The path he chose after his wife's death is the same one expected in later periods exclusively of widows, as a critical way to fulfill virtuous womanhood.

Wŏn's case—of a husband remaining faithful to his deceased wife—may have been atypical even during the Koryŏ dynasty.[2] How, then, was the chastity ideal perceived, and perhaps practiced, by people before the Chosŏn—a time of escalating numbers of women extolled for their dramatic and bodily performances of that ideal? Studies on chastity prior to the Chosŏn (and on women in general) are very few.[3] With materials fragmented even during the Koryŏ, it is hard to construct any cohesive or authoritative narrative, especially on women's experiences. Drawing from the scant number of records related to marriage practice, the existing scholarship assumes that chastity was neither a veritable norm nor a prevailing practice that penetrated the lives of Koryŏ people.[4] Such works hold that the idea of chaste women

1. Known as a loyal scholar-writer of the Koryŏ, Wŏn Ch'ŏnsŏk spent his last years on Mount Ch'iak in Kangwŏn Province, refusing to serve the new Chosŏn state after it replaced the Koryŏ dynasty.

2. Records of Wŏn Ch'ŏnsŏk remaining a widower are also found in other sources, including the *History of Koryŏ*, which comments that Wŏn's reason for following such a path was his pursuit of a Buddhist life. Kim Yunsŏp, "Koryŏ malgi yuga sadaebu chisigindŭl," 201–7.

3. Kwŏn Sunhyŏng is one of the few historians who has devoted extensive research to the topic of faithful women prior to the Chosŏn. See Kwŏn Sunhyŏng, "Koryŏ sidae ŭi sujŏl ŭisik kwa yŏllyŏ," 53–92; "Koryŏ mal yŏllyŏ sarye yŏn'gu," 29–62; and "Koryŏ sidae chŏlbu e taehan koch'al," 167–91.

4. For general studies on Koryŏ women, see Kwŏn Sunhyŏng, *Koryŏ ŭi honinje wa yŏsŏng ŭi sam*; Kim Ch'anghyŏn, *Koryŏ ŭi yŏsŏng kwa munhwa*; Hŏ Hŭngsik, "Koryŏ yŏsŏng ŭi chiwi wa yŏkhal," 64–83; and Yi Chŏngnan, "Koryŏ sidae honin hyŏngt'ae e taehan chaegŏmt'o," 5–26. On remarriage, see Pak Ŭngyŏng, "Koryŏ sidae

emerged with the arrival of Neo-Confucianism toward the end of the Koryŏ dynasty and that systematic dissemination of the chastity ideal occurred only after the establishment of the Chosŏn state, which issued volumes of legislation detailing the governing of gender relations based on Confucian principles and rituals.

Moreover, scholarship on chastity during the Chosŏn dynasty tends not to include a discussion of the earlier practice of chastity, instead starting with and focusing on the various ideological, textual, or legal devices that the early to mid-Chosŏn state carefully imposed, bringing the birth of chaste women to Korean history.[5] It is true that the legal sanctions for adultery and the social view of womanly virtues found in early histories of Korea do not mean that a woman's lifelong fidelity to one man—her deceased husband (or husband-to-be)—was formalized.[6] However, questions still remain. How radical was the birth of chaste women witnessed in Korean society in the beginning of the fifteenth century under the newly established Chosŏn state? Was chaste womanhood really a phenomenon that suddenly sprang to prominence out of previous obscurity?

To understand the rise of chastity discourse along the trajectory of larger historical changes, this chapter looks into the earlier records on female virtue in an attempt to revisit our fragmentary and perhaps overgeneralized view of the lives of women, and of women's relations to men, before the Chosŏn dynasty. Although the earliest records depicting women's lives before the Koryŏ dynasty all come from historical texts compiled during the Koryŏ, these texts, as examined below, vary in how they depict their protagonists and deliver moral messages. As I elucidate, the essence of the chastity ideal embedded in female virtue had already been valued in Korean society, and it was during the Koryŏ dynasty that the institutionalization of honoring wifely fidelity began. This was done primarily through an official

_____

chaega e taehan kŏmt'o," 111–39. On adultery, see Kim Ch'anghyŏn, "Koryŏ sidae kant'ong kwa kŭ sŏnggyŏk," 77–124. On English scholarship dealing with Koryŏ women and marriage, see Deuchler, *Confucian Transformation of Korea*, 29–88.

5. See Kang Myŏnggwan, *Yŏllyŏ ŭi t'ansaeng*.

6. Chinese histories record punishments for adultery in Old Chosŏn society and the ancient state of Puyŏ (second century BCE–494 CE). See the entry on Puyŏ (Ch. Fuyu) in Chen Shou, *Weishu*, 30:6b–8a

reward system for moral subjects and the regulation of elite women's sexual behavior—two pivotal projects inherited and continued by the Chosŏn government in later times.

Accounts of Virtuous Women: Early Times

Apart from some sporadic anecdotes from the Three Kingdoms period (fourth century to 676), textual evidence explaining the actual practice of female chastity before the Koryŏ dynasty is not easy to locate.[7] Most existing sources on exemplary women during the Three Kingdoms period come from the Koryŏ era; but some are found in didactic texts published during the Chosŏn, which also included and partially reorganized previously known sources. Although these added accounts are few in number and may have been written far later than the previously known sources, they do provide an adequate general picture.

The two sources best known as the earliest surviving records of pre-Koryŏ histories, myths, and various accounts are the *Historical Records of the Three Kingdoms* (*Samguk sagi*) and the *Memorabilia of the Three Kingdoms* (*Samguk yusa*). The compilation of the *Historical Records* was led by the Confucian scholar-official Kim Pusik (1075–1151) in 1145 on the order of King Injong (r. 1122–1146), based on chronological sequence.[8] The *Memorabilia*, compiled by the monk Iryŏn (1206–1289), is a collection of stories passed down in oral or written form and serves as an unofficial compilation of diverse narratives about monks and other people who piqued Iryŏn's interest.[9] Naturally, both works reflect their compilers' views throughout, mirroring

7. The existence of early women in Korean historiography is quite meager, with a slim list of studies, such as Yi Hyŏngu, "*Samguk sagi* yŏlchŏn," 97–127.

8. Although Kim Pusik was the chief compiler of the *Historical Records of the Three Kingdoms*, a group of fourteen or so scholars participated in the process. For a succinct introduction to the *Historical Records*, see Breuker, Koh, and Lewis, "Tradition of Historical Writing," 123–25. For a detailed study of Kim Pusik's work, see Breuker, *Establishing a Pluralist Society*, 322–49.

9. On the *Memorabilia of the Three Kingdoms*, see Baker, "Writing History in Premodern Korea," 125–31; McBride, "Is the *Samguk yusa* Reliable?," 163–89; and McBride, "Preserving the Lore," 1–38.

the contemporary ideals of their times. However, the fact that the stories collected in the two records had already persisted over the centuries, whether in written form because of their prominence or as oral transmissions because of their popularity, means that they disclose values that the earlier societies shared and appreciated.

The best-recognized and most-cited archetypal accounts of virtuous women in these collections are the stories of the Sŏl woman ("Sŏlssinyŏ") and of Tomi's wife ("Tomi"). Both are included in Kim Pusik's *Historical Records of the Three Kingdoms*, the oldest extant history of Korea.[10] Following the format of the Chinese historian Sima Qian's *Records of the Grand Historian (Shiji)*, Kim compiled accounts of notable people from the Three Kingdoms period in the "Biographies" ("Yŏlchŏn") section of his history, introducing these two female figures representing fidelity.[11] In contrast, the theme of womanly virtue is almost absent in Iryŏn's *Memorabilia*, even though the work does contain five stories about women in the "Filiality and Goodness" ("Hyosŏn") section, which recounts exceptional filial actions by both men and women.[12]

Contemporary scholars consider the accounts of the Sŏl woman and Tomi's wife the earliest examples of women's marital fidelity in Korean historiography.[13] Interestingly, the Sŏl woman's story begins with her filial devotion rather than with any notion of chaste womanhood. Concerned that her aging father is about to be conscripted, she decides to marry a man who is willing to fulfill her father's military obligation for three years. When her fiancé's return from the frontier is delayed for another three years, her father, worrying that his daughter is getting older, arranges a wedding with another man. The Sŏl woman refuses her father's wish that she marry, saying, "How can breaking faith

10. Kim Pusik, *Samguk sagi*, 1:705–7. In addition to these two accounts of female figures, the "Biographies" section of the *Historical Records* includes a story of the filial daughter Chiŭn ("Hyonyŏ Chiŭn").

11. Consisting of ten volumes, the "Biographies" section lists about sixty-nine figures from the Three Kingdoms period, devoting three of the ten volumes to the prominent Silla general Kim Yusin (595–673) and his offspring.

12. For example, stories of a filial daughter serving her mother and of a man cutting flesh from his leg to feed his father are recorded in this section of the *Memorabilia*.

13. Kwŏn Sunhyŏng, *Koryŏ ŭi honinje wa yŏsŏng ŭi sam*, 259–60.

and failing to keep one's word be a person's [sincere] heart (*injŏng*)?"[14] The story ends with her fiancé returning safely and marrying her after six years of extended waiting.

The story of the Sŏl woman and her faithful pledge to her fiancé reveals a conflict between its two central ideals—filiality and fidelity. The Sŏl woman decides to marry the man who saves her father from military service out of filial piety toward her father, but later declines to follow her father's order to wed another man so as to keep her promise to her husband-to-be. By going against her father's will, she emerges as a protagonist asserting her own choice—to accept the prolonged wait for her fiancé. But how far can we read her decision to wait as due solely to her determination to uphold the ideal of fidelity, when it might also spring from her feeling of gratitude toward her fiancé and/or from her personal commitment to keeping her word?

The account of Tomi's wife, in contrast, seems to have been read exclusively as the story of a wife's chaste devotion to her husband. This wife, endowed with beauty and upright conduct, is lured by the king of the Paekche state (18 BCE–660 CE), yet she rejects him by deception. Outraged, the king blinds her husband, Tomi, and banishes him, sending him away by boat. Her husband gone, Tomi's wife still resists the king, fleeing on a boat miraculously sent from heaven, and is eventually reunited with her husband. Reaching the mountainous land of the Koguryŏ state (37 BCE–668 CE), the couple live out their lives in poverty, with sympathetic Koguryŏ people helping them survive.[15]

When this story is read as a didactic text selected by the "Confucian" scholar Kim Pusik for his compilation, as has been conventionally postulated, the obvious message is how adamant Tomi's wife is in resisting the king's seduction, which later scholars present as the

14. Kim Pusik, *Samguk sagi*, 1:705–6. Here, I translate *injŏng* 人情 as "a person's [sincere] heart." The word *chŏng* 情, though often interpreted as "emotion," "feeling," or "affection," is challenging to convey accurately in English, and it is also translated as "compassion," "sympathy," "benevolence," etc. But in the context of the account of the Sŏl woman, I read it more as her sincerity stemming from her grateful feeling (heart) toward her fiancé, who has sacrificed himself for the sake of her father.

15. Kim Pusik, *Samguk sagi*, 1:707.

epitome of a faithful wife preserving her chastity.[16] Yet the story reveals more than her unconditional fidelity to her husband. Confident that he will succeed in enticing Tomi's wife, the king boasts to him: "In general, a wife's chastity (chŏnggyŏl) is regarded as the highest womanly virtue. But when [a woman] staying alone in a dark place is tempted with sweet words, there is hardly anyone whose heart will remain unshaken!" In responding to the king, Tomi nonetheless shows his faith in the marital bond, saying: "Although it is hard to fathom someone's heart (chŏng 情), my wife is not a person who will betray me, even at the risk of death."[17]

Despite numerous trials and agonies, Tomi and his wife maintain their marital trust and are reunited, just as Tomi believed they would be. Their life in exile may be a materially destitute one, yet it evokes the Neo-Confucian scholar Cheng Yi's dictum "To starve to death is a minor thing; to lose one's chastity is a great thing."[18] But is the story concerned wholly with the chastity that was imposed upon a woman? Although it is true that Tomi's wife steadfastly resists the king, it is Tomi's confident response to the king's boast that leads the infuriated monarch to order that Tomi be painfully blinded. The story's overall message does not simply valorize a wife's unconditional fidelity, as is the case in Cheng Yi's words. As the combination of Tomi's reaction to the king and his wife's unwavering commitment to Tomi illustrate, the virtue manifested in the story is accomplished only by the couple's reciprocal conjugal loyalty—that is, by the mutual faith between husband and wife, rather than by a wife's unidirectional devotion—and this may well be the message Kim Pusik hoped to deliver.[19]

16. See Breuker's criticism of modern scholarship that tends to group Koryŏ literati as Confucian, Buddhist, or Daoist, and to portray Kim Pusik as a thoroughly steadfast Confucian statesman. Breuker, *Establishing a Pluralist Society*, 267–72, 336–37.

17. Kim Pusik, *Samguk sagi*, 1:707.

18. Cheng Hao, *Er Cheng yishu*, 22B:5a. The English translation is from Ropp, "Passionate Women," 3.

19. Pointing out that "the narrative is usually referred to as 'The Biography of Tomi,' despite the wife's more prominent role," Lee Hai-soon notes that the title itself may complicate Kim Pusik's intention of having one primary protagonist—whether Tomi or his wife—in the story. In the "Biographies" section of *Historical Records*, the Sŏl woman and the filial daughter Chiŭn are only two females identified by their

In addition to the accounts of the Sŏl woman and Tomi's wife, *Historical Records* briefly introduces a wife's extraordinary revenge in a biography of her husband, Sŏk Uro. Sŏk was a general of the Silla state (57 BCE–935 CE) whose blunt words outraged envoys from the Wae (J. Wa) kingdom and who was eventually put to death by burning. Many years later, Sŏk's wife, having harbored her resentment, avenged her husband's death through the use of fire. At the end of the account, Kim opines that "she settled old scores, but [what she did] was an anomaly (*pyŏn* 變), not [taking] a right (*chŏng* 正) [path],"[20] thus recognizing her revenge yet criticizing the method she employed. In light of this commentary, it seems doubtful that Kim viewed her act as part of her wifely duty, for he does not praise her determination or the like. No further note tells us how the society at that time viewed Sŏk's wife's vengeful killing on her husband's behalf—whether it was treated as a commendable act or whether she was subject to punishment for the crime of reckless killing.[21]

Iryŏn's *Memorabilia of the Three Kingdoms* does not present an account of a virtuous woman, but it does mention the wife of a man whom the Silla king had sent to the Wae kingdom to rescue a prince. After faithfully waiting for her husband's return, the grieving wife took her own life on a hill gazing toward the Wae kingdom, and her body eventually turned to stone. Noting the later existence of a shrine to her on the hill, where people worshipped her as a godmother, Iryŏn does not celebrate the wife's fidelity per se but places the anecdote in the section devoted to "Unfamiliar Stories" ("Kii").[22] Interestingly, Kim Pusik's *Historical Records of the Three Kingdoms* includes the same story. Kim applauds the husband's formidable loyalty to the Silla king but does not mention the wife's long, futile wait for her husband's

---

own name (either family name or given name). See Lee Hai-soon, "Representation of Females," 81.

20. Kim Pusik, *Samguk sagi*, 1:664–65.

21. The issue of forgiving a wife's revenge of her husband's death occupied the Chosŏn court, becoming a subject of contentious debates over the boundary between fidelity and criminality. See Jungwon Kim, "Between Morality and Crime," 481–502.

22. Iryŏn, *Samguk yusa*, 205–9.

return; instead, his account ends with the husband's beheading after the Wae discover his rescue of the Silla prince.[23]

Kim Pusik and Iryŏn were the compilers rather than the authors of these accounts, and we cannot know to what extent they adapted them to fit either their own ideals or the Koryŏ ethos as they collected and selected stories circulating and available at the time. Nonetheless, along with reflecting Kim's ideas about Koryŏ politics and the social order, *Historical Records* may indeed echo various morals of his time. For example, the reciprocal conjugal loyalty of husband and wife seen in both the account of the Sŏl woman and the account of Tomi's wife was similarly acknowledged in Koryŏ society—as testified to in part by Koryŏ's reward system honoring righteous husbands (*ŭibu*), dis cussed in detail later in this chapter. Although it is difficult to accept these two stories as representing the whole picture of chastity practice before the Koryŏ dynasty, the fact that they had already survived for several centuries and been passed down to later generations does reveal the values that people cherished in early times. Most importantly, the debut of these two female protagonists in Korea's earliest extant official history resulted in the Sŏl woman and Tomi's wife being presented as early moral icons of female virtue in subsequent didactic texts for hundreds of years to come.

Principled Wives and Righteous Husbands: The Koryŏ Period

In the historiography of Korea, women under the Koryŏ dynasty are considered to have enjoyed a better position in society than women of the Chosŏn dynasty. What we know about Koryŏ women is, nevertheless, based on limited and fragmentary materials that reflect only a very small segment of the population. For example, the *History of Koryŏ*, one of the few major documents accessible for examining Koryŏ society, mentions women of royal or aristocratic families yet

23. The husband's last name is presented differently in the two compilations: whereas Iryŏn refers him as "Kim Chesang," Kim gives it as "Pak Chesang." Kim Pusik, *Samguk sagi*, 1:665–68.

rarely touches on the ordinary populace, including women. Despite this lack of materials, scholarly endeavor has thrown light on the lives of Koryŏ women from multiple angles and especially on the practice of marriage.[24]

Although the Koryŏ state tried to emulate the institutional features of the Tang dynasty (618–907 CE) by incorporating basic Confucian values, scholars agree that marriage remained rather "a loose institution, not restrained by a multitude of rules and regulations."[25] In Koryŏ society, uxorilocal marriage prevailed, and for a number of years after the wedding ceremony, a newly wed couple usually lived in the bride's natal home, raising their children there. The arrangement of uxorilocal marriage was often based on the bride's favorable economic status and was not linked to the need for an heir in a family without sons. Because it could benefit both bridegroom and bride, it was the preferred marriage pattern in Koryŏ society. There is also general consensus that Koryŏ women held equal status in inheritance and ancestor rites within the family. A wife's property devolved to her husband's family only through her children; if she was childless, it was returned to her natal family after her death or divorce. Since a woman could retain economic rights in her natal family even after she married, her position in the family remained relatively high. Sometimes her strong financial position made it possible for her to leave an unsatisfactory husband without risking destitution.

The privileges enjoyed by married women under the uxorilocal system extended into widowhood. Records show that some Koryŏ kings accepted remarried women as queens (even a woman with children from her previous marriage).[26] A representative case is that of Lady Hŏ, a royal consort of King Ch'ungsŏn (r. 1298, 1308–1313), who was a widow with three sons and four daughters when she married the king. While the arrangement may well have helped consolidate

24. See note 4 above for representative studies on Koryŏ women and marriage practice.

25. Deuchler, *Confucian Transformation of Korea*, 71.

26. The *Koryŏsa* records that the consorts of Sŏngjong, Ch'ungyŏl, Ch'ungsŏn, and Ch'ungsuk were remarried women: *Koryŏsa* 89:16b–17a, 89:11b–12a, 89:12a–13a, 110:3a–6b. See Kim Yongsŏn, *Yŏkchu Koryŏ myojimyŏng chipsŏng*, 736–41, 813–17.

his rule, it nevertheless shows that remarriage was not viewed as a flaw even in the case of royal unions.

Further evidence also indicates that a widow entering a new marriage was not an unfamiliar figure in Koryŏ society. An epitaph (Kr. *myojimyŏng*; Ch. *muzhiming*) dedicated to the high official Kim Yŏngbu (1097–1172) notes his eldest daughter's remarriage after her husband's death.[27] The fact that such information was included in a high official's epitaph hints at the society's open attitude toward widow remarriage. Not only could a widow choose to remain unmarried, but she was not stigmatized as an undesirable marriage partner, especially if she owned a great deal of property or had access to political power through her natal family. In another epitaph, written for the scholar official An Po (1302–1357), his wife Madam Ch'oe appears to have remarried after An's death. Instead of criticizing or hiding this fact, the epitaph's author explains that Madam Ch'oe was not able to maintain her fidelity to An because she had borne no child with him on whom she could rely for her remaining life as a widow.[28] The widowed mother of Yi Sŭngjang (1137–1191), in contrast, appears to have remarried after her husband's death primarily to be better able to raise her son. It seems that Yi's stepfather did not want to either send him to school or hire a tutor to teach him, using the excuse of the family's financial situation. His mother, however, asserted that she had remarried "for the sake of [securing] food and clothing. Now that a posthumous child has grown up and aspires to learning, we should let him follow in his father's [scholarly] footsteps. If not, how can I look upon my former husband's face after death?"[29] Yi was eventually able to attend a school, where his scholarship thrived. That his mother chose to remarry for the sake of her son from her first marriage shows that

27. Kim Yongsŏn, *Yŏkchu Koryŏ myojimyŏng chipsŏng*, 339–42. Adding 17 pieces to his earlier version, Kim Yongsŏn compiled about 325 epitaphs from the Koryŏ dynasty, of which 47 are dedicated to women.

28. The author of An Po's epitaph laments that no epitaph had been written for twenty-two years, mainly because An had no descendants. The author is known as the late Koryŏ scholar Yi Chehyŏn (1287–1367). Interestingly, Yi died ten years after An, so it is questionable why Yi stated "twenty-two years" in An's epitaph. Kim Yongsŏn, *Yŏkchu Koryŏ myojimyŏng chipsŏng*, 1052–58.

29. Kim Yongsŏn, *Yŏkchu Koryŏ myojimyŏng chipsŏng*, 425.

remarriage was not a shameful event but an option a widow could select, even though her children would no longer belong to her dead husband's family upon entering her second husband's household. The fact that the epitaph also states that "Yi's mother fulfilled her former husband's wish" by educating Yi indicates that after a widow remarried, it was not viewed negatively for her children by her first husband to continue to emulate their deceased father. It is therefore not surprising to find some family genealogies of the early Chosŏn recording the names of a woman's former and present husbands at the same time, a practice inherited from the Koryŏ.[30]

Buddhism, the most popular religion practiced by the royal house and aristocrats of Koryŏ, was another impetus for women's relatively liberated status in that society. An abundant number of epitaphs attest to how Buddhist customs were integral to everyday life and were more familiar to people than Confucian rites. As stated in an epitaph for a woman named Madam Yang (ca. 1156), who supported construction of a temple and publication of five thousand copies of Buddhist sutras, women were not restricted from visiting temples and played a central role both in financially assisting monasteries and in arranging family rituals through temples.[31] Madam Chŏng's epitaph (ca. 1210) also mentions that she offered consistent economic support to repair buildings, publish sutras, and provide labor to monasteries.[32] Most extant epitaphs dedicated to women list their active involvement in various Buddhist programs and festivals—including the two largest state Buddhist festivals, the Lantern Festival (Yŏndŭnghoe) and the Assembly of the Eight Prohibitions (P'algwanhoe)—as major donors and participants. Since such public gatherings were open to people of every class, somewhat easy contact between men and women was expected and allowed.

Although we may be able to make only precarious generalizations about Koryŏ marriage and inheritance practices, which unconditionally elevated women's position higher than in the Chosŏn dynasty,

30. Hŏ Hŭngsik, "Koryŏ yŏsŏng ŭi chiwi wa yŏkhal," 79–80.

31. Madam Yang herself died in a temple located north of the Koryŏ capital (Kaesŏng). Kim Yongsŏn, *Yŏkchu Koryŏ myojimyŏng chipsŏng*, 240–41.

32. Kim Yongsŏn, *Yŏkchu Koryŏ myojimyŏng chipsŏng*, 464–65.

regardless of individual circumstances, the Koryŏ's uxorilocal marriage system and favorable socioreligious environment do seem to have reinforced women's overall position. Koryŏ women, whom Martina Deuchler characterizes as "pre-Confucian," were hardly confined to the Confucian notion of serving one husband—the gist of chastity discourse.[33] They had multiple options when widowed because the society never completely absorbed patrilineal influence or moved to the strict patrilineal stage prescribed by the Neo-Confucian family rituals.[34]

From Principled Wives to Chaste Women

This does not mean that the ideal of a wife's fidelity was entirely neglected in Koryŏ society. Although the majority of Koryŏ women were given choices about remarriage, those who remained widows, especially for a long period, were noted and appreciated, as illustrated in their epitaphs. Madam Kim's epitaph (ca. 1149) praises her remaining faithful to her husband for thirty years after his death, as does the epitaph for Madam Yi (ca. 1350), who kept her widowhood for forty years.[35] Widows of high-ranking civil and military officials in particular were ennobled if they stayed loyal to their husband's families.[36] In addition, despite the fact that most sources on Koryŏ women, including epitaphs, center on upper-class women and that it is challenging to gauge general perceptions of the chastity ideal among the ordinary populace, the History of Koryŏ affirms that the Koryŏ state began to implement the state-reward system (chŏngp'yo), which officially recognized exemplary people with various types of awards.[37]

33. "Once entering a marriage, there should be no change until death. Therefore, [a woman] cannot marry even if her husband dies." Liji, 730.

34. Deuchler, Confucian Transformation of Korea, 82.

35. Kim Yongsŏn, Yŏkchu Koryŏ myojimyŏng chipsŏng, 149–50, 949–51.

36. Deuchler, Confucian Transformation of Korea, 277; Koryŏsa 75:34a.

37. Weijing Lu states that the state-reward system was "one of the central Confucian concepts of governance with benevolence and edification, and the practice dated back to the Chinese Han dynasty." According to Lu, it was during the Southern Song period (1127–1279) in China that the court conferred the imperial reward (jingbiao)

The first record in which the state recognizes principled wives dates to 989, the ninth year of the reign of King Sŏngjong (r. 981–997), when a bright comet (later known as Halley's Comet) appeared in the sky. Taking this event to be a sign of his own lack of virtue, the king rewarded principled wives, along with filial sons, as a way to display his benevolent kingship.[38] In 990, the king, honoring teachings from the Confucian classics, dispatched officials to the six provinces to look for virtuous individuals—filial children, obedient grandchildren, principled wives, and righteous husbands—as a way to promote Confucian moral values. Two women were recognized because they "became widows early but did not remarry, for the sake of taking care of their parents-in-law and raising children."[39] A memorial arch was built in their towns, and the state exempted the awardees' families from the corvée labor service and also offered other rewards in the form of rice, silver dishes, or cloth.

The reward practice continued throughout the Koryŏ dynasty until the last ruler, King Kongyang (r. 1389–1392), although it seems to have not been settled as an established system, as reflected in the late Koryŏ scholar Yi Kok's (1298–1351) writing:

Having traveled to China earlier, I saw many memorial arches in honor of [women's] chastity (chŏngjŏl), constructed even facing each other in towns. I thought such huge numbers to be strange at first. [But] later I learned that some families tried to avoid tax obligations by falsely citing chastity, and the [Chinese] government had officials always check the truth [of chaste acts before the reward was given]. [I believe erecting memorial arches] was done out of a good intention, strengthening human morality and rectifying the custom.[40]

---

on virtuous women and faithful maidens; see Lu, *True to Her Word*, 27. See also Ebrey, *The Inner Quarters*, 194–98.

38. *Koryŏsa* 47:17a–18b.

39. *Koryŏsa* 3:19a. Because the list of awardees includes one filial daughter, I translate *hyoja* 孝子 as "filial children" here.

40. Yi Kok, "Chŏlbu Chossi chŏn," *Kajŏng chip*, 1:8b–10a.

Yi Kok's observation is part of his biography of a principled wife, Madam Cho, who endured a long widowhood after her husband's death. Yi laments that the Koryŏ government, unlike the Chinese, did not recognize Madam Cho's virtue, which would thus be forgotten in the end. Whether Yi's statement mirrored the reality of Koryŏ reward practice or whether he simply wanted to alert people to Madam Cho's case is uncertain. But sources reveal that more than half the awards recorded were bestowed prior to the 1170 Military Revolt during King Ŭijong's reign (r. 1146–1170) and that the early rewards were mostly in the form of material goods, except in 990, when memorial arches were also offered.[41] Recognition of exemplary people, including faithful wives, was generally an expression of moral kingship and took place during events such as the king's enthronement or in response to a natural disaster or a state crisis. Rather than dispensing prized goods to individual awardees, kings sometimes invited those who had been recommended by their peers to the palace for banquets. The number of awardees each time is assumed to have been few. Seating at the banquets and receipt of royal gifts were based on the honoree's official title (or, in the case of a principled wife, on that of her husband or son), age, and hometown.[42] No concrete source gives us full information about the levels of prizes or standards of selection, since the *History of Koryŏ* does not record detailed stories of each person recognized for his or her virtue, except in a few cases. It only states, "[The king ordered] distribution of grain to filial sons and grandsons, righteous husbands, and principled wives based on their level of virtuous conduct."[43]

What, then, were the criteria for being a principled woman during the Koryŏ dynasty? Throughout the *History of Koryŏ*, it is the term "principled wives" that is used to refer to women of virtue in general. In a broader sense, a principled wife, or *chŏlbu*, could be a wife displaying either fidelity to her living husband or other aspects of virtue, such

41. Kwŏn Sunhyŏng, "Koryŏ sidae ŭi sujŏl ŭisik kwa yŏllyŏ," 178.
42. *Koryŏsa* 65:12b–29b. The Koryŏ court differentiated the seating and the kinds of gifts for awardees from the Western capital (Sŏgyŏng). This policy must have been affected by the rebellion in 1135 by Myoch'ŏng, who insisted on moving the capital to the Western capital.
43. *Koryŏsa* 4:1a–2a.

as filial piety to her husband's parents. As the reward cases in 990 indicate, however, those principled wives officially designated by the state were "widows who eschewed remarriage."[44] In addition, as early as 1108, the law clearly outlines that a married woman displaying promiscuous conduct would have her name entered in the *Register of Licentious Women* (*Chanyŏ an*).[45] A woman who committed adultery was also punished regardless of her marriage status.[46] The law further stipulated that a wife who left her husband or remarried recklessly was subject to punishment.[47] This indicates that widows who maintained faithfulness (and who also remained alive) generally met the conditions for principled wives, and that certain strictures were imposed on the sexual behavior of upper-class women in Koryŏ society.

It is only in the "Biographies" section of the *History of Koryŏ* that the terms "chaste women" and "chaste wives" appear. The history includes twelve cases of chaste women, along with cases of good officials, loyal and righteous subjects, and people distinguished for filiality and brotherly affection.[48] Under the category of chaste women, the preface introduces a definition as follows:

In the past, when a baby girl was born, she was taught by a nanny. After growing up, a female teacher (*tongsa*) instructed her.[49] Therefore, she became a wise daughter (*hyŏnnyŏ*) before wedding, a wise mother (*hyŏnmo*) when married, and a chaste wife upon encountering calamity. [Unfortunately,] disciplining women in later times did not reach the inner quarters. Oh, how difficult it would be for one to truly excel and keep integrity by laying down one's life under the blade of a knife in the midst of war! [This is why we] write biographies of chaste women.

44. *Koryŏsa* 3:17a–b.
45. *Koryŏsa* 84:41b.
46. *Koryŏsa* 84:38a–b.
47. *Koryŏsa* 84:42b–43a.
48. Although there are twelve entries, the total number of chaste women is fourteen because one case deals with three daughters jumping to their deaths in a river to avoid Japanese raiders in 1377.
49. *Tongsa* (Ch. *tongshi*) is an official title given to a court lady who takes care of matters in the palace.

By specifying that a married woman becomes a chaste wife "upon encountering calamity," the preface emphasizes political turmoil or war as circumstances when a wife's morality is tested and a chaste woman is produced. Indeed, of the twelve chaste women included in the *History of Koryŏ*, ten died during rebellions or the military conflicts with Mongol and Wae raiders, while the other two perished trying to save their husbands from fire or from being taken by a tiger.[50] Moreover, nine of these women lived during the last decades of the Koryŏ dynasty, under King Kongmin (r. 1351–1374) and King U (r. 1374–1388)—the reigns during which Koryŏ was plagued by the Red Turbans and Wae pirates.[51] Echoing the definition of chaste women provided in the preface, the twelve cases are closely linked to the notion of corporal sacrifice as an ultimate manifestation of wifely fidelity, reflecting perspectives of the early Chosŏn Confucian milieu in which the *History of Koryŏ* was actually compiled.

In its last phase, the Koryŏ dynasty faced a series of external threats as well as persistent political volatility inside the government; and the emphasis on female chastity developed together with a focus on political loyalty for men in the moral discourse. In praising an elite woman's choice of suicide to avoid Wae raiders in 1380, the late Koryŏ scholar Yi Sungin (1347–1392) bemoans the fact that "people always talk about the duties of subjects, children, and wives that are to be fulfilled, but there is hardly anyone performing [such duties] in the face of crisis. Madam Pae, as a mere wife taking her life, scolded Wae raiders without fear of death, exhibiting virtue higher than that of any loyal subjects in the past."[52] This sense of moral crisis invoked by dynastic crisis provided an important historical context in which the shifting rhetoric about female virtue—from principledness (*chŏl* 節) to chastity (*yŏl* 烈)—was gradually taking place at the dawn of the Chosŏn dynasty's formal establishment.

---

50. *Koryŏsa* 121:22b–27b.

51. The Red Turbans, a rebellion that occurred during the late Yuan dynasty (1271–1368) in China, attacked Koryŏ twice in 1359 and 1361 under King Kongmin. Wae pirates raided the coastlines of Korea from the thirteenth century, and King U's reign saw the most rampant raiding activities.

52. Yi Sungin, "Pae yŏlbu chŏn," *Toŭn chip*, 5:3a–4b. Madam Pae's story is also recorded in *Koryŏsa* 121:24b–25a.

Ŭibu: Righteous Husbands

Ch'oe Yunŭi (1102–1162), a high scholar and a descendant of the
prominent Confucian scholar Ch'oe Ch'ung (984–1068), left an epitaph for his deceased wife Madam Kim (ca. 1152). Whereas most
epitaphs for women were composed by other family members or by
an outside writer, Ch'oe is one of the three Koryŏ husbands we know
of who wrote his wife's epitaph himself.[53] Remembering the exact date
of their wedding, Ch'oe laments:

> Alas, I know it is natural logic that one is born, then dies. But your
> leaving me behind and perishing all of a sudden, after having been faith-
> fully at my side all these years, is truly distressing. Your sons are only
> seven to eight years old, and your daughters have not yet wed. Comfort-
> ing your soul and recollecting the past, my heart is torn. Holding a brush
> to briefly record your life, I cannot continue because of tears streaming
> down. Oh, there are paradise and heaven in Buddha's words; there are
> the Six Places and Three Pure Ones according to [the Daoist] hermits.
> Indeed, if there is a predestined bond in the afterlife, why cannot we
> promise [each other] the future? How sad! I close here.[54]

About ten years later, Ch'oe died. In the interim, he did not remarry
but raised five children successfully and saw four of them married.[55]
Following in the footsteps of his father Ch'oe Yong (ca. 1119), he became a renowned scholar-official serving many key roles at the Koryŏ
court, including that of selecting officials through the civil service
examination.[56] In his epitaph for his wife, however, Ch'oe appears

---

53. The two other extant Koryŏ epitaphs written by husbands for their wives are
those for Yŏm Kyŏngae by her husband Ch'oe Nubaek, and for Madam Ch'oe by her
husband Pak Chŏnji (ca. 1316). Kim Yongsŏn, *Yŏkchu Koryŏ myojimyŏng chipsŏng*,
134–37, 710–12.

54. Kim Yongsŏn, *Yŏkchu Koryŏ myojimyŏng chipsŏng*, 187. The Six Places 六洞
refers to the realm where Daoist immortals live, and the Three Pure Ones 三清 are
regarded as the highest Dao, or path, in Daoism.

55. Ch'oe Yunŭi's epitaph was composed by a scholar named Kim Ubŏn, at Ch'oe's
son-in-law's request. Kim Yongsŏn, *Yŏkchu Koryŏ myojimyŏng chipsŏng*, 313.

56. Kim Yongsŏn, *Yŏkchu Koryŏ myojimyŏng chipsŏng*, 311; *Koryŏsa*
95:8b–9a.

simply as a husband overwhelmed by deep grief at his wife's death, seeking comfort from Buddhist and Daoist teachings. Ch'oe's epitaph echoes the poem in the epigraph to this chapter, composed by the later scholar Wŏn Ch'ŏnsŏk, who also did not remarry after his wife's death. Just as widowed women had several choices of how to live out their lives in Koryŏ society, so Ch'oe's and Wŏn's cases raise the questions of what it meant for Koryŏ men to remain faithful to their deceased wives and how the society viewed their commitment to spousal fidelity.

Certainly, there was no legal stipulation directly regulating a husband's sexual integrity. In 1272, however, the state prohibited a husband's remarriage under certain circumstances. This provision was proposed when many officials not only remarried after their wives were captured by enemy troops during the 1270 rebellion, but then declined to accept the freed wives upon their return.[57] In the same year, the court ruled that a husband who abandoned his wife for no reason or without consulting his parents be suspended from his official position.[58] Given that women's fidelity was regarded highly, these legal clauses on men's remarriage denote the state's emphasis on mutual faith and marital responsibility at a time when divorce was practiced rather lightly in Koryŏ society, as also observed by the Chinese envoy Xu Jing (1091–1153) in his *Illustrated Account of Koryŏ* (*Gaoli* tujing).[59]

It may have been in this context that the Koryŏ state honored righteous husbands. Normally translated as "righteousness," the character 義 (*ŭi*) signifies one of the four core Confucian virtues, along with loyalty, filiality, and chastity, and is interlocked with the notion of faithfulness. From the very first rewards announcement in 989, the

---

57. *Koryŏsa* 84:41b–42a. Though not specified, this seems to refer to the Rebellion of the Three Elite Patrols in 1270—the year the Koryŏ court decided to end further resistance to the Mongols, thus disbanding the Patrols, which opposed the court's decision.

58. *Koryŏsa* 84:42a.

59. Xu Jing visited the Koryŏ capital in 1123. His *Illustrated Account of Koryŏ* provides a rare glimpse into Koryŏ people and social institutions. See Deuchler, *Confucian Transformation of Korea*, 31. For an English translation of Xu Jing's entire work, see Vermeersch, *Chinese Traveler in Medieval Korea*.

Koryŏ state created a category of "righteous husbands," along with those for other moral paragons such as filial children and faithful wives. Existing Koryŏ texts are silent about exactly which men were honored under this category and what their specific righteous actions were. The category of righteous husbands nevertheless remained in the active list of reward groups throughout the dynasty, resonating with the ideal of conjugal loyalty as evoked in the early tale of Tomi and his wife from Kim Pusik's *Historical Records*. A husband's faithfulness to his wife, as in the cases of Ch'oe Yunŭi and Wŏn Ch'ŏnsŏk, must have been valued, and the husband's honoring of his marriage would have served as an important defining criterion of his moral character in Koryŏ society.

The righteous husbands category continued to appear even after the establishment of the Chosŏn dynasty. The first royal edict by the dynastic founder, King T'aejo (r. 1392–1398), in 1392 stressed promotion of moral exemplars, as the Koryŏ kings had done.[60] During the first half of the dynasty, the state carried out a search for righteous husbands, along with other virtuous figures in local areas, although no concrete case is recorded. When several hundred names were recommended for rewards in response to the king's order in 1420, the government selected only forty-one people with "outstanding moral behavior," and the awardee list included not a single case of a righteous husband.[61] We cannot tell whether there were no nominees in the category or whether none met the "outstanding" standard set by the state. From the sixteenth century on, the term "righteous husbands" appears in the *Chosŏn wangjo sillok* (Veritable Records of the Kings of the Choson Dynasty; hereafter *Sillok*) only on two occasions—both during King Chungjong's reign (1506–1544), when it is used to refer to the Koryŏ practice. In the first case, the court official Sim Chŏng (1471–1531) proposed hosting a banquet for those filial sons, obedient grandchildren, righteous husbands, and principled wives who had followed the Koryŏ exemplars in their respective categories.[62] King Chungjong accepted Sim's idea, but the next day an officer of the Royal

60. *T'aejo sillok* 1:43a [1392/7/28].
61. *Sejong sillok* 7:10a–12a [1420/1/21].
62. *Chungjong sillok* 17:4a [1512/10/8].

Secretariat (Sŭngjŏngwŏn) opposed it as improper, declaring that it was Koryŏ's practice, not that of Chosŏn, to host such an event inside the palace.[63] When the term reappears in the *Sillok* in the early seventeenth century, its meaning has shifted, referring to "righteous men" in general rather than "husbands."[64]

The righteous husband category completely disappeared in the second part of the Chosŏn dynasty. It is premature to conclude that the existence of this category within the state-reward practice endorsed the ideal of marital fidelity for wives and husbands equally in Koryŏ (and even early Chosŏn) society. Nonetheless, the righteous husbands category attests to an important facet of the appreciation of conjugal values prior to the Chosŏn, as well as to a fluid notion of gendered behavior in pre-Chosŏn gender relations.

* * *

Koryŏ society applauded exceptional individuals who had lived up to its moral codes of conduct. However, Koryŏ examples of honoring principled wives do not suggest that Confucian values became dominant, governing the lives of Koryŏ people. In fact, as studies have shown, Buddhism and persisting native traditions continued to pose challenges for the Koryŏ state in adopting Confucian institutions and moral propriety.[65] Even women celebrated as principled wives in their epitaphs are still depicted as ardent devotees of Buddhism, and some widows chose to become Buddhist nuns instead of entering into a second marriage.[66] Such divergent forms of widowhood in turn reveal the multiple options that Koryŏ women had compared to women who were widowed in the following dynasty.[67] For Yi Sŭngjang's mother,

---

63. *Chungjong sillok* 17:4a [1512/10/9].

64. *Kwanghaegun ilgi* 42:53a [1617/11/24]. The last time righteous husbands are mentioned is in the Qing emperor's rescript to King Injo in 1645, as part of seventy clauses that should be promoted by the Chosŏn state. *Injo sillok* 46:4b [1645/2/18].

65. Duncan, *Origins of the Chosŏn Dynasty*; Joohang Cha, "Civilizing Project in Medieval Korea."

66. Kim Yongsŏn, *Yŏkchu Koryŏ myojimyŏng chipsŏng*, 736–41.

67. For example, Pak Ŭngyŏng argues that, when used in epitaphs, Confucian terms describing female virtue such as "fidelity" and "chastity" cannot be taken to

as we have seen, remarriage served a way to support her son's education and future career, even though her epitaph reveals that she was
aware of her choice "tainting the [spirit of the *Shijing* poem entitled]
'Cypress Boat' (Kr. 'Paekchu'; Ch. 'Baizhou')"—the classic symbol of
a woman's resolution to remain chaste.[68] Some Koryŏ widows vowed
fidelity to their deceased husbands under various circumstances and
with different motivations; many others selected remarriage, which
was not viewed undesirably, either.

Nevertheless, the idea of female virtue persisted as a moral value
to be applauded throughout the Koryŏ period. By the end of the dynasty, we see more widows who refused to remarry and relocated to
their husband's family. Although they had lived with their natal parents after the wedding according to the uxorilocal system, they decided
to leave their natal homes and join their late husband's household
when their parents pushed them to enter a second marriage.[69] As much
as Koryŏ women enjoyed a higher position thanks to socio-marriage
institutions and religious activities, the practice of wifely fidelity presents a complex picture of how women chose their courses of action,

---

indicate that women lived by these ideals because the authors of epitaphs were scholars
of Confucianism who probably preferred to use its rhetoric. Also, she contends that
those terms cannot necessarily be interpreted as Confucian because they were used not
only for widows but for wives with living husbands and also for unmarried women.
However, what she claims exactly fits the Confucian notion of the Three Followings
(*samjong*) to which a woman should adhere by following the orders of her father before
marriage, those of her husband after marriage, and those of her son when widowed.
Indeed, such a binary approach to determining whether Koryŏ women lived by Confucian norms or completely according to Buddhist practices may fail to capture a
complex picture of Koryŏ society, which operated within a matrix of Buddhism, Confucianism, and other native belief systems. Pak Ŭngyŏng, "Koryŏ sidae chaega e taehan
kŏmt'o," 132–35. On the pluralist orientation of Koryŏ society, see Vermeersch, *Power
of the Buddhas*; Breuker, *Establishing a Pluralist Society*.

68. "Cypress Boat," included in the "Yongfeng" 鄘風 section of the *Book of Poetry*
(*Shijing*), portrays a widow's loyal heart toward her dead husband and her refusal to
remarry. Another poem with the same title is found in the "Beifeng" 邶風 section, although this poem is about a wife retaining love for her husband who mistreats and
abandons her. In this epitaph, Yi Sŭngjang's mother refers to the poem in the "Yongfeng" section.

69. Yi Chae 李縡, "Yŏlbu Yissi chŏn," *Toamjip*, 25:12a–14a; Kim Chip, "Sŏnjobi
chŭng chŏnggyŏng puin Yangch'ŏn Hŏssi myogal," *Sindokchae yugo*, 8:1a–2b.

whether by adopting a form of moral propriety or fashioning one in their own ways.

The last years of the Koryŏ dynasty witnessed a growing concern with female sexuality in the face of political instability and external threats, and emphasis on female chastity increased in tandem with emphasis on male political loyalty. In response, the court legislated that the wife of a lower official was not allowed to remarry within three years of her husband's death; to do so was considered a loss of sexual integrity and was subject to punishment. Wives and concubines of higher officials who maintained fidelity after being widowed were to be honored with memorial arches and other prizes.[70] Given that these regulations were established through a proposal of the Privy Council (Todang) in 1389, only three years before the founding the Chosŏn dynasty, the extent to which they were put into effect in Koryŏ society may have been meager. Yet the legislation did not merely signify the Koryŏ court's temporary effort. Especially in the eyes of late Koryŏ Confucian reformers—who sought immediate reform of degraded Koryŏ customs and political immorality—female chastity, in parallel with male loyalty, became a critical political weapon, pushing forward a path to the more rigid Confucian definition of chastity that was to emerge in the new Chosŏn society. In sum, the chastity ideal championed during Chosŏn Korea cannot be understood separately from the practices and institutions inherited from Koryŏ society.[71] It was the Koryŏ dynasty that set the stage for the full formation of Chosŏn chastity culture, by enabling the new Confucian government to further deviate from the practices of its predecessor.

70. *Koryŏsa* 84:42b–43a.

71. This argument echoes John Duncan's influential study on the institutional continuity during the dynastic transition from Koryŏ to Chosŏn. Duncan, *Origins of the Chosŏn Dynasty*. For a new interpretation of the fourteenth-century dynastic change that revisits the conventional assumptions about the anti-Buddhist movement, see Juhn Y. Ahn, *Buddhas and Ancestors*.

CHAPTER TWO

Formalization of the Chastity Ideal

Alas, the fact that wives of the Eastern Country [of Korea]
are faithful, upright, and do not act obscene is thanks to
the teachings of the Eight Regulations (*p'alcho*). Coming
into this [Chosŏn dynasty] court, [the society] became
even more civilized, to the point that almost every household is invested with governmental recognition [for proper
decorum]. In addition, the law barring descendants of
remarried women from taking official positions became
strict, edifying [people] and [legally] prohibiting [remar-
riage practice] at the same time. In the late Koryŏ, this was
not the case, however. It was taken for granted that a
widow would remarry after a husband's death. In the old
[family] genealogies [of Koryŏ], therefore, [the widow's]
new husband's name was recorded when entering [the
names of a widow's] children, and this was not [even] considered shameless!
    —Yi Chae 李縡 (1680–1746)‡

In his biography of the Koryŏ dynasty "chaste woman" Madam
Yi, the late Chosŏn scholar Yi Chae denounces the Koryŏ custom
of remarriage. Madam Yi was pregnant when her husband, the scholar

‡ The epigraph is from Yi Chae, "Yŏlbu Yissi chŏn," *Toam chip*, 25:12a–14a. The Eight
Regulations refer to the laws believed to have been practiced during the Old Chosŏn
Kingdom (?–108 BCE). Of the eight regulations, only the three recorded in the *History
of the Han* (*Hanshu*) are known. Ban Gu, *Hanshu*, 1658.

Yang Susaeng (?–1377), died, yet her parents consistently pushed her to enter a second marriage. She therefore left her parents' home and moved to Namwŏn, where her in-law family's house was located. There she gave a birth to a son, the future scholar-official Yang Sabo (1377–?), whose descendants prospered and continued the Yang family line. For Yi Chae, Madam Yi's refusal to remarry was a remarkable act that preserved her chastity amid the disordered conditions of late Koryŏ society.[1] Although the virtue of fidelity had long been expected of wives of the Korean peninsula (or Eastern Country), as noted by Yi, his portrayal of Madam Yi's devotion as a rarity in Koryŏ times implies that the pervasive chastity culture of Chosŏn society was indeed a departure from the earlier customs. Yi's writing is hardly authoritative in offering a general picture of Koryŏ marriage practice (see chapter 3 for the context in which Yi wrote this particular biography), but reading it does leave the impression that the reforms carried out by the Chosŏn state, based on Confucian principles, had rectified both the remarriage practice and the morally "deprived" view of women's sexual integrity that had prevailed in Koryŏ society.

Compared with the rather fragmented references to precedents found in Koryŏ historical records, the Chosŏn dynasty boasts abundant textual and material evidence of chastity practice. The scope of Chosŏn chastity culture is unmatched in Korean history, for it dominated people's lives, from the most private realm of the women's quarters to the more open realm of public discourse. To remedy the seeming moral erosion in late Koryŏ society, the Chosŏn government embarked on significant steps of reformation, paving the way for the virtue of chastity to flourish. Yet chastity culture did not grow in isolation and cannot be understood as the product of any hegemonic historical or political force. Over the course of some five hundred years, the discourse of chastity closely reflected shifting expectations posed by special conditions during the dynasty. It corresponded to the early Chosŏn state's moral agenda in the fifteenth century, followed by the tumultuous wars in the late fifteenth and early sixteenth centuries, which in turn generated the society's obsession with extraordinary acts of virtue as well as a commemorative space for moral heroism in postwar

---

1. Yi Chae, "Yŏlbu Yissi chŏn," *Toam chip*, 25:12a–14a.

Korean society. The culture of chastity therefore cannot be generalized as a monolithic discourse, and its evolution speaks to each historical juncture of the Chosŏn dynasty. Not only the rhetoric of morally disordered late Koryŏ society but also the perceived moral deprivation of that earlier time (as implied in Yi Chae's statements about Koryŏ society) helped sustain the discourse and practice of chastity throughout the dynasty. Yet implementation of the chastity ideal was neither promulgated unidirectionally by the state nor promoted indiscriminately by scholar-officials. As I show in this chapter, chastity discourse emerged as and occupied a most contested site in Chosŏn society and continued to generate a wide array of debates and tensions in its political and intellectual spheres and beyond.

Institutionalizing Female Chastity: Regulating Sexuality and Virtue

Remarriage Debates in the Early Chosŏn Court

The chastity discourse that depicted women solely as moral objects began to appear in the late Koryŏ period, with the rise of scholars influenced by Neo-Confucianism. Backed by these scholars, the Chosŏn dynasty operated strictly on the principles of Confucian statecraft, which led to a new turn in shaping women's lives in Korean society. The theory was simple: since Confucian ideals were the political ideology connecting state and family, the state was seen as the family writ large—and the family was considered the model for the state. In an attempt to prevent social and familial disarray, Confucian reformers sought to correct the family and society by pushing Confucian rituals. Among them, as I illustrate in detail, marriage, which played a key role in establishing the Confucian vision of the family, was most intractably connected to the notion of women's chastity and became a subject of ardent debate at the early Chosŏn court.

Viewing women's proper conduct as the core of family relations, early Chosŏn reformers saw the custom of widow remarriage as a primary threat to both the family and social stability. Not only did they consider remarriage almost tantamount to adultery, but there were other socioeconomic concerns about remarriage, especially for the *yangban* elite class. For one thing, remarriage usually resulted in additional legitimate offspring who could inherit the father's status— and hence in too many qualified *yangban* sons with various privileges, including exemption from passing the civil service examination to hold an official title. Remarriage could also lead to schisms among sons of different mothers, disputes over division of property, and diffusion of the father's status.

The regulation of women's sexuality through remarriage began to undergo radical change in the fifteenth century. In 1407, Confucian bureaucrats, hardening their attitude toward remarriage, revived the Koryŏ practice of entering a thrice-married woman in the *Register of Licentious Women* and imposed harsher restrictions on the descendants of such women.[2] In 1485, with the legalization of listing thrice-married women in this register, the *Great Code of Administration (Kyŏngguk taejŏn)*—the basic law of the dynasty—further stipulated that the names of elite women who displayed misconduct (*sirhaeng*) or "(re)married more than three men (*kyŏngjŏk sambuja*)" be recorded and reported to the Ministry of Rites (Haejo), Ministry of War (Pyŏngjo), Office of the Censor-General (Saganwŏn), and Office of the Inspector-General (Sahŏnbu) under the "Laws on Penal Affairs" (Hyŏngjŏn).[3] At the same time, the "Laws on Ritual Affairs" (Yejŏn) of the *Great Code* specified that the sons and grandsons of such women would not be eligible to take the civil service examination.[4] Some elaborations were made later, but these two provisions on remarriage in the "Laws on Penal and Ritual Affairs" of the *Great Code* remained most fundamental and authoritative to the end of the dynasty.

While the Chosŏn state clearly regarded remarriage as sexual misconduct, this did not mean that every Confucian official at the early

2. *T'aejong sillok* 11:29a [1406/6/9].

3. *Kyŏngguk taejŏn* 5:8a–b. The earliest indigenous law promulgated in Chosŏn Korea was the *Six Codes of Administration (Kyŏngje yukchŏn)* in 1397. Shortly thereafter, compilation of the *Great Code of Administration* began during King Sejo's reign (r. 1455–1468). Several revisions of the *Six Codes* were produced before the final enactment and promulgation of the *Great Code* in 1485, the sixteenth year of King Sŏngjong's reign.

4. *Kyŏngguk taejŏn* 3:1ab.

Chosŏn court wholeheartedly supported the idea of enacting laws against remarriage. When this issue was raised in an audience with King Sŏngjong (r. 1469–1494) in 1477, the majority of officials presented the objection that the regulation would be too harsh for a young widow. Instead, they suggested upholding the existing provision on "not investing remarried women with noble titles and discriminating against descendants of thrice-marriage for the civil service examination."[5] Nevertheless, King Sŏngjong, under the banner of tightening the law to eradicate women's licentious conduct, espoused the minority voices advocating the remarriage provision.

Two years later, in 1479, an incident of a woman's overlapping marriage was appealed to the Chosŏn court. A daughter of Yi Kyŏngse had married a man years before, but it turned out that her family had previously agreed to her marriage to another man by performing a preliminary part of the wedding ritual (namnye).[6] When the family to which Yi Kyŏngse's daughter had been first engaged discovered her marriage, they submitted the petition.[7] According to the law, Yi's daughter should have been sent back to the man to whom her family had initially betrothed her.[8] But because she had already been another man's wife, sending her back would have signified that she would enter a second marriage. Demanding her return would have thus ultimately complicated the legislation against remarriage and would have undermined King Sŏngjong's stubborn attitude toward the remarriage issue. Caught in the challenging deliberation, First Royal Secretary (Tosŭngji) Kim Sŭnggyŏng (1430–1493) advised that "the

5. *Sŏngjong sillok* 82:6b–17a [1477/7/17]. This provision was proclaimed and included in the *Great Code of Pyŏngsul (Pyŏngsul taejŏn)*—one of the earlier versions of the *Great Code*—in 1466, the twelfth year of King Sejo. *Sejo sillok* 43:28a [1467/8/5].

6. The *namnye* (or *napch'ae*), as outlined in *Zhu Xi's Family Rituals (Zhuzi jiali)*, is a part of the wedding ritual in which the groom's family sends a wedding proposal that is then accepted by the bride's family.

7. *Sŏngjong sillok* 109:11a [1479/10/26].

8. *Kyŏngguk taejŏn* 5:8b. "In case [a family] accepts a marriage proposal but marries [a daughter to] another man, the marriage officiator will be punished and [the couple] will be divorced." Although this incident occurred several years before completion of the *Great Code*, this legal concept or code must have existed in the earlier versions of works such as the *Six Codes of Administration* that became the basis for the *Great Code*.

state has legislated a law prohibiting offspring of remarried women from being recruited for official positions. Taking her back to the man to whom she was betrothed earlier would be seen as official permission to remarry. In general, the marriage was to be arranged by a household head (*kajang*), not the woman [herself]."[9] Understanding Kim's point, the king laid responsibility on the patriarch of the woman's family, Yi Kyŏngse, and ordered that he be punished instead of his daughter being sent back to her first betrothed.[10] This decision reinforced Sŏng-jong's vision of consolidating the Confucian patriarchal family order and legitimating the law against woman's remarriage, both of which he sought to achieve by regulating female sexuality.

Once the remarriage provision was formally written into the *Great Code*, it immediately affected all the sons of remarried women (fathered by women's first and/or subsequent husbands), who then joined the sons and later descendants of secondary wives, local clerks, and criminals in being barred from sitting for the civil service examination.[11] In Chosŏn society, the civil service examination was the primary pathway to official positions and political prominence. Widows of *yangban* were thus most affected by this legislation, because if they remarried their offspring would be barred from obtaining governmental careers, jeopardizing the future success of the family. As some officials later noted, "Who would want to marry a widow, have his descendants be blocked [from the political path], and [finally] make them commoners (*sŏmin*)? Families would [thus] try not to lose their honor by [consistently] seeking ways for their offspring [to obtain] governmental positions."[12]

The general view of the remarriage provision holds that it was promoted and implemented by the Confucian-minded early Chosŏn kings and officials, then finalized during Sŏngjong's reign as an absolute law. This would seem to indicate that once this law was proclaimed in 1485 it was never contested. However, debates over the

---

9. *Sŏngjong sillok* 109:11a [1479/10/26].
10. *Sŏngjong sillok* 109:11a [1479/10/26].
11. While the civil service examination was open to commoners, sons of the lowest-status individuals, such as slaves, merchants, and so on, did not have the right to sit for it. See Wagner, "Civil Examination Process," 22–27.
12. *Yŏnsan'gun ilgi* 28:32a [1497/12/12].

remarriage provision continued at the Chosŏn court, with some officials considering it to have the potential to inadvertently encourage
moral decay due to the agonies that young widows would, realistically,
face. In 1497, the third year of the succeeding King Yŏnsan (r. 1494–
1506), a memorial by a Confucian scholar-teacher of Tansŏng region,
Song Hŏndong, intensified the discussion about revising the remarriage
stipulation. Among the seventeen items proposed in his memorial, the
first one reads:

> The prohibition of a young widow's remarriage is [done] to respect [her]
> fidelity (*sung chŏrŭi* 崇節義) and commemorate [her] sense of honor (*sang
> yŏmch'i* 尙廉恥). However, eating food and being a man or a woman
> are the greatest desires of a human being.[13] Thus [if someone is] born as
> a man, he wants to have a wife, and [if born] as a woman, she wants to
> get married. This is people's innate nature that cannot be forcibly
> stopped. As for a woman, she has the righteousness of the Three Fol-
> lowings: following her father when unmarried, following her husband
> after being married, and following her son when widowed. This is what
> the *Book of Rites* teaches [us].[14]
>
> However, there are women who become widows in [only] three days
> or within a year after the wedding, and who also become widows in their
> twenties and thirties. If they are able to keep their chastity like Lady
> Gongjiang and [Lady] Cho, that is it.[15] [Yet in a case where the widow]
> has no parents, siblings, or child, she will [soon] be wandering on the
> road, [or] will be threatened by a man going over the wall [to enter her
> room], and there will be many who eventually lose their chastity.[16] I

---

13. The original text simply writes "men and women" (*namnyŏ*), but I translate it
as "being a man or a woman" to denote a sexual difference or sexual desire.

14. 婦人從人者也 幼從父兄 嫁從夫 夫死從子. *Liji*, 732.

15. Lady Gongjiang composed a poem refusing the remarriage forced upon her by
her natal parents after the death of her husband, Gongbo, the prince of the Wei 衛 state
(?–209 BCE). This poem, entitled "Cypress Boat," is included in the *Book of Poetry*
and appears in many Chosŏn official histories and private writings as the prime reference to female virtue. See chapter 1, note 68. See also the *Elementary Learning* (Kr.
Sohak; Ch. *Xiao xue*), which carries Lady Gongjiang's story. Zhu Xi, *Xiao xue*, 146.
Both ladies cited here must have been known for their virtue and commitment to serving only one husband, but I was not able to locate detailed information on Lady Cho.

16. The original text reads that such a widow will be "wet with street dew"
(*haengno chi sojŏm*). *Yŏnsan'gun ilgi* 28:32a [1497/12/12].

therefore request that a widow under twenty years old without a child be
allowed to remarry and have the plan to live with pleasure.[17]

Song's point was not to revert to the existing remarriage provision
but to take into account the reality of young, childless widows without
economic or familial resources, who were likely to become targets of
sexual attack and a further source of moral disorder in society. During
the extended discussion of this issue, which about thirty high officials
from the State Council (Ŭijŏngbu) and the Six Ministries (Yukcho)
attended, many indeed espoused Song's proposal for revision by raising two points. First, they argued, the provision, which had never
existed in previous reigns of the dynasty, had been adopted solely by
former King Sŏngjong himself, despite the strong opposition of many
court officials.[18] Thinking from the outset that such a provision would
not be feasible, these officials had voiced their opinion that it would
be impossible for a young woman to live as a widow for the rest of her
life, given human beings' biological propensity for sexual desire. Yet
Sŏngjong had not heeded their advice, declaring that "even if a later
king changes [the provision], [I] should implement [it now]."[19] The
officials backing Song's memorial thus argued that the remarriage
provision had been legalized only in obedience to the king's order,
without reflecting the majority concern at the court that its strictures
ignored the basic sexual component of human nature.

Second, the officials maintained that the existing remarriage stipulation would increase not only young widows' resentment at their lot
but their chances of losing their chastity because of their prolonged,
impoverished widowhood, and that this would eventually have a
harmful effect on the larger society. Moreover, the state would no
longer be able to appoint a man of unusual talent if he happened to be
the son of a woman who had remarried; and a family with only one

17. *Yŏnsan'gun ilgi* 28:31b–32a [1497/12/12].
18. The *Sillok* uses the term *sinch'ung* 宸衷 ("king's inner mind" or "king's agony,"
as in 成宗斷自宸衷而立 and 出自宸衷) to imply the uneasy position the king found
himself in when making the decision, even though he did so voluntarily. *Yŏnsan'gun
ilgi* 28:33a [1497/12/12].
19. *Yŏnsan'gun ilgi* 28:33b [1497/12/12].

daughter (and no sons) would be in danger of dying out if she remained a childless widow. The officials further opined that chaste women and devoted wives appear rarely in the world, implying that chastity was not something that every woman could easily achieve. In the end, they argued, requiring all women to abide by the new regulation against remarriage was not viable, and its implementation would only engender many ills and harmful consequences. Instead of controlling female sexuality through such an inflexible remarriage provision, the state should cultivate the moral and patriarchal order of the society by utilizing the state-reward system of honoring chaste women, if there were any to be found.[20]

In contrast, those officials who wanted to keep the remarriage legislation as it was claimed that the provision legitimated by former King Sŏngjong could not be hastily revised, especially at the recommendation of Song Hŏndong, a mere Confucian scholar from the countryside. Though agreeing with Song's points to some extent, they highlighted the fact that "the provision in the *Great Code* does not prohibit a widow's remarriage itself, but only bans the government's employment of her son in a high-ranking position."[21] Further, they contended that the remarriage provision was never so harsh as to punish fathers who allowed the remarriage of their widowed daughters.[22] However, the *Sillok* later records the case of a father who was condemned for marrying his widowed daughter to a second husband. In 1528, the Office of the Inspector-General accused the station officer

20. *Yŏnsan'gun ilgi* 28:32a–33a [1497/12/12]. Later, an eminent Neo-Confucian scholar, Song Siyŏl (1609–1689), also took a negative stance toward a legal ban on women's remarriage on similar grounds of sexual desire, economic survival, and concern for offspring. Instead of legal enforcement, Song claimed that a widow's choice of remarriage should come from "spontaneous manifestation of her moral nature." Hwa Yeong Wang, "Chastity as a Virtue," 4–6. For more detailed analysis of Song's position on widow remarriage legislation, see Hwa Yeong Wang, "Against the Ban on Women's Remarriage."

21. 大典之法 非禁再嫁也 但其所生 不得敍顯職耳. *Yŏnsan'gun ilgi* 28:32a [1497/12/12]. While the *Great Code* simply states that descendants of remarried women are barred from taking the civil service examination, the *Sillok* notes a little elaboration here: they cannot serve in high-ranking positions. In other words, they could still enter the bureaucracy via the protection privilege (*ŭmjik*) and serve in low-ranking offices.

22. *Yŏnsan'gun ilgi* 28:33b [1497/12/12].

(*ch'albang*) Chŏng Yu (1503–1566) of having his recently widowed daughter remarry. When investigating this case, the office raised the point that punishing Chŏng for this matter would go against the existing law because the *Great Code* simply proscribed descendants of remarried women from taking the civil service exam. To uphold the moral sprit of the state, the office nevertheless recommended firing Chŏng from his post because he was a patriarch and therefore responsible for his daughter's remarriage.[23] Interestingly, this happened in the same year that Chŏng himself passed the lesser examination (*samasi*) as a classics licentiate (*saengwŏn*), so the post from which he was dismissed would have been his first official position. Nine years later, in 1537, Chong finally passed the civil service examination. After that, he held numerous key government positions, including those of Censor-General (Taesagan), Winter Solstice Envoy to China (Tongjisa), and Inspector-General (Taesahŏn).[24] Chŏng remained a highly esteemed officer in the reigns of the next two kings—Injong and Myŏngjong (r. 1545–1567)—notwithstanding the earlier incident of his daughter's remarriage.

These rigorous debates over revision of the remarriage legislation were therefore not confined to the Confucian ideology of women's virtue but encompassed realistic matters such as a widow's sexual desire, her risk as a potential sexual target, her economic situation, matters of family succession, and the problem of official appointment of talented men.[25] In contrast to the conventional portrayal of Chosŏn remarriage discourse, which is centered on the abstract notion of the chastity ideal, the ongoing debate about the remarriage regulation was never uniform, for it highlighted more practical concerns and their adverse impacts on society. In addition, the way this law discriminated against the sons of remarried women did not seriously affect the sons of non-elite widows. Although the Chosŏn civil service examination

23. *Chungjong sillok* 64:12a [1528/yun10/19].
24. *Injong sillok* 1:31a [1545/yun1/18]; *Myŏngjong sillok* 10:84b [1550/9/21]; 17:28a [1554/8/18]; 18:14a [1555/2/29].
25. Later, the *Continuation of the Great Code* (*Sok taejŏn*) added a provision that impoverished chaste widows begging for food should be supported with rice and clothing annually, via reports to the king by the Ministry of Rites for those residing in Seoul, or reports by provincial governors in other regions. *Sok taejŏn* 2:26b–27a.

was in theory open to non-*yangban* commoners, it was hardly possible for them to afford the time and financial means required to prepare for the exam. Since the remarriage provision had little direct influence on the lives of non-elite widows and their families, it is doubtful that they felt compelled to stick to it firmly, especially when dealing with the more pressing issue of sheer survival. Moreover, as the remarriage of the officer Chŏng Yu's daughter shows, the immediate impact of the remarriage provision did not necessarily stop *yangban* families from opting for remarriage (whether of the head of a widow's family or of a widow herself), regardless of the potential disadvantage to descendants.

More importantly, remarriage itself was never directly outlawed, as already articulated in the statement by officials at the early Chosŏn court that "the provision in the *Great Code* does not prohibit a widow's remarriage in general, but only bans the government's employment of her descendants."[26] As seen in the debates over the remarriage provision and in the case of Chŏng Yu as well, the Chosŏn court was extremely sensitive about keeping the legislation's original meaning intact in its application and was thus careful that it never exceeded its intended boundaries for demerit or punishment. In other words, the remarriage provision was intended solely to obstruct the descendants of remarried women from pursuing official careers—an aim that indirectly led to the rectification of the remarriage practice—rather than as an absolute law indiscriminately punishing women who chose to remarry.

Toward the end of the dynasty, however, the remarriage provision seems to have gradually attained the status of an anti-remarriage law. For example, the eighteenth-century scholar Sŏng Taejung (1732–1809) remarked that "our country prohibits remarriage" (*aguk kŭm chaega*), echoing the general perception that remarriage almost came to be deemed the target of legal sanction in the late Chosŏn.[27] By 1894, as part of the Kabo Reform, the government allowed "a widow to decide about a remarriage [matter] of her own will, regardless of social

26. *Yŏnsan'gun ilgi* 28:32a [1497/12/12].
27. Sŏng Taejung, *Ch'ŏngsŏng chapki*, 361.

status," responding to reform-minded officials' criticism of the remarriage prohibition for ruining young widow's lives.[28] Yet as a memorial submitted by Min Ch'ihŏn (1844–1903) in 1900 reveals, the reform edict had virtually no impact on how people viewed women's remarriage. Min points out:

> The reason the court banned descendants of remarried women from taking high office was because scholar-officials cherished propriety and their official positions. In teaching women's proper conduct, they sternly imposed the principle without any leniency, to such an extent that remarriage had become taboo in this country. . . . [Even after the 1894 reform,] the society is still bound to the old practice against remarriage.[29]

Min's memorial indicates the shift in people's perception about women's remarriage that had occurred in the course of the long Chosŏn dynasty. While the provision itself rarely punished or banned remarriage, the notion that Chosŏn law prohibited remarriage had become entrenched in the minds of Korean people by the turn of the twentieth century. In a sense, the term "the law prohibiting remarriage" (*chaega kŭmjipŏp*), which was coined by modern scholars, may correctly describe late Chosŏn society's popular perception or attitude toward remarriage practice.[30] What factors, then, contributed to remarriage being more stringently prohibited than in the law as originally

28. *Kojong sillok* 31:44a [1894/6/28].
29. *Kojong sillok* 40:109a [1900/11/30].
30. There is a long list of Korean scholarship examining the problems of widowhood and remarriage during the Chosŏn dynasty. As early as 1937, Yi Sangbaek analyzed the *Great Code of Administration* provision related to the sons of remarried women; see Yi Sangbaek, "Chaega kŭmji sŭpsok ŭi yurae e taehan yŏn'gu," 205–48. Yi did not see this provision as a law absolutely prohibiting remarriage. It was Kim Tuhŏn who first used the term *chaega kŭmjipŏp*; see Kim Tuhŏn, *Han'guk kajok chedo yŏn'gu*. Since then, Korean scholars have widely employed this term in referring to the remarriage provision, belying its accurate meaning as outlined in the *Great Code*; see O Hwanil, "Chosŏn sidae chaega kŭmjipŏp yŏn'gu," 121–44. Only recently have some scholars begun using a phrase taken directly from the *Kyŏngguk taejŏn*, "the law banning offspring of remarried women from office" 再嫁女子孫禁錮法, which more accurately conveys the law's legal implications.

prescribed by the early Chosŏn state? How did the deepening of chastity discourse contribute to shaping people's practice of and views on remarriage toward the later Chosŏn era?

Reward Debates and Problems

THE WIDOW LANDS PROGRAM

Discouraging the practice of remarriage was indeed most intimately related to the issue of promoting women's sexual integrity. Studies on chastity practice in both Chosŏn Korea and late imperial China contend that the emphasis on female chastity stemmed from the male elites' anxiety about preserving Confucian patriarchy in a period of social change.[31] John Duncan, taking the example of early modern France, maintains that there is a close relationship between men's assertion of control over female sexuality and their own political power. "The increasing legal subjugation of wives by their husbands," according to Duncan, "was seen as a guarantee of the obedience of both men and women to the slowly centralizing state."[32] Although the early Chosŏn remarriage debates, including the issue of women's sexual desire mentioned earlier, complicate Duncan's argument, this may still explain why the Chosŏn state sought to relate the remarriage provision to political opportunity by imposing a legal sanction on the families of remarried women.

In institutionalizing chastity, the Chosŏn state pursued two fundamental methods: control and reward. Control was exercised through the remarriage legislation, which aimed at regulating women's sexuality, while the state employed various rewards to honor widows who maintained their sexual integrity. In the early Chosŏn, the state endowed widows who remained unmarried with the right to collect tax on certain lands through the "widow lands program" called *susinjŏn* (literally, "lands of keeping fidelity"). Originally inherited from the Koryŏ system that provided the family of a deceased or retired soldier

---

31. Ju-K'ang T'ien, *Male Anxiety and Female Chastity*; Angela K. Leung, "To Chasten Society," 1–32; and Duncan, "*Naehun* and the Politics of Gender," 26–57.

32. Duncan, "*Naehun* and the Politics of Gender," 45–46.

with land (*kubunjŏn*), the widow lands program was created in 1391 (still under the Koryŏ dynasty), when the rank-land system (*kwajŏn-pŏp*) was proposed by the Confucian reformers who soon joined in founding the Chosŏn dynasty.[33] Although the early fifteenth-century Chosŏn court made a number of changes in putting the program into effect, the basic provision was as follows: upon the death of a governmental official—a subject who had received a prebendal right on lands from the state—his widow and children inherited the same right to all the lands the husband had held the right over.[34] If the couple had no child, the widow's right was reduced to half of her deceased husband's prebendal right. However, if the widow remarried, she completely lost her eligibility to inherit the right, or she had to return it to the state if she had already inherited it.[35] This program thus supported a widow and her children financially on the condition that she maintain permanent fidelity (*susin*) to her deceased husband.

In theory, land granted under the rank-land system was not inheritable. Yet special lands bestowed in exceptional cases, including the widow lands program, were often passed on to the next generation.[36] Because of difficulties in tracing improper inheritance practices, which caused confusion as to the proper ownership of prebendal rights among different family members, the government revised the rank-land system and made it the office land system (*chikchŏnbŏp*) in 1466, tightening its noninheritable nature.[37] With this new law enacted, the widow lands program was abolished. In 1473, however, a group of officials headed by First Counselor (Pujehak) Yi Kŭkki (?–1489) of the Office of the Special Counselors (Hongmungwan) submitted a

33. According to the *History of Koryŏ*, *kubunjŏn* was given to families of deceased or retired soldiers in 1024 and 1047. *Koryŏsa* 78:13b, 14a.

34. According to the rank-land system, the state did not grant officials ownership of any land, only the prebendal right. This meant that widows accordingly inherited only the right to the tax on the allotted land.

35. *T'aejong sillok* 12:33a [1406/11/1].

36. Martina Deuchler notes that illegal inheritance of lands through *susinjŏn* and *hyuryangjŏn* (land to safeguard upbringing) was done quite easily despite the regulation under the rank-land system. See Deuchler, *Confucian Transformation of Korea*, 203–4.

37. *Sejo sillok* 39:34b [1466/6/25]. Under this new office land system, only incumbent officials were supposed to receive the lands, with no exceptions.

memorial to restore the rank-land system and also to revive the widow lands program, on the grounds that the latter would eventually contribute to the moral edification of populace. The debates over the restoration of the rank-land system ended without reaching an agreement so the discussion on the widow lands program continued.[38]

In 1478, when the king held an audience over the problem of Buddhist temple lands (*sasajŏn*), a group of officials suggested resuming the widow lands program by breaking up lands belonging to Buddhist temples and transferring them to the widow lands program.[39] King Sŏngjong did not take the advice of the officials, who almost confronted him out of concern that he might come to favor Buddhism in the end.[40] Two years later, in 1480, officials again proposed reestablishing the widow lands program by taking the Buddhist temple lands. They argued:

> Only after people have enough food and clothing can they cultivate righteousness and practice rituals. In the past, [the state] fostered virtue by granting widows the prebendal right [through the widow lands program]. Yet [due to this right] having been abolished upon the implementation of the office land system, a widow must remarry after her husband's death because of lack of [financial] support. Moreover, a son of a remarried woman would not be hired [by the government, and] how can this be the [right] way to nurture virtue? We request the restoration of the

38. *Sŏngjong sillok* 32:18a [1473/7/30]. Another memorial in 1477 continued to propose restoration of the rank-land system; see *Sŏngjong sillok* 75:10b [1477/1/13].

39. *Sŏngjong sillok* 95:19b [1478/8/25]. By referring to this court discussion on 1478/8/25, Yi Sugin assumes that there was a brief revival of the widow lands program between 1473 and 1478, based on officials' assertion that the program could not be abolished 不宜廢也. See Yi Sugin, *Chŏngjŏl ŭi yŏksa*, 82. However, it is clear from the following court meeting held on 1478/8/29 that the widow lands program never resumed once it was stopped. The court officials argued that "rewarding a chaste wife and assisting the poor populace through the widow lands program were good systems, but were abolished by King Sejo through implementation of the office land [system]." *Sŏngjong sillok* 95:23a [1478/8/29].

40. At the end of the meeting, officials asked why the king had refused to accept any advice with respect to the Buddhist temples and monks. King Sŏngjong replied, "Since I do not like Buddhism, why does it matter?" Then an official replied, "Although you do not at this point, I am deeply afraid you may gradually favor [Buddhism]." *Sŏngjong sillok* 95:19b [1478/8/25].

widow lands program by abolishing the lands bestowed on Buddhist temples.[41]

Citing the dictum "A chaste woman does not serve two husbands," Sŏngjong did not accept the proposal, maintaining that "chastity should be achieved regardless of economic conditions."[42] Further, he criticized officials for bringing up the widow lands program to divest the Buddhist temples of their lands—the issue that had earlier divided the king and various court officials. The king was steadfast in maintaining that "King Sejo gave the monks the lands, and I cannot take [the land from them]" 世祖旣與僧人予不忍奪.[43] Though agreeing with the king on the essence of widow virtue, Yi Kŭkki, who had previously raised this issue in 1473, appealed to him again, contending that the widow lands program was necessary if the country truly prized "the way of fidelity and righteousness" 節義之道 most highly. Sŏngjong nevertheless declined to restore the program, on the grounds that the previous king had already abolished it, and thus it should not be easily revived.[44]

More memorials on the widow lands program reached the king both from high officials and from scholars in the countryside, but nothing changed his mind. In 1481, a local Confucian scholar named Yi An submitted a memorial that included revival of the widow lands program on the basis that many widows could not even afford food for dinner after their husband's death.[45] In 1491, King Sŏngjong generously met with the low-ranking scholar Cho Yuhyŏng, who had memorialized the throne about the indictments of the time, and listened to his opinions on governing the country, which pointed out the indispensable restoration of the rank-land system as well as the widow lands program.[46] Although the king complimented Cho on his insights

41. *Sŏngjong sillok* 118:12a [1480/5/19].
42. *Sŏngjong sillok* 118:12a [1480/5/19].
43. *Sŏngjong sillok* 117:12a [1480/5/19].
44. *Sŏngjong sillok* 117:12a [1480/5/19].
45. *Sŏngjong sillok* 130:6a [1481/6/9].
46. Cho Yuhyŏng's memorial arrived on the sixth day of the twelfth month in 1490. *Sŏngjong sillok* 248:6b [1490/12/6]. The next day, the king ordered that a meeting be arranged with Cho. *Sŏngjong sillok* 248:7a [1490/12/7]. His audience with Cho took

and ordered that he be rewarded with bags of black pepper, his position remained unchanged and he reiterated that restoration could not
be done.[47]

The discussion on the widow lands program continued into the
next reign. In 1515, the tenth year of King Chungjong, some court
officials again proposed that the widow lands program be reenacted.
Chief State Counselor (Yŏngŭijŏng) Yu Sun (1441–1517) not only
supported its reinstatement but suggested that the Ministry of Rites
take the lead in its reimplementation, in light of a possible land short-
age in regions surrounding the capital if the program were restored.
Other officials, however, disagreed with Yu's assertion that "no woman
of a *yangban* family these days would not keep her fidelity, nor would
it be [at this point a matter of] the previous king's order being over-
turned hastily."[48]

The consistent pleas for restoring the widow lands program after
it was abolished in 1466 did not yield any fruitful outcome. No further
discussion on this issue is found in official records after the 1515 court
meeting. It was King Sŏngjong who was at the center of the debates
on both the remarriage provision and the widow lands program in the
early Chosŏn court, and he adamantly refused to accept criticisms and
challenges from scholar-officials. Why did Sŏngjong, who wanted to
foster the chastity ideal to strengthen the moral life of the state, not
support the widow lands program as a means to pursue his goal? Both
matters were tightly connected to a widow's economic standing after
her husband's death. Unlike the remarriage regulation, however, the
widow lands program could generate further problems that could directly affect the state's fiscal health, leading to a deficiency of state
land that should be given to incumbent governmental officials. Moreover, it could perpetuate possession and accumulation of the lands
in question by the *yangban* families of chaste widows, concentrating
wealth and potential power in the elite families. On the surface, the
king and his officials all used the same rhetoric of female "chastity and

---

place about a month later. The *Sillok* identifies Cho as both a classics licentiate and
literary licentiate (*chinsa*).

47. *Sŏngjong sillok* 249:2a [1491/1/5].

48. *Chungjong sillok* 21:58b [1515/2/22].

righteousness" (*chŏrŭi*) to justify their assertions—regardless of whether these were to abolish or to restore the widow lands program. To be specific, the king stressed the greater depth of a widow's chaste spirit irrespective of her economic difficulties, whereas the officials saw economic stability as indispensable for sustaining chaste widowhood. However, as echoed in the extended debates and underlying tensions over the court officials' proposed use of the widow lands program to divest the Buddhist temples of their lands and the king's determination to oppose this, the issue of widow chastity was subtly interwoven with the political interests of both sides—interests that may well have extended far beyond the boundaries of the chastity ideal.

THE STATE-REWARD SYSTEM

To be sure, the legal sanctions against remarriage and the widow lands program that we have seen so far were focused on regulation of upper-class women's sexuality and conduct. To achieve the goal of moral indoctrination in the broader society, the state formally implemented a reward program to recognize paragons of virtue among the ordinary populace. This was not a novel policy on the part of the Chosŏn government. A story found in Kim Pusik's *Historical Records of the Three Kingdoms* mentions a Silla king who rewarded a filial daughter with a huge amount of grain, a house, and exemption from taxes, while designating her town "a village fostering filiality" (*hyoyang-bang*).[49] In Iryŏn's *Memorabilia of the Three Kingdoms*, too, filial sons and daughters are rewarded for their exemplary conduct. The rewards normally consisted of gifts of rice or the building of houses that were later donated as temples. The *Memorabilia*, like the *Historical Records*, contains an account of a Silla king rewarding a filial daughter who served her mother with utmost care despite their poverty. The area where she resided was also recognized as "a village nurturing filiality"

49. Kim Pusik, *Samguk sagi*, 1:704–5. The original text reads 標榜其俚孝養坊, meaning "designating the town 'a village fostering filiality' to promote [virtue]." The terms indicating the reward system, such as *chŏngp'yo* 旌表 or *chŏngnyŏ* 旌閭, emerged in later dynasties.

(*hyoyang-ri*).[50] Though collected in two separate sources, these stories of filial daughters read quite similarly and, more interestingly, are recorded as having happened under two consecutive Silla kings— Chŏnggang (r. 886–887) in Kim Pusik's *Historical Records* and Chinsŏng (r. 887–897) in Iryŏn's *Memorabilia*. Whether such recognition was part of a regular reward program is not known, but this certainly hints that virtuous people were celebrated as early as the Three Kingdoms period. As discussed in chapter 1, state-level awards began in and continued throughout the Koryŏ dynasty, albeit unevenly because of political disarray and external threats such as military coups and the Mongol Invasions. Building on the Koryŏ practice, early Chosŏn kings and Confucian statesmen worked to stabilize the reward system as the core of the Chosŏn's dynastic mission.

Accordingly, as soon as the founder of the Chosŏn dynasty, King T'aejo, took the throne in the seventh month of 1392, he issued a royal edict that reinforced the tradition of praising loyal subjects, filial children, righteous husbands, and faithful wives as part of his vision for governing the new country. Urging local officials to search for exemplary people, the king confirmed that the state would officially honor them by the erecting of memorial arches.[51] In the fourth year of T'aejo (1396), the state made the first awards, to nine filial sons and four faithful wives, after each province submitted lists of names to the government.[52] Although the *Sillok* records only eight women celebrated for their fidelity during the six years of T'aejo's reign, the number of recipients increased gradually as time went on, reaching a total of about 270 women by the reign of King Myŏngjong.[53]

In addition, the state actively identified hidden examples of chaste women from the Koryŏ period. Acting on a recommendation by the State Council, King Sejong ordered the honoring of chaste women from the previous dynasty who had not been properly rewarded in the

50. Iryŏn, *Samguk yusa*, 466–67. The original text reads 旌坊爲孝養之理, meaning "indicating the area as a village nurturing filiality."

51. *T'aejo sillok* 1:43a [1392/7/28].

52. *T'aejo sillok* 8:5a [1396/9/16].

53. This number is based on the *Sillok*, counting up to King Myŏngjong's reign, shortly before the Imjin War broke out in 1592.

past.[54] Most of all, unlike the remarriage provision and widow lands program, which affected mainly upper-class women, the state-reward system embraced people of any social status. The state's vision of making it a formal institution was based on the larger mission of the new dynasty, which placed a set of essential moral values at the center of its moralizing project. A royal message from King Sŏngjong articulates this point:

> Filial sons and chaste wives sometimes come from those ignorant men and women of the lowest class. This is because they do not lose their human nature of keeping the normative principle. Thus, once it [human nature] is evoked, a good heart is implanted—that is why we strongly support [their virtuous actions] by inspiring them with rewards. . . . In indoctrinating the ordinary populace and moralizing the society, nothing is more imperative than [running the state-reward system]. Have local officers in the provinces look for filial sons and chaste wives, then press them to send reports to the king.[55]

What, then, were the legal and official procedures for rewarding chaste women? At the beginning of the Chosŏn dynasty, chastity awards were carried out through the governmental recognition of moral paragons, as initiated by the king's order to search out exemplary subjects in local areas. By Sŏngjong's reign, the reward policy was formally legislated under the "Encouragement" ("Changgwŏn") section of the Ritual Codes in the *Great Code of Administration*, which reads as follows:

> Those who display virtuous deeds such as filiality, brotherly affection, fidelity, and integrity—including filial children and grandchildren, faithful wives, descendants of loyal subjects, harmonious family members, and people helping out others with difficulties—should be annually recorded by the Ministry of Rites at the end of every year and recommended to the king for rewards. [These] include offering official positions or material rewards. Erection of a memorial arch, along with exemption from

54. *Sejong sillok* 106:15a [1444/10/20].
55. *Sŏngjong sillok* 241:14a [1490/6/20].

miscellaneous duties, should be done for cases of extraordinarily virtuous conduct. Also, [when] the wife of a loyal subject who died for
the sake of the country keeps her fidelity, [she] can be exempted from the
miscellaneous duties.[56]

This statute became a pillar of the state-reward policy throughout the
Chosŏn dynasty. A noticeable modification from the previous practice
was the elimination of the "righteous husbands" category as one of
the recipient groups. Classified under the state-reward system, the
kinds of award granted to chaste women usually consisted of one or
two of the following: (1) the erection of a memorial arch or a tombstone (chŏngnyŏ); (2) exemption of the household from miscellaneous
duties (pokho); (3) the award of rice, cloth, land, and houses (sangmul); (4) awarding or upgrading official positions for the sons of
chaste wives (sangjik, sŏyong, kaja); and (5) releasing women of the
lowest status from their social class and making them commoners
(myŏnch'ŏn). Building upon the previous practice in Koryŏ, the
Chosŏn court newly added two items—offering official positions and
upgrading social status—to the list of rewards. In Chosŏn society,
where social mobility was extremely limited, changing one's societal
status received at birth was almost impossible. The reward of changing
one's social class was thus highly significant to those in the lowest
group, presenting as it did an official way to remove the stigma of low
status for those who excelled at its chastity standards. For the most
superior moral conduct, the state conferred a memorial arch, often in
combination with other material rewards or tax exemptions.

It was only in 1785, with the compilation of the *Great Code for
Ruling the State (Taejŏn t'ongp'yŏn)*, that the state added supplementary provisions for a detailed procedure to the existing statute:

For the matters of conferring memorial arches, posthumous official
rank, and exemption from taxes, the Royal Secretariat distributes copies
of the king's order to the central and local governments. As for filial sons
and chaste women who are worthy of being rewarded with arches and
tax exemption, they should be nominated by the provinces and reported

56. *Kyŏngguk taejŏn* 3:40a–b.

to the king. At the beginning of every three-year [period], three officials of the Ministry of Rites should hold a meeting to evaluate [those recommended] and forward [their decisions] to the State Council. Only then should the select list be submitted to the king for his approval.[57]

Besides the king's calling on local officials to search for exemplary subjects, the 1785 *Great Code for Ruling the State* put local governors in charge of carefully detecting any extraordinary acts of filiality and chastity in their districts, then reporting them to the higher office.[58] The new provisions connote the more structured reward system established by the eighteenth century, particularly in the procedure for assessing a person's merit. With an increasing number of families requesting their members' recognition by tendering petitions, the government also regulated such petitioning activities, criticizing them as evil practices engaged in simply to seize the rewards. A 1789 royal edict clearly prohibits petitioning to honor chastity or filiality either on behalf of a family member or someone else. It prescribes that the recommendation be made through a collective agreement (*kongŭi*), followed by a formal report from the provincial governor (*tobaek*) to the king.[59]

It seems, however, that these regulations may not have been effective. By the mid-nineteenth century, the Chosŏn court again adopted a similar provision stipulating punishment when a request for a chastity reward was not formally administered through the provincial governor. If someone reported the matter to the king via written petition (*sangŏn*) or presumptuously appealed to him via oral petition (*kyŏkchaeng*) during a public procession in his carriage, the request would not be accepted and became subject to punishment by law.[60]

---

57. *Taejŏn t'ongp'yŏn* 3:42a.

58. *Taejŏn t'ongp'yŏn* 3:42a.

59. *Sugyo chŏngnye*, 66–68.

60. *Taejŏn hoet'ong* 3:50b. The oral petition was one of the lawful ways for people to appeal a grievance or submit a request to the king during the Chosŏn dynasty. Rather than petitioning through local government, people could present their problems by stopping the king's carriage during a royal procession and submitting prepared petitions, bypassing the local and provincial steps. For studies on late Chosŏn petitioning activities, see Han Sanggwŏn, *Chosŏn hugi sahoe wa sowŏn chedo*; Cho Yunsŏn,

Moreover, appeals for two concurrent awards—a memorial arch and posthumous official rank—for a single virtuous case were legally banned, though such a combined reward had been common in the past. The Ministry of Rites forwarded all matters related to these two types of awards to the king and reinvestigated them accordingly.[61] These newly added provisions not only denote the particular kinds of rewards that people preferred but indicate the mounting interest in attaining rewards for family members in the latter part of the Chosŏn society.[62]

Several added provisions in statutes concerning chastity awards also reveal people's obsession with official recognition and the critical issues that the Chosŏn government faced in its effective execution of the reward system. The fundamental problem was the specific criteria for determining the merit of an exemplary subject, which are not found in the Chosŏn legal codes. The chastity reward itself is usually mentioned together with other exemplary cases, such as loyalty and filiality, within the context of the larger state-reward policy. The Chosŏn government outlined neither a clear standard for the chastity reward nor a detailed guideline of the evaluation procedure that led to official recognition. In general, upon hearing the government's announcement calling for recommendations, local magistrates encouraged neighbors or family members to submit the names of qualified female candidates to the local court, which passed them on to the capital. In China, the Board of Rites set legal qualifications for chaste women, such as an age requirement, as early as the Yuan dynasty (1271–1368), and the state established the detailed criteria for being designated a chaste woman based on social status and number of years of preserving fidelity.[63] The Chosŏn reward policy, in contrast, was relatively

---

Chosŏn hugi sosong yŏn'gu; Kim Kyŏngsuk, "Chosŏn hugi yŏsŏng ŭi chŏngso hwaltong"; and Jisoo M. Kim, Emotions of Justice.

61. Taejŏn hoet'ong 3:50b.

62. Chapter 3 details the background factors that intensified these appeals for awards, finally prompting new legislation by the Chosŏn state.

63. The age requirement in China was born of the ethnic tension between Mongol rulers and Han-Chinese literati, as the former tried to regulate the latter's obsession with the reward. Bossler, Courtesans, Concubines, chap. 9. See also Sommer, "Uses of Chastity," 80. Although Angela Leung states that the cult of women's chastity in

lenient and inclusive: no law stipulated prerequisites for chastity candidates; rather, the award was open to all women, regardless of social status, age, and aliveness, by following the customary nomination procedure.[64]

Despite the lack of standardized criteria and the variations in awards according to a candidate's socioeconomic status, two categories of action were generally considered worthy of state recognition— (1) remaining chaste after one's husband's death, and (2) bodily resistance to sexual assault—both stances that could be displayed to the extreme by committing suicide. Various official and unofficial records reveal that Chosŏn society evaluated a candidate's chastity based on her response to external challenges such as widowhood and sexual assault. Once they had identified a woman displaying one of these two categories of action, family members or local Confucian scholars described her conduct in detail and forwarded the account to the local office. The local magistrate in turn sent his report of the case to the central government for official recognition. After reviewing testimonials to the woman's merit, the government decided whether to canonize the case and grant the award. This practice—which was largely dependent on individual, familial, and communal recommendations through collective endeavor and declarations in response to the government's calls for candidates—became routine and continued without substantial modification to the end of the Chosŏn dynasty.[65]

Although openness and relative flexibility characterized the Chosŏn reward policy, one key factor that automatically disqualified a woman from receiving the reward, no matter how remarkable her display of virtue, was remarriage. In 1498, a provincial governor of Kyŏngsang reported the suicide of a widow named Okkŭm to the king. After a slave man had threatened her on the street, Okkŭm had hung

China was initially meant to be valid only for the lower class, Mark Elvin argues that elite women were not really debarred from awards for fidelity. See Angela K. Leung, "To Chasten Society," 2–3; Elvin, "Female Virtue and the State," 124.

64. *Karim poch'o*, 675–76.

65. Sun Joo Kim's study on a scholar of P'yŏngan Province, Yi Sihang, shows how he mobilized his network to receive state recognition of his ancestor's filiality and how the collective effort was integral to a successful case. See Sun Joo Kim, *Voice from the North*.

herself. The report highlighted Okkŭm's unwavering resistance in the face of the man's repeated threats and how she had finally taken her own life to preserve the chastity ideal. The virtuous spirit that she had displayed more than matched that of women who had been designated chaste in the past, and hence she was deserving of public recognition, which would then inspire the ordinary populace. However, the Ministry of Punishment (Hyŏngjo) raised the suspicion that she had been a remarried woman. If that were proved to be true, it would imply that Okkŭm had already lost her chastity and would be ineligible for the official reward because a chaste woman does not serve two husbands in her life. The king, agreeing with this point, ordered further investigation as to whether or not Okkŭm had formally remarried.[66] The *Sillok* provides no information about the investigation result, but about two months later, the Ministry of Rites recommended rewarding Okkŭm based on the *Great Code*, and the king accepted the recommendation.[67] In determining Okkŭm's case, two contrasting opinions brought up by the Ministry of Punishment and the Ministry of Rites reveal interesting points. The former argues that, from the legal point of view, Okkŭm would have become a woman without fidelity (*silchŏl*) upon entering a second marriage and would have remained such a woman, no matter how exceptional the virtue she performed with respect to her second husband. The latter, in contrast, holds that Okkŭm's chaste act itself could perfectly well serve as a moral exemplar for the people.

Since remarriage itself was *not* punishable and the state tried to apply the remarriage provision as carefully as possible to actual cases (as discussed earlier in this chapter), Okkŭm's case appeared as a complicated one at the early Chosŏn court. Toward the later part of the dynasty, a woman's marriage history became a critical precondition of reward eligibility. In 1711, for instance, a remarkable story of a wife fighting a tiger for the sake of her slave husband came to the court. Witnessing the tiger killing and eating her husband, she had attacked the tiger and secured her husband's dead body. Recognizing her heroic action of righteousness and chastity (*ŭiyŏl*), the Ministry

---

66. *Sŏngjong sillok* 287:9b–10a [1494/2/13].
67. *Sŏngjong sillok* 289:7b [1494/4/10].

of Rites initially recommended that she be honored. Yet a county magistrate (*pusa*) of Samch'ŏk County, where she resided, noted that she had remarried about a year before and might not be qualified for such an award. The Ministry of Rites accordingly withdrew the earlier proposal, and the king consented.[68] A woman's decision to remarry thus meant absolute abandonment of her fidelity, and the lofty principle of a woman's devotion to a single husband was of critical importance, even for a woman of lower status, in evaluating her merit. Although the government delineated no specific criterion for the chastity reward, the two contrasting opinions about the relevance or irrelevance of remarriage in the 1498 case of Okkŭm versus the unilateral condemnation of remarriage in the similar case of 1711 signifies a shift in how female chastity was perceived between the early and the latter part of Chosŏn society.

TRIALS AND ERRORS WITH THE STATE-REWARD SYSTEM

After this shift, the basic structure of the Chosŏn state-reward program did not undergo much drastic change in operation, serving as a major means of promoting the state's orthodox vision of female sexuality and gender relations to the general populace. During the early Chosŏn, however, though the state-reward program functioned as the core of the moralizing campaign, its local-level administration was not always as zealous as the state wished it to be. Official records often disclose difficulty in obtaining the names of virtuous people from local governments. In 1458, the State Council criticized provincial governors and local magistrates for neglecting their duty to search for and provide the names of worthy people despite the fact that the reward program had already been legalized.[69] Again, in 1465, officials at the Office of the Inspector-General were dispatched to investigate and punish provincial governors for any inattentive case.[70] And in 1489 the Ministry of Taxation (Hojo) pointed out that local magistrates frequently maladministered one type of reward—exemption of a chaste

---

68. *Sukchong sillok* 50:3a [1711/1/10].
69. *Sejo sillok* 12:12a [1458/4/23].
70. *Sejo sillok* 36:9b [1465/5/30].

woman's household from miscellaneous duties—thereby releasing such households from other tax obligations as well.[71]

The most persistent problem was, however, the absence of lucid screening guidelines when it came to authenticating candidates for rewards. As a consequence, selection of a qualified chaste woman often resulted in disputes among Chosŏn court officials. In 1443, the State Council noted that the authenticity of each case was not checked carefully once the name was submitted and that rewards were given out to candidates unworthy of such recognition. It urged the Ministry of Rites to search for concrete evidence of candidates' extraordinary actions after each province had submitted the nominees for faithful wives.[72] In 1453, the king again emphasized that explicit proof of a candidate's merit, prepared by administrative officials, should accompany any nomination for the reward.[73] Nonetheless, determining the genuineness of a woman's virtuous conduct continued to lead to controversy at the court.[74] War in the late sixteenth century exacerbated the situation, as the state ardently sought to reward a large number of chaste women as a crucial part of restoring postwar society. In the midst of the war, in 1595 and 1596, the government had ordered a search for cases to be recognized, but in 1601, the Office of the Censor-General stated that the order was still not being enacted because of trouble in sorting through the huge number of nominees and winnowing out false cases from true ones. Fearing that undeserving people would take an advantage of the reward program, the government commended meticulous investigation for each case.[75]

It was the local magistrate who first reviewed nominations initiated by village elders or county schools (hyanggyo) and then forwarded them to the provincial governor, who, after going over the names again, submitted them to the Ministry of Rites for the king's final approval. Not being equipped to assess the truth of each case, the government mostly relied on local sources of information, which

71. *Sŏngjong sillok* 232:9a [1489/9/21].
72. *Sejong sillok* 101:28b [1443/8/13].
73. *Tanjong sillok* 1:3b [1452/5/18].
74. *Chungjong sillok* 101:35a [1543/10/24]; *Hyojong sillok* 5:3a [1650/8/20].
75. *Sŏnjo sillok* 139:12a [1601/7/9].

hinged on recommendations from family members or from scholars in the community of the nominee. Whether answering a call to submit names by local officers ordered to do so by the state or whether voluntarily reporting an outstanding person of virtue, it was lineage members and local leaders who vouched for the veracity of a candidate's reputed conduct. In the case of a *yangban* woman, family members usually drafted an eloquent statement detailing her virtuous attributes, which were then confirmed by the head of the lineage. For a non-*yangban* woman, village elders or Confucian literati who had heard of an exceptional wife or daughter wrote and submitted reports to the local office.

The family's central role in the nomination process would be expected in the Chosŏn social context, but it was highly problematic nonetheless. First, the social standing of a lineage in the local context affected how an application was received. It was not so much the candidate's moral achievement as her family's reputation in the community that could initially influence the nomination at the local level. Second, because rewards often ensured either elevation or entitlement to an official rank, producing a chaste woman was directly related to the family's future through her sons' and/or their descendants' professional success in the government. There is ample evidence of a chaste widow's son (or adopted son) appealing to the state, out of filial duty, for official canonization of his mother's chastity.[76]

From the seventeenth century on, when growing numbers of descendants requested the state's retroactive recognition of their already deceased female family members, the awards sometimes went to living male members of a chaste woman's lineage, who were offered official titles without having to pass the civil service examination. Such practice had already caused a serious problem within the government, because many of those who secured an official position through the

---

76. For example, Ha Hakho, the adopted son of the widow Madam Yi (1716–1784?), kept memorializing the court for two years and finally succeeded in having her designated an official chaste woman. Madam Yi had become a widow at the age of twenty-seven and had committed suicide decades later, on the anniversary of her husband's death, after taking care of her in-law family as well as her children for forty-three years. A memorial arch was erected in 1790 upon the order of King Chŏngjo (r. 1776–1800). Chŏng Pŏmjo, "Sŏ Yissi chŏngyŏ sasil," 38:23b–24a.

reward program displayed incompetence in performing governmental tasks.[77]

The core of the problem, therefore, was how to gauge the genuine cases of chaste conduct. With the skyrocketing number of reward requests that were made toward the later Chosŏn, checking the authenticity of every case became almost impossible.[78] Struggling to separate valid from fraudulent claims, some officials in charge of verifying candidates were bribed even in making up their list of nominees.[79] The *Sukchong sillok* confirms that the outpouring of requests to honor recent ancestors triggered a proliferation of problems: besides rewards being given without adequate testimonials, some previous awardees' names reappeared on lists of new reward recipients.[80] In other words, the names of women who had already been recognized were resubmitted for another type of reward by their descendants.

The government discussed possible ways to prevent these problems, yet no viable solution was adopted in the absence of constructive selection guidelines. In 1796, King Chŏngjo responded as follows to the Ministry of Rites' recommendation on reward recipients:

Execution of the state-reward [program] is a task that should be done carefully. How much more so for posthumously honoring someone's virtuous behavior! Now sixty-nine people have been selected and recommended [for their exemplary conduct], yet isn't this too many? These days, *officials tend to demonstrate their benevolence by giving out frequent rewards, which then reflects great credit on them.* However, they do not seem to have a cautious and prudent attitude at all [in making nominations]. Indeed, this has been a serious problem for the Ministry of Rites. [I command that] such officials' salaries be reduced to the fifth grade and that other officials [at the Ministry of Rites] be interrogated.

77. *Sŏngjong sillok* 45:8a [1474/7/23].

78. Han Sanggwŏn's analysis shows that 592 petitions for recognition by the state-reward system were submitted during King Chŏngjo's reign alone. Han Sanggwŏn, *Chosŏn hugi sahoe wa sowŏn chedo*, 127–29.

79. *Myŏngjong sillok* 26:33b [1560/5/24].

80. *Sukchong sillok* 64:30a [1719/11/10].

Among the tasks [of the state-reward system], erection of a memorial arch should be done for a case that manifests the most superior virtuous conduct. How deplorable that those officials do not know this simple logic [and allow excessive erection of arches]! I have already deleted some names of people on the list of recommendations and have returned [it to the Ministry of Rites], . . . so discuss this issue again with other officials and inform me [of the revised list] by [later] today.[81]

In addition to familial and local-level problems with the reward-selection procedure, King Chŏngjo aptly points out that court officials used records of reward nominations as an integral part of their career performance and evaluation. Without appropriate review, the erection of a memorial arch—the mark of "the most superior virtuous conduct," as the king states—was offered thoughtlessly, an indication of the popular demand for chastity arches in late Chosŏn society. The king's reaction to the long list of reward candidates submitted by the Ministry of Rites displays his resolution to rectify chronic problems in the overall reward practice. Interestingly, during the fifty-two years of King Yŏngjo's (r. 1724–1776) reign, the Sillok records about 98 people honored for loyalty, filiality, or chastity, and some 140 were recognized during the twenty-four years of King Chŏngjo's reign.[82] Considering the lengths of the two reigns combined, these numbers are relatively small, especially compared with the number granted on a single occasion in the eleventh month of 1713, when King Sukchong (r. 1674–1720) endorsed rewards for about 400 people at once.[83]

Why were Yŏngjo and Chŏngjo, despite their prominence as active promoters of the state-sanctioned moralizing campaign to the populace, reluctant to give out too many awards? Known as the two brightest Chosŏn kings in the eighteenth century, Yŏngjo and Chŏngjo

81. Chŏngjo sillok 45:62a [1796/12/28]; emphasis added. The recommendation was prepared by Minister of Rites Min Chonghyŏn (1735–1798), Second Minister of Rites Yi Chosŭng (1754–1805), and Third Minister of Rites Yi Chŏngdŏk (1752–1801).

82. This calculation is based on the Yŏngjo sillok and Chŏngjo sillok. During Yŏngjo's reign there were forty-three awards for loyalty, twenty-five for filality, and twenty-one for chastity; during King Chŏngjo's reign, sixty-six awards for loyalty, thirty-nine for filiality, and thirty-five for chastity.

83. Sukchong sillok 54:36b [1713/11/21].

showed a great interest in the state-reward program and a willingness
to facilitate it. Yŏngjo was particularly concerned with the discriminative practice of the reward policy that favored the *yangban* elites. In
1772, he ordered that "those elites with outstanding conduct have no
problem in receiving the memorial arch as a reward. However, the
awards for the non-elites, even if they have achieved more remarkable virtues, are usually confined to mere material benefits. How can
the kinds of award depend on one's social status?"[84] The *Sillok* also
frequently notes Chŏngjo's active enforcement of the reward system
throughout the country, by encouraging officials both at the center
and in the provinces to recommend more candidates at the beginning
of each year.[85] Meanwhile, as reflected in his response to the Ministry
of Rites in 1796, he was fully aware of the tendency to abuse the reward program only to enhance the officials' own credit (and authority).
Keeping its original spirit, both Yŏngjo and Chŏngjo strove not to
dilute the value of the reward system.

The problems of who could be honored and how to determine the
qualifications for chastity nevertheless remained complex and continued to be contested among court officials and Confucian scholars. By
the end of the eighteenth century, borrowing the Qing edicts on the
award policy, Chŏng Yagyong (1762–1836) laments:

> Laws on the Chinese reward system are clearly defined. Respecting
> these [laws], they honor filial sons and chaste women. Moreover, in
> Chinese law, the award is granted in various ways, including giving
> silver, constructing walls, composing essays in a panel, and erecting
> tombstones. Yet [in Chosŏn, memorial] arch construction is the single
> way prescribed in the law.[86]

Chŏng confirms the lack of concrete chastity-reward criteria as a relent-
less problem in the selection of truly deserving women for public recognition. However, his criticism of the memorial arch as the only type of

---

84. *Yŏngjo sillok* 79:12a [1772/1/25].
85. *Chŏngjo sillok* 15:18a [1783/1/21]; 16:59a–67b [1783/10/29]; 23:42b–43b
[1787/4/8]; 41:33b [1794/11/4].
86. Chŏng Yagyong, *Mongmin simsŏ* 7:55a.

award somewhat contradicts the kinds of official reward outlined by the basic Chosŏn law—the *Great Code of Administration*. We know that the Chosŏn government conferred varied types of rewards, as was also done in China. One of the most brilliant scholar-officials of the era, whose works encompassed virtually all disciplines, Chŏng was an expert in administration and law and should have been well versed in the Chosŏn legal codes. It is puzzling why he points out here that the sole method of reward in the Chosŏn was memorial arch construction.

Intriguingly, an independent term, "the law granting a memorial arch" (*chaksŏl chi chŏn* 綽楔之典), which is not found in official records prior to the late seventeenth century, gradually appears in the *Sillok* toward the later Chosŏn.[87] According to Chŏng, the term *chaksŏl* 綽楔 means the elongated wooden lintel of a door, which was what had originally been used as a memorial arch in the past. For Chŏng, "the past" indicated the early Chinese state, not the recent past of the earlier Chosŏn, for he discusses this issue in the context of the edification campaign led by a local governor in the Chinese Jin 晉 state (625–149 BCE). Correcting the misuse of the term *chaksŏl*, instead of the correct term *t'aksŏl* 楍楔 (wooden arch), by people during his time, Chŏng notes that the usage of *chaksŏl* was groundless in Chosŏn practice.[88] Indeed, it was the term *t'aksŏl* that was officially used in referring to a memorial arch, as evidenced in the *Sillok* until the end of Chŏngjo's reign.[89] By the end of the nineteenth century, however, the term *chaksŏl chi chŏn* was exclusively adopted for referring to a memorial arch and was employed to represent almost the entire state-reward system (*chŏngnyŏ*). The abridged term *chaksŏl* and

87. The term *chaksŏl* is first seen in the *Yŏngjo sillok* 54:1a [1741/7/1], and increasingly toward the end of the Chosŏn dynasty until 1906. *Kojong sillok* 47:21b [1906/4/17].

88. Chŏng Yagyong, *Mongmin simsŏ* 7:53a. (Mis)uses of the term *t'aksŏl* do appear in nineteenth-century investigation reports on death cases. For example, *t'aksŏl* is used in a magistrate's postscript written for a widow suicide case, indicating the reward program itself. It states, "Nowadays, there are no grades in *t'aksŏl* (the reward program [for chaste women])." *Kŏmanch'o* (*kon*) (vol. 2), 95.

89. The earliest appearance of the term *t'aksŏl* in the *Sillok* is in the *Hyojong sillok* 6:21a [1651/4/8], and the last use of the term is found in the *Chŏngjo sillok* 51:72a [1799/5/28]. But *t'aksŏl* still appears in some local and legal documents of the mid-nineteenth century.

even the single word *chak* were also widely used alternatively with the existing terms *t'aksŏl* and *chŏngnyŏ*.

The increasing use of the term *chaksŏl chi chŏn* may explain Chŏng's remark about "arch construction as the single way prescribed in the law," criticizing the excessive granting of a memorial arch as the state reward par excellence in eighteenth-century Chosŏn society. It also elucidates the background of legislating a supplementary statute on regulating the arch reward in the 1865 *Comprehensive Collection of Dynastic Codes (Taejŏn hoet'ong)*.[90] As the highest marker of exceptional virtue, the memorial arch was favored over all other types of rewards, especially by the *yangban* elite. In fact, the majority of reward recipients were *yangban* women, and an arch served as incontrovertible public proof of a family's status as a moral standard for the community. Similarly, the memorial arches erected during a local official's tenure bore perpetual witness to his own outstanding ability to promote virtue in the area, as well as to his contributions to the moral governance of the state. Although the chaste reward system was implemented upon the egalitarian sense of inviting participation by women from all societal backgrounds, it continued to generate a wide array of issues and tensions that often epitomized the interests of *yangban* groups.

Inscribing Chastity:
Moral Handbooks and Illustrations

With the remarriage legislation and official reward system as essential institutional devices, the Chosŏn state actively promoted didactic handbooks as part of its moralizing project. The state's primary goal was to achieve a stable society based on a healthy patriarchy by propagating Confucian norms and rituals and to root out any lingering Buddhist customs. In 1515, for example, King Chungjong ordered that additional didactic books be printed and sent to Kaesŏng, the former Koryŏ capital, where Buddhist practice remained prevalent and revered.[91] To reinforce its rule by Confucian virtue, the Chosŏn state devoted enormous

90. *Taejŏn hoet'ong* 3:50b.
91. *Chungjong sillok* 22:30a [1515/6/9].

energy to publishing and circulating moral texts in which the ideal of virtuous women was always central, in addition to delineating legal measures to regulate women's sexuality, as discussed earlier.

One of the most distinct examples of these moral handbooks is the *Illustrated Guide to the Three Bonds* (*Samgang haengsilto*), which was first compiled in 1432, the fourteenth year of the reign of King Sejong. In his meticulous study of the *Illustrated Guide*, Young Kyun Oh notes the Ming Chinese connection to the publication of this handbook. According to Oh, many Ming *shanshu* (books to promote good deeds) were introduced to the early Chosŏn court, including copies of *Biographies of Exemplary Women of the Past and Present* (*Gujin lienü zhuan*), possibly influencing publication of the *Illustrated Guide* around the same period.[92] Detailing 330 moral exemplars of the Three Bonds (*samgang*)—those between ruler and subject, father and son, and husband and wife—the *Illustrated Guide* includes poems celebrating distinct moral achievements as well as illustrations of each account that would have helped advance the understanding of ordinary people (fig. 2.1).[93]

The "Chaste Women" section of the *Illustrated Guide* presents 110 chaste women, of which 95 were selected from Chinese cases and 15 from Korean. Of the 15 Korean women, only one is from the Three Kingdoms period—Tomi's wife—while 9 are from the Koryŏ dynasty and 5 from the Chosŏn. Whereas the two other archetypal stories of female fidelity featured in Kim Pusik's *Historical Records of the Three Kingdoms*—those of the Sŏl woman and Sŏk Uro's wife—are not included in the *Illustrated Guide*, the story of Tomi and his wife is. It was newly entitled "Tomi's Wife Eating Grass" ("Mich'ŏ tamch'o" 彌妻啖草), underlining the wife's role as the main protagonist.[94] Of the 9 Koryŏ women whose stories are contained in the *Illustrated Guide*, 7 overlap with the 12 chaste women found in the "Biographies"

92. Young Kyun Oh, *Engraving Virtue*, 67–68. Oh provides a thorough examination of the evolution of the *Illustrated Guide to the Three Bonds* from multiple angles of its linguistic, printing, and ideological history.

93. *Sejong sillok* 59:32b [1433/2/24]. The *Sillok* notes that the *Illustrated Guide* carries 110 examples for each category—loyalty, filiality, and chastity.

94. See chapter 1 for a detailed discussion of the Tomi story, originally titled simply "Tomi" in Kim Pusik's *Historical Records*.

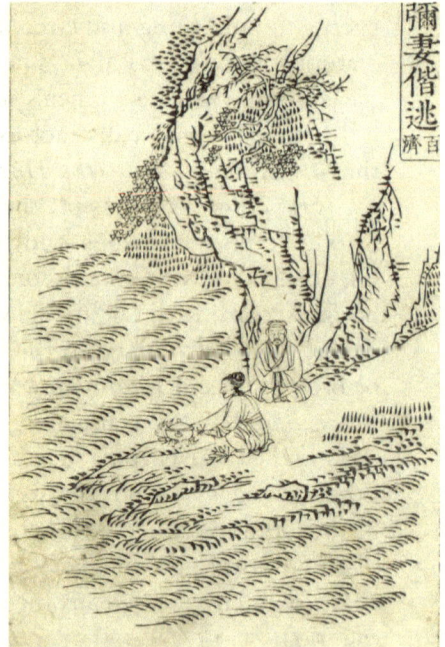

2.1. Left: an illustration of the story of Tomi's wife, included in the 1432 *Illustrated Guide to the Three Bonds* with a new title, "Tomi's Wife Eating Grass" ("Mich'ŏ tamch'o"). Right: an illustration of the same story in the 1797 *Illustrated Guide to the Five Relations*, with the revised title "Tomi's Wife Running Away Together (with Her Husband)" ("Mich'ŏ haedo"). Manuscript; ink on paper. Kyu 138, Karam ko170-Y510-v.1-4. Photographs courtesy of Kyujanggak Institute for Korean Studies, Seoul National University.

section of the *History of Koryŏ*. Given that the *Illustrated Guide* and the *History of Koryŏ* were compiled around the same time (in 1432 and 1451, respectively), it is not surprising that they share many of the same accounts. However, it is difficult to know on what basis the compilers of both made their selection decisions, or how 5 more cases were added to the 7 in the *Illustrated Guide* to total the 12 that appear in the *History of Koryŏ*. If we recall King Sejong's order in 1444 to locate chaste women from the previous dynasty, that search may have indeed contributed to discovering additional cases.[95]

95. *Sejong sillok* 106:15a [1444/10/20].

Having completed the *Illustrated Guide* project in 1432, and with the invention of the Korean script in 1443, King Sejong wanted to have it translated into Korean script (*ŏnmun*) and widely disseminated so that it could reach the vast majority of the population who were not trained in literary Chinese.[96] Some officials opposed the idea, however. During an audience between Sejong and his officials, First Counselor Ch'oe Malli (?–1445) of the Office of the Special Counselors, strongly disagreed with the notions of the wider use of Korean script and of printing publications in the vernacular. Another official, Chŏng Ch'angson (1402–1487), Fourth Counselor (Ŭnggyo) of the Office of the Special Counselors in the Hall of Worthies, also asserted that the degree to which the general populace could be indoctrinated was a matter not of the readability of the *Illustrated Guide* but of people's innate ability to learn and absorb moral norms. Chŏng specifically stressed that "publication of the Korean version would not result in major edification of people."[97] Confronted by various scholar-officials, the king was nonetheless determined to advance his plan and dismissed Chŏng from his position.[98]

The vernacular Korean edition of the *Illustrated Guide* finally appeared in 1490, under King Sŏngjong's sponsorship, with the Korean translation of each story in the top section (fig. 2.2).[99] Prior to this, in 1481, Sŏngjong had ordered publication of the "Chaste Women" section in Korean script: titled the *Illustrated Guide to the Three Bonds and Chaste Women* (*Samgang haengsil yŏllyŏdo*), it specifically targeted the female audience in the country.[100] The publication of an

96. The Korean alphabet (known as *han'gŭl* in the modern era) was referred to as *ŏnmun* during the Chosŏn dynasty. Literally meaning a "language of the lower class," the term *ŏnmun* carries a connotation of inferiority in comparison to literary Chinese, which elite circles used exclusively.

97. Chŏng Ch'angson's remark about people's inborn nature seems to reflect what Confucius says in the *Analects*: "The Master said, The common people can be made to follow a course, but cannot be made to understand why they should do so." Confucius, *Analects*, 8:9.

98. *Sejong sillok* 103:19b [1444/2/20]. On the invention of the Korean script and King Sejong's political leadership, see Mirim Yoo, "King Sejong's Leadership," 7–38; and Kim-Renaud, *Korean Alphabet*.

99. *Sŏngjong sillok* 239:1a [1490/4/1].

100. *Sŏngjong sillok* 127:7a [1481/3/24].

2.2. "A Chaste Wife Entering the River" ("Yŏlbu ipkang") is an account of Madam Pae, who jumped into a river after leaving her baby on the river-bank in order to avoid Japanese pirates at the end of the Koryŏ dynasty. From the 1432 *Illustrated Guide to the Three Bonds*. Manuscript; ink on paper. Kyu 138. Photograph courtesy of Kyujanggak Institute for Korean Studies, Seoul National University.

independent *Chaste Women* text was not a sudden, isolated event.[101] Around this time, the debate over legally prohibiting remarriage was already underway. Adding to this, a series of adultery scandals involving court officials and upper-class wives reinforced Sŏngjong's determination to rectify female conduct by all possible measures, from legal sanctions to the distribution of moral texts. To facilitate the propagation of the texts, the Ministry of Rites further proposed to the king

101. Young Kyun Oh states that one can also posit the separate publication of two other sections—on loyal subjects and filial children—despite the fact that no copies are extant. Young Kyun Oh, *Engraving Virtue*, 130–31.

that, for *yangban* households of the capital area, the male patriarch should teach the text to female members and that erudite elders needed to be chosen for the same task in the remote countryside. The state should also compliment those in charge of edification, along with virtuous women themselves.[102] The 1485 *Great Code of Administration* formally legalized these recommendations—publishing the vernacular version of the *Illustrated Guide* and circulating it through the instruction of patriarchs, elders, and Confucian teachers.[103] In 1490, an abridged vernacular edition (*sanjŏngbon*) of the *Illustrated Guide* was completed with the stories of 105 exemplary men and women. Taking a court official's advice that the extensive contents of the original three-volume edition would hinder people's understanding of the text, this shortened one-volume version contained stories of 35 chaste women—29 Chinese and 6 Korean. In other words, of the 15 cases of chaste Korean women included in the original version, only 6 were selected—the case of Tomi's wife, 2 Koryŏ cases, and 3 Chosŏn ones—as the stories considered to most effectually inspire people.[104]

By the time of King Chungjong's reign, publication of the *Illustrated Guide* was thriving, as was the publication of other didactic texts. In 1511, the king had the Office of Editorial Review (Kyosŏgwan) publish and distribute about 2,940 copies of the *Illustrated Guide* to both central and local areas.[105] Although the proportion of those

102. *Sŏngjong sillok* 128:11b [1481/4/21].

103. *Kyŏngguk taejŏn* 3:43b.

104. Pak Sungjil (?–1507), a provincial governor of Kyŏnggi, was the official who proposed the abridged vernacular edition, an idea that King Sŏngjong enthusiastically accepted. *Sŏngjong sillok* 229:1a [1489/6/1]. However, because the records were not revised from their original form, the abridged version simply contained fewer stories of exemplars in its single volume. *Sŏngjong sillok* 229:16b [1489/6/18]. This abridged edition contains, in addition to the women included in the "Chaste Women" section, four stories of Chinese filial daughters or daughters-in-law in the "Filial Children" section, but no case of a Korean filial daughter.

105. *Chungjong sillok* 14:39b [1511/10/20]. Since the *Illustrated Guide* consists of three separate books—on loyal subjects, filial children, and chaste women—the total number of books was about 8,820. It was published additionally by six regional facilities: Haeju (Hwanghae Province), Samch'ŏk (Kwangwŏn Province), Namwŏn and Namp'yŏng (Chŏlla Province), and Sŏnsan and Sŏngju (Kyŏngsang Province). See Kang Myŏnggwan, *Yŏllyŏ ŭi t'ansaeng*, 233.

printed in Korean script versus literary Chinese is not stated, this huge number of copies nonetheless denotes the state's commitment to popularizing the work among the ordinary populace. Shortly thereafter, in 1512, the king began to urge compilation of a sequel with additional exemplars not included in the original text.[106] As a result, in 1514, twenty-eight more women were added to the "Chaste Women" section, of which twenty were Chosŏn cases and eight, Chinese.[107] The same year saw publication of the *Revised Illustrated Guide to the Three Bonds and Chaste Women of the Eastern State (Tongguk sok samgang haengsil yŏllyŏdo)*, again seeking to capture the attention of female audiences. King Chungjong continued to push the printing of other moral handbooks in Korean script, such as the *Elementary Learning*, *Biographies of Chaste Women (Yŏllyŏjŏn)*, *Instructions for Women (Yŏgye)*, and *Regulations for Women (Yŏch'ik)*. Production of a longer list of texts was recommended by the Office of the Special Counselors on the grounds that the *Illustrated Guide*, though an excellent didactic text, only recorded outstanding exemplars from times of crisis and was not easily adapted to instilling moral conduct in people in everyday life.[108] The printing and circulating of didactic texts that had been initiated by King Sejong and that had continued under King Sŏngjong's sponsorship thus reached its apogee during King Chungjong's reign. Chungjong's efforts to indoctrinate society through the application of Confucian norms must have been inseparable from the political context in which he had dethroned his predecessor King Yŏnsan, whose reign had been dotted with countless immoral incidents. To legitimate his reign and establish his image as a Confucian sage-ruler, Chungjong promoted the edification of society through the inscription and distribution of moral tales—a matter in which Yŏnsan had shown little if any interest.[109]

106. *Chungjong sillok* 17:4a [1512/10/8].

107. *Chungjong sillok* 20:38b [1514/6/27].

108. *Chungjong sillok* 28:21b–22a [1517/6/27].

109. The State Council had memorialized King Yŏnsan for promoting the *Illustrated Guide* to women in the countryside, but he had virtually ignored them. *Yŏnsan'gun ilgi* 38:20a–22b [1500/8/29]. Yŏnsan once gave the *Illustrated Guide* to court officials, but only by way of mentioning the difficulty of finding truly loyal subjects. *Yŏnsan'gun ilgi* 55:23a [1504/9/18].

In the meantime, distributing the moral texts to the general populace did not always go smoothly. In 1515, King Chungjong, as already noted, pressed officials to send more volumes of the *Illustrated Guide* to Kaesŏng, where people still worshipped the previous Koryŏ rulers, engaged in Buddhist practices, and did not know the Confucian rituals.[110] In 1518, he again expressed concern as to whether people in local areas were being instructed according to the distributed text.[111] By 1536, court officials reported that people regarded the *Illustrated Guide* as something old and published in the past, and almost ignored the text. Proposing to produce a new version of the book, officials emphasized the need to print its vernacular version for the illiterate population.[112] The king also had provincial governors address the importance of inculcating people with its lessons when they toured their local areas.[113]

Moral texts in Korean script were certainly more accessible to ordinary people than those written in literary Chinese. To further assist comprehension, particularly by illiterate people, compilers added illustrations to each story either below the text or on the next page, and these proved to be powerful tools. On the assumption that written text would distract people from observing the "illustrations of chaste women" (*yŏllyŏdo*) that first appeared in the 1432 version of the *Illustrated Guide*, each image was designed to take up most of a page (see fig. 2.1). According to the Korean art historian Ko Yŏnhŭi, the format of Korean illustration in the *Illustrated Guide* was modeled on the Ming Chinese one, but employed sophisticated engraving skills inherited from the advanced Koryŏ printing culture of Buddhist texts.[114] This fifteenth-century format remained the prototype for later moral textbooks.[115]

Nevertheless, the immediate impact of the illustrations may have been rather limited. As Young Kyun Oh observes, "The flow of scenes

110. *Chungjong sillok* 22:30a [1515/6/9].

111. *Chungjong sillok* 32:27a [1518/3/11].

112. *Chungjong sillok* 81:54b [1536/5/12].

113. *Chungjong sillok* 93:41a [1540/6/22].

114. Ko Yŏnhŭi, "Chosŏn sidae yŏllyŏdo koch'al," 189–225. It is not clear who drew the illustrations in the moral textbooks.

115. For a thorough study on this topic, see Sin Sugyŏng, "Yŏllyŏjŏn kwa yŏllyŏdo ŭi imiji yŏn'gu," 171–200.

in the illustration does not follow any conceivable order in the *Illustrated Guide,* and it is hard to imagine how these illustrations made sense—with or without the written text."[116] Although the primary reason for inserting illustrations was to help the illiterate populace understand moral messages through visual images, people had difficulty fully engaging with a visual sequence of each account when they had no prior knowledge of the story or linguistic ability to read the text first (whether in literary Chinese or Korean script).[117] The illustrations also did change over the time. For example, as figure 2.1 shows, the later illustration of Tomi's wife's story is far simpler than the original version. Whereas the illustration in the 1432 *Illustrated Guide to the Three Bonds* depicts the story in sequence, with cartouches identifying both Tomi and his wife, the one in the 1797 *Illustrated Guide to the Five Relations* does not offer an order of events but only portrays the end of the story, with the new title "Tomi's Wife Running Away Together [with Her Husband]." It would be almost impossible to grasp the thread and message of the account from only the illustration without having already read or heard the whole story. Although the simplified illustrations in the later moral handbooks may have been prompted by increasing literacy in the Korean script over time, these images provided no useful clues for those who remained illiterate.

To what extent, then, did moral handbooks reach the general populace even in the remote countryside, as intended by the state? Finding such books in a *yangban* household (or in the house of a rich commoner) is no doubt plausible. Different editions and printed versions of the *Illustrated Guide* are extant today, some of which are preserved in libraries, archives, and museums.[118] This certainly indicates the high level of distribution and accessibility of the text throughout Chosŏn Korea. Although it is difficult to gauge how extensively ordinary people read these texts, the state clearly persisted in using them to edify the wider populace by selecting moral paragons, inscribing their stories,

116. Young Kyun Oh, *Engraving Virtue,* 117.

117. Young Kyun Oh, *Engraving Virtue,* 117.

118. For example, the Kyujanggak Archive itself holds a total of twenty volumes of the *Illustrated Guide* in different editions, seventeen of which have unknown years of publication.

transcribing them in Korean script, and engraving illustrations for them, as an indispensable tool to expedite the indoctrination process.

Visualizing Chastity: The Power of Red Arches

As examined in the previous section, illustrations were added to the didactic handbooks to facilitate the dissemination of morals to people beyond the literate elite group. The idea was that even those who were completely illiterate in classical Chinese and Korean script could learn from encountering pictorial material. A few remarkable accounts of chaste women had long been passed down orally, but the bulk of such stories remained available only in written form, as biographies, poetry, and essays in texts that circulated only within educated circles.

In 1470, the first year of King Sŏngjong, Queen Dowager Chŏng-hŭi (1418–1483) sent a blank screen (*sobyŏng*) to the Royal Secretariat (Sŭngjŏngwŏn) and ordered:[119]

> Let the censorial officers collect ancient words of inspiration and vigilance, then write them on the screen. Place [the screen] on the right and left sides of the king's seat, so that [the words on the screen] can be read for morning and evening reflection. *Books are seen only by opening them. [Yet words] written on a screen are always in front of your eyes and it is impossible not to look at them.* This should be helpful.[120]

Chŏnghŭi was the first queen dowager in Chosŏn history as well as the first queen to serve as regent, which she did for seven years on behalf of her grandson, the young King Sŏngjong, who was enthroned at the age of thirteen. Unlike her daughter-in-law, Queen Sohye (1437–1504), the king's mother, who was known for her exceptional education and for writing her own moral text, the *Inner Instruction* (*Naehun*),

---

119. Although referenced only as Queen Dowager in the *Sillok* entry, this must have been King Sŏngjong's maternal grandmother, known as Queen Dowager Chŏnghŭi, who was regent from 1470 to 1476. Chŏnghŭi is a posthumous title bestowed after her death in 1483.

120. *Sŏngjong sillok* 4:15a [1470/4/1]; emphasis added.

Chŏnghŭi was not trained in literary Chinese and learned Korean script relatively late in life. She would therefore have been aware of how much seeing visual material every day could aid the learning process. Responding to her wish, King Sŏngjong ordered the production of folding screens decorated with paintings of prominent figures in Chinese history and had the screens placed in the inner palace, not only to cultivate his own morality but to indoctrinate palace women with pictures of ten exemplary queens and secondary consorts known for their virtue.[121] Sŏngjong's biography also notes that he had painters make folding screens with paintings, stories, and poems about both exemplary and non-exemplary kingly figures in history, and admonished himself by viewing them, whether when sitting or lying down.[122] The use of folding screens for the moral edification of palace residents continued, as evidenced in the later *Sillok*. In 1531, in response to the attempted rape of a palace maid by Hong Uryong, a memorial headed by Censor-General Hwang Sau (1486–1536) called for strict governing of the palace and mentioned the production of a folding screen with paintings of virtuous consorts during Sŏngjong's reign as a means to articulate the palace's proper inner-outer boundary.[123]

Toward the latter part of the dynasty, folding screens were employed as didactic aids not only within the palace but among *yangban* families (fig. 2.3). For example, after viewing an eight-panel folding screen illustrated with virtuous women's stories that a nephew's wife had brought with her upon wedding, the scholar-official Cho Hyŏn-myŏng (1690–1752) complimented the noble insight of her parents vis-à-vis their daughter's education. In dedicating a preface to this particular folding screen, Cho wrote that it is "made of eight panels with stories of exemplary wives whose conduct can be enlightening and imitable, covering themes from domestic lessons, food

121. *Sŏngjong sillok* 71:4a [1476/9/13].

122. *Sŏngjong sillok* 297:18b–19a. For more records, see *Sŏngjong sillok* 61:3b [1475/11/9] and 72:7b–16a [1476/10/21].

123. *Chungjong sillok* 70:33a [1531/3/22]. Hong Uryong was a brother of Lady Hong (1494–1581), a consort of King Chungjong. Hong visited Lady Hong to pay his respects but was charged with attempting to rape her maid at night. For details of the Hong Uryong case, see *Chungjong sillok* 71:31a–b [1531/3/18].

2.3. The ten stories on this folding screen were selected from the *Illustrated Guide to the Five Relations*, compiled in 1797 at the order of King Chŏngjo. Each story is recorded as a painted illustration as well as in both literary Chinese and Korean script at the top of the panel. *Ten-Panel Folding Screen with Paintings on the "Illustrated Guide [to the Five Relations]" (Haengsilto sipkok pyŏngp'ung)*. 19th c. Folding screen; ink and color on paper. 87.6 × 39 cm. Ku 2248. Photograph courtesy of National Museum of Korea, Seoul.

preparation, [and] upbringing of children to proper spousal relations."[124] Instead of sending luxury items such as silk and jewelry as gifts for a daughter's wedding, Cho recommended that parents prepare more meaningful items like the folding screen because, "in inspiring one's mind, nothing is comparable to listening with one's ears and seeing with one's eyes. Viewing [a folding screen illustrated with virtues] would draw the sincere attention of even a woman of misdeeds

124. Cho Hyŏnmyŏng, "Yŏllyŏ pyŏngsŏ," *Kwirok chip*, 18:1a–3a.

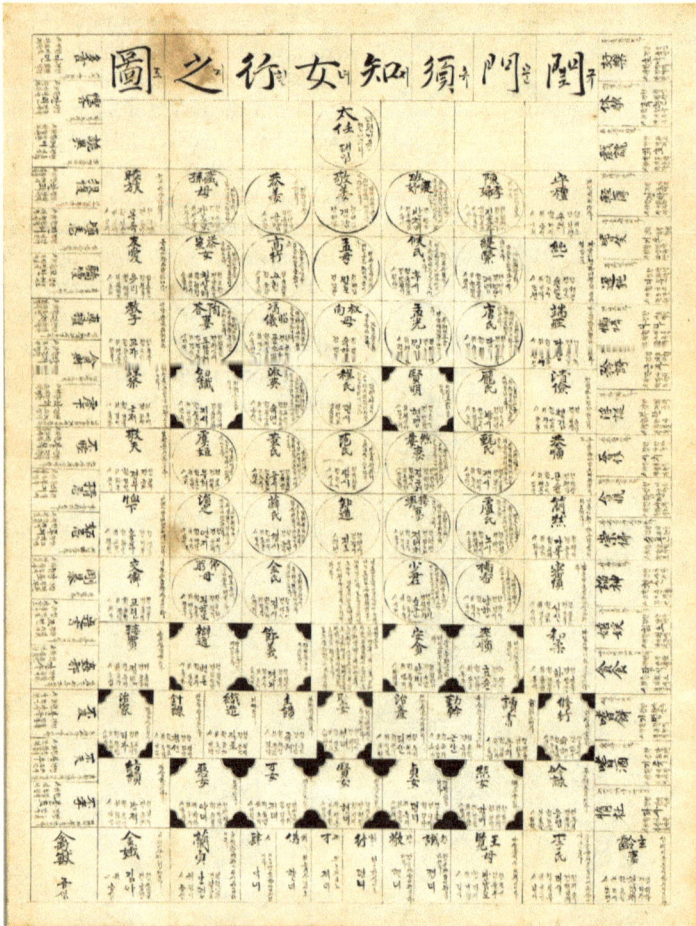

2.4. This board game presents a chart of behaviors that a woman should learn. It also provides the names of exemplary women drawn from the *Inner Instruction*, *Four Women's Classics* (*Yŏsasŏ*), and the *Illustrated Guide to the Three Bonds*, as well as those of some evil female figures in history. It is known that Queen Inhyŏn (1667–1701) personally devised this illustrated chart while residing outside the palace for six years after being deposed by her husband, King Sukchong. According to her brother, Min Chinwŏn (1664–1736), "The Queen created this to inspire women to proper conduct as they play the game. She thought that this foldable board could be put in a woman's pocket any time, whether [she] is young or old." "Illustration of Women's Essential Knowledge and Conduct in the Inner Quarters" ("Kyumun suji yŏhaeng chi to"). Ink on paper. 91.2 × 67.7 cm. Sŏul Yŏksa Pangmulgwan, *Chosŏn yŏin ŭi sam kwa munhwa*, 175–76. Ku 7204. Photograph courtesy of National Museum of Korea, Seoul.

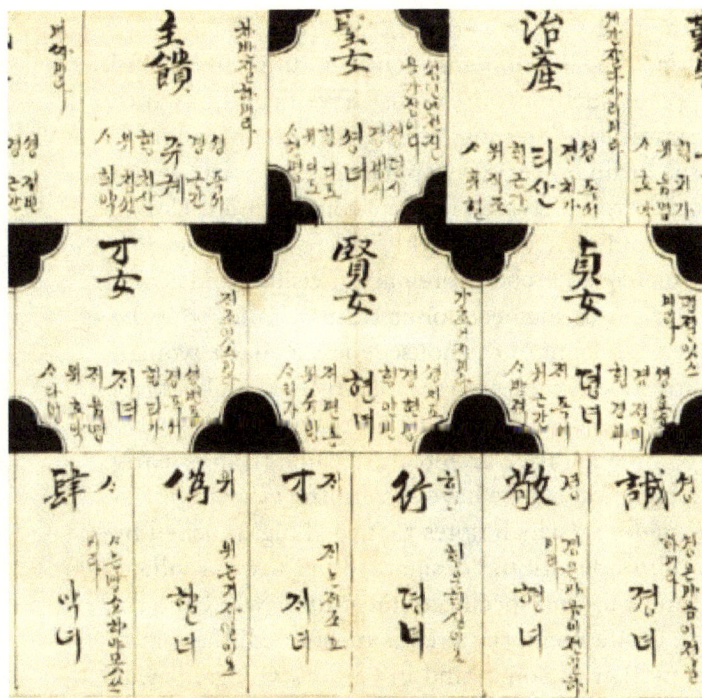

2.4 DETAIL: The bottom line features six starting points, each representing women's characteristics, which are also engraved on six-faced dice. Based on the roll, players advance to one of the upper columns, such as "talented woman" (*chaenyŏ* 才女), "virtuous woman" (*hyŏnnyŏ* 賢女), or "faithful woman" (*chŏngnyŏ* 貞女).

and would be awakened. How much more so for a bride born with a beautiful nature!"[125]

When the scholar Pak Yunwŏn (1734–1799) was consulted about a folding screen to be placed in the bedroom of his nephew's wife, he carefully selected the most noteworthy passages about womanly virtue from texts such as the *Elementary Learning, Instructions for Women*, and *Book of Poetry*. Pak then had his nephew, the husband himself, write each passage onto an eight-panel folding screen. Pak noted that "a wife would become as exemplary as the ancient women of virtue by observing [the folding screen] all the time and putting into action in person [what those women's virtue inspired]."[126]

125. Cho Hyŏnmyŏng, "Yŏllyŏ pyŏngsŏ," *Kwirok chip*, 18:1a–3a.
126. Pak Yunwŏn, "P'alcho yŏgye sŏ chongjabu Yissi ch'imbyŏng," *Kŭnjae chip*, 13:8b–10b.

Although it is clear that people were fully aware of the didactic power of visual materials, the use of items such as folding screens and board games (fig. 2.4) for such purposes must have been limited to women of *yangban* families. The most effective and approachable didactic objects for the ordinary female populace, in contrast, would have been the memorial arches erected in their communities. Unlike moral handbooks and folding screens—which were expensive, privately owned items—memorial arches were public, visible, and accessible to everyone regardless of socioeconomic status. Standing at the entrance to the village or in front of the house where a chaste woman had lived, the story embedded in the arch was clearly discernible to all passersby.

The practice of commemorative architecture came from as early as the Three Kingdoms period, as we have seen in the *Historical Records of the Three Kingdoms*, which notes that the king, touched by the filial daughter Chiŭn's devotion, "designated her town a village fostering filiality."[127] Although no specific architectural award or term referring to the erection of a memorial arch is mentioned, there may have been a physical marker of some kind in Chiŭn's village. It was during the Koryŏ dynasty that the building of monuments to commemorate moral achievements was established as one form of official award. During the Chosŏn dynasty, the state endowed memorial arches regularly as part of institutionalizing the state-reward system. Memorial arches became far more visible as the number of awardees increased, and by the end of the dynasty, it was not unusual to find memorial arches even in extremely remote rural areas and on distant islands.

Diverse in form, location, and architecture, memorial arches were considered the most prestigious of all the honors conferred upon the recipients of chastity awards in Chosŏn society. As with the criteria for chastity, however, concrete state guidelines for arch construction are difficult to find. There is rich evidence in official records about the conferring of memorial arches, but insight into how the award was actually executed in local areas is scarcely available. How and why

127. Kim Pusik, *Samguk sagi*, 1:704–5.

were these arches built, who patronized them, and how were they received by the local people?

Existing scholarship discusses the practice of erecting memorial arches simply as one type of prize within the state-reward system, and as an abstract symbol of honoring a chaste woman and her family. Studies on the dissemination of the chastity ideal have concentrated exclusively on textual analysis, and virtually no study has explored the materiality of these arches and their larger socio-visual impact on the community, or the detailed process of constructing the arches at both the governmental and local levels. Yet, in examining memorial arches, we can still "retrieve the message conveyed by the technical practices and products, to see how social roles were naturalized through that most powerful form of indoctrination, the bodily habit."[128] Indeed, the Chosŏn court did not grant a memorial arch simply as a reward but emphasized its significance as the medium through which the chastity ideal was transmitted to the illiterate local populace. Nothing was more influential than seeing, touching, or walking by and through architecture built to commemorate chaste women, many of whose (extreme) stories were quite remote from contemporary women's experiences, both spatially and temporally. The key purpose in building them was "not only to promote the chastity ideal, but to evoke [it in people's minds] by seeing [the arches] and hearing [about chaste acts], thus letting [the virtuous conduct] become part of ordinary people's lives."[129] Material rewards directly benefitted the virtuous woman and her family, but arches could have a wider impact beyond the familial circle, on people in the community and even on strangers from outside.

128. Bray, *Technology and Gender*, 2. In her analysis of the structure of late imperial Chinese houses, Bray points out how the building embodies the hierarchies of gender, generation, and rank inherent in the Chinese social order.

129. Yulian Wu, "Let People See," 111–63. In her careful examination of the material and cultural implications of chastity arches constructed in the Huizhou region during the High Qing period, Yulian Wu powerfully shows the dynamic and contested interactions between the imperial court, local merchants, and residents over the chastity cult in Chinese society at that time. Ever since I attended Wu's talk at the 2014 Annual Meeting of the Association for Asian Studies, her work has greatly inspired me to think of Chosŏn chastity arches from the visual angle.

The Chosŏn kings understood the overarching implications and advantages of arch construction. For instance, when one wife was nominated for her superior virtue in 1529, King Chungjong responded: "The wife of Chang Chŭngmun, Madam Kim, displays [extraordinary] fidelity. If the government exempted her household from miscellaneous duties (*pokho*) and rewarded her with rice, how would people in the remote countryside know that her virtue is exceptional? Nothing is more effective than the memorial arch in moving people's minds and leading them to see and observe. Add [this] correction and resubmit [the document]."[130] About two months later, a memorial arch was granted on behalf of Madam Kim's virtue.[131] And in 1786, when a woman named Kim P'allyŏn killed herself with poison after a neighbor named Kang Ch'wimun spread the false rumor that he had had adulterous relations with her, King Chŏngjo ordered a memorial arch to be built in her honor and for Kang to be interrogated "under P'allyŏn's arch."[132] When she died, P'allyŏn was only eighteen years old and was soon to marry her fiancé. Valuing her righteous spirit highly, the king used the memorial arch to commemorate the young woman's commitment and to alert village people that anyone violating a woman's sexual integrity would be punished like Kang in a vivid scene of public interrogation.

Memorial arches usually contained an engraved record that identified the honored woman and provided a brief account of her virtuous conduct. Although such inscriptions, written in literary Chinese, were comprehensible only to the literate, the overriding purpose of constructing a memorial arch was to inspire people irrespective of their education, social status, age, and gender. This is expressed in Yi Imyŏng's (1658–1722) tomb inscription written for Madam Yi: "Alas! Those who do not have tears in their eyes after passing by the tombstone or reading what is inscribed on it are no longer human beings."[133]

130. *Chungjong sillok* 65:21a [1529/4/6].
131. *Chungjong sillok* 65:64b [1529/6/19].
132. *Ch'ugwanji*, 1:451–54.
133. Yi Imyŏng, "Yuin Yussi myop'yo," *Sojae chip*, 40:10b–13a. Here Yi uses the term *yuin* to show his respect for the deceased wife of a Confucian scholar without any governmental position. On the visual impact of tombstones, Sun Joo Kim discusses ancestor tombstones and elaborate gravesites as effectively displaying Chosŏn *yangban* families' status in local society. Sun Joo Kim, *Voice from the North*, 29–30.

Often built in front of the village or the house of a moral exemplar, the memorial arches and their unique architecture easily caught people's attention. With their distinctive color, architectural style, and materials, the arches served as a salient representation of the official honor bestowed upon a chaste woman and her family in the town. For travelers and visitors, a memorial arch was also a clear sign of the moral edification that the local community had achieved.

Meanwhile, despite the state's zeal for memorial arch construction to edify the broad populace, their erection in local areas proved a challenging task. Whereas it was the state that approved and granted the award, it was the local government that carried out the actual work. Once the reward was announced, the designated local government was in charge of supplying both the funds and the labor required for construction and thus came under a heavy burden in executing the reward. Not only that, but low-ranking clerks in the Ministry of Rites often mislaid an order from the court between other documents, where it could remain forever.[134]

Maintenance of the arches could also be problematic. In 1477, the Ministry of Rites accused local magistrates of negligence in maintaining the arches. Instead of building them with proper form and at an appropriate location, they simply placed a log on the side of the street without any marker so that it was hardly seen as a chastity arch. Moreover, when the wood rotted as the years went by, the local government repeatedly pressured the chaste widow in question to repair it herself, rather than doing it on her behalf. Not having the financial means to do so, the widow had to beg funds from neighbors to repair it.[135] To remedy such problems, the Ministry of Rites proposed that "though we had villages following the Chinese example—building a rack and hanging a plaque to display the moral deed—the foremost purpose should be promotion of virtue, not colorful elaboration of the arch. . . . Inheriting our old, existing practice, we need to build a [false] gate (hŏmun) with a plaque, then erect a stone underneath [the gate] where the name and moral conduct of the honored are engraved."[136]

134. *Chungjong sillok* 98:76b [1542/7/27].
135. *Sŏngjong sillok* 79:17b [1477/4/22].
136. *Sŏngjong sillok* 79:17b [1477/4/22].

2.5. Memorial arch granted to the chaste wife Madam Yi, wife of the late Koryŏ scholar Yang Susaeng, presumed to be one of the oldest chastity arches from the Chosŏn dynasty extant in South Korea. The award was conferred in 1467, but the monument house erected over the stone was built in 1774, replicating the "cinnabar and blue-green" memorial building style. Photograph courtesy of Culture and Tourism Department, Sunch'ang-gun, North Chŏlla Province.

By making the components of memorial arches simpler, the Ministry of Rites tried to resolve local governments' inattentive attitude toward chastity arches in their regions.

Yet again, in 1542, a discussion on memorial arches returned to the court: it centered on criticism of local magistrates who often had local clerks engrave recipients' names on tombstones, instead of writing the names themselves. Because of the clerks' lack of calligraphy training, the engraved characters appeared ugly and small and could barely be deciphered. The Chosŏn court therefore proposed constructing a tall building with pillars to protect the tombstone, instead of erecting a gate-style arch, and even painting the roof in bright "cinnabar and blue-green" (tan'ch'ŏng)—that is, in elaborate patterns of red, green, blue, and yellow (fig. 2.5).[137]

The stylistic specifics that the Ministry of Rites suggested became the basic features of the chastity arch in Chosŏn society, reflecting the long tradition of building memorial arches. In addition to the house-type memorial arch, a gate style was often built in the town or in front of a chaste woman's house. The area underneath the gate was open, with no doors, and people could walk through. Typically known as a chastity gate (yŏllyŏmun), the structure was also called a red gate (hongmun) given the paint color used on it. Because both types of memorial arch are simply referred to as chŏngnyŏ in historical records, without differentiation, the textual sources cannot provide clues to the actual arch design.[138] As with the red gate, the house-type arch was also constructed with red-painted wood. No source mentions when and how the arches came to be painted red, but the color represented single-hearted devotion and had long signified loyalty, filiality, and chastity in Korea.[139] Along with this moral symbolism, the red color

137. *Chungjong sillok* 98:76b–9a [1542/7/27].

138. I use the terms *memorial arches* and *chastity arches* to refer to all buildings granted under the *chŏnggyŏ* and *chŏngmun* categories in the original texts, although there were several different styles of arch, predominantly the house style and the gate style.

139. The red gate called *hongsalmun* was also built at the entrance of the king's grave or other Confucian shrines in Chosŏn Korea, implying that the color red symbolized "sacred."

allowed the arches to be clearly visible "even far in between villages" and was highly effective in inspiring people.[140]

Moreover, memorial arches manifest different regional cultures and material resources. Architectural style became more diverse in conjunction with the large number of chastity rewards granted toward the latter part of the Chosŏn dynasty. In some regions, the inside of a memorial house was empty, for performing rituals. In others, such as Madam Chang's arch on Cheju Island (fig. 2.6), a large stone filled the space. Whereas wood was commonly used for chastity arches in other areas of the Korean peninsula, most Cheju arches were built of the basalt unique to the island. Lightweight and with countless holes, basalt is the result of the island's past volcanic activity. Although no record tells us why Cheju people used this material, the reason could be both practical and deliberate: using the widely available slabs of basalt would have saved wood for fuel, and the special stone material highlights the distinct moral spirit of the Cheju region—an island on the outermost periphery of the country, remote from the continental center.

At the same time, the arches naturally display the hierarchies of social status embedded in Chosŏn society. Memorial arches built for members of illustrious families were larger in size and more elegantly decorated than those for ordinary recipients. Yet because arches were awarded to anyone of exceptional virtue irrespective of social class, these monuments reinforced the state's commitment to the overall moral project of reaching and edifying the entire society. Especially in the second part of the dynasty, both textual and material evidence shows that several arches were even erected for slaves whose moral conduct was recognized by the scholarly community and the state. In 1794, Sim Naksu (1739–1799), a secret inspector to Cheju Island, recommended a reward for a female slave of the Pak family, Kosorak. Even refusing to marry, Kosorak devoted her life to serving the chaste widow Madam Pak. Touched by this story, King Chŏngjo ordered the

---

140. *Yŏngjo sillok* 66:18b–20a [1747/10/2]. In memorializing about the unfavorable conditions in the Southwestern Region (Honam), Wŏn Kyŏngha (1698–1761), an officer in charge of the region's agriculture, remarked upon the traditionally virtuous spirit of the region by pointing out the many red gates erected in the area that were visible even from afar.

2.6. Memorial arch in the town of Aewŏl on Cheju Island inscribed "Madam Chang, the loyal, filial, and chaste wife of the scholar-official Ko Chŏngŏn" (T'ongjŏngdaebu Ko Chŏngŏn ch'unghyoyŏl Changssi ryŏ). The inscription was painted red after being engraved. The back of the memorial stone reads "Madam Chang wished to die instead of her ill husband, but heaven did not prolong his life. She served her mother-in-law with utmost filial piety and performed mourning rituals with devotion. In the year of chŏngmi (1907) when the country was in crisis, she donated money to the government by selling her clothes. What she did was chastity for her husband, filiality for her mother-in-law, and loyalty to the king!" Photograph courtesy of Jeju Studies Archive, Center for Jeju Studies.

erection of an arch commemorating both women together, by recording "the name of the slave *one line below* the name of her owner on the arch."[141] The king also added, "As far as people passing by the arch, those riding on horses should give salute to it and those walking should pay respect to it by pointing to the arch."[142]

141. *Chŏngjo sillok* 39:65b–66a [1794/4/22]; emphasis added.
142. *Chŏngjo sillok* 39:65b–66a [1794/4/22].

The arches dedicated to slaves served several purposes. For the state, they demonstrated that the state's orthodox moral vision extended to the bottom of the social hierarchy, while also serving as public symbols that would simultaneously inspire people and reiterate dynastic power. For the society's most marginalized members, the arches provided a sense of belonging to the ethical realm prescribed by the state. By witnessing the arch's physical presence or being involved with an arch, whether as a recipient or a laborer, illiterate subjects had the opportunity to foster their society's moral judgments about the chastity ideal. As the number of chastity arch awardees increased dramatically in the late Chosŏn, so did the building of arches. The more arches that were built, the more visible they became. The immediate impact of seeing the arches and passing by or through them was far more direct than any other indoctrination project implemented by the Chosŏn state. Proudly placed in locations that ensured wide viewership, memorial arches were very much part of communal life and served as venues for making private morality tales part of the public memory of the communities. Pursued by the state, elites, and local communities for different reasons, and prompting a variety of reactions among the populace, chastity arches became integrated into local people's lives as vital elements of the spaces where they engaged in their everyday moral practices.

Commemorating Chastity:
The Wars and Honorable Death

The Chosŏn culture of chastity was shaped by legal, material, textual, and visual efforts on both the central and local levels. Although the state initiated and tried to systemize the moralizing project, the task of inculcating the populace with the chastity ideal was constantly interwoven with debates and dialogues between the king and Confucian officials in response to ceaseless reports and memorials submitted by local offices and local scholars. Institutional changes targeting both elite and ordinary women accelerated the systematic promotion of female chastity, setting the pace for the burgeoning chastity culture throughout Chosŏn Korea. Nevertheless, it is not an overstatement that the war experiences in the late sixteenth and early seventeenth centuries played a pivotal role in shaping the route of chastity discourse and practice in the later Chosŏn dynasty.

The shattering Imjin War and Manchu Invasions ushered in an era of chaste martyrdom in which many women were honored for choosing heroic death in defense of their sexual dignity. In the chaos of wartime, women died while avoiding sexual violence from invading soldiers, since violating conquered women was often considered a way to do violence to the invaded country and its men as well. Numerous official and other accounts record the intensive sexual violence of the invading armies during these wars.[143] In 1593, still in the midst of the Imjin War with Japan, court officials memorialized the king to publicize the names of loyal subjects and chaste women as a way to reinstate social control and moral order. In addition to identifying people who displayed loyalty and chastity, the officials wanted these subjects to be documented in a book that would be distributed widely.[144] The king approved the project, yet the exigencies of war seem to have blocked any tangible action. Two years later, in 1595, the Office of the Inspector-General and the Ministry of Rites again urged a search for exemplary people in the face of the destruction of human morality, stressing that commemorating people's honorable deaths was a task as critical as military defense. After repeated pressure by the state, provincial governors submitted a long list of names for public recognition.[145]

By 1613, the Office of the Special Counselors was put in charge of publishing the records of chaste women. But the matter of veracity became problematic given the lack of evidence of chaste acts. Because many women who were under consideration for being chaste had died before anyone could attest to their chastity, it was difficult to trace their genuine intentions or to know whether they had in fact eventually lost their chastity in cases where, for example, they had been taken prisoner and transported to Japan. Their families could have submitted

143. For example, *A Miscellaneous Record Written during the War* (*Nanjung chamnok*) by Cho Kyŏngnam (1570–1641), who participated in a righteous army during the Imjin War, describes Chosŏn women's miserable situation during the war.

144. *Sŏnjo sillok* 42:35b [1593/9/29].

145. *Sŏnjo sillok* 65:33a [1595/7/18]; 65:34a [1595/7/19].

false reports, concealing the truth, to seek posthumous benefits on behalf of these women. The court officials were concerned that honoring unworthy women would prompt ridicule from the populace instead of inspiring people with virtuous cases.[146]

Despite such doubts, the state eventually compiled eighteen volumes of the *New Expanded Illustrated Guide to the Three Bonds of the Eastern State* (*Tongguk sinsok samgang haengsilto*) in 1617.[147] Even with the desperate postwar fiscal condition, the government's investment in printing the extensive volumes of the *New Expanded Illustrated Guide* testifies to its pledge to honor deaths that were deemed worthy. Written both in literary Chinese and Korean script, eight volumes were dedicated to chaste women, accounting for a total of 719 cases. Except for 2 women from Paekche and Silla and 24 from the Koryŏ dynasty, the rest had lived during the Chosŏn, among which 553 women were contemporary to King Sŏnjo's reign (r. 1567–1608). Moreover, the stories of 441 of these women were directly related to the war with Japan (whereas the names of only 59 male loyal subjects are registered therein). Of those 441 women, 437 had perished—or chosen death—while avoiding sexual assault by invading soldiers.[148]

The large number of female martyrs included in the *New Expanded Illustrated Guide* shows that death had emerged as the core criterion singled out by the state, or as the embodiment of the ideal of chastity at any given moment in time. In other words, chastity now had to be demonstrated through death if a woman was to be eligible to become what Tobie Meyer-Fong has termed the "dynasty's dead."[149] Commemorating chaste women continued in the wake of the Manchu Invasions, and the *Sillok* records that the government designated more than 200 chaste women during the twenty-six years of King Injo's reign alone. This number is remarkable when compared with the total number of reward recipients up to the Imjin War—about 272 women

---

146. *Kwanghaegun ilgi* 73:78a–b [1613/12/12]. The historian of the *Sillok* comments that, after the books with new names of chaste women were published, some people even used their pages as wallpaper or to cover a cooking pot as a lid.

147. *Kwanghaegun ilgi* 39:58b [1617/3/11].

148. Hŏ Namlin, "Yŏllyŏ tamnon kwa Imjin waeran," 185–86.

149. Meyer-Fong, *What Remains*, 137.

recognized for chastity are found in *Sillok* between the reigns of King T'aejo (r. 1392–1398) and King Myŏngjong.

The impressive numbers of chaste women honored after the wars with Japan and the Manchus have been generally understood to reflect women's internalization of the chastity ideal, driven by the state's ardent promotion during the first half of the dynasty.[150] Some recent studies, in contrast, revisit the role of the Imjin War in shaping of the postwar chastity discourse in conjunction with the state's mobilization of female sexuality as a device to rebuild the country and sustain patriarchal mores in the postwar Korean society.[151] Nam-lin Hur, in particular, highlights the male ruling elites' invocation of the chastity ideology as a way to restore their status in the postwar society, which in turn glorified the violent nature of chaste action.[152] In considering bodily performance (i.e., suicide) to be the utmost expression of the chastity ideal in the second part of the dynasty, such a view indeed endorses the postwar period as a turning point for the chastity discourse in Chosŏn society.

In delving into the issue of the war experiences and the dramatic rise of chaste women, however, we also need to situate the society's growing obsession with female chastity and chaste suicide in relation to the dynasty's broader commemorative culture, which I see as the critical momentum for the phenomenon. Although the Koryŏ state had venerated moral subjects, the commemoration of virtuous paragons became a central part of state-initiated rituals only with the foundation of the Chosŏn dynasty. Hand in hand with seeking to promote the orthodox, state-sanctioned values of chastity, filiality, and loyalty to the entire society, the crucial task of honoring and remembering exemplary people of all social classes—whether alive or dead— remained essential to the Chosŏn state's ideological legitimacy. With a strong sense of posterity, many authors of commemorative writings

150. Pak Chu, *Chosŏn sidae ŭi chŏngp'yo chŏngch'aek*, 143.

151. Yi Sugin, "Imjin War and the Official Discourse," 137–56. Another study examining the Imjin War and female chastity by Michael J. Pettid points out the fissure between the records in didactic texts and those in unofficial accounts, revealing contrary representations of chaste women during the war. Pettid, "Fashioning Womanly Confucian Virtue," 357–77.

152. Hŏ Namlin, "Yŏllyŏ tamnon kwa Imjin waeran," 183–210.

emphasized how critical it was that these individuals' moral achievements not be forgotten by later generations and so must be transmitted to people still alive. Indeed, ensuring collective memory appears often to have been these writers' primary motivation for taking up their brushes.

The Imjin War and the military conflicts marked by the Manchu Invasions dominated almost a half century in the mid-Chosŏn, producing countless war dead. Especially for Koreans, the fall of the Ming represented the loss of the center of civilization to barbarians, ultimately threatening the very basis of Korean cultural identity.[153] The changing world order in East Asia, along with the domestic crisis generated by the war experiences, required the Chosŏn state to search for "a new episteme of the world and the self" as a way to preserve its political and cultural identity.[154] Despite ongoing dispute in the seventeenth-century intellectual community about this new mission, the Chosŏn court was empowered by a keen consciousness that it was the last bastion of Confucian civilization.[155] The widespread belief that the country established by those [Manchu] barbarians will not have the fortune to last even a century continued to prevail in the eighteenth-century Chosŏn court, combined with a piquant sense of loyalty to the Ming. The Chinese empire ruled by the Manchus was no longer considered the center of the world, and a number of maps of East Asia produced in seventeenth- and eighteenth-century Chosŏn continue to depict China at the time of the Song or Ming dynasty.[156]

Under this changing intellectual view of the Chosŏn state's role in East Asia and duty to uphold Confucian morality, the state-sanctioned

153. Haboush, "Constructing the Center," 46–90; and Haboush, "Dead Bodies in the Postwar Discourse," 416–17.

154. Haboush and Deuchler, *Culture and the State*, 5.

155. In examining the ritual controversy of seventeenth-century Chosŏn, JaHyun Kim Haboush shows how members of the intellectual community clashed over the issue of Korea's search for a new cultural and ideological identity. In contrast to conventional Korean scholarship that has generally accepted the postulation that seventeenth-century Korea embraced the idea of *Chosŏn chunghwa* (Chosŏn-centered ideology), Haboush probes the diversity in scholarly discourse that existed at that time. Haboush, "Constructing the Center," 46–90. For a representative study on *Chosŏn chunghwa* in Korean scholarship, see Chŏng Okcha, *Chosŏn hugi Chosŏn chunghwa*.

156. Pae Usŏng, "Chosŏn hugi kukt'ogwan kwa ch'ŏnhagwan," 335–50.

commemoration of the righteous dead thrived. The discourse on dead bodies and on martyrdom preoccupied Chosŏn politics as the court set about the daunting task of reinstating Korean society after the devastating wars.[157] Moreover, that society was largely left with—and split between—those who had survived the wars and those who had chosen death as their ideal. Deciding who would be commemorated or not emerged as a contested task, and since only those who were still alive could make these decisions, the discourse of martyrdom became extremely intricate. For the dead, having perished proved their commitment to righteousness and virtue; yet for the living, commemorating the dead could highlight their own humiliating path of avoiding death out of fear.[158] One of the most illuminating examples of the latter is seen in the thorny disputes in the postwar Chosŏn court concerning the so-called brought-back women.[159] During the turbulence and hostility of the Manchu Invasions, many Chosŏn women were captured by invading troops and taken to the home country of the enemy as prisoners of war. Those who survived and returned to Chosŏn then faced questions regarding their chastity, and the issue of "brought-back" women posed a dilemma for the government when their in-law families sought divorces from these women for their "possibly" lost sexual integrity.[160]

<hr/>

157. Haboush, "Dead Bodies in the Postwar Discourse," 415–42. For a compelling study on commemorating the war dead in post-Taiping China, see Meyer-Fong, *What Remains*, 99–174.

158. Haboush, "Dead Bodies in the Postwar Discourse," 415–42; Kim Ho, "Politics and the Discourse," 45–70.

159. The term *hwanhyang-nyŏ* 還鄉女 (literally, "homecoming women") has been widely used to refer to these women in Korean society, and most Korean scholars also employ this term. See, for example, Yi Sugin, *Chŏngjŏl ŭi yŏksa*, 146–49. However, this term in fact does not appear in Chosŏn official records. In the *Sillok*, these women are referred to as *p'iro chi nyŏ* 被虜之女 or *sokwhan p'iro punyŏ* 贖還被虜婦女—the women who were brought to [China] and came back to [Chosŏn].

160. On the study of "brought-back" women, see Morioka Yasu, "Syokanhiryohujin no riimondaini tsuite," 56–93. The case of Chang Yu (1587–1638), a high official and the crown prince's father-in-law, is a well-known divorce request for a brought-back woman. Chang petitioned the Ministry of Rites that he could not readmit to his family his daughter-in-law, who had been taken to China during the war and would have lost her chastity. Most officials supported Chang's request, but King Injo did not

Although the culture of commemoration had long been the core that gave structure to Chosŏn society, it thus grew and deepened greatly through these traumatic war experiences in the late sixteenth and early seventeenth centuries, extending its main performers from the central government to the local populations. Responding to the state's call, families and communities not only participated in the state-led commemoration activities for their own war dead but also gradually engaged in local modes of remembering the dead through collective efforts. Countless pieces of writing, including petitions and circular letters to secure the state's recognition of local martyrs, illuminate how the second part of the Chosŏn dynasty became engrossed with the discourse of martyrdom.[161] Among the numerous war dead, women became a keen focus because of their heroic actions, which often took the form of suicide to avoid falling prey to enemy forces. In a society where the Confucian patriarchal norms governed gender relations and women had limited visibility beyond the domestic realm, this commemorative space, generated through tumultuous war experiences and exigencies, allowed women to be publicly remembered. It was in this historical context that the chastity discourse continued to evolve throughout the rest of the dynasty.

*   *   *

This chapter has focused on the evolution of chastity culture, asking why the idea of female chastity was valued more highly by the Confucian reformers with the dawn of the Chosŏn dynasty than in the previous times; how the socio-political-cultural environment rendered the discourse of chastity important in Chosŏn society; and why the Chosŏn state attempted to formalize the concept of chastity.

---

permit it, following the opinion of Prime Minister Ch'oe Myŏnggil (1586–1647) instead. *Injo sillok* 36:23b–24b [1638/3/11].

161. On the postwar discourse of martyrdom, see Sun Joo Kim, "Culture of Remembrance," 563–85; Saeyoung Park, "Expansion of Ideal Subjecthood," 45–74; Haboush, *Great East Asian War*; and Christina Han, "Scholar-Soldier in Mourning Robes," 61–92.

The culture of chastity in Chosŏn was developed as part of the broader orthodox, state-led moralizing project through four major means of indoctrination: institutionalizing, inscribing, visualizing, and commemorating the core chastity ideal. In institutionalizing chastity, the state legalized acceptable modes of feminine behavior and administered the state-reward system. Didactic texts recounting numerous tales of chaste heroines inscribed the virtue of chastity in the minds of people by their state-sponsored compilation and publication. Memorial arches dedicated to chaste women served as the most powerful material resource for visualizing the chaste paragons practicing virtue among the ordinary populace in everyday interactions. The late sixteenth and early seventeenth-century war experiences reinvigorated the practice of commemoration that had long existed in Korean culture as the state-sanctioned public space where chaste martyrs ultimately became an endorsement of the political legitimation of the state.

Indeed, the evolution of Chosŏn chastity culture was a long process that inherited the previous practice of praising women's virtuous conduct. It was promoted by the new dynasty's ideological campaign to instill Confucian morals and encountered continuous shifts in meaning throughout the dynasty. All these driving forces behind the growth of chastity culture were enmeshed and interwoven with different interests and cannot be understood as the outcome of any single hegemonic historical or political factor. Emphasis on female chastity in the Chosŏn was not a mere device for monitoring and regulating women's sexual behavior; rather, it emerged as a critical nexus where the agenda of the Confucian state, the proprieties of elite *yangban* families, and the views of various individuals intermingled and were intensely contested by different groups for their own objectives.

The most fascinating aspect of chastity practice during the Chosŏn is that it functioned in a dual context in relation to one's social status. On the one hand, although the Chosŏn state maintained a strict societal hierarchy, honoring chastity through the state-reward system operated in a remarkably inclusive way that was open to every woman in the society, including slaves, regardless of class, age, and regional background. On the other hand, a clear distinction between the socioethical expectations of *yangban* women and non-*yangban* women persisted. Although any woman of exceptional virtue could be nominated for state recognition, chastity performed by a woman of lower status was applauded far more highly than for an upper-class woman, because of the assumption that lower-class women lacked an inborn capacity for moral cultivation. Chastity thus occupied the heart of the virtue paradigm that informed significant notions of women's position in the society, and the implications of chastity came to be disproportionately amplified given the concrete social and political value of female virtue as an attribute of individual, family, and community moral integrity and reputation—a theme that is further discussed in chapter 3.

CHAPTER THREE

The Politics of Chastity Discourse

Since every widow in this country keeps her chastity, her family cannot be recognized as something remarkable unless she commits suicide.
—Pak Chiwŏn

There is nothing more malicious in the world than killing oneself. . . . If a wife takes her life to follow a husband who died in peace, this is only an empty suicide without righteousness at all.
—Chŏng Yagyong‡

These statements by two prominent late Chosŏn scholars have been widely understood to criticize the fanatical extremes of female chastity practiced since the eighteenth century. Pak Chiwŏn laments the fact that suicide is the utmost representation of a widow's chastity, and Chŏng Yagyong judges taking one's own life as irrational self-destruction, not an act to be revered. Indeed, the vast numbers of chastity accounts produced after the Imjin War and Manchu Invasions attest to this obsession with widow celibacy and suicide, as illustrated not only in official histories and local gazetteers but also in biographies, fiction, poetry, songs, and countless eulogies, epitaphs, and essays

‡ The epigraphs are from Pak Chiwŏn, "Yŏllyŏ Hamyang Pakssi chŏn," *Yŏnam chip*, 1:34b; and Chŏng Yagyong, "Yŏlburon," *Kugyŏk Tasan simunjip*, 5:151–54.

composed in most cases by Confucian literati. Along with visual evidence such as the numerous memorial arches constructed and preserved in local areas, the late Chosŏn society's ardent devotion to women's chaste actions has convinced modern scholars that the ideological roots of chaste suicide lie in the Confucian patriarchal norms and their notions of purity, though the question remains as to how and why chastity culture flourished so excessively in the second half of the dynasty.[1]

The country's war experiences in the late sixteenth and early seventeenth centuries certainly intensified the state's embrace of Confucian principles as part of the reordering of the postwar society, including active commemoration of virtuous deaths. In addition to this official initiative, reflections about the perceived moral decadence of society increasingly dominated literary writings in the postwar period. This perceived moral decadence was not a literary reaction unique to this time. It had occupied the minds of earlier Confucian literati as well, who accentuated exemplary acts of the uneducated lower classes and of women as a way to discipline their own morals.[2] The traumatic events of the wars and the collapse of the Ming dynasty renewed this reaction and had a profound epistemological and emotional impact as the entire society navigated the postwar turmoil.[3] Eulogies, epitaphs,

1. Concrete numeric data for "extant" Chosŏn-era chaste arches are not available because many were destroyed during the Korean War as well as during South Korea's urbanization. Also, we do not know the exact number of surviving arches in North Korea because of the division of the peninsula. However, it is not difficult to locate traces of many arches in the countryside, extending as far as Cheju Island (see chapter 2, "Visualizing Chastity"). For instance, a 2016 survey of existing commemorative buildings (including arches, tombstones, and shrines) in Yech'ŏn County of Kyŏngsang Province tallied twenty-three arches and tombstones dedicated to female chastity in that region. Kim Ponggyun, *Yech'ŏn ŭi hyoyŏl*, 425–30.

2. For example, Kim Pusik, in his *Historical Records of the Three Kingdoms*, frequently uses the word "even though" (*yu* 唯) in describing these people, such as "even as a woman" or "even if they were poor," denoting his intention to alert men and members of the upper class, respectively, to the importance of cultivating virtue themselves. Yi Hyesun, *Koryŏ chŏn'gi hanmunhaksa*, 422.

3. In discussing the dramatic obsession with the faithful maiden in mid-seventeenth-century China, Weijing Lu also points to the major historical events—the fall of the Ming and the suicide of the last emperor—that ultimately shaped the elite's own political vision and action, connecting them to those "heroic young women." Weijing Lu, *True to Her Word*, 49–50.

and biographies of chaste women were not written simply to uphold an ideal that Confucian scholars had envisioned; rather, the massive corpus of chastity accounts that emerged from the eighteenth century on, which became more and more elaborate in language and tone, served as the critical site where scholars inscribed their own self-reflections about moral visions and virtuous paths through life.

At the same time, Confucian scholars' fervent participation in commemorating chaste suicide generated intense deliberations over the choice of death that these women made. While still caught up in applauding such chaste acts, some scholars began to be puzzled by the fanatic violence inherent in the expression of the chastity ideal. These scholars viewed the choice of suicide not as a sacrifice to the greater virtue of absolute chastity but as a manifestation of patriarchal selfishness, as Chŏng Yagyong expresses in the epigraph above. Yet such critical voices did not have the power to affect the phenomenon at large. Rather, in embracing the government's continuing pursuit of the moral vision that operated through the existing state-reward system, male literati supported the state's interests more enthusiastically than ever before. If, prior to the mid-seventeenth century, the state promoted the chastity ideal central to its larger moral edification propaganda, it was local literati in the eighteenth and nineteenth centuries who took the lead in buttressing and realizing that ideal through the webs of various personal, academic, political, and social mechanisms, ultimately reshaping its discourse and practice. By the nineteenth century, their active local participation in honoring chastity resulted in the overflowing number of chaste women who were officially recognized, exceeding even the large number produced in early seventeenth-century postwar society. Gradually replacing the state as the key arbiter of the moralization project, local Confucian literati re-created the culture of chastity on their own throughout the latter part of the dynasty.

Shifting Discourses: From Center to Local

In 1648, not long after the Chosŏn state's humiliating conclusion of tumultuous military struggles with the Manchus, the community compact of the Miryang region included two entries about chastity practice in the long list of compact articles. First, in case a commemorative arch needed to be renovated, the local office should be informed to carry this out; second, if any act of filiality and chastity was known, it had be reported to the local office following the steps of public consensus (*kongnon*).[4] Modeled after Zhu Xi's Lü Family Community Compact (Lüshi xiangyue 呂氏鄉約) in Song China, the community compact was introduced to Korea in the early sixteenth century and was embraced by scholar-officials such as Chu Sebung (1495–1554), who advocated its implementation to instill morals in people in the local areas.[5] Toward the later sixteenth century, eminent Neo-Confucian scholars such as Yi Hwang (also known by his pen name T'oegye; 1501–1570) and Yi I (Yulgok; 1536–1584) promoted community compacts as part of their moral edification project in local areas. The Yean and Haeju community compacts—drafted by Yi Hwang and Yi I, respectively, based on their local administrative experience—became the basis for compacts proposed by later generations of Neo-Confucian scholars. Emphasizing virtuous conduct and mutual propriety to realize harmonious community, these two early compacts list some immoral behavior, such as lascivious acts toward women, as acts to be punished.

The seventeenth century saw the blooming of community compacts across the countryside, led by local *yangban* scholars. At the same time, the earlier compacts were revised to meet changing social circumstances and local demands, by adding more detailed articles on community issues. The two articles included in the Miryang Community Compact of 1648—an article on memorial arches and an article on public consensus on chaste acts—clearly indicate the community's

---

4. The original text reads 一曾有旌門處報官修築; 一境內有孝貞烈之行從公論報官. Miryang Hyanggyo, "Ipŭi."

5. A governor of Kyŏngsang Province, Kim Anguk (1478–1543), translated Zhu Xi's Lü Family Compact into Korean script and published the text under the sponsorship of King Chungjong. *Chungjong sillok* 27:47b–48a [1517/3/15]. There is a long list of Korean scholarship on the subject of community compacts in Chosŏn Korea. For studies in English, see Deuchler, "Practice of Confucianism," 291–334; Deuchler, *Under the Ancestors' Eyes*, 159–62, 230–32; Sakai, "Yi Yulgok and the Community Compact," 328–45; and Palais, *Confucian Statecraft and Korean Institutions*, 705–61.

growing interest in the chastity ideal and practice. Mid-seventeenth-century society was quite far from the sixteenth-century milieu in which Yi Hwang and Yi I had formulated their community compacts. Having witnessed the destructive wars, the state and the elites saw as their most urgent task the reestablishment of the socio-moral order. As discussed in chapter 2, the postwar Korean court honored a huge number of women for taking their own lives during wartime, setting the rhetoric of moral heroism as the major discourse governing society.

Although the Chosŏn state continued to pursue its initial goal of moral edification via the state-reward policy, the excessive official rewards granted during this postwar juncture changed the direction of chastity practice, gradually reshaping people's perception of what it meant to be an officially acknowledged virtuous subject of the Chosŏn state. The questions of who was to be honored and on the basis of what criteria arose as primary concerns for the literati as they navigated shifting political environments, social demands, and their places in postwar Korean society. In the midst of intensive debate over surviving the humiliating war years and what constituted a meaningful death, nothing was more influential than having a virtuous family member formally commemorated for public accolade. Such recognition not only distinguished the awarded family from other families and restored the lost moral identity of remaining family members through their connection to the virtuous subject but also interlinked family members to the moral reputation of the local community in which the family had its roots. Since the foremost duty of a *yangban* literatus was to die for the king and the state with a loyal heart, being connected to such a legacy and community moralism was a sign of family members' own moral commitment and cultivation, tightening their position within the postwar sociopolitical sphere. In other words, the honorable death of a female family member was viewed not simply as her personal manifestation of the chastity ideal but as embodying the virtues of the entire family, which then extended into the realms of the larger political and social lives of the community. Of course, the ideal of chastity had never been separate from political interests since the beginning of the dynasty. Over time, however, it became an even more pronounced political virtue, until it scarcely remained a private pursuit of wifely virtue.

As delineated in the Miryang Community Compact of 1648, local Confucian literati voluntarily called for the repair of memorial arches damaged or destroyed during the war years. Although the original purpose of such repair projects may have been to rebuild the community's outward appearance, the projects came to entail more than the physical restoration of the living sites, opening a renewed space for local literati's collective identity with the region to which they belonged.[6] The public consensus that was required for the chaste-woman recommendations, as specified in the Miryang Community Compact, also extended far beyond a mere reflection of the discussion among Confucian literati. Prior to being sent to the local or provincial offices, cases of chastity had to fulfill the moral criteria expected by the community of scholars in the area, and even further, the cases selected had to be approved by the collective sentiment of the local people. While the state-reward system continued to function as the core mobilizer, the local Confucian literati's incorporation of chastity-reward procedures into their community regulations marked a crucial point in both the reward system and the chastity discourse in late Chosŏn society, making a shift from the center to the local level.

Localization of Chastity: Glorifying Suicide

As Pak Chiwŏn's epigraph at the beginning of this chapter indicates, a woman's chastity was central to the honor of her household and family. A loss of chastity damaged her own integrity as well as that of her extended family. Upholding chastity, in contrast, promised everlasting glory that would be bestowed upon both the woman and her family generation after generation. In the second half of the dynasty, families increasingly produced and employed didactic books instructing their daughters in a set of behavioral standards, and male members actively sought to avoid disgrace to the extended family. In 1785, for example, a man named Yi Ŏn acted against his nephew's widow when

6. On the topic of late Chosŏn local *yangban* efforts to gain state recognition that would enhance their standing in their local areas, see Kawashima, "Study of the Hyangan," 3–38. On "the localized *sajok* [aristocratic families] turned local" and "*sajok*'s localist strategies," see Deuchler, *Under the Ancestors' Eyes*, 237–65.

it was rumored that she had been promiscuous: he put a gag of thick leather in her mouth and threw her into a river to drown—with the help of the widow's own brother.[7] Yi, a senior member of the lineage, was afraid that the rumor would ruin the repute of his lineage, and the widow's brother held the very same concern for his own family. Yi's action was an extreme one, yet such incidents are not uncommonly found in legal cases of the time. And just as a woman's unvirtuous behavior (or even a rumor of it) could alter the fate and the status of her natal and marital families, so her virtuous conduct became a key opportunity to display the family's high morality and thus fortify its position in society.

Indeed, producing a formally recognized woman of virtue was a critical way for a family to distinguish itself from others, especially in late Chosŏn society, which saw growing tensions among *yangban* groups. As it gradually became less feasible for any given *yangban* man to obtain one of the coveted official positions at the center of government, more *yangban* families returned to and settled in their local hometowns than had done so earlier in the dynasty. Moreover, this growth of the *yangban* population led to competition for authority in the local community. As Sun Joo Kim notes, "The effort of the established *yangban* to maintain their grip on power and prestige met with various challenges and generated considerable friction in local society," further complicating the identity of the local elites toward the end of the Chosŏn dynasty.[8] Female chastity, as the prime virtue appreciated, honored, and visibly rewarded by the state, was an authoritative public indicator of a family's collective moral level, a path to qualifying its members for admission to the elite realm. The concept of chastity was therefore ever more vigorously mobilized to make a family's status distinctive from that of others.[9]

---

7. *Ilsŏngnok* 297:151–52 [1789/3/29]; 302:95–96 [1789/5/22]; 349:70 [1790/8/16].

8. Sun Joo Kim, *Marginality and Subversion in Korea*, 30. Martina Deuchler also notes that "locality assumed an ever more vital significance in negotiating high social status with [*sajok*'s] prospects of office holding dimmed and their status affirmation by the state in jeopardy." Deuchler, *Under the Ancestors' Eyes*, 243.

9. On this subject, see Yi Hŭihwan, "Chosŏn malgi ŭi chŏngnyŏ wa kamun," 141–70. In his study, Yi introduces the efforts of the Yŏngch'ŏn Yi clan, originally a *chungin* (middle-class commoner) clerk family, to upgrade their status in the local

The obsession with obtaining a state reward in turn encouraged further systematic collaboration among *yangban* to produce "public consensus" in their communities. As a crucial element in the reward selection procedure at the local level, securing an official awardee often involved collective activities that reached beyond familial efforts, such as circular letters, joint petitions, and publication in local gazetteers (*ŭpchi*), which elevated the recognition of chaste women into a form of communal identity and justice. In the case of Madam Kim's (1883–1904) chaste suicide, a family petition for an official recognition, which initially held the signatures of 10 male members of her husband's family, eventually expanded to a provincial-level petition with the signatures of 580 literati residing in Kyŏngsang Province.[10] Although Madam Kim's lofty death would have motivated these scholars, the gigantic support across the entire province clearly signifies the family's position in the local community and its various scholarly and marriage connections; almost all writings dedicated to Madam Kim point out that she was a descendant of the prominent Confucian scholar Kim Koengp'il (1454–1504) and the illustrious Sŏhŭng Kim family.[11]

Male literati's active participation in collecting, drafting, editing, rewriting, and transmitting chaste-woman stories was prompted largely by their sense of membership in elite and local networks. The impact of local Confucian elites' collective inscribing stories of virtuous women was far-reaching and was not limited to glorifying a given lineage. Rather, their influence extended beyond the elite sphere and could make a tale a runaway favorite that symbolized the region's moral image for centuries thereafter. In their writings to celebrate chaste women who resided in remote frontier, island, or countryside locales, Confucian scholars also point out that these women's moral achievements are all the more exceptional given the less civilized

---

community by erecting nine memorial arches between 1861 and 1905. Yi Hŭihwan, "Chosŏn malgi ŭi chŏngnyŏ wa kamun," 163–64.

10. *Chongyongnok*, 2:20b–24a. In between the family petition and the provincial-level petition, there was another petition with thirty-two local scholars' names, followed by a district-level petition signed by forty Confucian scholars.

11. For a detailed discussion on Madam Kim's case and her family background, see Jungwon Kim, "Deeper than the Death," 163–82.

culture of such marginalized areas, where moral edification hardly reached.[12] Such rhetoric appears for the most part in stories about non-elite chaste women, implying the literati's immediate linking of any individual woman's virtue to a sense of regional pride.

The story of Hyangnang, a commoner woman of Sŏnsan in Kyŏngsang Province whose remarkable commitment to fidelity was celebrated to the extreme, is worth exploring here in detail because it negotiates the line between the elites' efforts to disseminate moral values to the non-elites via chaste-woman stories and an extensive reproduction of her story for their own local, political interests. Hyangnang, who killed herself in 1702, posthumously enjoyed greater fame than any other woman recognized for chastity during the Chosŏn, even to the extent that scholars have labeled the eighteenth and nineteenth centuries "Hyangnang's era": about thirty literary pieces were dedicated to her, including six biographies and thirteen poems by eminent scholars of the time.[13] A song that Hyangnang (supposedly) composed shortly before her suicide came to be included in a later collection of folk poetry (sogakpu), indicating its wide circulation among people at that time.[14] In 1814, more than a century after her death, a scholar named Kim Sohaeng (1765–1859) wrote a novel entitled Samhan sŭbyu (An Addendum to Korea) based on her life story. Many of his contemporary literati competitively composed prefaces to Kim's novel, immortalizing a mere commoner wife as a countrywide celebrity.

What aspect of Hyangnang's story inspired so many Confucian literati to take up their brush to sing her praises? How was her death different from other chaste women's suicides? With the popularity of her story, the Sillok records King Sukchong's grant of a memorial arch commemorating her chastity in 1704. It describes how Hyangnang, as a woman of an ordinary household, managed to marry an irritable

12. For examples, see Kim Chingyu, "Ae Oyang yŏlbu sa," Chukch'ŏn chip, 6:10b–12; and Yu Ŏnho, "Cheju O chŏllyŏ chŏn kyŏngsul," Yŏnsŏk, 13:9b–12b.

13. There is a long list of studies on Hyangnang in the field of premodern Korean literature, including two book-length works: Sŏ Sinhye, Yŏllyŏ Hyangnang ŭl marhada; and Chŏng Ch'anggwŏn, Hyangnang, sanyuhwa ro chida.

14. Yi Yuwŏn, Imha p'ilgi 16:69a–69b. Yi notes that a song entitled "Mountain Flowers" ("Sanyuhwa") was included in the collection of folk poetry.

husband who often beat her. After enduring this painful life for many years, she returned to her natal home, where her violent-tempered step-mother did not welcome her. With no place to live, Hyangnang went to the home of her uncle, but he pushed her to remarry. She therefore went back to her husband's home. There, her father-in-law, unable to change his son's hostility toward Hyangnang, also encouraged her to remarry, even issuing a divorce document. Finding herself with no one to rely on, Hyangnang decided to die by throwing herself into a river. Shortly before doing so, she met a girl on the riverbank. Weeping, Hyangnang told her about the miserable life she had suffered and asked the girl to pass on her final words to people, saying: "I had no spousal trust throughout my marriage.[15] Yet having already surrendered by my body to a husband, how can I remarry? If I die without any evidence [of his abuse], my parents and in-laws will assume that I followed another man. How unjust that would be!"[16] With these last words, Hyangnang jumped into the river and died.

The *Sillok* notes that, after Hyangnang's story was circulated to the community (presumably by the girl whom she asked to convey her last words), a provincial governor, while punishing the dead woman's hus-band, stepmother, and father-in-law, submitted her case to the central government for an official reward. Yet the first commendation request was denied, and Hyangnang's case was excluded from discussion for a long time. Only Left State Counselor (Chwaŭijŏng) Yi Yŏ (1645–1718) brought up the case again, arguing, "As an ignorant woman of the countryside, Hyangnang understood the righteousness of not serving two husbands, protected her integrity by dying, and publicized her death [by telling her circumstances to the girl]. No chaste woman listed in the *Illustrated Guide to the Three Bonds* is superior [to Hyangnang], who thus deserves a memorial arch to rectify customs and morals."[17]

The very first account written on Hyangnang was by Cho Kusang (1642–1712), who became district magistrate of Sŏnsan in 1702, the

---

15. For "spousal trust," the original text reads 夫婦之道, literally, "spousal way." However, 道 here is difficult to translate neatly as "way," and I read it more as spousal respect, affection, or feeling.

16. *Sukchong sillok* 39:50a [1704/6/5].

17. *Sukchong sillok* 39:50b [1704/6/5].

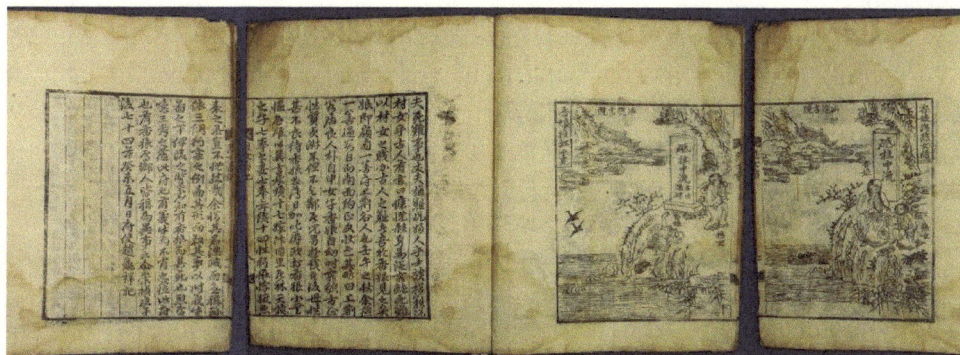

3.1. A woodblock-printed book presenting Hyangnang's story in two illustrations captioned "Hyangnang speaks to a girl woodcutter" (*Hyangnang yŏ ch'onyŏ ŏ*) and "Hyangnang jumps into the water and dies" (*Hyangnang t'ugang susa*). A tombstone commemorating the late Koryŏ Neo-Confucian scholar Kil Chae is clearly engraved in both illustrations. *Illustrations of the Righteousness and Chastity of Sŏnsan (Ilsŏn ŭiyŏlto*, 1703). Manuscript; ink on paper. KYU, Karam ko 398.4-Il9. Photograph courtesy of Kyujanggak Institute for Korean Studies, Seoul National University.

same year Hyangnang took her life. Only a few days after assuming his position, a head of the community compact reported Hyangnang's suicide to the magistrate's office, leading to an investigation of her death. When the provincial governor's recommendation of Hyangnang was declined, Cho, disappointed, composed an account of her life based on the report, fearing that otherwise "Hyangnang's extraordinary virtue would be forgotten."[18] Following the format of the *Illustrated Guide to the Three Bonds*, Cho also published a woodblock-printed version of Hyangnang's story in illustrations in the fifth month of 1703, to which his account was attached, even before the government formally made her a chaste martyr of the Sŏnsan region in 1704 (fig. 3.1).

It is impossible to know whether Cho Kusang predicted the state's eventual endorsement of Hyangnang's commendation. In either case, what is notable is the fact that Cho decided to make Hyangnang's story public and immortal by writing and printing it regardless of the state's recognition. The production of illustrations to her story also indicates

18. Cho Kusang, "Yŏllyŏ Hyangnangdo ki," *Yuhyŏn chip*, 455–60.

local elites' considerable involvement in Cho's project, for their support would have been indispensable to him as a magistrate just beginning his tenure in the region. Unlike early local magistrates who were often criticized for not diligently reporting the names of exemplary people (as discussed in chapter 2), Cho was enthusiastic about Hyangnang and took a different path—one that may have been more viable than seeking an official chastity reward, given the extreme uncertainty of the state-reward system. Instead of waiting for an official decision, he and Sŏnsan elites apparently saw that biographical accounts, especially with illustrations, could exert much wider and more immediate moral and social influence on the community.

Yet, reading Hyangnang's actual life story, questions remain as to why scholars and officials, including Cho himself, became so ardent about the death of an ordinary wife, and what made them persistently memorialize and write about her last deed. Compared with the suicides of many previously celebrated chaste women, Hyangnang's case was nothing spectacular. The only part of her story deserving of applause was the fact that, as a non-elite woman, despite economic necessity, she refused to remarry, choosing death instead. Perhaps because lower-class women often selected remarriage for financial reasons (a subject examined in detail in part 2), Hyangnang's decision against remarriage could be seen as exceptional. Having left her husband's house while he was still living, Hyangnang was also not an archetype of chastity, since the ideal chaste woman was usually a widow.

In looking more closely at the illustrations produced by Cho and local elites (see fig. 3.1), we see that on the edge of the riverbank where Hyangnang talks to the girl and then casts herself into the water, there is a huge tombstone dedicated to Kil Chae (pen name Yaŭn; 1363–1419), one of the most respected Neo-Confucian scholars of the late Koryŏ and early Chosŏn dynasties. Regarded as the progenitor of the Chosŏn Neo-Confucian lineage, Kil Chae settled in his hometown of Sŏnsan after the Chosŏn replaced the Koryŏ dynasty, declining an official position in the new dynasty. On the illustrated tombstone, the four characters 砥柱中流 (a pillar in the middle of the stream) are engraved (along with Kil Chae's pen name in the second illustration), pointing to his unwaveringly loyal heart during the chaotic dynastic transition. In both illustrations, the roof of a building in the background is indicated as Yaŭn Sŏwŏn, the local Confucian academy built in the region as a place to worship Kil Chae and study under his scholarly legacy. Although the illustration is dedicated to Hyangnang's chastity, it clearly emphasizes the moral thread connecting Kil Chae, Hyangnang, and the Sŏnsan region. Did Hyangnang accidentally throw herself into the river right next to Kil Chae's tombstone? Did she intentionally choose the site to highlight her chaste resolution? Or did Cho Kusang and other literati add the tombstone to the illustration to give it the greatest possible moral impact on the community and fully articulate the moral heritage of the area?

Throughout the dynasty, a local region's fortunes rose and fell not only with the political and scholarly success or decline of people from the area, but also with the fluctuating morality of the region's residents. It was not infrequent for a town's administrative level to be downgraded if the town produced someone who violated familial moral principles or was disloyal to the throne. For example, in 1515, when a man named Yi Maktong killed his own mother, younger brother, and nephew while fighting over a trivial matter, the Chosŏn government deemed his crimes extremely heinous and punished him for violating the essential moral duties.[19] His house was also demolished and the site made into a pond. Moreover, the government downgraded his hometown from prefecture (kun) to county (hyŏn) level.[20] And in 1776, when the Confucian scholar Yi Ŭngwŏn submitted a memorial requesting the punishment of those who had plotted in the Imo Incident (the death of Crown Prince Sado), King Chŏngjo, taking the memorial as disloyal to the former King Yŏngjo, ordered Yi's execution and demoted his hometown, Andong, from the status of special city (pu) to county town.[21] By doing so, the state alerted people to the fact that a resident's immoral act could directly affect the

19. *Chungjong sillok* 21:53b [1515/2/13].
20. *Chungjong sillok* 21:56a [1515/2/15].
21. *Chŏngjo sillok* 2:2b–8b [1776/8/6]; 2:14a [1776/8/19].

community's overall moral status, shaping the collective fate of the
local area to which they had long belonged.

Indeed, Sŏnsan was known as a region that had produced many
prominent Confucian scholars over the generations. The eighteenth-
century geographical encyclopedia *Classic for Choosing Settlement*
(*T'aengniji*) describes Sŏnsan as follows: "Half of Chosŏn's men of
talent live in the Yŏngnam region [in the southeast part of the Korean
peninsula], and half of these Yŏngnam men are residing in Sŏnsan."[22]
For Confucian scholars, Sŏnsan was a proud place that had produced
many eminent figures in the past. This may be why Sŏnsan elites responded so enthusiastically to the chaste suicide of a mere commoner
woman, Hyangnang: they wanted to spotlight their community's in-
comparably high morality, inherited from Kil Chae's time, that had
extended to and inspired even people at the bottom of the society.
Properly packaged, Hyangnang's death had the potential to maintain
Sŏnsan's genealogy of moral paragons and to regalvanize the region's
virtuous spirit.

Interestingly, Cho Kusang's paternal grandfather, Cho Ch'anhan
(1572–1631), had also served as magistrate of the same district, Sŏnsan. While in his post, Cho Ch'anhan published an illustrated account
of a righteous cow (*Ŭiudo*) that had fought a tiger that attacked the
cow's owner. Although the owner was rescued, he soon died of injuries
inflicted by the tiger. Refusing fodder for three days, the cow followed
its owner into death. In his preface to the account, Cho Ch'anhan
states that such an unheard-of case was possible thanks only to the
moral transformation of the region, which had inspired even a mere
animal, and that this was why he was publishing this story with four
sections of detailed illustrations.[23] Aware of his grandfather's work,
Cho Kusang, at the end of his biography of Hyangnang, notes: "There
was a righteous cow when my grandfather Cho Ch'anhan was serving as district magistrate of Sŏnsan. Upon his humble grandson Cho
Kusang's appointment [to the same town], we have just heard of
Hyangnang's virtuous death. People all say a series of peculiar things

22. Yi Chunghwan, "Kyŏngsangdo," *T'aengniji*, 35.
23. Cho Ch'anhan, "Ŭiudo," *Ilsŏn ŭiyŏlto*, 3a–8b.

have happened!"[24] The existing 1703 copy of *Illustrations of the Righteousness and Chastity of Sŏnsan* (see fig. 3.1) is a compilation of the accounts and the illustrations of both cases—that of the righteous cow and of Hyangnang. A postscript by the renowned Neo-Confucian scholar Kwŏn Sangha (1641–1721) is also attached, complete with Kwŏn's acclamation of Sŏnsan as an area of superior loyalty and righteousness.

Glorification of Hyangnang's suicide was, therefore, the collaborative fruit of Cho Kusang's efforts and local elites' enthusiastic support. For Cho, a newly appointed magistrate without a deep sense of connection to the region, Hyangnang's case could strengthen his position in the area. Cho in fact never passed the civil service examination, yet his official career began with the rank of *ŭmjik*, the position given to descendants of illustrious *yangban* lineage-holders. Somewhat lacking in his credentials as a local official, Cho nevertheless established himself as a virtuous magistrate by linking Hyangnang's suicide with his grandfather's commemoration of the righteous cow, as well as by publicizing Hyangnang's virtue to extol Sŏnsan as a moral exemplar for other regions. For local elites, whose collective identities were formed and represented through regional networking and mobilization of the literati community, the production and recognition of chaste women was a critical step in promoting the community's moral level and cultural prestige. The fact that the head of the community compact made the first report of Hyangnang's suicide to the magistrate also confirms local scholars' sensitivity to an incident that was compelling enough to help them achieve their mission.

The Hyangnang project illuminates local elites' eagerness to produce local moral exemplars as a path to upholding their own positions in the community and the distinction of their region. Interestingly, in contrast to the undiluted praise of Hyangnang's moral character typical of later literati biographies of her, earlier anecdotes point to more complicated aspects of her personality. The scholar-official Sŏng Taejung, for example, notes her wild behavior—as a young girl she had ongoing conflicts with her stepmother, and conflicts continued with

24. Cho Kusang, "Yŏllyŏ Hyangnangdo ki," *Yuhyŏn chip*, 455–60.

her husband after marriage.[25] Tired of Hyangnang's shrewishness, her husband sent her back to her impoverished natal home. Sŏng adds, "The case of Hyangnang, a woman of Sŏnsan, is remarkable. There is even a song about her life that has been made and circulated. Yet what those ordinary people in Sŏnsan all say is that Hyangnang was a woman of violent and quick temper who would never have been able to manage a household. If even a man of great merit usually has an ill disposition, how much more so might a woman?"[26] There is no way we can tell to what extent Sŏng's information is trustworthy. Nevertheless, the prompt local creation of Hyangnang as a heroine of chastity clearly suggests a second important facet of late Chosŏn chastity culture besides familial interest in an enduring virtuous reputation: the value to local elites' own political interests of strengthening their region's cultural and moral distinction through collective activism that identified and promoted local paragons of virtue.

The Hierarchy of Virtues: Chastity and Filiality

Whereas Sŏng Taejung references Hyangnang's aggressive nature, later biographies portray her as an obedient young girl who never expressed any anger despite being insulted and beaten by her stepmother. Highlighting her stepmother's ill temper, the biographies portray Hyangnang as courteous, well behaved, and filial—the virtue almost inseparable from a discussion of female chastity. The biographies are also silent about her choosing to commit suicide, which was an obvious defilement of filial piety since it meant abandoning the body her parents had given her. Filiality and chastity were considered fundamental Confucian principles and were equally valued. Numerous accounts complimenting virtuous women cite both their filial devotion

25. Born an illegitimate son (*sŏŏl*) with no right to take the civil service examination, Sŏng Taejung was able to hold an official position thanks to King Yŏngjo's flexible policy on hiring talented illegitimate sons (*sŏŏl t'ongch'ŏng*). Although Sŏng's writing style as a Kyujanggak scholar-official was strictly based on the Confucian classics, he also left a miscellaneous volume that is full of anecdotes and unofficial stories about people of every social status.

26. Sŏng Taejung, *Ch'ŏngsŏng chapki*, 343–44.

and their chastity, accentuating the women's perfect moral character. Yet in the case of a chastity-driven death, an explanation is required to justify the seemingly unfilial act of taking one's own life. Whereas in the first half of the dynasty, death was not necessarily viewed as the ultimate expression of a woman's integrity, the conundrum of whether to follow filiality or chastity became increasingly complicated when Chosŏn society began to witness a large number of chaste suicides from the seventeenth century on, as presented in the following story.

One night in 1688, a woman known as Madam Pak committed suicide by poisoning herself. She had married a man named Kim Kukpo at the age of sixteen, but he became ill shortly thereafter and died despite her greatest efforts to save him. Because she expressed no desire to continue life as a childless widow, Madam Pak's family watched her closely in case she attempted to follow her husband into death. Half a year later, she killed herself by drinking bittern. After Madam Pak's death, her in-law family members and villagers all suggested reporting her case to the magistrate's office for official recognition, noting that her suicide was motivated by the virtue of chastity. Her tearful father, however, stopped them from doing so. He insisted, "Although my daughter may be called a chaste wife because she achieved her own wishes [of dying], she cannot be a filial daughter for her causing [me] heartrending sorrow. It is [also] not the will of the deceased (my daughter) to do this [kind of public memorialization]." Disregarding his request, Madam Pak's husband's family and others nevertheless decided to report the case, insisting that "[doing] this is not a matter related to [her] natal family." Gathering at a village elder's house, they drafted and compiled relevant documents detailing Madam Pak's life and death, then made a petition for honoring her virtuous deed to the Ministry of Rituals. Four years later, in 1692, the government responded, formally rewarding Madam Pak with a memorial arch.[27]

The commemoration of Madam Pak against her own father's wishes reminds us again of the subtle tension between two moral duties—filial piety and wifely fidelity—as implied in most writings on female chaste suicide. While filiality, as the universal value, obliged

27. Pak Chiwŏn, "Pak yŏlbu sajang," *Yŏnam chip*, 10:8b–10a.

men and women alike to be selflessly devoted to their parents, women were supposed to transfer their daughterly duty to their parents-in-law when married. In other words, a woman's filiality was complicated by its transfer from her natal parents to her parents-in-law, whereas a man's filiality remained confined to the family into which he was born regardless of marriage.[28] As Madam Pak's case shows, even though the state, Confucian literati, and local communities glorified a woman's chaste suicide as a didactic tale, this often caused her natal and in-law families to clash: whereas Madam Pak's father took her prioritizing of chastity to be a denial of filial piety, her marital family viewed her death as the utmost fulfillment of her wifely duty. Certainly, a chaste woman would become the glory of both her families in the end. Yet the fact that a woman's seemingly honorable act of killing herself could simultaneously be an act of profound unfiliality to her parents revealed both that a married woman's moral identity lay somewhere in between filiality and fidelity and that there was the prospect of conflict and negotiation between her two families.

Nor was the tension between these two potentially conflicting moral duties limited to married women. Many accounts tell us of the dilemmas that male literati and generals encountered over the contending demands of loyalty and filial piety, especially during wars and other dynastic crises. Caught between his duty of loyalty to the king and his filial obligation to his parents, a man became a hero if he chose to die for his ruler.[29] Such accounts often portray the state distinguishing the man as a loyal subject (*ch'ungsin*) and his parents as having encouraged him to choose loyal duty over filiality. In 1637, when the news arrived that Manchu soldiers had surrounded King Injo in Namhan Fortress, Yi Sŏ (1580–1637) had to lead an army to save the king. Having already lost his father during the Imjin War, he

28. For further discussion on the debates and tensions between filiality and fidelity for a married daughter during the late Chosŏn, see Jungwon Kim, "Between Morality and Crime," 481–502. See also Haboush, "Filial Emotions and Filial Values," 129–77.

29. In his fascinating study on instances of irresolvable value conflicts in Confucian thought, Michael D. K. Ing notes, "Confucians have debated how to reconcile the tension between loyalty and filial care for over 2,000 years." Ing, *Vulnerability of Integrity*, 151–55.

hesitated, thinking of leaving his mother behind. But Yi's mother, embroidering his military robe with colorful thread, urged him to go, saying, "The time has come for you to redirect [your] filial piety [for me] to the king by being loyal [to him]."[30] Respecting his mother's words, Yi made a deep bow to her and left for the battlefield. Fighting bravely against the enemy troops, Yi lost his life. The state posthumously honored him for his loyal devotion and granted material rewards to his descendants.[31]

In ranking loyalty above filial duty when both could not be performed concurrently, Yi's mother understood that the public duty of loyalty was more imperative than the private matter of filial devotion. A person was expected to sever personal attachment for the sake of a higher moral ideal, and only someone who overcame such emotional torment to fulfill that greater virtue was deemed an exemplary subject to be commemorated. Although the conflicting responsibilities of filiality, loyalty, and fidelity were grounded in the individual person's moral understanding and choice, it was the state that publicly sanctioned the sacrificing of one's life in an act that apparently violated the duty of filial piety.

It was this same logic that sanctioned a woman's unfilial suicide for the sake of maintaining her marital fidelity, since chastity was seen as the female counterpart of a man's loyalty to the king. Any violence committed out of devotion to the chastity ideal—even suicide that both killed a woman and disfigured the body her parents had given her—was legitimated in this context within the hierarchy of Confucian virtues. This understanding is encapsulated in an epitaph commemorating Madam Kim's chaste suicide in which the Confucian scholar Kwŏn Tugyŏng (1654–1725) wrote as follows:

Someone might ask, "Was it too cruel for Madam Kim to follow her deceased husband, leaving everyone from her parents-in-law to five

---

30. "Ŭiyŏlsa t'ongmun," in *Komunsŏ chipsŏng* 9, 626–34.

31. "Ŭiyŏlsa t'ongmun," in *Komunsŏ chipsŏng* 9, 626–34. The *Sillok* does not record this official recognition, though it mentions his death. *Injo sillok* 34:2a [1637/1/2]. Yet Yi Sŏ is listed under the "loyal subject" category in the local *Ch'ilgok Prefectural Gazetteer*. See *Kugyŏk Ch'ilgok chi* 4:343.

children behind?" In response, the Sage says, "Was it really? Not at all, not at all. To die or live is important." As a scholar, how is it you cannot make a correct moral judgment [on this]? Taking her life quietly, Madam Kim proved her righteous spirit.[32]

To Kwŏn, what Madam Kim had achieved was the highest virtue a human being could attain: in the words of Confucius himself, "Killing oneself to perfect one's humaneness."[33]

Nevertheless, the tension between moral values and human emotions cannot always be resolved as clearly as such logic might suggest and could deeply affect even the king, whose official validation usually functioned to resolve such conflicts. In 1758, Princess Hwasun (1720–1758) killed herself fourteen days after her husband died. Born the second child of King Yŏngjo and Lady Chŏng (1694–1721), Princess Hwasun married Kim Hansin (1720–1758), who was the same age she was and who had been chosen as her spouse through the official selection process when they were thirteen years old. Unfortunately, Kim died of an illness, and the couple had no child. Determined to follow her husband into death, the princess refused to eat and drink. Concerned about this, the king visited and urged his daughter to take sustenance.[34] But the princess did not listen to him and continued to fast until she starved to death.

In recording the princess's death, the historian in the *Sillok* extols her notable achievement of "chastity" (*chŏng*)—the only woman's "way" (*to*)—as a royal woman.[35] What made her death even more exceptional, the historian writes, was her fortitude in keeping her pledge to die of starvation when a quick suicide would have been easier to accomplish. Court officials also requested that her chaste act be formally commemorated. After attending the princess's funeral, the king returned to the palace, replying as follows to their request:

32. Kwŏn Tugyŏng, "Yi yŏlbu Kimssi chŏngmun myŏng pyŏngsŏ," *Ch'angsŏljae chip*, 15:31a–33b.

33. "The Master said, The man of high ideals, the humane person (*ren* 仁), never tries to go on living if it is harmful to humaneness. There are times when he sacrifices his life to preserve humaneness." Confucius, *Analects*, 15:9.

34. *Yŏngjo sillok* 91:4a [1758/1/8].

35. *Yŏngjo sillok* 91:6b–7a [1758/1/17].

It is unfilial for a child not to obey a father's words and to starve herself to death. As a father who could not simply sit by and see his child dying, I repeatedly tried to persuade her to take medicine. . . . Yet [she] did not follow her parents' wishes and died in the end. She fulfilled chastity, but [she] was not filial. If she had died immediately, my agony would have been a little less. Because [she] declined to eat for ten days, it greatly distressed my mind. The proposal by the minister of rites to honor [her death] was wrong. Such a method of a father rewarding a child's virtuous [but unfilial] conduct should not be perpetuated; furthermore, doing so will generate a harmful effect later.[36]

Because he felt that Princess Hwasun's choice of death had been unfilial, King Yŏngjo did not approve the building of a memorial arch for her. In contrast to the historian's admiration for the princess's unwavering determination to end her life by starvation, Yŏngjo stated that this prolonged method had caused him even more distress than if she had ended her life immediately. What the court officials lauded as an exceptionally virtuous death had meant only increased excruciating pain to the princess's father. While agreeing with the king's stance as a parent, the officials continued to appeal to him to recognize his daughter's chastity, which they felt should not be forgotten. However, the king did not change his mind, insisting that "it is the spirit of chastity, not the [material] reward, that will not disappear for hundreds of generations to come."[37] The historian, altering his position in the *Sillok* entry for that day, then concludes, "The princess's chaste death is already known to people and will be recorded in histories. Why do we look for such an unimportant memorial arch?"[38] Adding that it would be inappropriate for the king to honor his own child's virtuous death, the historian justifies Yŏngjo's reaction as right and fair.

It was King Yŏngjo's successor, King Chŏngjo, who granted a memorial gate for Princess Hwasun in 1783 (fig. 3.2). The gate was built at the entrance to the village where her husband's family resided. Comparing her faithful death to the "Cypress Boat" story in the *Book*

---

36. *Yŏngjo sillok* 91:6b–7a [1758/1/17].
37. *Yŏngjo sillok* 91:6b–7a [1758/1/17].
38. *Yŏngjo sillok* 91:6b–7a [1758/1/17].

3.2. Memorial gate for Princess Hwasun (Hwasun ongju chi mun) located in Yesan, South Chu'ungch'ŏng Province. Photograph courtesy of Culture and Tourism Department, Yesan-gun, South Ch'ungch'ŏng Province.

of Poetry, Chŏngjo noted that the princess's chastity had been incomparable, for there was no other such case in the entire history of the ancient Chinese imperial family.[39] Not only was her death proof of the existence of a faithful woman in the Eastern State (Chosŏn), but it illuminated the beautiful mores of his own family (the Yi royal family).[40] Chŏngjo also commented on the reason the princess had rejected her father Yŏngjo's pleas that she resume eating, as follows:

> Her Highness Princess Hwasun, who was benevolent and filial, must have understood the principle that she should follow the words of her father, the king. The reason she did not waver once she had made up her mind is that the filiality of abiding by [her father's] order is a small matter, but

39. For an account of the "Cypress Boat" story, see chapter 1, note 68.
40. *Chŏngjo sillok* 15:20a–b [1783/2/6].

killing herself [to follow her husband into death] is the greater virtue of fidelity. Alas, this is indeed chastity![41]

Referring to the princess as a woman of high virtue (*kunja*), King Chŏngjo promised that he would compose a ritual oration for her on the day the gate was erected.

Chŏngjo's hierarchical understanding of a married daughter's filial piety being superseded by a wife's fidelity represented the official position of the Chosŏn state, yet it exactly opposes Yŏngjo's conviction that the princess's chaste act was an unfilial one. Unlike King Chŏngjo's words extolling Princess Hwasun's choice, King Yŏngjo's funeral ode to his daughter is full of lamentation and regret about his inability to change her decision, even with his personal visit and also sending her a long letter urging her to eat. He sees his daughter as a chaste wife but grieves that she did not consider how a gray-haired father relies on his child, and thus finds her undutiful. Gulping down his tears, the king ends the ode, "How sad! Having a chaste daughter, I have no grudge remaining [in my heart]. [Yet] gazing into the distance, my tears gush out . . . how sad and how sad."[42]

In 1752, just six years before Princess Hwasun's death, Yŏngjo had awarded a widow named Madam Chŏng a memorial arch for her chaste death. Like the princess six years later, Madam Chŏng had starved herself to follow her deceased husband into death.[43] Acclaiming Madam Chŏng's formidably faithful heart, Yŏngjo recognized her internalizing of wifely fidelity as a virtue higher than filial devotion. But when faced with his own daughter's chaste suicide, he could not bring himself to do the same. Rather, he declared, "As a king and mentor [of the country], I do not want to have a harmful effect [on people by rewarding my own daughter]."[44] Yet would not the princess's chastity have potentially been more exemplary—and more effective in delivering a moral message to the populace—than the chaste acts of an ordinary wife?

41. *Chŏngjo sillok* 15:20a–b [1783/2/6].
42. Yŏngjo, "Yŏngjo ŏje Hwasun ongju yujemun," in *Yŏngjo chason charyojip*, 5.
43. *Yŏngjo sillok* 76:23b [1752/5/23].
44. *Yŏngjo sillok* 91:6b [1758/1/17].

Indeed, in our effort to comprehend the extremity of commitment to the chastity ideal and practice in Chosŏn Korea, it becomes clear that the ideological clash between the two fundamental values of filial piety and chastity remained a matter to be intensely contested and negotiated. Harming one's body and/or dying before the deaths of one's parents was a serious desecration of filial piety—the backbone of Confucian norms—and was proscribed in the *Classic of Filial Piety*.[45] Nevertheless, by commending and even encouraging such unfilial actions (through the reward system), the state placed wifely fidelity above filial piety. This emphasis on chastity often had ironic and poignant consequences, as demonstrated in the case of King Yŏngjo's deep grief at his own daughter's slow suicide by starvation. The dilemma posed by this ideological conflict is also illuminated in another father's eulogy for his married daughter, Madam Kim, who committed suicide to follow her deceased husband, Sim Chaedŏk (1887–1903), at the age of nineteen. The father mourns, "A wife following her deceased husband is a completely righteous thing. Nevertheless, how can a father [not] wail upon a child's death? What kind of logic is this? . . . I only try to suppress heartbreaking sorrow."[46] As a Confucian scholar himself, this father comprehended the grand meaning of chaste suicide as the ultimate expression of a wife's fidelity but had naturally hoped that his beloved daughter would not have to face such a predicament. Despite official endorsement of the hierarchal notion of chastity taking precedence over filiality, the process of recognizing and honoring a chaste woman reveals fissures in how people perceived and navigated the two competing virtues of filiality and chastity in Chosŏn society.

45. For self-harming acts and their potentially heterodox implications for Confucians from the Chinese religious perspective, see Jimmy Yu, *Sanctity and Self-Inflicted*, 62–88. On the act of finger-severing and its validation in Confucian culture, see Sixiang Wang, "Filial Daughter of Kwaksan," 175–212. For a detailed discussion of the contradictions between filial piety and filial sacrifice, see Cho Namuk, "Yuga hyoron kwa yuksin hyohaeng ŭi munje," 123–45. On a widowed daughter's dilemma vis-à-vis filial emotion and marital fidelity, see Jungwon Kim, "Deeper than the Death."

46. *Chongyongnok*, 3:26a. For further discussion of Madam Kim's father's position toward his daughter's death, see Jungwon Kim, "Deeper than the Death."

Legitimating Violence:
How to Perform Chaste Death

Confucian scholars writing on chaste suicide often faced the arduous task of validating the rationale behind a woman taking her own life. Even the titles of women's biographies show that male scholars were exacting in evaluating women's righteous actions. For instance, titles of two eighteenth-century biographies written around the same time— "The Biography of Madam Ha" ("Hassinyŏ chŏn") and "The Biography of Chaste Wife Madam Hong" ("Hong yŏlbu chŏn")—differ in how they refer to the two women whose stories they tell.[47] Madam Ha deliberately killed herself at the local magistrate's residence to publicize the guilt of her husband who, out of his desire to seize her entire inheritance, had murdered her younger brother. Her husband was eventually sentenced to death.[48] The widow Madam Hong (?–1685), in contrast, had been falsely accused by her brothers-in-law of having an affair and giving birth to the child of another man during a stay at her natal home. The younger brothers of Madam Hong's deceased husband were covetous of the inheritance left to Madam Hong. Wishing to take the inheritance, they planned to eliminate her by having their father (Madam Hong's father-in-law) accuse her of illicit sexual conduct. Although they expected Madam Hong's immediate suicide out of humiliation, she proved her innocence by showing her naked belly in public. Only after her in-laws were punished did Madam Hong commit suicide.[49]

47. The author of "The Biography of Madam Ha" was a Confucian scholar, Im Kyŏngju (1718–1745). There are two biographies dedicated to Madam Hong—one by Yi Chae 李栽 (1657–1730), entitled "Hong yŏlbu chŏn" 洪烈婦傳, and the other by Yi Sisŏn (1625–1715), entitled "Yŏllyŏ Hongssi chŏn" 烈女洪氏傳.

48. According to the biography, Madam Ha was a beautiful woman who received a large inheritance from her deceased father. She continued to raise her younger brother even after she married and planned to give him the entire property when he grew up. Madam Ha's husband did not agree with her idea, and so killed the brother secretly to secure her inheritance for himself. Im Kyŏngju, "Hassinyŏ chŏn," *Ch'ŏngch'ŏnja ko*, 3:24a–25a.

49. Yi Chae, "Hong yŏlbu chŏn," *Miram chip*, 16:1a–6b.

The author of Madam Ha's biography comments that "although Madam Ha never uttered a single word against her husband [during her testimony], it is clear that she killed herself to avenge [the murder of her brother] . . . Her death was done with the spirit of *yŏl*, yet she failed in fulfilling the [wifely] way."[50] Since Madam Ha had put her brother's welfare above that of her husband, she had been derelict in her wifely duty and was not eligible for the label of "chaste wife" in the title of her biography. In contrast, Madam Hong's death met the criteria for being a "chaste wife" because she "verified" her sexual loyalty to her late husband. Her act of publicizing her father-in-law's false accusation was unfilial, but it ultimately served to prove her marital fidelity, and she also made a plea for mercy on his behalf. By designating her a "chaste wife," the author of Madam Hong's biography acknowledges that wifely duty surpasses filiality as a married woman's foremost moral accomplishment.

Reading the copious chaste-woman biographies, accounts, and eulogies, we see that they function almost like didactic texts, scarcely venturing beyond moral inspiration and reflecting their male authors' eagerness to encourage people through virtuous tales. To be sure, biographical writings were not composed only to commemorate chaste women, and male scholars used to take up their brushes for political reasons. The early Chosŏn scholar Nam Hyoon (1454–1492) wrote the "Biographies of Six Officials" ("Yuksinjŏn" 六臣傳), an account of six men who had opposed King Sejo's usurpation of his nephew King Tanjong's (r. 1452–1455) throne, both to demonstrate the loyal hearts of the six subjects and to display Nam's own political position and righteousness. Continuing political conflicts and purges also inspired the Confucian literati to produce writings intended to applaud the uprightness of one's political faction. Modern readers tend to find these biographical works monotonous in style and plot, with shared themes and characterizations, because of the fact that the biographer "usually gathers a few anecdotes from the life of the given person, . . . in accordance with the general image and stylization the given person

---

50. Im Kyŏngju, "Hassinyŏ chŏn." *Ch'ŏngch'ŏnja ko*, 3:24b-25a

has created by tradition."[51] It is true that biographical writings, though often supplementing historical records, portray exemplary people as single-mindedly taking radical action to follow Confucian values. This is also the case in most of the works dedicated to chaste women, who are profiled as martyrs to marital loyalty and heroines of morality. The recurring trope of suicide stories in chaste women's biographical writings thus heavily exalts their dramatic wifely devotion while obfuscating the voices of female actors who select such a path.

Yet these accounts do not solely acclaim death as the final outlet for chastity. In articulating the symbolic power of women's deaths under the banner of the chastity ideal, male authors also strove to explain the moral logic behind women's violent choice and to legitimate suicidal acts as valid expression of their high moral caliber. As Joan Judge notes, "Biography function[s] in the Confucian cultural tradition not only as a means of commemoration but, more importantly, as a technology of the self."[52] Though inscribed in formulaic language and Confucian rhetoric, writings about chaste death offered a textual space in which male literati not only navigated the contested values between female fidelity and filiality but also ruminated on their own moral convictions.[53]

In the second part of the dynasty, Confucian literati's records of chaste women grew significantly in number and changed in tone and style, along with the shifting chastity discourse centered on corporal performance of its ideal. Whereas earlier works praise women's virtue in general, eighteenth- and nineteenth-century writings on chaste women focus on the performative aspect of the ideal. This shift is not surprising given the increasing practice in late Chosŏn society of women taking their own lives after their husbands' deaths. The mounting

51. Prusek, "History and Epics in China," 29. There were diverse styles and genres of writing on chaste women, ranging from epitaphs and eulogies to biographies and poems. Here I use "biographical works" or "biographical writings" to encompass a wide range of these records because they all detail the lives of chaste women. On the subject of premodern biographical writings, see Judge and Hu Ying, *Beyond Exemplar Tales*, 4–5.

52. Judge and Hu Ying, *Beyond Exemplar Tales*, 4–5.

53. Weijing Lu, "Faithful Maiden Biographies"; Judge and Hu Ying, *Beyond Exemplar Tales*, 89–91.

numbers of requests for honoring these chaste women intensified the
competition for an official reward, with the result that merely lauding
a woman's fidelity was no longer sufficient. As communities of scholars
aggressively sought to distinguish the cases they were championing from
other contenders for recognition, male authors had to persuasively
explicate why the woman in question had been morally justified in
choosing to end her own life.

On the one hand, the debates over keeping chastity alive versus
dead continued to occupy the writings of male literati. In his epitaph
for Madam Yi (1678–1732), the Confucian literatus Yi Kwangjŏng
(1674–1756) states that "dying to follow a dead husband for chastity is
not as formidable as maintaining [chastity] while alive."[54] Madam Yi,
despite her husband's early death leaving no child, remained a faithful
widow. She adopted a son of her husband's cousin and continued to
serve her parents-in-law with filial devotion. Yi Kwangjŏng emphasizes
how challenging it was for a widow to carry on her wifely duty alive,
rather than recklessly killing herself upon her husband's death. On the
other hand, another scholar of Yi's time, Nam Yuyong (1698–1773),
praises the suicide of Madam Kim, who, like Madam Yi, did not have
a child, but who killed herself on the same day her husband died. Nam
distinguishes Madam Kim's commitment to chastity from that of a
widow who prolongs her life on the excuse of raising an heir, as Madam
Yi did. Madam Kim's suicide was a loftier expression of her long-held
resolution to die with her husband—a righteous act that Nam concludes
was a matter of realizing her "supreme virtue" (*in*; Ch. *ren* 仁).[55]

Though Madam Yi and Madam Kim were both childless widows,
the two male writers who recorded their stories offered contrasting
views of their different choices: whereas Yi Kwangjŏng still valued a
widow's remaining alive to fulfill her wifely responsibilities, Nam
Yuyong held death to be the ultimate form of a widow's internalizing

---

54. Yi Kwangjŏng, "Hyo yŏlbu Yigongin myojimyŏng," *Nurŭn chip*, 14:13b–15b.
55. Nam Yuyong, "Yŏlbu Kimyuin aesa," *Noeyŏn chip*, 18:38a–39b. Although the
character 仁 connotes "comprehensive ethical virtue" in Confucian thought, with an
exact meaning that cannot be pinned down, it has commonly been translated as "benevolence, humaneness, and goodness." I appreciate a reviewer's comments on translating this term, suggesting "supreme virtue," in this particular context of a woman's
self-killing, to describe her behavior for "being fully human."

the chastity ideal. It is interesting that Nam understood a widow killing herself to be an act of "supreme virtue" attained by upholding righteousness (ŭi). Another scholar of the same era, An Chŏngbok (1712–1791), offers further elaboration on the moral reckoning behind chaste suicide. In his postscript to a biography of another Madam Yi, An also vindicates her suicide as a legitimate action upholding the chastity ideal. Although An views a woman's exemplary behavior as stemming from her benign nature, he writes that it is her ardent spirit (chŏngyŏl) that leads her to take the final action of committing suicide. Aligning benignancy with supreme virtue and ardor with righteousness, An sees no absolute separation between the two pairs of traits. But he points to righteousness as far more difficult to perform than supreme virtue, because benignancy conforms to the situation, whereas an ardent spirit goes against it.[56] Whereas Nam Yuyong situates the two moral norms of righteousness and supreme virtue as functioning in parallel with each other, An seems to emphasize righteousness. Like Nam, however, An confirms "chaste suicide" (sunjŏl) as the superlative evidence of female moral integrity, and both men deem righteousness and supreme virtue the core of the moral impetus in women's chaste deaths.

Although some scholars, such as Yi Kwangjŏng, praise remaining alive as more crucial than taking one's own life, the greater number of eighteenth- and nineteenth-century biographical writings focus on chaste suicide. These late Chosŏn scholars' recourse to the notion of supreme virtue, or in, in interpreting suicide as the greatest moral accomplishment was derived from Confucius's saying "They sought in and attained in—what resentment could they have?"[57] Literati writings on chaste women indeed frequently cite this particular passage when rationalizing self-killing. For example, in a eulogy dedicated to a chaste woman known as Madam Ch'oe, the scholar Yi Kwangsa (1705–1777) stresses how difficult it was even for (male) exemplars of the past to achieve in by killing themselves, and hence how astonishing it is for a mere woman residing in a remote frontier area to do so.[58] Yet though scholars supported the Confucian idea of "killing oneself

56. An Chŏngbok, "Che yŏllyŏ Yŏhŭng Yissi haengnok hu," Sunam chip, 19:9b–11b.
57. 求仁而得仁 又何怨. Confucius, Analects, 7:14.
58. Yi Kwangsa, "Ch'oe yŏlbu ch'an," Wŏn'gyo chip, 8:10a–11a.

to perfect [one's] humaneness," they did not simply justify suicide—an act that breached one's filial duty—but also accentuated the peace in chaste women's hearts when putting their moral priority into action.[59] The Confucian scholar Wi Paekkyu (1727–1798), in his petition to honor another chaste widow called Madam Ch'oe, starts with this saying of Confucius, too, explicating that "she did not hesitate to take her life because her mind was comfortably set to die, once fulfilling her moral duty."[60] In describing the scene of her suicide, Wi depicts her unflinching determination to die with her husband: "She bound her neck with a hemp rope as tightly as possible, connecting the end of the rope to the coffin in which her dead husband was placed. She was found dead right next to the coffin, with the rope held in her hands."[61] Wi adds that such a death is the highest death possible, incomparable to anything else in the world. The twenty-year-old childless widow Madam Ch'oe was able to attain this stage because she had "no regret and shame about her resolution."[62]

Sensational stories followed one after another, highlighting chaste women's tenacity about following their husbands into death. Numerous writings illustrate how they persisted and eventually succeeded in killing themselves, even after family members rescued them from multiple earlier attempts. Madam Cho (1705–1758) was one of many such women, being saved several times by people who knew that she had intended to kill herself during her husband's funeral. After having been prevented from doing so, she lived "without combing her tangled hair or washing her body, on which lice were crawling in between her clothes. She did not care, covering her body with a blanket that had been used to wrap her husband's corpse."[63] On the second anniversary of her

---

59. See note 33 above. Although some biographers quote the famous saying of Confucius about "killing oneself to perfect [one's] humaneness," the passage "They sought *in* and attained *in*—what resentment could they have?" appears most frequently in writings on chaste women by late Chosŏn scholars.

60. Wi Paekkyu, "Ch'ŏngp'o yŏllyŏ Ch'oessijang tae," *Chonjae chip*, 4:7a–9a.

61. Wi Paekkyu, "Ch'ŏngp'o yŏllyŏ Ch'oessijang tae," *Chonjae chip*, 4:7a–9a.

62. Wi Paekkyu, "Ch'ŏngp'o yŏllyŏ Ch'oessijang tae," *Chonjae chip*, 4:7a–9a.

63. An Chŏngbok, "Yŏllyŏ sugin Chossi chŏngmun," *Sunam chip*, 17:34a–35b. In addition to this official report, An, a close friend of Madam Cho's husband, also wrote a biographical record of Madam Cho.

husband's death, she tried to poison herself but was saved once again. About ten days later, she succeeded in committing suicide by poison. An Chŏngbok, the author of a report on Madam Cho's conduct, provides an exhaustive narrative of each step she took toward death, for she refused to compromise in the face of external pressure and steadfastly put her own chastity practice ahead of her own life.

The Confucian scholars' linking of chaste suicide to the idea of seeking *in* and attaining *in* is crucial to understanding how they legitimated women's extreme behavior under the banner of realizing the chastity ideal. By juxtaposing suicide as the bodily manifestation of the chastity ideal with the supreme virtue of humaneness (*in*) in the Confucian canon, suicide was not merely justified but was promoted to the highest level of virtue. Moreover, this approach implied that *not* all chaste suicide was the same. For instance, when a report on the case of the chaste wife Madam Yu, signed by fifty Confucian scholars from her hometown, was submitted to the king, the court discussion centered on how long Madam Yu had lived as a widow—her suicide took place five years after her husband died. The court viewed her five years of moral perseverance as superior to the suicides of "those women who impatiently killed themselves out of grief and the harsh reality a widow would face."[64] In another petition, written for the chaste wife Madam O, Wi Paekkyu also underscored that "it is easy to kill oneself impulsively, yet far harder to endure agony with a painful heart for a considerable time [until death]."[65] Instead of immediately killing herself, Madam O had starved herself for ten months and finally died. Such a death could be achieved only through tenacious moral commitment, exactly resonating with Confucius's saying that "They sought *in* and attained *in*—what resentment could they have?" Ranking a premeditated death higher than suicide committed out of spontaneous passion, Wi acclaims Madam O's chaste suicide to be "a death that could happen [only] once in a thousand years" in his appeal to the state to honor the deceased chaste widow.[66]

64. Kim Chingyu, "Ch'ŏng Yu yŏlbu chŏngp'o myŏnju," *Chukch'ŏn chip*, 7:20b–23b.
65. Wi Paekkyu, "Ch'ŏngp'o yŏlbu Ossijang tae," *Chonjae chip*, 4:3b–7a.
66. Wi Paekkyu, "Ch'ŏngp'o yŏlbu Ossijang tae," *Chonjae chip*, 4:3b–7a.

The vindication of a woman's suicide as virtuous action meant that death alone was no longer enough to make a case extraordinary. As stated in Wi Paekkyu's record, "Tens to hundreds of chaste-woman cases reach the provincial governor's office; the Ministry of Rites receives thousands of petitions from the eight provinces each year. People spend seventy to eighty years or even one hundred years in Seoul to obtain the state recognition, but some succeed and some do not."[67] Amid intense competition for official recognition, records of chaste women often overflowed with dramatic details about the women's suicidal actions, portraying the women almost as protagonists found in fiction. What made a story unparalleled was not just the death itself but "how she performed the death," and the premier form of chastity was found in a woman's unwavering heart that was set on "dying quietly," transcending her private desires.[68]

In dramatizing the metaphorical power of chaste suicide in Confucian morality, biographical writings on chaste women reveal late Chosŏn scholars' own moral convictions in their defense of women's violent choices. Deliberating on the enduring nature of conflicting values and their modes of practice, these male literati accentuated the performative aspect of self-killing, deeming the underlying tensions in chaste suicide "conflicts of commitments rather than virtues often associated with roles or commitments."[69] As Confucian authors strove to incorporate their moral reckoning into their writings on chaste women, they neither composed mere testaments to the virtue of chastity nor delivered uniformly didactic voices, but instead illuminated the shifting rhetoric about—and ideological tensions over—the ideal of chastity in late Chosŏn Korea.

---

67. Wi Paekkyu, "Yŏllyŏ Kimssi chŏngmun Okkwa ki," *Chonjae chip*, 21:16a–18a.

68. Contemplating Zhu Xi's dictum, "Dying out of indignation is easy; dying quietly is difficult" 感慨殺身者易 從容就義者難, a quiet death (suicide) committed with an indomitable heart became a dominant theme in the writings on chaste suicide in eighteenth- and nineteenth-century Chosŏn Korea. See Jungwon Kim, "*Yŏl* (烈): Chaste Martyrdom."

69. Ing, *Vulnerability of Integrity*, 151.

Criticizing Extremes:
Selfish Fidelity and Meaningful Death

In his reply to Kwŏn Si (1604–1672), Song Siyŏl comments as follows on Kwŏn's inquiry about remarriage, in an enclosure separately attached to his letter:

> The moral foundation for a loyal subject not serving two kings is juxtaposed with [the moral foundation for] a chaste wife not serving two husbands. Why has our country failed to set up a law preventing officials from serving two kings while strictly enforcing the rule against a woman serving two husbands?[70]

As indicated by his posthumous title Songja (Master Song), Song was the most revered and influential Neo-Confucian scholar-official in Chosŏn history. While Song buttresses the idea of widow chastity as an eternal value elsewhere in his reply, he also argues that it should be promoted through a gradual edification process, not by harsh legal methods. He quotes a question that Zhu Xi was asked about the two Cheng brothers allowing a niece to remarry even though this went against their belief that a widow should not serve two husbands. While supporting the Cheng brothers' widow-chastity ideal, Zhu Xi had replied that some cases are beyond human control. Praising the three great Neo-Confucian scholars' approach to the ideal of chastity, Song reinforces his original assertion, noting that current legal prohibitions with respect to remarriage are not effective. Also, as an essential aspect

70. Song Siyŏl, "Tap Kwŏn Sasŏng," *Songja taejŏn*, 39:28b–30b. For a detailed analysis of Song's position on widow remarriage legislation, see Hwa Yeong Wang, "Against the Ban." Kwŏn Si and Song Siyŏl were in-laws, and Sasŏng was Kwŏn's courtesy name. Because Kwŏn supported Yun Sŏndo (1587–1671), who was against Song's position during the 1660 ritual controversy, it caused a breach in their relationship. All three letters to Kwŏn included in Song's scholarly collection are dated before the ritual controversy, and this particular one was written in 1659. Interestingly, Kwŏn's literary collection contains about eighteen letters sent to Song, titled "Letters to Song Yŏngbo" ("Yŏ Song Yŏngbo"), for Yŏngbo was Song's courtesy name. See Kwŏn Si, *T'anong sŏnsaeng chip*. For an English study of the ritual controversy, see Haboush and Deuchler, *Culture and the State*.

of human morality, fidelity should be expected equally of both men (being loyal to one king) and women (being faithful to one husband). Although Song's comment may be read as a direct attack on the remarriage practice in the Chosŏn society, he was actually targeting male intellectuals who had lost their political morality through factional conflicts while nevertheless imposing the lofty value of lifelong chastity on women.

In the midst of the deepening discourse on chaste death, the eighteenth century began also to witness some literati questioning the era's extreme performance of widow suicide. Pointing to the new intellectual quest that had emerged during the latter part of the dynasty, existing scholarship emphasizes that scholars of so-called practical learning (*sirhak*) proposed differing perspectives, criticizing the rigid attitude toward chastity practice predominant in Chosŏn society. The problem of defining and grouping those practical scholars into one coherent school has been contested in Korean historiography and is beyond the scope of the present discussion.[71] However, as much as a clear delineation of practical-learning scholars is still under debate, it is also precarious to denote all so-called *sirhak* scholars as having expressed ambivalence about the chastity ideal. For example, Yi Ik (1681–1763), a scholar recognized as a pioneer of practical learning, praised the chastity practice in Chosŏn society by writing a recommendation for honoring a faithful maiden who had starved herself to follow her fiancé into death and noted that her determined suicide had been a righteous action. Also, in his essay entitled "Coercive Fornication" ("Kanggan"), Yi calls for women's steadfast commitment to the chastity ideal in the face of sexual offense (see chapter 4 for a detailed discussion). And Yi's disciple An Chŏngbok, who was also known as a *sirhak* scholar, extolled chaste suicide as the utmost indicator of wifely virtue, as examined in the preceding section. Most of these scholars do not seem to have critically distanced themselves from notions of the ideological legitimacy of chastity.

Indeed, it is virtually impossible to classify scholars as holding a negative view of chaste suicide from their writings collected in the

71. On this issue, see Baker, "Use and Abuse of the Sirhak Label," 183–254. See also No Kwanbŏm, "Kŭndae ch'ogi sirhak ŭi chonjaeron," 447–73.

official histories and in private publications.[72] Moreover, in their personal accounts only a handful of late Chosŏn Confucian literati—whether they are labeled *sirhak* scholars or not—either disapprove of or feel uncomfortable with the society's fanatical adoration of the chastity ideal as manifested through death. The literatus Yi Ok (1760–1812), though certainly not a *sirhak* scholar, is one who is often considered a critic of a widow's tendency to take her own life. Despite his literary talent, Yi Ok remained an iconoclast whose controversial writing style and unconventional stories were regarded as violating Neo-Confucian literary norms. He left extensive writings in various genres, including four biographical accounts of female chastity.[73] Especially in his "Tale of a Living Chaste Woman," Yi condemns the trend of female suicide in the country:

A widow who refuses to remarry is a chaste woman. . . . Women in mourning clothes in this country were all faithful women in old times. Now, however, the government honors only widows who commit suicide after their husband's death; thus "all chaste women in Chosŏn" refers only to those who have already died.[74]

The protagonist of this tale, Madam Sin, cut a piece of flesh from her thigh to feed her dying husband, in the hope of curing his illness. Thanks to her self-harming sacrifice, his life was saved, and Madam Sin recovered from her injury. Nevertheless, because her selfless act did not take the ultimate form of exhibiting the ideal—death—Madam

---

72. For instance, Neo-Confucian scholar Yi Hwang is known for encouraging a chaste widow to carry out filial responsibility alive, instead of committing suicide after her husband died, and for letting his own widowed daughter-in-law remarry. Taking pity on his young widowed daughter-in-law, who was the only offspring of her natal family, Yi Hwang allowed her to return to them. Several years later, when Yi traveled to the Tansŏng region, he spent a night at a *yangban*'s house, where he realized that a daughter-in-law of the household was his own son's widow, who had remarried and was now happily living with her new husband and children.

73. These four biographies by Yi Ok are "Tale of Such'ik" ("Such'ik chŏn"), "Tale of Sangnang" ("Sangnang chŏn"), "Tale of Chaste Wife Madam Yi" ("Yi yŏlbu Yissi chŏn"), and "Tale of a Living Chaste Woman" ("Saeng yŏllyŏ chŏn").

74. Yi Ok, "Saeng yŏllyŏ chŏn," *Yŏkchu Yi Ok chŏnjip*, 2:217–18.

Sin's devotion was not recognized by the government. Considering only the excerpt quoted above, Yi Ok seems to oppose the society's obsession with the chastity ideal in general. However, a close reading of his full account of Madam Sin's life reveals that Yi is targeting the Chosŏn state's discriminative reward policy itself, which prioritized the performative aspect of chastity and thus eventually drove women to extreme action. Therefore, as Yi opines in his "Tale of Such'ik," "it would be far harder to keep one's chastity while alive than to do so through death," which aligns with his position in his "Tale of a Living Chaste Woman."[75] In a third biography, "Tale of Chaste Wife Madam Yi," Yi Ok nevertheless lauds Madam Yi's tenacious determination to remain faithful to her deceased husband by killing herself after successfully giving birth to a son and completing the three-year mourning period for her husband. Like his contemporaries, Yi Ok says nothing about abandoned maternal duty and emotion but merely praises Madam Yi's suicide as something she did not carry out in a great hurry but as a manifestation of her "painful fidelity" (kojŏl).[76]

Yi Ok's ambiguous attitude toward chaste suicide echoes Pak Chiwŏn's conversation with two Chinese court officials during his trip to Qing China in 1780. Pak first explains that widow chastity is one of the most beautiful customs of Chosŏn Korea. But when the two Chinese officials voice concern about their own country's infatuation with the faithful-maiden cult, Pak joins them in criticizing the violent aspect of the chastity practice prevalent in Chosŏn society. The three scholars then agree that if unrealistic stories like accounts of "plucking a [blooming] bamboo shoot from the snow and catching carp [jumping] from an ice hole" counted as proofs of one's true virtue, this would only indicate a disturbance in the energy between heaven and earth.[77] Pak's doubts are also reflected in his biography of the widow Madam Pak, who poisoned herself to death after mourning her deceased husband for three years. Expressing his sympathy about Madam Pak's choice of suicide, Pak states that "dying might be better than living

75. Yi Ok, "Such'ik chŏn," Yŏkchu Yi Ok chŏnjip, 2:212–16.

76. Yi Ok, "Yŏllyŏ Yissi chŏn," Yŏkchu Yi Ok chŏnjip, 2:210–11.

77. See the discussion in the introduction on this conversation. Pak Chiwŏn, Yŏrha ilgi, 621.

because a young widow would be treated pitifully and remain a target of gossip in the community."[78] Pak thus expresses concern about the social conditions that left women without an alternative to death, yet he never rejects the culture of chastity as a whole.

Perhaps the most ardent opponent of chaste suicide was Chŏng Yagyong, a scholar conventionally placed within the practical-learning circle along with Pak Chiwŏn. In his epitaph written for a woman named Madam Ch'oe, who was the wife of his second cousin, Chŏng emphasizes that he is recording nothing but the truth about her death, unlike typical epitaphs that glorify chaste deaths. After Madam Ch'oe hanged herself to follow her dead husband, literati of her town discussed the matter and decided to make her case public, asking Chŏng to draft a petition to honor her suicide. However, Chŏng writes, he turned down the request, instead following the lead of the scholar Chŏng Sihan (1625–1707), who once stopped Confucian literati from petitioning the state to reward a widow's suicide by saying, "Dying to follow a husband without a reason is not rightly [performing] wifely fidelity; airing the virtue in public is not bringing fortune to the family."[79] Taking Chŏng Sihan's words to heart, Chŏng Yagyong criticizes a widow's unreasonable suicide as an insular decision to neglect her remaining duties. Instead of petitioning on behalf of his cousin's wife, Chŏng therefore decided to write an epitaph to be placed in her grave.

As one of the most prolific scholars of the dynasty, Chŏng Yagyong wrote about almost every aspect of Chosŏn society. Unlike his contemporaries who celebrated female chastity in various writings, Chŏng wrote a critical essay on the topic, entitled "Discussion on Chaste Wives" ("Yŏlburon"). In it he asks:

> If a son dies to follow his deceased father, is it filial piety? No. . . . If a subject dies to follow the deceased king, is it loyalty? No. . . . What about celebrating a wife dying to follow her dead husband, by erecting a

<hr/>

78. Pak Chiwŏn, "Yŏllyŏ Hamyang Pakssi chŏn," Yŏnam chip, 1:34b.
79. Chŏng Yagyong, "Chŏlbu Ch'oessi myojimyŏng," Kugyŏk Tasan simunjip, 7:203–4.

scorching red gate and exempting her family from taxes? That is not chastity but an eccentric [act].[80]

For Chŏng, all chaste deaths carried out under the banner of morality are meaningless unless they meet specific requirements that legitimate them. He confines the definition of "chaste wives" to (1) those who follow their husband into death after the two of them fought robbers or beasts side by side; (2) those who commit suicide on the verge of being raped by a stranger or forced to remarry by parents or other relatives; and (3) those who are punished with death after failing to clear their deceased husband's name at court.[81] Except under these radical circumstances, Chŏng viewed a wife's suicide as a meaningless sacrifice and irresponsible act done without consideration for surviving in-laws and children.

The conviction that underlies Chŏng Yagyong's criticism of chaste suicide is that it does violence to the core value of filial piety. As earlier sections have examined, Chŏng's contemporaries, though holding a range of opinions and feelings, persistently sought to legitimize chaste suicide by deprioritizing filiality when it clashed with hypothetically higher virtues such as loyalty and chastity. In Chŏng's other writings, however, such as *Treatise on Government* (*Kyŏngse yup'yo*) and *Admonitions on Governing the People* (*Mongmin simsŏ*), which cover a wide spectrum of topics on governing society and edifying people, he clearly rejects the dominant rhetoric that justified women's suicide by subverting filiality, as follows:

Filial piety is the utmost virtue of human beings. Yet people fear that townspeople will rarely know whether they perform filial piety if they serve [their parents merely] with a benign attitude and mild countenance. Many thus cut their fingers or thighs, making their filiality [into] violent righteousness. Ordinary people cannot easily achieve such an extraordinary act, nor did the Emperor Shun and Master Zeng (505–435 BCE) cut their fingers and thighs; the Duke of Zhou and Confucius never

80. Chŏng Yagyong, "Yŏlburon," *Kugyŏk Tasan simunjip*, 5:151–54.
81. Chŏng Yagyong, "Yŏlburon," *Kugyŏk Tasan simunjip*, 5:151–54.

mention [such a practice], nor do the Nine Classics record and prove [it]. The sage man is cautious about mentioning [such extreme behavior].

Auspicious events such as sparrows [allowing] themselves to be caught, carp jumping out of [holes in the] ice, bamboo shoots blooming [in the snow], and pine trees drying out are miracles that occur only once in a thousand years. *Yet these days such [miraculous] stories are always included in drafting family petitions and community letters [for reward requests], although I do not think that there could be that many miracles from Heaven. . . .*

Rewards of chaste women should be vigilantly inspected and reasonably practiced. After being corrupted by thieves or enemies, [women] may respond by killing themselves. Still, a thorough investigation is required for the case of a young widow who, not being able to overcome the shame and resentment [of her miserable situation], follows her narrow-minded personality and hangs or poisons herself—[such a case] should never be commemorated or encouraged.[82]

Chŏng asserts that the superfluous violence people perform for the sake of demonstrating their virtue is a form of grandstanding and is mentioned nowhere in the Confucian classics. Although some exceptional cases may have been combed from the classics to support the moral ideal in accounts of chastity, he maintains that the current unprecedented levels of bodily sacrifice lack a canonical foundation. Chŏng also questions the authenticity of auspicious signs that were often rumored to accompany harming one's body. Though increasingly included in letters and petitions seeking official recognition of a deceased woman's chastity, such claims are mostly vacuous embellishments, he implies. Most of all, it was the state-reward system that promoted the delusion that chaste suicide was exemplary conduct. Although the state's initial motivation had been to edify the populace, honoring the extreme behavior of suicide gradually valorized a selfish form of fidelity that caused serious harm—such as women abandoning their other familial and moral duties.[83]

Moreover, Chŏng argues, by "commemorating the evil practice [of suicide] by reducing the taxes of the household," the government

---

82. Chŏng Yagyong, *Mongmin simsŏ*, 4:37–40; emphasis added.
83. Chŏng Yagyong, *Kyŏngse yup'yo*, 3:312–13.

"encourages [ignorant] people to follow the most malicious act in the world."[84] Such material compensation drove women to take their lives while fostering "an unhealthy craving for posthumous glory" and a vulgar impetus to obtain economic benefits from the reward program.[85] A wife's fidelity should be praised only when she fulfills her responsibilities as a devoted mother and filial daughter-in-law, not when she hollowly abandons her life after her husband dies of natural causes. To prevent such empty deaths, Chŏng stresses the need for a careful investigation of chaste suicides claimed by women's families and townspeople. A local officer in charge must first scrutinize the background of the chaste death and its righteousness, since many cases are embellished with untrue events to stand out among the myriad requests for an official reward. While nothing in the world is more difficult than killing oneself, the death should nevertheless be honored only if it was carried out with utmost sincerity.

Like Yi Ok and Pak Chiwŏn, Chŏng Yagyong never challenged the chastity ideal itself nor the lifelong widowhood imposed on women. Chŏng's criticism of the extreme performance of chaste suicide was part of his broader concerns about the moral authenticity of "virtuous sacrifice" conducted under the flag of loyalty, filiality, or chastity.[86] Chŏng insisted that the state should establish an objective set of criteria to distinguish one's sincerity from the falsity that could lie behind action. He blamed the misguided state-reward policy for the increasing numbers of women who chose death as a moral outlet, condemning the government for celebrating such immoderate moral performance in Chosŏn society. Chŏng's criticism of the extreme nature of chastity practice remained too marginal to compete with the predominant emphasis on bodily sacrifice in the late Chosŏn and hence did not produce a collective voice or active criticism among literati. Chŏng's points, nevertheless, certainly departed from the mainstream chaste discourse at a time when the Chosŏn state viewed chaste suicide as one path toward a moralized society, which was the ultimate goal of the

84. Chŏng Yagyong, "Yŏlburon," *Kugyŏk Tasan simunjip*, 5:151–54.
85. Ropp, "Passionate Women," 7.
86. On Chŏng Yagyong's view on virtuous sacrifice and moral authenticity in late Chosŏn Korea, see Kim Ho, "Politics and the Discourse."

dynasty. Most significantly, Chŏng's criticism was the product of prolonged tension among late Chosŏn literati over the conflicting values of filiality and fidelity and the question of what constituted an honorable death—tension that had intensified for two centuries after the Imjin War and Manchu Invasions. The vigorous debates that took off during the postwar period gradually opened up a vital moment when scholars such as Chŏng Yagyong were able to reflect on renegotiating the very notion of chastity.

The Nineteenth Century and Chastity Exaltation

Along with the production of rich literati accounts on chaste suicide, the nineteenth century saw the largest number of official rewards for chastity ever made in Chosŏn history. During the thirty-four years of King Sunjo's reign (r. 1800–1834), based solely from the *Sillok* records, the state rewarded 315 chaste women, which exceeded the 209 chastity rewards conferred during King Injo's reign.[87] Although Injo's reign was not as long as Sunjo's, we must recall the urgent context in which his court was established and the fact that the rewards were granted in the immediate aftermath of two traumatic wars and the political disturbance during which Injo was enthroned. Moreover, Sunjo's court bestowed about ten times more chastity rewards than that of his father, Chŏngjo. Not surprisingly, then, the nineteenth century also witnessed the largest numbers of chaste heroines at the local level: unofficial biographies and local chronicles recount innumerable stories of women who triumphed over the agony of living as widows by following their deceased husbands into the grave. In a sense, the nineteenth century marked a paradoxical time for Chosŏn women: although they had lost considerable familial and social standing under the steady penetration of the patrilineal system, their very private virtue of chastity also brought them more public recognition and visibility than ever before.

The state's motivation for rewarding so many chaste paragons cannot be separated from the political climate of the era. Having succeeded

---

87. Combining loyalty, filiality, and chastity awards, Injo's government rewarded a total of 573 people during his reign, compared to 983 recipients under Sunjo's reign.

his father Chŏngjo to the throne in 1800, at the tender age of eleven, Sunjo was too young to display formidable kingship. Major governmental power gradually became concentrated in the hands of the powerful Andong Kim lineage, opening the so-called era of in-law government.[88] In addition, the state's finances faced extreme difficulties as severe famines swept the country and rampant embezzlement was practiced by local clerks.[89] Early to mid-nineteenth-century Chosŏn was also punctuated by several major peasant uprisings across the country that ultimately undermined the stability of the society. Continuation of unfavorable economic conditions heavily burdened the people, while weakening the state's capacity to sustain the social order based on Confucian norms. Honoring virtuous subjects therefore proved again an important way of demonstrating the state's grip on the unstable society, as it had in the aftermaths of the Imjin War and Manchu Invasions in earlier centuries. In 1812, when the Hong Kyŏngnae Rebellion was finally quelled, for example, the government recognized about 130 people with the highest-level rewards, 12 of whom were commended for being loyal subjects—the largest number recognized for loyalty in any one year of Sunjo's reign.

Considering the tight reward policies under his two predecessors, moreover, Sunjo's court appears to have become lenient. Whereas Chŏngjo had stipulated the number of candidates to be recommended from each region, to prevent certain provinces from monopolizing the rewards, Sunjo tended to approve proposals for rewards without seriously questioning their authenticity and regardless of whether they were submitted through the Ministry of Rites, court officials, or even

88. As soon as Sunjo was enthroned, Queen Chŏngsun (1745–1805), who was a queen of King Yŏngjo, administered state affairs "from behind the veil" on behalf of the young king. However, political power was soon dominated by Kim Chosun (1765–1832), Sunjo's father-in-law, and by his Andong Kim family, which, except during the short reign of Hŏnjong (r. 1834–1849), remained powerful to the end of nineteenth century, when it was challenged by Hŭngsŏn Taewŏn'gun (1820–1898), the famous regent and father of King Kojong (r. 1863–1907).

89. For a detailed discussion of the early nineteenth century's fiscal situation, see Karlsson, "Royal Compassion and Disaster Relief," 71–98.

local Confucian scholars.[90] Perhaps because of the unprecedented number of rewards granted, descriptions of the awardees' chaste deeds are much shorter in the *Sunjo sillok* than in the *Sillok* of previous reigns, which usually contain detailed stories of each recipient's individual moral achievements. In 1832 alone, when eighty-eight women were nominated for the honor of receiving a memorial arch, the *Sunjo sillok* is silent about any review of the recommendations or further discussion on the final selections, simply listing recipients' names and hometowns.[91]

What distinguished the early nineteenth-century reward system was, therefore, the state's gradual inability to control the selection process that preceded official recognition, and this tendency seems to have lasted until the end of the dynasty. When the government recognized a great number of chaste women during King Kojong's reign, including one hundred virtuous subjects who had died during the Manchu Invasions in the early seventeenth century, only a few of their individual stories were recorded and court officials expressed concern about the inefficient reward system.[92] The high number of official rewards meant that the state granted prizes in various forms, including tax release, which became an added burden to the already deteriorated financial condition of the government. In an 1870 audience with King Kojong, Chief Minister of Rites Kim Pyŏnghak (1822–1879) pointed out two chronic problems with the reward system: (1) the loose screening procedure did not thoroughly scrutinize an applicant's merit, and (2) the tax-exemption reward customarily remained in effect even after the death(s) of the family member(s) or of the immediate descendant(s) of the awardee.[93] The next year, Kim again brought up these issues, stating that "immunity from corvée [given to those of outstanding merit] is a special favor arranged by the state. Recently, there has been

90. King Chŏngjo limited the annual number of nominations to ten for the two southern provinces (Kyŏngsang and Chŏlla), to six or seven for Kyŏnggi and Ch'ungch'ŏng, and to four or five for the northwestern provinces. *Chŏngjo sillok* 46:15a–16a [1797/2/10].

91. *Sunjo sillok* 32:21a–22a [1832/4/13].

92. *Kojong sillok* 4:41a [1867/9/15].

93. *Kojong sillok* 7:30a [1870/yun10/10].

rampant release from corvée whenever cases of filiality and chastity have been reported. . . . Filial children and chaste wives have become [indeed] only superficial titles for getting exempted from the tax."[94]

Although Kim Pyŏnghak mentions the questionable legitimacy and the obvious ineffectiveness of the reward system, his primary concern was how to collect hidden taxes when the state was facing serious fiscal drain. To remedy the situation, Kim proposed a thorough inspection of all the households in the eight provinces that had overtly benefited from such cases, but did not suggest any specific methods to rectify the reward system and prevent its misuse.[95] Whether or not the government conducted the inspection is uncertain. Yet it seems the abuse of the reward system persisted or even worsened toward the end of Kojong's reign, as described in a memorial submitted by the court official Yi P'ilhwa:

> Although it may be inappropriate for me to speak about the problem of education, . . . there are several matters about which, as a loyal subject, I am compelled to speak [to Your Highness]. The first is about the Bureau of Rites Administration (Changyewŏn 掌禮院), which has routinely collected money from people for the cost of erecting a memorial arch. In general, the practice of honoring loyal subjects, filial sons, and chaste wives is the pillar [of the state mission] that has been established as a vital way to promote moral norms. . . . These days, the government grants [the reward] based not on the truth about actual virtuous behavior, but on [whether the applicant can] afford to pay [the fee for the reward]—800 wŏn. Therefore, the exemplary conduct is considered nothing; the ability to submit the customary money has become the main point. Even if there are people whose actions are remarkably loyal, filial, and chaste, such would not be known to the world [if the fees for reward requests were not paid]. This is far from the state's original intention in legislating the reward policy. [I ask you to] immediately discipline the officials in charge [of administrating the rewards] and to permanently abolish the so-called payment required to receive the reward (chŏngnyŏ yenapchŏn). Provincial governors must carefully investigate cases to be nominated for the state reward before making an official request. In case

94. *Kojong sillok* 8:53a [1871/9/15].
95. *Kojong sillok* 7:30a [1870/yun10/10].

an official who was privately bribed fabricated the story of [someone's] virtuous act, both the [corrupt] official and the one who asked for [the fabrication] should be punished.[96]

Yi's memorial criticizes the state for dropping its initial vision of the reward policy and even reaching the point of collecting money in the name of granting a memorial arch. Officials in charge of managing the rewards burdened applicants with monetary requirements. Whether this was done simply to boost the state's coffers or was initiated to offset the fiscal drain engendered by the increasing numbers of awardees, it implied that a morally superior person would not qualify for official recognition without also being able to afford the required payment. When the "sale" of rewards began is hard to know, but the practice seems to have already prevailed in the nineteenth century. Yu Insŏk's "Biography of Chaste Wife Madam Yi" includes an anecdote of how her in-law family became dejected when the Ministry of Rites demanded payment upon receiving their request to honor her chaste suicide. The family's relative residing in Seoul also stopped the appeal, lamenting the distorted reward practice that was rampant at that time.[97]

While such evidence indicates the state's loss of conscientiousness in moralizing the society through the state-reward system, the local-level search for chaste paragons remained vibrant, especially in combination with mounting familial and regional interests, as discussed earlier. Furthermore, claiming a new reward—or requesting that the reward level granted in the past be upgraded—was considered an imperative filial duty for *yangban* descendants. To generate a greater number of memorial arches—the highest of all material honors—and galvanize the visibility of a family's morality, descendants submitted chains of petitions for a higher level of reward to the court, and even made payments in some cases. To them, "representation" of their lineage or region was paramount, and memorial arches met the purpose more than anything else. It was not rare for a lineage to erect several arches in the same area (as the Hyŏnp'ung Kwak lineage did, described

96. *Kojong sillok* 47:22a–b [1906/4/17].
97. Yu Insŏk, "Yŏlbu yuin Yissi chŏn," *Ŭiam chip*, 50:19a–20b.

in chapter 4), boasting a high spirit of morality that would fortify its position in the local community. Even if the state did not accept a reward request, the fact that it had "actually" been written and submitted made a great difference, partially fulfilling a filial obligation, and such effort was occasionally recorded on the memorial arches built for other awardees of the same town.[98] Nominating ancestors who had died several hundred years before required even more extensive collective endeavors that called upon wider literary, political, and regional networks. In fact, local gazetteers, documents in private literati collections, and other extant writings carry far longer lists of chaste-woman names produced from various local areas than are found in the *Sillok* records themselves. This raises the question of whether or not all these women received official chastity awards from the state. In either case, what mattered most for the sake of familial and regional significance was the inscribing of their names in these local publications.[99]

Even when the nineteenth-century Chosŏn government was no longer able to regulate the state-reward system or correct its problems, remarkable stories of chaste women and their moral champions flourished at the local level more than ever before. Seizing upon their role as the ultimate guardians of local order and morality, the local *yangban* undoubtedly utilized this official system to solidify their status. At the same time, each region's collective efforts to identify local chaste paragons gave *yangban* the opportunity to assert their cultural authority over the discourse of chastity in the region. The large numbers of non-official chastity awardees whose names also appear in local gazetteers and local histories reveal the extended, localized interpretations and criteria of chastity. The nineteenth-century exaltation of chastity reflects how the commemoration of chaste heroines in postwar Chosŏn

98. Yi Hŭihwan, "Chosŏn malgi ŭi chŏngnyŏ wa kamun," 159–61.

99. According to Yi's study, which examines the existing memorial arches built in the Namwŏn area of Chŏlla Province during Kojong's reign, about 103 people received rewards in that area, yet only 165 cases are recorded nationwide in the *Kojong sillok*. This relatively small gap suggests either the *Kojong sillok*'s negligence in documenting all rewards from all local areas or the possibility of manipulation to inflate the number of awards listed in the local gazetteers. Yi Hŭihwan, "Chosŏn malgi ŭi chŏngnyŏ wa kamun," 150–51.

society was gradually transformed into a crucial venue for negotiating the identities of local families and communities, creating a distinctive juncture in which they shaped their own culture of chastity.

* * *

The extreme content of chaste-woman stories was born in a historical context that was rife with memories of disturbing war experiences, intrigued with new modes of commemoration, and preoccupied with reestablishing socio-political order. While the Chosŏn court continued to cherish women's chastity via various methods of indoctrination, the turbulent Japanese and Manchu wars in the late sixteenth and early seventeenth centuries led to a watershed in the evolution of chastity discourse and practice. The postwar debates over what constituted a meaningful death gave Confucian literati a renewed space where intense deliberation about how to perform chastity surfaced and flourished. Although chaste-woman tales were retold in similar rhetoric so as to meet the heroic standards required of virtuous women, the large corpus of chastity accounts encompasses divergent interpretations of the conflicting moral duties of daughterly filiality and wifely fidelity, elucidating the literati's own reflections on the moral conviction implicit in legitimating a woman's violent choice to take her own life.[100]

The changing discourse on women's chastity was also closely related to the dynamics of various social powers in the second part of the dynasty. The state-reward system continued to function as a fundamental driving force in deepening chastity culture, yet individual female chastity was increasingly viewed as the embodiment of the entire family's virtue, which then extended into the realms of larger community and politics. Cognizant of their roles as moral leaders and of the intensified competition for state rewards, local elites actively engaged in a range of collective calls to produce officially honored chaste women. Such activism certainly fulfilled their duty to instill an awareness of moral values in ordinary local people, but it ultimately strengthened the elite membership in local communities by solidifying

100. Carlitz, "Desire, Danger, and the Body," 123.

social ties and local networks, and embellishing the moral lore of the community.

The nineteenth-century culmination of chastity culture was therefore a combined product of the state's long-term moral vision of the society and the chastity activism of local elites who gradually took over the leadership of the moralization project in their local communities. Ironically, however, when the culture of chastity reached its pinnacle, the government was no longer effectively in control of the state-reward process. A range of political and socioeconomic problems incapacitated the reward program, generating corruption in the selection procedure and exacerbating the chronic issues of verifying the authenticity of a woman's chaste action. This does not mean that the state-led system was completely decentralized, defunct, or replaced by the localization process. Although the Chosŏn state had lost its earlier fervor for managing and engineering chastity practice, its role as the only legitimate, official patron of chastity awards remained unaffected to the end of the dynasty, and local elites continued to seek resources within the existing system. Once there was no central court to canonize chaste martyrs after the official demise of the dynasty in 1910, local-level chastity activism eventually stood in for the state, carrying on with the reward activity through its own local modes of commemorating chaste women.[101]

---

101. See the epilogue for a discussion of local scholars' activities to honor chaste women during the colonial period.

PART II

SOCIAL POWER AND NEGOTIATION

In the *Compilation of Korean Oral Literature (Han'guk kubi munhak taegye)*, there are eighteen stories about so-called fake chaste women (*katcha yŏllyŏ*).[1] Fourteen of them mention the activity of a well-known secret royal inspector, Pak Munsu (1691–1756), who was dispatched to local places to investigate whether the region's chaste-woman cases were really true. Interestingly, ten of the eighteen stories are about members of the illustrious Kwak family of Hyŏnp'ung, renowned for producing more virtuous members over the generations than any other family in Korean history. Originating in Hyŏnp'ung village in Kyŏngsang Province, the Kwak family had built twelve memorial arches and been recognized for a total of one loyal subject, eight filial sons, and six chaste wives.[2] Acknowledging the family's role as a moral paragon that had produced the largest number of chaste wives and filial sons since the years after the Imjin War, the Chosŏn state in 1724 gave the family a memorial house with twelve rooms—glorious proof of the family's virtuous reputation (fig. P.1).

Though there are different versions, these stories of fake chaste women related to the Kwak family recount Secret Inspector Pak Munsu's

---

1. Han'guk Chŏngsin Munhwa Yŏn'guwŏn, *Han'guk kubi munhak taegye*. I used digital versions available from the Changsŏgak Archives (http://yoksa.aks.ac.kr/jsp/ur/Directory.jsp?gb=3).

2. Pak Chu, *Chosŏn sidae ŭi hyo wa yŏsŏng*, 362–70.

visit to the Talsŏng region, where the Kwak family resided. Curious as to how a single family had yielded so many state-rewardees, Pak, hosted by a male member of the family, intentionally stayed in the Kwak family's house. One night after his host had gone out, Pak accidentally discovered a widow of the Kwak family having relations with an outside man (in most versions a monk) and killed both the widow and the man on the spot. When his male host (who turned out to be the widow's brother-in-law) returned home and learned what Pak had done, he fabricated the story that the widow had committed suicide out of fidelity and had his slaves secretly bury the dead man's body. The family then spread word about her chaste suicide, building a memorial arch and throwing a banquet to commemorate her chaste death. Shortly thereafter, the brother-in-law burned down the arch to erase any incriminating evidence that might be uncovered later, lying that it had been accidentally set on fire by a beggar. Impressed by the brother-in-law's quick thinking in turning a case of adultery into a widow's chaste suicide, Secret Inspector Pak offered him an official title for his brilliance in preserving the family reputation.[3]

Because these stories were transmitted orally among the ordinary populace, rather than in written form, we cannot know to what extent they reflect the facts. Perhaps all the chaste suicides reportedly committed by women of Kwak family were indeed their own virtuous and sincere actions. It is possible that stories transmitted on the lips of generation after generation were embellished and even distorted from the original versions. It was also not uncommon during the latter part of the dynasty for a family to erect more than one memorial arch in the same area, thereby boasting of a high spirit of morality that would concomitantly fortify its position in the community. But what do the existence and circulation of such stories tell us?

Part 1 has demonstrated the tensions in and the historical trajectories of the making of Chosŏn chastity culture—tensions and trajectories that also underlay its political and ideological significance during the dynasty. Shifting from the external settings that had shaped the concept of female chastity to reflect the subjectivity of women when faced

3. Han'guk Chŏngsin Munhwa Yŏn'guwŏn, *Han'guk kubi munhak taegye*, 7.15:545–48. Yi In'gyŏng, *Yŏllyŏ sŏrhwa ŭi chaehaesŏk*, 245.

P.1. Memorial house with twelve elaborate rooms, bestowed on the Kwak family of Hyŏnp'ung, Talsŏng-gun, Taegu. Photograph courtesy of Cultural Heritage Department, Talsŏng-gun, Taegu Metropolitan City, North Kyŏngsang Province.

with various allegations, part 2 explores the micro level of how chastity was perceived and practiced among the ordinary populace in Chosŏn society. If, by the second part of the dynasty, the Confucian transformation had somehow reached people at the bottom of society—people who were supposed to emulate the behavior of the *yangban* elites—then what visions might these non-elites have had for their lives? What moral instruction could ordinary people have gained from their observation of the elites' obsession with their own moral status, as sustained and strengthened through the constant production of virtuous heroes and heroines? Do oral stories introduced earlier hint at a possible fracture between the normative ideology and its actual practice attached to the ideal of female chastity? If so, to what extent does Confucianization explain or fail to explain such a fissure? In part 2, I address these questions by locating a variety of people's voices and attitudes toward female chastity regardless of their own socio-marital status.

To access how chastity functioned in the sociocultural settings in which ordinary people lived, I analyze legal codes and court testimonies dealing not only with sexual crimes such as adultery and rape but with suicide. Ironically, the practice of chastity may be best uncovered by examining crimes against chastity. Legal cases in particular interweave the complex responses to social norms that arose from everyday interactions between ordinary Chosŏn men and women whose lives are scarcely visible in other sources. Stories woven in legal testimonies also unveil choices women made when their moral integrity was threatened and questioned, indicating the dynamics of women's reactions to various marital, familial, and legal conditions—whether their goal was to compromise, reject accusations, or obtain revenge.

Some women ran away from a profligate or irresponsible husband to live with a man capable of giving them a better life, and others plotted to murder their husband in the hope of maintaining their illicit relationship. Despite Chosŏn society's negative attitude toward remarriage, many widows in fact sought a new life in this way. Other widows became victims of sexual violence and killed themselves out of shame; still others, who were brought before the court for having illicit relations, were able to tell their stories to defend their positions. As chapter 6 illuminates, a number of women who chose death also raised their voices, whether in verbal or written form, hoping not only to properly punish and avenge their attackers but to reinscribe their personal or moral integrity through their own words. Revealing a surprising degree of fluidity in marital practices and illicit sexuality, the evidence amply shows that people interpreted and utilized the chastity discourse for their own purposes and according to their circumstances. Although the populace may have had a good understanding of the official norms on chastity and propriety by the latter part of the dynasty, I argue that the definition of women's chastity was consistently contested both by women themselves and by their interactions with others—and that the fissures between the state orthodoxy toward chastity and the popular practice of chastity were dynamic yet not invisible.

CHAPTER FOUR

Chastity in Law and Legal Trials

On the second day of the eleventh month in 1796, a death was reported to the local magistrate's office of P'yŏngsan in Hwanghae Province.[1] A man named Yi Ch'undae had beaten to death Yang Sŏnghang, another man residing in the same village. When the magistrate of P'yŏngsan arrived at the spot where Yang's dead body was located, it turned out that the report had been made in error by the dead man's cousin: Yang had in fact poisoned himself to death. The testimonies of Yang's family members and people related to Yang's death revealed that he had maintained illicit relations with a daughter of Yi Ch'undae who lived near the house of Yang's adopted father. Because the affair had gone on for about three years, it became widely known to the townspeople.

On the twenty-eighth day of the tenth month, Yi Ch'undae had visited Yang's two fathers (biological and adopted) to reclaim his daughter's wooden hairpin, which Yang had snatched and kept in his pocket. According to Yi, Yang intentionally broke the hairpin in half and showed it to people in the hope of making Yi's daughter his concubine. Though impoverished, Yang's family was *yangban* class, whereas Yi Ch'undae was a commoner. Yang's fathers saw Yi's rude attitude as an affront and declined his request but were shortly confronted by

1. *Pyŏgyŏng surok* 10:18b–25a.

Yi armed with a knife. Yi was ultimately stopped by his brother, who had accompanied Yi at that time, but the *yangban* Yang family felt deeply humiliated. They reproached their son Yang Sŏnghang, deploring the way he had disgraced the good reputation of their ancestors and blaming themselves for failing to educate him in proper filial conduct. Frustrated, Sŏnghang left home, but later that night he was found in the yard of his home in severe pain. He soon died, after uttering his last words: "Rather than place my fathers in endless plight, I prefer to die painfully by drinking bittern."[2] Believing Yi Ch'undae to be the root cause of Sŏnghang's death, the Yang family moved Sŏnghang's corpse to a room in Yi's house in protest.

Following the testimonies of Yang's family members and the accused Yi Ch'undae, Yi's eighteen-year-old daughter, Yi Chokkŭmaji, was brought to the trial. She testified:

> Last year while I was picking beans in the field, Sŏnghang appeared from a mountain all of sudden and teased me. [He] took me to the corner to [sexually] harass me, but he did not dare to do so with tens of people's eyes [watching us] in broad daylight. A few days later, when I was washing cotton in the stream, Sŏnghang stole a wooden hairpin I was wearing on my head. With [the hairpin], he made up a story of secret fornication [between me and him] to force a marriage and make me his concubine. This is how things have reached this point. How on earth can there be ambiguity? I only wish to die soon.[3]

While Chokkŭmaji was denying her adulterous relations with Sŏnghang, a postmortem of Sŏnghang's body began. Because the room where the body had been placed in Yi Ch'undae's house was too small to turn the body over for examination, Yang's corpse was moved to a plank in the yard. When a silver pin was inserted in both upper and lower parts of his body, the head of the pin became black, but it turned white after washing. Also, after boiling the liquid used to wash the pin, salt was extracted, signifying that he had ingested bittern. The

---

2. *Pyŏgyŏng surok* 10:19b.
3. *Pyŏgyŏng surok* 10:21b.

investigator thus concluded the true cause of Sŏnghang's death as bittern poisoning.[4] In the meantime, the Yang family continued to blame Yi Ch'undae for Sŏnghang's suicide, arguing that Sŏnghang was "always well-behaved as a *yangban*'s son."[5] In opposition, Yi and his daughter maintained that Sŏnghang had brought about his own death both by pestering Chokkŭmaji and by fabricating a story of illicit relations with her.

Given the contrasting accounts of the Yang and the Yi families, how did the magistrate judge the case based on the postmortem and a series of people's testimonies? He viewed Sŏnghang's death as a result of conflict between *yangban* and commoner, rather than focusing on the man's licentious relation with Chokkŭmaji. He wrote in his postscript, "At first glance, this case looks like Sŏnghang's groundless suicide, but investigating carefully, the Yang are *sajok* and the Yi are commoners."[6] Sŏnghang had killed himself out of a deep feeling of guilt that his behavior had resulted in the non-*yangban* Yi Ch'undae insulting both his biological and his adopted *yangban* fathers. The magistrate was himself a descendant of a *yangban* family that had held official posts for generations, so he understood well that Sŏnghang's sense of nobility could not stand the mortification of the commoner Yi confronting his fathers.

Yi Ch'undae was hence designated as the accused. Although he did not commit the crime of killing Sŏnghang by his own hand, from the magistrate's point of view, he had triggered the suicide.[7] Further, the magistrate determined that Chokkŭmaji was a "licentious woman"

4. *Pyŏgyŏng surok* 10:22a–24a. Although the *Sinju Muwŏllok* (Newly supplemented *Coroner's Manual for the Elimination of Grievances*), which was compiled in 1438 based on the Chinese *Wuyuanlu*, had long been used to conduct postmortems in Chosŏn, an article on "Death by Poisoning with Bittern" was only added to the *Chŭngsu Muwŏllok* (Amplified and Corrected *Coroner's Manual for the Elimination of Grievances*) in 1792. See *Chŭngsu Muwŏllok ŏnhae* 3:62b. For further discussion of a detailed postmortem procedure, see Sun Joo Kim and Jungwon Kim, *Wrongful Deaths*.

5. *Pyŏgyŏng surok* 10:20b.

6. *Pyŏgyŏng surok* 10:23b.

7. *Pyŏgyŏng surok* 10:24a.

(*ŭmnyŏ*) whose obscene conduct had been disclosed, causing a clash that had led to a man's death. The magistrate saw her crime as deserving such grave punishment that it would hardly be a pity if she were sentenced to death. Ordering that she be imprisoned wearing a cangue, he further decreed that Chokkŭmaji be made a government slave (*kwanbi*).[8]

In responding to the P'yŏngsan magistrate's investigation report, however, the provincial governor reversed the initial decision. Although still seeing Sŏnghang's suicide as stemming from Yi Ch'undae's abasement of Sŏnghang's fathers, the governor understood Yi Ch'undae's resentment about the rumor of illicit relations between his unmarried daughter and Sŏnghang, which would block his daughter's marriage prospects. Nevertheless, he concluded that Yi's crime of threatening Sŏnghang's fathers with a knife was an evil act deserving of one round of beating with a heavy stick. Concerning Chokkŭmaji, the provincial governor wrote:

> Picking beans in the field and washing cotton in the stream are the typical work of ordinary women. How could stealing [the woman's] hairpin while flirting *not* be considered [Sŏnghang's] intention to establish illicit relations with her? [Also,] registering a commoner woman as a government slave is not a trivial matter. Without a direct witness [to this incident], moreover, the claim that she is a licentious woman is too superficial [evidence] to meet [the crime of adultery]. Therefore, [I command that] Aji (Chokkŭmaji) leave town by marrying [a man] of her father's choice.[9]

Chokkŭmaji was therefore freed. People's testimonies had confirmed the existence of the rumor of her illicit relations with Sŏnghang, yet the provincial governor pointed out that, without an eyewitness, this was not enough to condemn her of the crime of adultery. His judicial

---

8. *Pyŏgyŏng surok* 10:24a–b. Wearing a cangue indicated a heavy crime, above flogging. Despite the 1747 regulation prohibiting the use of a cangue on women, it seems that such punishment was not completely eradicated. See Sun Joo Kim and Jungwon Kim, *Wrongful Deaths*, 221.

9. *Pyŏgyŏng surok* 10:25a.

decision implies that, as Chokkŭmaji testified during her trial, it may indeed have been Sŏnghang who made up the story by showing her hairpin to the townspeople with the intention of making her his concubine.

How could the P'yŏngsan magistrate and the provincial governor come to such completely different verdicts on Chokkŭmaji? Regarding the magistrate's perspective on this case as a *yangban* versus non-*yangban* conflict, we might point to the power of the *yangban* Yang family in the local community. The magistrate clearly empathized with Sŏnghang's situation as a *yangban* son, but he did not comment on his harassment of an unmarried young woman and blamed only Chokkŭmaji for lewd conduct. In the magistrate's view, Chokkŭmaji's enraged father, Yi Ch'undae, must necessarily stand accused of Sŏnghang's suicide, while Chokkŭmaji herself deserved to be severely punished for her licentious conduct. In the meantime, Chokkŭmaji had a chance to speak for herself at the court, and her testimony was heard and inscribed in the magistrate's report. Her words eventually reached a higher office and were taken into consideration in the final verdict despite her non-*yangban* status.

Of course, not all women called to the court for their sexual misbehavior succeeded in defending their positions, and women's sexual purity was the most pivotal criterion for female virtue in Chosŏn society. Indeed, this one legal case displays how issues of female sexuality, moral integrity, and social status were all interwoven in intricate ways and factored differently in contrasting judicial decisions. Taking the themes of illicit sexuality and sexual offenses as analytical lenses for examining how the ideal of chastity functioned and was perceived, I first examine the legal framework within which the category of sexual crimes was situated in Chosŏn law. Drawing upon judicial decisions and court testimonies, I then consider a variety of challenges and interactions inherent to accusing, prosecuting, convicting, and punishing crimes against female chastity. Most of all, I demonstrate how a commoner woman such as Chokkŭmaji, who was accused of being "licentious," could still carve out her position within the shifting legal terrain and judicial boundaries of sexual crimes—shifts that responded to myriad sex acts and actors of all genders, ages, social statuses, and economic positions.

Stolen Virtue: Sexual Crimes
in Chosŏn Criminal Law

As illustrated in Chokkŭmaji's case, the practice of chastity may, ironically, be best uncovered by examining the sexual crimes against it.
Legal cases entwine the complex reactions to social norms that arose
from everyday interactions between men and women in Chosŏn society. Among the many types of Chosŏn legal documents, investigation
reports containing detailed postmortem and trial procedures at local
courts grant us the extremely rare opportunity of hearing people's
vivid testimony in colloquial form. Although the voices of the people
in these reports have been filtered through the minds and ink brushes
of the local clerks who recorded them (as noted in the introduction),
they still illuminate the potential for accommodation and reproduction
between the existing law and the people's response to and use of the
law, which ultimately influenced the course of punishments on the often
ambiguous boundaries of sex crimes.[10]

The Chosŏn laws delineating punishments for sexual crimes show
that the state viewed crimes, homicides, and suicides revolving around
female sexual integrity as the most daunting threats to chastity. In
Chosŏn society, crimes violating the fundamental Confucian norms
(*kangsang*) of loyalty, filiality, and chastity were absolutely unpardon-
able regardless of extenuating circumstances. Crimes against a woman's
sexual integrity were viewed as equivalent to other immoral crimes
that deserved the heaviest punishments, because they ultimately posed
a challenge to the moral foundation and patriarchal constructions of
state and society. In other words, sex crimes were not simply individual
and familial matters but were directly connected to social harmony
and dynastic health.

Detailed statutes punishing sex crimes were outlined in the penal
code of the 1485 *Great Code of Administration*, which was founded
upon the *Great Ming Code*. Adoption of the Ming penal code had
been officially announced in the enthronement edict of King T'aejo,
the founder of Chosŏn, right after the dynasty was established in

---

10. Dunn, *Stolen Women in Medieval England*, 5–6.

1392.[11] As the first line of the penal code section in the *Great Code of Administration* clearly denotes, the Ming Code served as the basis of Chosŏn criminal law.[12] However, though it remained influential to the end of the dynasty, the Ming Code was never the only criminal law in use during the Chosŏn, since Korea's judicial approaches to matters such as places of exile, social status, and kinship degrees were distinct from those of China. The Chosŏn court soon compiled the *Direct Explanation of the Great Ming Code* (*Taemyŏngnyul chikhae*) in 1395, by rendering the Ming Code into the clerks' readings (*idu*) to help Korean officials understand the abstract and foreign law. The *Direct Explanation of the Great Ming Code* did not merely translate the Ming Code. Providing thorough explanation of each code, it complemented the Ming penal codes by omitting those that did not suit specific Chosŏn situations, offering translations that differed from the received meaning of the original codes, and even adding new codes not found in the Ming Code.[13] Furthermore, like the Qing state, which was built upon the Ming Code yet greatly expanded its legislative scope to fit the new regime's agendas, the Chosŏn state constantly enacted supplementary legislation in response to its own demands and problems throughout the dynasty. Already in 1492, compilation of newly issued royal edicts (*sugyo*; "received instructions") began, resulting in the *Supplementary Great Code* (*Taejŏn songnok*), which was followed

11. *T'aejo sillok* 1:43a [1392/7/28]. The Chosŏn court did not absolutize the Ming Code at the beginning of the dynasty, and the state also utilized other existing codes inherited from the Koryŏ dynasty. Chŏng Kŭngsik, "Chungguk yullyŏng ŭi suyong kwa han'guk chŏnt'ong sahoe," 149–50.

12. *Kyŏngguk taejŏn* 5:1a. Scholars have noted that traces of the Ming Code were still found in the 1905 version of the penal code (*Hyŏngpŏp taejŏn*), until it finally disappeared with the promulgation of the "Chosŏn Penal Order" (*Chosŏn hyŏngsaryŏng*) by the Japanese colonial government in 1912. See Chŏng Kŭngsik and Cho Chiman, "Chosŏn chŏn'gi Taemyŏngnyul ŭi suyong kwa pyŏnyong," 205–41. William Shaw, in examining the early nineteenth-century criminal case book *Conspectus of Laws and Precedents* (*Yullye yoram*), maintains a view similar to that of Chŏng and Cho. See Shaw, *Legal Norms in a Confucian State*, 4, 29.

13. Sim Chaeu, "Chosŏn malgi hyŏngsapŏp ch'egye wa Taemyŏngnyul ŭi wisang," 125–27. Throughout the Chosŏn dynasty, the *Direct Explanation of the Great Ming Code* was referred to simply as the "Great Ming Code" without distinguishing it from the original *Great Ming Code*. It was the Japanese colonial government that added "direct explanation" (*chikhae*) to the title to distinguish it from the Chinese Ming Code.

in 1543 by the *Continued Supplementary Great Code* (*Taejŏn husong-nok*) with added edicts.

The increasing complexity posed by the war experiences of the late sixteenth and early seventeenth centuries, as well as subsequent economic and social changes, further required the state to periodically issue additional statutes to cope with new challenges. New edicts continued to be proclaimed through the late Chosŏn, and the mounting volumes of edicts led to publication of a series of compilations in which all received royal edicts were brought together for more effective judicial application and to provide vital references for administrators. In 1698, the *Collected Royal Edicts* (*Sugyo chimnok*) was compiled under the order of King Sukchong, containing all edicts issued after the prewar publication of the 1543 *Continued Supplementary Great Code*. In 1743, the government completed its expanded version, the *Newly Supplemented Collected Royal Edicts* (*Sinbo sugyo chimnok*), by adding new edicts as well as the ones previously omitted.[14] The Chosŏn state's supplementary legislation process reached a high point during the eighteenth century, when two kings—Yŏngjo and Chŏngjo—placed an elevated value on law and legislation for social reform.[15] Whereas there are only 82 special provisions in the *Great Code of Administration* to supplement the Ming Code, 588 such provisions appear in the *Continuation of the Great Code*, compiled in 1746.[16] The state's efforts to produce comprehensive codes in one place continued, culminating in the 1785 publication of the *Great Code for Ruling the State* (*Taejŏn t'ongp'yŏn*), again followed in 1865 by the

14. Royal edicts "could themselves be complemented, modified, and emended according to new ad hoc decisions dictated by unforeseen situations" and supplemented the *Great Ming Code* and the *Great Code of Administration* as "operating regulations with legal authority." Jérôme Bourgon and Pierre-Emmanuel Roux see this as distinct from Chinese codification procedure. Bourgon and Roux, "Chosŏn Law Codes," 29–30.

15. Shaw, *Legal Norms in a Confucian State*, 9–12; and Shaw, "Traditional Korean Law," 305–6. For more detailed discussion of the early Chosŏn reception of the Ming Code from a legal perspective, see Mun Hyŏngjin, "Taemyŏngnyul kwa Kyŏngguk taejŏn," 199–213.

16. Sim Chaeu, "Chosŏn sidae pŏpchŏn p'yŏnch'an kwa hyŏngsa chŏngch'aek ŭi pyŏnhwa," 254–56; Chŏng Kŭngsik and Cho Chiman, "Chosŏn chŏn'gi Taemyŏngnyul ŭi suyong kwa pyŏnyong," 239.

Comprehensive Collection of Dynastic Codes. Moreover, unlike the *Great Code of Administration*'s articulation of the exclusive use of the Ming penal code, the 1746 *Continuation of the Great Code* eloquently decreed that "Chosŏn statutes and edicts be prioritized in case of competing with the Ming Code."[17]

It is therefore difficult to discuss sexual crimes without carefully understanding the changing backgrounds and practices of the related codes in the making of Chosŏn criminal law. Although the Ming Code was employed as basic criminal law, copious volumes of special edicts issued throughout the dynasty point to the state's changing stances in dealing with sex crimes, not only to effect the dynastic agendas of that time but to meet unique Chosŏn situations. In other words, as much as legal codes were pivotal in shaping and directing the legal lives of people, the codes' vitality and meaning were achieved through their application and reinterpretation during specific trials—which was accomplished by inviting everyone to weigh in, from provincial governors or local magistrates (the judges representing the official view) to victims, defendants, and witnesses, as illustrated in Chokkŭmaji's case described above. The "Committing Fornication" ("Pŏmgan") section, therefore, underwent a series of modifications and revisions up until the 1746 *Continuation of the Great Code* was compiled (see tables below).

In what follows, I discuss crimes against chastity both through the shifting practices of Chosŏn criminal law on sex crimes and by delving into actual legal cases with detailed oral testimonies. How the court listened to the voices of people, especially those of women as victims, defendants, or witnesses; how it framed the duties of people within the dynasty's legal and ethical principles; and how it punished different crimes—all these are critical to comprehending the practice of adjudicating sex crimes in Chosŏn society. Conversely, people's strategies during the court testimony sessions uncover the space made for construal of the laws and normative prescriptions, highlighting the

---

17. It states, "Apply the *Great Ming Code* as outlined in the *Great Code of Administration*. However, in case the statutes are included in the *Great Code of Administration* and the *Continuation of the Great Code*, use them instead." *Sok taejŏn* 4:1a.

complex relation between the abstract ideal and the actual practice when it comes to the virtue of female chastity.

The Crime of Consensual Fornication: Adultery

As in the *Great Ming Code* itself, the Chosŏn penal codes on sex crimes are found in the "Committing Fornication" section of the *Great Code of Administration*, which includes the categories of consensual fornication (*hwagan*; Ch. *hejian*), seduction-led fornication (*chogan*; Ch. *diaojian*), and forcible fornication (*kanggan*; Ch. *qiang jian*).

In fact, the most widely used term implying fornication in Chosŏn legal archives is *t'onggan* (通姦 or 通奸).[18] Unlike forcible fornication, in which the female victim could be of any marital status, consensual fornication was commonly understood as extramarital sexual intercourse between a man and a woman not married to each other. However, as Chokkŭmaji's case shows, its definition was flexible in Chosŏn, expanding to include any intercourse outside legitimate marriage, such as illicit relations between a (married or unmarried) man and unmarried (or widowed) woman.[19] Although today the English term "adultery" usually denotes "voluntary sexual relations between an individual who is married and someone who is not the individual's spouse," I use this term throughout this book to indicate consensual fornication in a broad sense, as applied in Chosŏn Korea.

The key element defining consensual fornication is the nature of "mutuality," since it always entails the consent of both parties. In punishing adultery, as table 4.1 shows, the Chosŏn state prescribed eighty strokes of beating with the heavy stick for anyone who committed adultery, regardless of status or gender distinction, as outlined in the Ming Code. If the woman had a husband, her penalty increased to

18. The two characters with the same sound (*kan*)—姦 and 奸—appear interchangeably in various official records and legal cases.

19. In searching for the definition of a sexual offense during imperial China, Matthew Sommer states that it had three elements: (1) intercourse between male and female, (2) intercourse outside legitimate, normative marriage, and (3) an assault by an outside male that threatens to interfere with another man's lineage. Sommer, *Sex, Law, and Society*, 33–36.

Table 4.1. Basic Punishments for Sexual Crimes

Type of sexual crime	Punishments in the *Great Ming Code*, "Committing Fornication" section
Consensual fornication	–Eighty strokes of beating with the heavy stick regardless of gender.
	–Ninety strokes of beating with the heavy stick for married women.
	–The punishments of forcible fornication applied if committing consensual fornication with young girls twelve years old or younger.
	–Men and women punished with this same [eighty-stroke] penalty if committing fornication with consent or by [partial] seduction
Seduction-led fornication	–One hundred strokes of beating with the heavy stick regardless of gender.
Forcible fornication	–If consummated, strangulation for men only; women not punished.
	–If unconsummated, one hundred strokes of beating with the heavy stick and life exile to [a distance of] 3,000 *li*.*

SOURCE: Yonglin Jiang, *Great Ming Code*, 214.

* Instead of 3,000 *li*, the 1395 *Direct Explanation of the Great Ming Code* (*Taemyŏngnyul chikhae*) does not specify the distance of exile, revising the punishment to "one hundred strokes and life exile to a remote place." *Taemyŏngnyul chikhae*, 549–57.

ninety strokes while the man was still punished with eighty strokes, underlining a married woman's heavier moral responsibility for committing adultery. However, punishing adultery was not as simple as was prescribed in the law. Every individual engaged in the crime was identified under different socio-political-familial statuses, according to official positions, family and relative relations, and master-servant hierarchy, all of which necessitated careful judicial reasoning in delivering the verdict of punishment.

Table 4.2 illustrates how the punishments for adultery consistently underwent revision and elaboration until the *Continuation of the Great Code* in 1746. Although earlier collected volumes of royal edicts became key sources for the *Continuation of the Great Code*,

Table 4.2. Royal Edicts and Statutes on "Committing Fornication": Adultery

Year and Royal Edict*

1553‡ – For deprived yangban (sajok) widows who cannot live by themselves, thus gathering firewood and drawing water with their own hands, if they have men with whom they are committing secret consensual fornication, they shall not be treated by the punishment of yangban women's consensual fornication. Those adulterers shall be freed without investigation.

1575 – For a palace woman committing consensual fornication with an outside man, punish by decapitation without waiting.

1585 – For women of conscripted soldiers (chŏngbyŏng) or wives of palace guardsmen (naegŭmwi) committing consensual fornication with a clerk at the station, treat [them] with the law corresponding to the punishment of yangban (sajok).

1649‡ – In the case of [a man] committing consensual fornication with his brother's daughter (niece), the head of the family cannot be exempted and shall be punished by exile for an indefinite period.

1667‡ – For palace women who use illness as an excuse and secretly commit consensual fornication with a brother-in-law while visiting their father's home, then becoming pregnant, [execute] the punishment [of decapitation] without waiting for the 100 days' [exemption after delivery]. (Note: See also the 1575 Royal Edict)

1677 – In the past, palace guardsmen were generally yangban (sajok) and many conscripted soldiers came from yangban families. However, things have changed by now and it is impossible to apply the same statute [as before]. Revise this after having discussions among high officials.

1679 – Those yangban committing consensual fornication with wives of relatives within the fifth degree of mourning shall be punished by the statute [in the Ming Code] without waiting.

1681 – A slave husband committing consensual fornication with his wife's mistress shall be punished by decapitation without waiting.

Statute[†]

If a [*yangban*] woman is deprived and cannot live by herself after being expelled, *she is not different from non-yangban women who wander around like beggars relying on other men. In that case, she shall not be punished along with the adulterer because her status is no longer considered to be yangban.*

For a palace woman committing consensual fornication with an outside man, punish *both man and woman* by beheading without waiting.
In a case where [the woman] is pregnant, execute the punishment after childbirth, yet without applying the law of 100 days' exemption after delivery.

Those *yangban* committing consensual fornication *with relatives within the fifth degree of mourning* or wives of relatives within the fifth degree of mourning shall be punished *by strangulation* without waiting. *Those committing consensual fornication with a concubine's relative within the third degree of mourning shall be punished by decapitation. Those non-yangban committing consensual fornication with their mother-in-law shall be punished by decapitation. [Those non-yangban] committing consensual fornication with sisters of the same mother and a different father shall be punished by strangulation. Those committing consensual fornication with wives of uncles or cousins shall be punished with one hundred strokes with the heavy stick and exile to [a distance of] 3,000 li.*

A slave husband committing consensual fornication with his wife's mistress shall be punished by decapitation without waiting.

(continued)

Table 4.2. *(continued)*

Year and Royal Edict*
1690[‡] – For *yangban* wives committing licentious acts, if [such actions] were forced by being seduced by strangers while staying in another place, [they] shall be considered differently from voluntary consensual fornication and the reduced punishment of exile shall be applied.
1724[‡] – For those committing consensual fornication with uncles' nephews and becoming pregnant, they shall be punished by decapitation without waiting. However, wait for delivery, then execute the punishment.
1734[‡] – For *yangban* (*sajok*) committing consensual fornication with cousins' commoner concubines, they should be recorded; for *yangban* wives voluntarily committing consensual fornication, they shall be [punished by] strangulation under the statute on corrupting public morality.

SOURCES: *Sugyo chimnok* (1698); *Sinbo sugyo chimnok* (1743); *Sok taejŏn* (1746).

* Edicts compiled in the 1698 *Collected Royal Edicts* (*Sugyo chimnok*) and/or the 1743 *Newly Supplemented Collected Royal Edicts* (*Sinbo sugyo chimnok*). Edicts included in the 1743 version are marked with a double dagger (‡).

not all previously issued edicts were retained for codification. For example, when reporting an incident of adultery between cousins with different surnames in 1684, Minister of Punishment (Hyŏngjo) Kim Tŏgwŏn (1634–1704) asked King Sukchong about determining the right punishment. According to Kim, the law (the Ming Code) prescribed "one hundred strokes of beating with the heavy stick and penal servitude for three years."[20] Yet punishment for a similar crime in 1679 had been decided instead under the 1543 *Continued Supplementary Great Code*, which instead specified that "a *yangban* woman who corrupts morality by committing adultery shall be strangulated along with the adulterer." Also, in accord with a recommendation by an official at that time, Kim continued, the crime was eventually punished "by decapitation without waiting," and this was subsequently codified

20. Yonglin Jiang, *Great Ming Code*, 215.

Statute[†]

Women of yangban families (sajok) who taint custom and corrupt morality by committing licentious acts shall be punished by strangulation along with male adulterers.

In general, punishment of criminals who committed consensual fornication shall be executed without waiting. Yet if the criminal was pregnant, wait until delivery and then punish.

[†] Modifications and additions made in the 1746 *Continuation of the Great Code* (*Sok taejŏn*) to an earlier edict are indicated with italics.

in a new edict. Kim therefore inquired whether the adultery case in question should be punished under the newly added 1679 edict. The king's answer, however, was *no*. He noted that the edict had been issued for the moral rectification of that particular time but was not meant to become a permanent statute.[21] Yet, as table 4.2 shows, the state preserved this 1679 royal edict, along with considerable modification and expanded statutes, in the *Continuation of the Great Code* completed in 1746.

The discussion between King Sukchong and the Minister of Punishment illuminates the complexity in judging each adultery case. There is no question that the Ming Code served as the fundamental penal law, but the Chosŏn government was cautious in applying the most appropriate code(s), depending not only on the social statuses

21. *Ch'ugwanji*, 2:268–69.

and backgrounds of those accused but also on existing judicial options and precedents.[22] Reflecting the specific Chosŏn conditions of a specific time—for example, whether recent immoral crimes had endangered the public morality—the punishment could be heavier or lighter, as Sukchong's response to the Minister of Punishment shows. Indeed, the 1746 *Continuation of the Great Code* dictates that "in deliberating on the judicial decision, commutation of punishment should rely on extenuating circumstances; though not codified in the *Continuation of the Great Code*, refer to [previously] collected royal edicts."[23] Although the "Committing Fornication" section remained unchanged from the compilation of the 1746 *Continuation of the Great Code* to the end of the dynasty, the Chosŏn government continued to issue royal edicts in between completions of the last dynastic codes in the nineteenth century. In the meantime, those non-codified royal edicts on adultery (see table 4.2) did not become defunct. Although only those selected for the dynastic codes became codified as permanent laws (*chŏn*), the Chosŏn court continued to apply previously announced edicts in other official records, as well as in the various volumes of collected royal edicts (*tŭngnok*), as crucial statutes whenever necessary.

The Ambiguous Crime: Seduction-Led Adultery

The Chosŏn penal law on committing fornication includes another type of adultery—*chogan*—that may be unfamiliar to modern readers. In the *Great Ming Code*, *chogan* is outlined as "fornication brought about by seduction that shall be punished with one hundred strokes of beating with the heavy stick."[24] While it delineated no independent punishment for a seduced woman, she was supposed to be punished according to the crime of adultery—eighty strokes of beating with the heavy stick (see table 4.1).

22. Bourgon and Roux note that Chosŏn kings "gave advantages to dynamic case law over fixed codified law," a characterization with which I agree. Bourgon and Roux, "Chosŏn Law Codes," 24.

23. *Sok taejŏn* 4:25a; Yi Chongil, *Taejŏn hoet'ong yŏn'gu*, 4:188.

24. Yonglin Jiang, *Great Ming Code*, 214.

The crime of *chogan*, which I translate herein as "seduction-led adultery," was vague in Chosŏn officials' view. In explicating the definition of this foreign code, the 1395 *Direct Explanation of the Great Ming Code* provides an elaborated translation explaining that "those who seduce or half-coercively seduce a woman into having sexual intercourse shall be punished with one hundred strokes of beating with the heavy stick,"[25] adding the element of "coerciveness" to the seduction. Although seduction-led adultery ended up being *consensual*, the crime had to have been initiated by a man's (possibly coercive) seduction of the woman and was thus different from mutually consensual fornication. The crime's coercive aspect gave the male offender the heavier punishment of one hundred blows compared with eighty strokes as punishment for the adultery itself. Whereas adultery was clearly defined as a crime of mutual consent during the Chosŏn dynasty, and rape as a man's crime against a nonconsenting woman, the crime of seduction-led adultery was tricky to pin down because it left room for different judicial interpretations and blurred the line between consensual and forcible fornication.

The difficulty in interpreting the crime of seduction-led adultery is presented in conversations between Korean court officials and a Ming Chinese envoy in 1450. Given the opportunity to inquire about the Ming legal code, the Korean official Sŏng Sammun (1418–1456) asked the Chinese envoy about the exact meaning of the crime. The envoy answered that seduction-led fornication occurs when "an adulterer lures an adulteress out to a third person's place and commits adultery."[26] Without expounding the definition further, he added only that in China the crime of consensual fornication was punished more severely under some circumstances than the written code specified.[27] It is unclear whether the envoy was fully acquainted with Chinese

---

25. *Taemyŏngnyul chikhae*, 550.

26. *Sejong sillok* 127:26a [1450/yun1/9].

27. The Chinese envoy explained that an adulterer with a wife or an adulterer with an official title would receive more severe punishment than that actually written in the law. *Sejong sillok* 127:26a [1450/yun1/9].

cases of seduction-led adultery, but in any case the Korean officials seem to have remained confused about its exact meaning.[28]

In 1485, when it was discovered that a royal messenger named Kim Yunson had seduced a female entertainer of base status and fornicated with her in the daytime, the Chosŏn court decided that Kim was to be punished with one hundred blows of the heavy stick, as stipulated in the Ming Code. In addition, Kim was stripped of his governmental position and exiled to a remote place. Because the female entertainer had lived with a man named Yi Chŏng, who was a member of the royal family, and was lured to a third place, Kim's crime was deemed a case of seduction-led adultery. However, some officials argued that his crime was not grave enough to warrant the usual punishment of one hundred blows, not to mention exile as well, because Yi Chŏng was known for inviting every local female entertainer visiting the capital to his house, so the woman in question could not necessarily be considered Yi's concubine. During the trial, Kim also asserted that he, not Yi Chŏng, had had sexual intercourse with her first. After a lengthy debate, the court chose to stick to its original decision of seduction-led adultery, deeming Kim's crime as fornication by seduction of another man's wife or concubine. Besides, since the female entertainer had already entered Yi Chŏng's house when Kim seduced her, Yi could be considered her owner regardless of whether Kim had sexual relations with her before Yi did.[29]

After this 1485 case, no further application of the seduction-led adultery law is found in official sources. It was not until about a hundred years later, in 1573, that discussion of seduction-led adultery reappeared at the Chosŏn court, when First Counselor Yu Hŭich'un (1515–1577) of the Office of the Special Counselors reported difficulty in deciphering its definition. Having served as an examiner in the

28. The Chinese legal historian Yonglin Jiang sees that the Ming Code of *diaojian* (fornication brought about by seduction) has its origin in the Yuan law on *youjian futao* (fornication through seduction and flight with the woman). While *diaojian* indicates taking the woman to another place through seduction, *youjian futao* refers to both "fornication" and "flight," hinting at a possible connection, with some modification, in two statutes. Email communication with Yonglin Jiang (November 13, 2016).

29. *Sŏngjong sillok* 185:14a [1485/11/16].

miscellaneous examinations, Yu noted that examinees in the field of law had not known the meaning of this crime at all when being tested on the "Committing Fornication" section of the penal code. Referring to the Chinese envoy's answer in 1450, Yu opined that seduction-led adultery must be worse than adultery itself because the character *cho* ㅋ in the term *chogan* means "pulling," signifying the coercive nature of the crime. Yu also pointed to an incorrect commentary provided in the Chinese legal text *Clear Elaboration on the Great Ming Code* (*Luxue jieyi*), which defined *cho* ㅋ as a "gong," implying the luring of a woman with music and then committing adultery with her. Yu's interpretation of the meaning of seduction-led adultery is reminiscent of the elaborated translation of the code in the *Direct Explanation of the Great Ming Code*, with its emphasis on the aspect of coerciveness. Finding the lack of a lucid definition of the crime to be puzzling and problematic, Yu proposed creating a higher official position in the field of law as a way to produce more experts in legal texts.[30]

Except for a few mentions in lists of sexual crimes, seduction-led adultery does not appear in any further entry in the later *Sillok* or other Chosŏn records. However, the 1690 edict included in the 1743 *Newly Supplemented Collected Royal Edicts* (see table 4.2) hints that the court still judged crimes involving seduction differently from other sex crimes. Though the exact term *chogan* is not used, the edict states that "for *yangban* wives committing licentious acts, if [such conduct] was forced by their seduction by strangers while staying in another place, [then these actions] shall be considered differently from voluntary consensual fornication and the reduced punishment of an exile shall be applied."[31] A *yangban* woman's consensual adultery was subject to the heaviest punishment—strangulation—but the Chosŏn court recognized the forcible element of seduction-led adultery and therefore lessened the woman's punishment to exile. Also, the *Conspectus of Laws and Precedents* (*Yullye yoram*) compiled in 1841 specifies that Buddhist monks and Daoists who seduced women visiting monasteries

---

30. *Sŏnjo sillok* 7:19b [1573/4/20].
31. *Sinbo sugyo chimnok* 2:107b.

should be punished two degrees higher than specified in the usual seduction-led adultery law.[32]

Despite its ambiguous place in the "Committing Fornication" section of the Chosŏn penal code, the seduction-led adultery statute remained in effect to the end of the dynasty. Its absence in Chosŏn legal documents has nevertheless led to a near-complete absence of scholarship closely examining this crime, except for a brief discussion in Chang Pyŏngin's study. Chang sees the main factor distinguishing seduction-led adultery from consensual adultery as the public facet of the crime: taking a woman to a third place publicly indicated the man's explicit intention to commit adultery with her, whereas fully consensual adultery took place in secret. Because openly committing adultery was uncommon and almost impossible, Chang notes that there were scarcely any cases to which this law might have applied throughout the dynasty.[33]

However, I see the core element distinguishing seduction-led adultery from consensual adultery as its coerciveness rather than the act of taking the woman to a third place. As gender historians of other early modern societies have noted, the boundary between seduction and consent was extremely obscure in sexual crimes, frequently complicating the judicial discourse.[34] In the 1781 incident of a man trying to violate a fifteen-year-old young woman, for instance, the Ministry of Punishment reasoned that "a woman being seduced differs from her being forcibly violated" and concluded that the case was one of consensual fornication. Finding this statement to be vague, however, King Chŏngjo criticized its far-fetched legal reasoning and urged that the ministry review the case again. It was not strange that the young woman should have been seduced at first, but seduction itself did not justify the conclusion that she had engaged in consensual fornication. Indeed, whether the situation had ended with consensual or coercive fornication was difficult to tell.[35] Given the dual nature of the crime, situated as it was in between consensual and forcible, it was highly

32. *Yullye yoram*, 302–3.
33. Chang Pyŏngin, *Chosŏn chŏn'gi honinje wa sŏngch'abyŏl*, 284–86.
34. Binhammer, *Seduction Narrative in Britain*.
35. *Ilsŏngnok* 95:202–3 [1781/1/22].

possible that the validity of the allegation of seduction-led adultery could be contested through the testimonies of each party during the court sessions. And if a woman's claim that she had been coerced was taken to be true, the crime would then be determined to be forcible fornication, and the court would eventually free her, whereas such a decision would make the man in the case subject to graver punishment than for the crime of consensual adultery. Yet without eyewitnesses to a man's seductive acts, as well as to their consequences, it could be precarious to convict him of seduction-led adultery—which may explain why court cases of seduction-led adultery are so few. This also denotes that the crime's convoluted definition and scope inadvertently offered space for potential accommodation between the existing law and people's use of the law, which ultimately influenced the course of trials as well as the punishments for the crime—the subjects to be discussed in detail later in this chapter.

The Crime of Forcible Fornication: Rape

Among the three sexual crimes defined in Chosŏn law, forcible fornication was considered the most powerful threat to female chastity in Chosŏn society. In a literal sense, the result was the same in all three situations—a woman's chastity was violated, regardless of whether the crime took place by mutual consent, by seduction tinged or mixed with coercion, or by a man's unidirectional coercion. However, there was a huge dissimilarity between mutual consent and sheer force in terms of the woman's position: consensual adultery represents a woman's voluntary abandonment of her chastity and/or betrayal of marital fidelity toward her husband, whereas forcible fornication connotes a woman's determination to preserve her sexual integrity. Moreover, in a society where all sexual activity was interpreted as possession of the woman by the man, coercively violating a female body also meant that the rapist was guilty of assaulting a patriarchal figure (husband, father, brother) of the female victim.[36]

36. On the language of all sexual activity as a language of male ownership of the female body, see Walker, "Rereading Rape and Sexual Violence," 1–25.

In modern Korea, forcible fornication is commonly referred to as *kanggan*, which is translated as "rape" in English.[37] During the Chosŏn dynasty, terms such as *kŏpt'al* (taking things by force) and *kŏpkan* (violating a woman's body) were used interchangeably with *kanggan* to indicate forcible fornication. During the early Chosŏn, the definition and use of the term *kŏpt'al* had been limited to "taking and damaging others' assets by force." Yet it became widely employed for forcible fornication in the latter part of the dynasty, officially replacing the term *kanggan* in the 1746 *Continuation of the Great Code*, which specifies cases in which women of different social statuses were forcibly abducted and sexually violated (table 4.3).[38] Also, the state added a sub-statute in the "Theft" section of the *Continuation of the Great Code* to explain the specific use of the term *kŏpt'al* in the case of forcible fornication, noting that "a man coercively violating a woman would be treated and punished like someone plundering in the marketplace during the daytime."[39] The concept of rape thus became remarkedly rigid in Chosŏn society. And part of the impetus behind this rigidness was that rape was understood to be the theft of a woman's chastity. In other words, unlike modern concepts of rape, forcible fornication was deemed exclusively a man's crime against a woman not his legal wife: at least, no opposite case (of a woman committing such a crime against a man) is found in the records. Though the word "rape" does not completely reflect what constituted the crime of forcible fornication as it was perceived in Chosŏn Korea, I nevertheless use "rape" to refer to this specific crime hereafter in this book.[40]

37. On competing dictionary definitions of "rape" and ambiguities of this term in modern society, see Greenfield, *Interpreting Sexual Violence*, 3–4.

38. *Sok taejŏn* 4:27b.

39. *Sok taejŏn* 4:10b. This added status reflects how "rape was viewed a property crime, a form of theft" in early modern society, as Garthine Walker discusses. Walker, "Sexual Violence and Rape," 437.

40. Concepts of rape have varied historically and culturally, and historical definitions of rape differed from those in modern societies. For example, see Caroline Dunn's study on the shifting notions of the term "raptus" in medieval England, which has been narrowly taken to mean "rape" by scholars. Dunn, *Stolen Women in Medieval England*. And in his study of rape law in late imperial China, Matthew Sommer points out that "rape" as a modern Western legal term is not comparable to the "illicit coercive sexual intercourse" defined in Qing law. Sommer, *Sex, Law, and Society*, 66.

As with the adultery law, with shifting socio-legal demands leading to new rape statutes, the Chosŏn state issued a series of special
edicts throughout the dynasty complementing the Ming Code. All rape
victims were women, and the primary purpose of legislation against
rape was to punish those who violated women's sexual integrity. Because the state implicitly required all women, regardless of marital
status, to submit to the sexual monopoly of a (past, present, or future)
husband, the penalties for rape were the most severe of all the punishments for crimes of illicit sex (see table 4.1). The crime of rape was
viewed as the ultimate threat to the ideal of female chastity and the
patriarchal order in a Confucian society. In other words, the victim
of rape was not limited to the woman, but extended to her husband
or father—the man to whom she belonged.

Because rape was taken to be a man's crime, the female victim's
reaction to the menace of coercive sexual intercourse was the key
factor in determining the accurate punishment: if the crime was ad-
judged as rape, male assailants were punished accordingly, while
women victims were exonerated. After a woman became a subject of
sexual attack, she was given the formal opportunity to assert her sexual innocence and to punish the male offender. However, drawing a
lucid judicial boundary for rape was crucial, since sexual crimes were
mostly committed in a private setting where direct witnesses and
proofs were hard to come by. Defining and determining the range of
rape often led to controversies both at the central and local government levels, generating intense debates, from the early dynasty on, as
officials faced the intricacies posed by each rape case.

In 1430, a military official named Sin T'ongnye had raped a married slave of the government named Ko Ŭmdŏk. According to the Ministry of Punishment's report, when Ŭmdŏk was first abducted and
forced to have sexual intercourse, she refused by crying, yet she eventually committed adultery with Sin. If her initial resistance were taken
into account, the case was a rape and Ŭmdŏk should have been freed.
Nevertheless, because she eventually had sexual intercourse with Sin,
Ŭmdŏk was recommended for the punishment of ninety blows with the
heavy stick for her illicit conduct as a married woman. But the problem
remained of whether the case should be settled as one of adultery or
rape. Facing the hurdle that it would be odd to punish the man and

Table 4.3. Royal Edicts and Statutes on "Committing Fornication": Rape

Year and Royal Edict*
1671 – Those who forcibly fornicate with an unmarried *yangban* woman shall be punished by decapitation without distinguishing the principal offenders or accomplices. In cases of forcibly fornicating with a woman of non-*yangban* (*sanghan*) [status], punish under the usual [forcible fornication] code [in the Ming Code].
The edict announced in 1684 revises that, for those committing forcible fornication with a non-*yangban* woman, the principal offender shall be punished by strangulation while the accomplice (only himself) shall be sent to the frontier as a slave.
1682 – Those forcibly fornicating with *yangban* women in the street and taking their goods shall be punished by decapitation without waiting.
1702‡ – Those committing forcible fornication with the daughter of a *yangban*'s concubine shall be punished by the statute on forcible fornication with *yangban* women.
1702‡ –Those committing forcible fornication with the daughter of a *yangban*'s concubine shall be decapitated without waiting and without distinguishing the principal offenders or accomplices.
1702‡ – Those committing forcible fornication that was unconsummated with the daughter of a non-*yangban* shall be punished by exile [to a distance] of 3,000 *li*. [For the same crime,] those committing forcible fornication with the daughter of a *yangban* shall be decapitated.
1738‡ – For those committing forcible fornication that was unconsummated with a third cousin, if the woman [victim] poisoned herself to death out of humiliation, then punishing [the man] under the statute of unconsummated forcible fornication with heavy beating and exile is too light, while it is [also] inappropriate to execute the law of "using coercion to cause others to die" directly. Considering the situation, punishment shall [thus] be exile to a remote island. For the woman, a memorial arch shall be erected.

Those who forcibly fornicate with *a wife or daughter* of a *yangban* shall be punished by decapitation without distinguishing principal offenders or accomplices *and without waiting, whether [the forcible fornication] was consummated or unconsummated. The same punishment shall be applied for those committing forcible fornication with a concubine or with a daughter of a yangban.*

In cases of forcibly fornicating with a non-*yangban* woman, *if it was consummated*, the principal offender shall be punished by strangulation, while the accomplice (only himself) shall be sent to the frontier as a slave. *If [forcible fornication] was unconsummated, he shall be punished with 100 strokes with the heavy stick followed by exile to [a distance of] 3,000 li.*

These [punishments for consensual fornication with relatives] apply equally to men and women, yet in the case of forcible fornication, men shall be decapitated while women shall be exempted. All other cases shall be applied by the usual statute [in the Ming Code pertaining to committing fornication with relatives].

(continued)

Table 4.3. *(continued)*

Year and Royal Edict*

SOURCES: *Sugyo chimnok* (1698); *Sinbo sugyo chimnok* (1743); *Sok taejŏn* (1746).

* Edicts compiled in the 1698 *Collected Royal Edicts* (*Sugyo chimnok*) and/or the 1743 *Newly Supplemented Collected Royal Edicts* (*Sinbo sugyo chimnok*). Edicts included in the 1743 version are marked with a double dagger (‡).

woman involved in the same incident by different laws—the man for rape and the woman for adultery—the case was forwarded to the king. After a thorough review, Sejong made the final decision that Sin should be punished according to the rape law, but reduced by one degree, while the punishment for Ŭmdŏk remained unchanged.[41]

This 1430 case was considered more on the male offender's side, but judgment on a similar sexual crime was made differently a century later. In 1531, a governor of Koryŏng County, Yi P'aengnyŏng, was accused of committing adultery with Sun'gŭm, the daughter of a slave. Witnesses—and Yi himself—claimed it had been adultery, and Sun'gŭm's father even doubted whether it could be considered rape because she had previously lived with another man, meaning that her sexual integrity was already lost. But Sun'gŭm argued that as a weak woman she had not been able to resist Yi and ended up spending two nights with him. Unlike the 1430 case, the court honored Sun'gŭm's words while punishing Yi under the rape law.[42]

Such conflicting views in determining rape cases persisted into the late Chosŏn and were further complicated by the issue of whether there had been sexual intercourse. Reviewing Yu Sudol's attempted rape of

41. *Sejong sillok* 50:11a [1430/10/25].
42. *Chungjong sillok* 71:5b [1531/yun6/10].

Statute†
In cases of consummated forcible fornication, the same punishment [i.e., decapitation] shall be applied to the man, but the woman shall be freed. In cases of unconsummated forcible fornication, the man shall be decapitated after waiting for prosecution of the crime. However, if the man is the slave husband of a commoner mistress, he shall be punished by the above statute as hired labor (*kogong*) only if he is married and lives with the woman.

† Modifications and additions made in the 1746 *Continuation of the Great Code* (*Sok taejŏn*) to an earlier edict are indicated with italics.

a widow in 1777, for instance, King Chŏngjo stressed the unconsummated aspect of Yu's crime. Although the crime of rape itself was grave, the king underlined that there was a clear difference between consummation and lack of consummation in rape.[43] A few years later, in 1782, when an eighteen-year-old commoner woman named Kim Idan hanged herself after a *yangban* man, Yi Ch'angbŏm, forced her to have sexual intercourse with him, the provincial governor, focusing on Yi's word that the intercourse was only "attempted," judged that it was an unconsummated rape attempt. The Ministry of Punishment then reversed the provincial governor's verdict, viewing Yi's crime as completed rape. Carefully going over the testimonies given in the case, King Chŏngjo reversed the decision once more, holding that the crime had been unconsummated. He also reproached the ministry for construing unconsummated rape as consummated rape, on the basis that this not only infringed upon the course of legal reasoning but could taint the perception of Kim Idan's fortitude in keeping her chastity. Yi thus received a reduced punishment of exile for life to the northern frontier rather than strangulation—the punishment pertinent to rape—and Kim Idan's

43. *Ilsŏngnok* 50:204 [1777/5/11]. It seems that Yu Sudol was eventually freed later in the same year, after the court discussion on acquitting imprisoned criminals. *Ilsŏngnok* 56:171 [1777/11/25].

family was recommended for a material reward. Though lessening Yi's punishment, the king also ensured that Yi received three rounds of heavy beating before going into exile to alert people to the gravity of his crime against female sexual integrity.[44]

King Chŏngjo's verdict in Kim Idan's case discloses his concern about correctly judging cases of rape as well as his sympathy for female victims. Why did it matter to the Chosŏn court whether a rape had been consummated? And how could one draw a clear line between forcible and consensual fornication? On the complexities of judging a rape case, the eminent Confucian scholar Yi Ik wrote the following in his essay "Coercive Fornication" ("Kanggan"):

> There is an old saying that "rape does not exist in the world." This means that if a woman is determined to protect her chastity at the risk of her life, [her chastity] cannot be violated. In the past, Lu Yongqing had two strong men strip off a woman's clothes to judge a question of adultery versus rape.[45] At last, all her clothes had been removed except her underwear, which she was grasping hard, resisting to the death. Therefore, Lu concluded that the case was not rape but adultery, and people complimented him for his great adjudication.
>
> I think, however, that [the way Lu reached his conclusion] is only an argument without logic. If a man *attempts* to rape a woman who *refuses*, it is already rape, without even mentioning what might happen afterward. . . . The man bears the guilt [for violating the woman]. If we follow

---

44. *Simnirok* 9:84a–86a; also in *Ilsŏngnok* 121:139–41 [1782/11/14]. For a record on Kim Idan's chastity recognition, see *Ilsŏngnok* 121:161 [1782/11/16].

45. This story is found in the twenty-eight-volume compilation entitled *Zhinang* (*Sack of Wisdom*) by Feng Menglong (1574–1646), a well-known writer of Ming China. Feng completed the *Zhinang* in 1626, when he was fifty-four, to transmit great old stories reflecting Chinese wisdom to future generations. The *Zhinang* contains about two thousand anecdotes and examples that deal with complicated matters in a wise way. As soon as it was published, it gained tremendous popularity in China. Considering the fact that Yi Ik's lifetime roughly corresponds to that of Feng's, the *Zhinang* must have become known to Chosŏn scholars of that time, and Yi Ik would have certainly read the *Zhinang* before writing his essay on coercive fornication. However, we do not know when exactly Yi Ik wrote his essay because his collected works, *Sŏngho sasŏl* (*Sŏngho's Discourses on the Minute*), which carries the essay, was posthumously compiled around 1740 by his descendants and was published only during the colonial period.

this adjudication by Lu Yongqing, we may cause abuse; that is why I discuss this matter.[46]

Yi Ik challenges a judgment made by the Chinese official Lu Yongqing, who, in his position as governor-general, had to distinguish rape from adultery in a controversial case. Whereas the man insisted it had been consensual adultery, the woman claimed it had been coercive fornication. Because in the test before the court, the woman was able to hold onto her underwear to the end, Lu decided that the case was one of adultery rather than rape (i.e., rape could not have been consummated since the woman would also have managed to keep her underwear on during the occasion considered in the case). Lu comments, "If a woman tries to preserve her chastity to the death, two strong men cannot do anything with her; how much less so one normal male?"[47]

Yi Ik's point, in contrast, is that argument over rape versus adultery is irrelevant because one cannot draw such a hard and fast line between consummation and nonconsummation. According to Yi, if the offender carries out an intention of rape and the woman resists, his attempt itself is a crime. Moreover, even if the female victim fails to resist to the end (so that the rape is consummated), this does not mean that she has consented. For Yi, the crime still lies with the male offender, so it should not be regarded as adultery: in other words, Yi seems almost to agree with Susan Brownmiller's claim that rape is not a sexual crime but "a crime of violence."[48]

Yi Ik's assertion delineates the importance of a woman's attitude in adjudging rape cases, reinforcing the idea that the criminal act is entirely on the man's side. At the same time, however, Yi blames a woman of loose conduct if her (frivolous) behavior tempts the offender. He indicates that if the woman looked adamant and resolute in her chastity, the male offender would not even dare to think of violating her. Though Yi places more responsibility on the man, supporting the

46. Yi Ik, *Sŏngho sasŏl*, 16:11a.
47. Feng Menglong, *Zhinang*, 2:153–54.
48. Seeing the root cause of female oppression throughout history as springing from patriarchal structure, Susan Brownmiller maintains that rape is a crime of violence, not a sexual crime. Brownmiller, *Against Our Will*.

woman under coercive circumstances and her efforts to protect her bodily integrity, he accepts the eternal canard that "the woman was at fault in her behavior which led to the act of sexual violence."[49] These seemingly dual attitudes that Yi Ik presents in his essay reflect the Chosŏn state's perception of and position on the discourse of rape in a broader sense: it maintained that rape was a men's crime, while also emphasizing the importance of women's proper behavior.

Given the subtleties involved in defining rape cases, disputes over the veracity of rape continued to be controversial at the Chosŏn court, and some officials even expressed concern about the way adultery could be embellished and presented as rape. On the former official Sin Sukchŏng's rape case in 1512, for example, court officials complained that the judgment was based solely on the female victim's claim, while ignoring the fact that illicit relations took place in broad daylight and that Sin took the woman to a room by holding her waist. If she had been fully determined to protect her chastity, she would have resisted him. Therefore, "it must have been adultery at first; yet when the husband and neighbors became aware of it, she insisted it was rape. There are many legal cases like this."[50] In other words, the contentious judicial line between adultery and rape could be shaped and determined by how men and women testified and the extent to which their testimonies were believed at the court. Rape cases therefore illuminate the multiplicity of attitudes that could be held by the victim, rapist, judge, and the court and cannot be encapsulated in a one-dimensional cultural or legal view of rape. In what follows, moving back and forth between normative legal prescriptions and practices in the Chosŏn court, I analyze specific legal cases on various sexual crimes and people's testimonies in detail. In doing so, I demonstrate how gender mattered in the way sexual crimes were reported and punished and how women, as energetic complainants with full legal capacity, were

49. On the "victim-blaming" myth circulated in early modern society, see Gammon, "Researching Sexual Violence," 13.

50. *Chungjong sillok* 15:22a [1512/2/21].

able to carve out their position within the legal sphere of an evolving discourse on sexual crimes in Chosŏn society.[51]

Chastity in Trials and Testimonies

Examining legal cases on sexual crimes offers an important window onto previously understudied perceptions and practices of female chastity. It elucidates, first, how the state negotiated the conflicting boundaries of virtue and law; second, how the notions of sexual crimes shifted in response to the state's moral agendas; and finally, how people reacted to the prescribed gender norms and legal stipulations.

Despite growing interest in women's status and gender relations from various perspectives in the field of Chosŏn history, existing scholarship on the topic of sexual crimes is quite meager.[52] Still, one of the representative studies is Chang Pyŏngin's analysis of the statutes on and punishment of sexual crimes in the first half of the dynasty, in which Chang finds that almost all cases reported to kings in the *Sillok* involved members of the elite, such as court officials and members of the royal family. Seeing this as an indication of the state's intention to tightly control the *yangban* group, Chang argues that the sexual

51. On women's legal capacity as active agents in the realm of the petition system, see Kim Kyŏngsuk, "Chosŏn hugi yŏsŏng ŭi chŏngso hwaltong"; Kim Kyŏngsuk, "Chosŏn hugi kyŏlsongiban kwa yŏsŏng sosong ŭi chuch'e," 325–57; Haboush, "Gender and the Politics of Language"; Hwisang Cho, "Feeling Power in Early Chosŏn Korea," 7–32; and Jisoo M. Kim, *Emotions of Justice*.

52. Two book-length studies on this subject are Chang Pyŏngin, *Chosŏn chŏn'gi honinje wa sŏngch'abyŏl* (1997); and Chang Pyŏngin, *Pŏp kwa p'ungsok ŭro pon Chosŏn yŏsŏng ŭi sam* (2018). Chang's 2018 publication is based on her earlier book, revised and modified by incorporating her published articles. Other representative studies are Chang Pyŏngin, "Chosŏn sidae sŏngbŏmjoe e taehan kukka kyuje ŭi kanghwa," 228–50; Chŏng Kŭngsik, "Uri nara kant'ongjoe ŭi pŏpchesajŏk koch'al," 139–42; Hong Yanghŭi, "'Sŏllyanghan p'ungsok' ŭl wihayŏ," 317–41; Kim Hyŏnjin, "Simnirok ŭl t'onghae pon 18-segi yŏsŏng ŭi chasal silt'ae wa kŭ sahoejŏk hamŭi," 197–230; Kim Sŏn'gyŏng, "Chosŏn hugi yŏsŏng ŭi sŏng, kamsi wa ch'ŏbŏl," 57–100; Paek Minjŏng, "Hŭmhŭm sinsŏ ŭi yŏsŏng kwallyŏn pŏmjoe punsŏk ŭl t'onghae pon Chŏng Yagyong ŭi yŏsŏng insik kwa sidaejŏk ŭimi," 161–200; and Pak Sohyŏn, "Choson hugi sŏngbŏmjoe ŭi kyuje wa ch'ŏbŏl," 185–225.

behavior of the non-*yangban* population was not a focus of the state's attention.[53] In her later studies covering cases from the second part of the *Sillok*, Chang detects far fewer adultery cases than in the early *Sillok*. For factors contributing to such a remarkable decrease, Chang points to widespread chastity ideology in later Chosŏn times and (*yangban*) families' concealment of adultery incidents to avoid damaging their reputations.[54] The overall implication of Chang's pioneering studies is that the state's primary interest lay in the protection of *yangban* women's sexual integrity and that it did not intervene in the sexual crimes of non-*yangban*.[55]

Some other studies, examining legal decisions on various sexual crimes, also limit themselves by locating "the state" at the center of their discussions and by assuming that all women were repressed under the patriarchal system, the core of the social order. Mostly analyzing eighteenth- and nineteenth-century legal hearings, they assert that the Chosŏn state oversaw the lives of women by strictly applying the ideal of chastity to safeguard and regulate women's sexuality.[56] These studies maintain that the variety of women's reactions to external challenges only confirms both the collective social phenomenon that celebrated women's sacrifice under the banner of chastity discourse and Chosŏn women's general indoctrination with the ideal.

Examining Chosŏn legal testimonies on sexual crimes, however, sheds additional light on the dynamic interactions between the state and the people, especially the much-varied choices and responses women of all classes made when the question of their sexual integrity was raised. To a certain degree, the state's zeal to popularize chastity seems to have shattered in the second part of the dynasty, as a woman's

53. Chang Pyŏngin, *Chosŏn chŏn'gi honinje wa sŏngch'abyŏl*, 284–359; Chang Pyŏngin, *Pŏp kwa p'ungsok ŭro pon Chosŏn yŏsŏng ŭi sam*, 265–66.
54. Chang Pyŏngin, "Chosŏn sidae sŏngbŏmjoe e taehan kukka kyuje ŭi kanghwa," 228–50. Chang notes that an adulterous woman was even forced to kill herself by the family before her crime was discovered.
55. Chang Pyŏngin, "Chosŏn sidae sŏngbŏmjoe e taehan kukka kyuje ŭi kanghwa," 232–35.
56. Kim Sŏn'gyŏng, "Chosŏn hugi yŏsŏng ŭi sŏng, kamsi wa ch'ŏbŏl," 96–100; Kim Hyŏnjin, "*Simnirok ŭl t'onghae pon* 18-segi yŏsŏng ŭi chasal silt'ae wa kŭ sahoejŏk hamŭi"; Paek Okkyŏng, "Chosŏn sidae ŭi yŏsŏng p'ongnyŏk," 93–126.

societal status and protection of elite interests came to be emphasized over the prosecution of sexual crimes through codification. Nevertheless, people at every level of society were aware of state-defined orthodoxy with respect to female chastity and had their own understandings of it. The standards applied to all regardless of social status, but violations and transgressions of female chastity, as revealed in legal testimonies, signify how people negotiated the application of them in diverse ways depending on their socioeconomic situations. They illuminate the ways women interpreted the norms of virtue in accordance with their personal values, realistic needs, and the resources they possessed, obfuscating a uniform picture of women's endurance in patriarchal Chosŏn society.

Adultery, Violence, and Domestic Disorders

In his magnum opus, *New Treatise on the Legal System* (*Hŭmhŭm sinsŏ*), Chŏng Yagyong (see chapter 3) introduces several Chinese and Korean legal anecdotes on the judgment of ambiguous homicides. All anecdotes concern wives' killings of their husbands who were initially thought to have died of other causes. Chancing to hear the wives crying in ritual grief for the deceased, the investigator in each case detected an element of fear in their weeping and a lack of sincere sorrow. Eventually, it turned out that wives had murdered their husbands to hide their adulterous relations with outside men. When no appropriate statute was found in law books for the crime being investigated, Chŏng urged Chosŏn officials to look for other texts and judicial examples from the past that demonstrated brilliant methods of unearthing the principal offenders in such incidents.[57]

Chŏng Yagyong's inclusion of these anecdotes was aimed primarily at warning Chosŏn officials about the importance of making a careful and thorough judicial decision when dealing with human lives. It also implies challenges in mapping out the crime of adultery, especially when it became involved with various forms of violence, including homicide—the most extreme manifestation of spousal and emotional conflict. Although not every case of adultery resulted in

57. Chŏng Yagyong, *Hŭmhŭm sinsŏ*, 1:88–92.

such violence and no fixed pattern emerges in the adultery-related homicide cases that I have examined, legal records do disclose how adultery can lead to a desire for revenge and end in brutal violence. A homicide usually occurs when a husband learns about a wife's illicit relations with another man or when she is caught in the act of committing adultery. Moreover, while it is taken for granted that a cuckolded husband is more likely to kill than be killed, legal cases also show that other family members, including husbands of adulteresses, frequently become victims, being murdered by the wife, her lover, or both. In other words, an adulteress kills her husband to maintain her affair, or joins in a conspiracy to kill him with her partner in adultery, and an adulterer, too, is inclined to murder his lover's husband to retain her.

As table 4.4 shows, a husband is exempted from the death penalty for homicide if he catches and "immediately" kills his adulterous wife and her lover at "the place of adultery." This means that the state tolerated vengeful homicide by a wronged husband, validating the infringement of a husband's rights ensuing from his wife's sexual misconduct. In contrast, an adulterous wife is sternly punished—sentenced to death by slicing—if she is involved in killing her husband either directly by her own hand or indirectly by joining in her lover's plot to kill him. Justifying a husband's violent reaction to his wife's violation of fidelity, the law on adultery-led homicide was sympathetic to husbands, whereas the adulteress would fall into the most adverse situation possible if her wrongdoing was discovered.

Given such sentiments, the punishment was often reduced for a husband who killed his adulterous wife and her lover at a time and place other than the spot where the adultery took place. In 1689, a man named Ingbok was on the verge of being punished by decapitation for killing two people, according to the provincial governor's judgment. Learning about his wife's adultery, Ingbok had captured his wife along with the adulterer and thrown them both into a river to their deaths. Under the Chosŏn law's stipulation that taking a person's life is the gravest crime, homicide must be repaid with the criminal's own life.[58] Moreover, because Ingbok's crime did not satisfy the spatial

58. Yonglin Jiang, *Great Ming Code*, 169.

Table 4.4. Punishments for Killing Adulterous Lovers

Punishments in the *Great Ming* Code, "Homicide" section
–In all cases where a wife or concubine commits adultery with another [man], if [her husband] himself catches the adulterer and the adulterous wife at the place of adultery and immediately kills them, he shall not be punished.
–If he [the husband] kills only the adulterous lover, the adulterous wife shall be punished in accordance with the code [on committing fornication] and shall be remarried or sold by her husband.
–If the wife or concubine, because of adultery, plots [with her adulterous lover] and kills her husband, she shall be sentenced to death by slicing. The adulterous lover shall be punished by decapitation.
–If the adulterous lover himself kills the husband, the adulterous wife shall be punished by strangulation even if she does not know the circumstances. She is a criminal for violating moral principles.

SOURCE: Yonglin Jiang, *Great Ming Code*, 171.

requirement for an exemption—that he must catch and kill them immediately at the place of adultery—the provincial governor held that he certainly deserved the punishment for homicide. However, King Sukchong adjudicated that Ingbok's actions did not differ from catching and killing the adulterous couple on the spot and therefore reduced his punishment to exile.[59] In 1707, the state even made the verdict in Ingbok's case into a royal edict, which was eventually included in the 1743 *Newly Supplemented Collected Royal Edicts*, as table 4.5 shows.

Furthermore, a husband who committed homicide after discovering his wife's adultery was completely exempted even if the conditions did not meet the judicial provisions. In 1782, a man named Yi Tŭkp'yo of P'yŏngan Province killed his wife's lover, Im Tŏkchung, by stabbing him with a knife. Caught by Yi while engaging in adultery with Yi's wife, Im fled, but was soon seized and killed by Yi. The provincial governor recommended that Yi be acquitted under the law of "not questioning the guilt" (*mullon*) in cases where a husband kills his adulterous wife and her lover immediately on the spot.[60] Viewing this judgment

59. *Ch'ugwanji*, 2:239. The original document has no information about Ingbok's social status. With no family name, he must have been non-*yangban*.

60. *Simnirok* 9:97a.

Table 4.5. Royal Edicts and Codes on Homicides Stemming from Sexual Crimes

Year	Royal Edict*
1690[‡]	If a husband stabs his wife's adulterous partner after she committed consensual fornication a while ago, he should receive the reduced punishment of exile [instead of] the death penalty.
1691[‡]	In case a husband captures his wife committing consensual fornication with a relative and then running away, and cuts her ears which causes her death, this is different from a planned homicide of the wife. The husband's punishment should be reduced to exile [instead of] the death penalty.
1697[‡]	If a son kills a man resting his head on the pillow with his mother, he should receive the reduced punishment of exile in consideration of the extenuating circumstances.
1707[‡]	As for a wife committing consensual fornication with a man, if [her husband] captures the man and wife on the spot, but ties and moves them some distance, then throws them into water to their deaths, this should be considered "killing immediately on the spot [of adultery]."
1712[‡]	As for a wife committing consensual fornication with a man, if her husband, together with his son by the adulteress, beat the man to death, the husband should be exonerated and her son exiled in consideration of the extenuating circumstances.
1746	
1785	
1865	

SOURCES: *Sugyo chimnok* (1698); *Sinbo sugyo chimnok* (1743); *Sok taejŏn* (1746); *Taejon t'ongp'yŏn* (1786); and *Taejŏn hoet'ong* (1865).

* Edicts compiled in the 1698 *Collected Royal Edicts* (*Sugyo chimnok*) and/or the 1743 *Newly Supplemented Collected Royal Edicts* (*Sinbo sugyo chimnok*). Edicts included in the 1743 version are marked with a double dagger ([‡]).

Statute†

Continuation of the Great Code: *If a mother commits consensual fornication and her son kills her partner on the spot of adultery, he should receive the reduced punishment of exile in consideration of the extenuating circumstances.*

Great Code for Ruling the State: If an unmarried daughter is forced to commit fornication and her father beats the aggressor to death on the spot where the forcible fornication was committed, the father should receive one hundred blows with the heavy stick under the law on recklessly killing a man deserving the death penalty.

Comprehensive Collection of Dynastic Codes: As for not obtaining evidence of consensual fornication on the spot of adultery, if a place where the man and woman had a meal together is the same as the adultery spot, do not close the case but report to the king in writing.

† Modifications made in the 1746 *Continuation of the Great Code* to the corresponding 1712 edict are indicated with italics.

as too light, the Ministry of Punishment proposed that Yi be exiled for life instead, since he had not murdered Im at the exact spot of adultery. King Chŏngjo supported the provincial governor's ruling and ordered that Yi be acquitted, however, maintaining that it made no difference precisely where the homicide and the adultery had taken place. Additionally, the king criticized his court officers for not properly punishing Yi's adulterous wife, who had betrayed her long marital relations with Yi. In the end, he sentenced her to lifelong exile on a remote island, after demoting her to slave status and subjecting her to three rounds of beating with the heavy stick—a more grievous punishment than stipulated in the adultery law, which specified ninety blows of the heavy stick for an adulterous married woman.[61]

Indeed, acquittals of husbands who committed adultery-led homicide appear quite frequently in Chosŏn legal cases. Two similar incidents a couple of years later, also in P'yŏngan Province, exemplify the state's lenient attitude. In 1785, a man named Yun Kŭm caught Yi Kwangbaek while Yi was committing adultery with Yun's wife in broad daylight. Frightened, Yi ran away but was soon chased and stabbed by Yi in the yard. Because the killing did not take place in the room where the adultery had been committed, the Ministry of Punishment, as in the case of Yi Tŭkp'yo above, raised concern about applying the law of "not questioning the guilt."[62] Nevertheless, Yun was, in the end, exonerated. The king commented:

> It is not human nature for a husband not to react [by doing something] such as stabbing [the adulterer] upon witnessing his wife committing adultery in the middle of the day. . . . Regardless of [whether the adultery took a place in] the room or the yard, the house itself can be [broadly considered] the site of adultery. It was reasonable to kill [the adulterer, Yi]; if he [the husband, Yun] had not [done so], he would not have the heart of a human being. . . . Considering the edicts of 1758 and 1773 [discussed in the next section in this chapter], there should be no question about this verdict. Release Yun Kŭm immediately.[63]

61. *Simnirok* 9:97b–98a; *Ilsŏngnok* 121:54 [1782/11/5].
62. *Ch'ugwanji*, 2:260–61.
63. *Ch'ugwanji*, 2:260–61; *Ilsŏngnok* 178:103–4 [1785/7/22]; *Simnirok* 16:144b.

Later in the same year, another man named Pak Ch'ojŏng, upon seeing his wife having sexual intercourse with a man in the woods, became furious and murdered them both right away. Pak was aware of the punishment for homicide but did not know the specific statute of "not questioning the guilt" applicable to adultery-led homicide. Terrified that he would receive the death penalty, Pak hid his murder by making it look as though his wife and her lover had voluntarily hanged themselves. Being brought to the court, however, Pak confessed his crime. He was still recommended for exoneration because his crime, despite his initial attempt to conceal it, met both the temporal (immediacy) and spatial (on the spot) requirements. Reviewing the case, King Chŏngjo agreed, understanding that Pak's plot to cover the homicides had been due to his ignorance of the law as an ordinary man. Citing the case of Yun Kŭm, who had been released for a similar incident earlier that year, the king stressed that Pak's case was to be treated in the same way.[64]

The reasoning behind the leniency in punishing husbands' adultery-led homicides is fully illuminated in the king's statements. Taking for granted a husband's rancorous heart toward an adulterous wife, his crime of homicide was regarded as something not to be blindly subjected to the law but to be empathized with under the "heavenly way and human nature" (ch'ŏlli injŏng).[65] It was not surprising to see a husband become infuriated to the point of committing brutal violence upon witnessing the very moment of his wife's adultery.[66] If he did not take immediate action against the adulterous scene, he became liable to disdain as a man of weak temper, "an insensible and obtuse husband without emotion and heart, suppressing his anger unnecessarily long."[67]

---

64. Ch'ugwanji, 2:247–48; Ilsŏngnok 178:104 [1785/7/22]; Simnirok 16:143b.

65. Simnirok 11:195b; Ilsŏngnok 145:178 [1784/3/15]. While the court justified a husband's feeling of vengeance against his adulterous wife, a wife's jealousy over a husband's concubines was viewed as a negative emotion to be regulated for a virtuous womanhood. On the topic of gendered emotion and women's jealousy, see Jisoo M. Kim, "From Jealousy to Violence," 91–100.

66. Simnirok 11:159b.

67. Ch'ugwanji, 2:248–49; Simnirok 21:81b.

The state's compassionate stance was not limited to an adulteress's husband but extended to other family members as well. In 1698, Kim Tujong of P'yŏngsan found that his father's cousin, Nonnam, was committing adultery with his mother by taking advantage of his father's absence. Overcome with indignation, Kim stabbed Nonnam to death. Since Nonnam was Kim's uncle, his crime fell into the category of killing a senior family member—the most heinous homicide in terms of Confucian moral principles—and was subject to punishment by decapitation.[68] However, the king ordered that Tujong be spared the death penalty and receive the reduced punishment of exile instead. Not only did Kim's outraged act of murder upon witnessing the adultery between his own mother and his uncle garner him sympathy in line with the "heavenly principle and human nature," but more importantly, Nonnam was considered to be the one who had "first" violated moral order within the family. Therefore, Kim Tujong's killing of Nonnam was not circumscribed under the law on homicide of a (senior) family member; rather, it was seen as a rightful action on behalf of Kim's absent father to avenge the adulterer's heinous acts.[69]

Eventually, as table 4.5 shows, the state issued an edict in 1712 that, in cases of a husband killing a wife's adulterous partner with the collaboration of his son, the husband was to be exonerated and the son, though deserving the death penalty for homicide, was to receive the reduced punishment of exile. This 1712 royal edict was formally written into the 1746 *Continuation of the Great Code* as an independent sub-statute on a son's killing of a mother's adulterous partner. Several decades later, in 1780, when a father killed a neighbor man who had seduced his fourteen-year-old unmarried daughter for fornication, the Ministry of Punishment, though understanding the father's resentful emotion after reviewing the investigation report, recommended sentencing him to death. Although a husband's killing of his wife's adulterer could be pardoned by the law, the Ministry of Punishment underlined that this could not be extended to the father-daughter relationship because to do so would lead to people abusing the law. Citing the statute on a son's killing of his mother's adulterer in the

68. Yonglin Jiang, *Great Ming Code*, 170.
69. *Ch'ugwanji*, 2:270–72.

Continuation of the Great Code, however, the king asked, since a daughter was supposed to follow her father while unmarried, "If a son was vindicated in his mother's case, why not a father for his daughter?"[70] Claiming that punishing the father under the homicide law would go against the spirit of the law (*pŏbŭi*) and only foster further sexual assaults on young women, the king commanded that the father receive a reduced punishment.[71] Furthermore, reflecting this case, the Chosŏn state codified a statute on a father killing a sexual aggressor of his unmarried daughter in the 1785 *Great Code for Ruling the State* (see table 4.5). The series of newly promulgated codes endorsed an expanded scope of eligible male members in a family (from the husbands to sons and fathers) who could punish violators of women's sexual integrity and whose violent action toward adulterers was tolerated by the state.

THE RIGHT TO KILL THE ADULTEROUS

As such modified final verdicts on punishments made by kings and added royal edicts attest, ruling on various types of adultery-led homicide or death cases posed mounting challenges to both local and central government officials. Because of the concealed nature of the crime, a lucid judgment was hard to arrive at, and investigators faced significant hurdles to successful prosecution. Although the state continued to issue edicts to supplement existing law, many cases of adultery or adultery-led violence confused investigators in the absence of direct witnesses or concrete evidence pertaining to the incident. Moreover, as the notion of chastity gradually gained in importance during the latter part of the dynasty, the boundaries of sexual transgression became even subtler, to the extent that the act of pulling a woman's skirt (*mansang taeban*) began to be judged as no different from illicit sexual intent.

As described earlier, in 1785 King Chŏngjo exonerated Yun Kŭm from his crime of killing his wife's adulterous partner. At that time, the

---

70. "A woman should follow or obey her father before marriage, her husband after marriage, and her son when widowed." Legge, *Li Chi, Book of Rites*, 441.

71. *Ch'ugwanji*, 2:237–38.

provincial governor had inquired whether a 1758 royal edict could be used to rule the case, whereas the Ministry of Punishment had recommended sticking strictly to the law rather than applying the more recently decreed edict. In accordance with the law on killing adulterous lovers in the Ming Code, Yun should have received the punishment for homicide since he had killed the adulterer beyond the very spot where the adultery took place. Citing two edicts issued in 1758 and 1773, however, the king did not accept the Ministry of Punishment's recommendation, and instead freed Yun.

What, then, were the two edicts of 1758 and 1773 quoted throughout Yun's case? The 1758 edict, proclaimed during King Yŏngjo's reign, states that a man's acts of pulling a woman's skirt and having a meal in the same room with her should be deemed to be adultery. In other words, an outraged husband murdering a man who had simply pulled his wife's skirt or sat opposite her at the meal table would receive a favorite judicial decision—a reduced punishment or even exoneration.[72] Again, in 1773, Yŏngjo announced another edict requiring local officers to submit investigation reports to the central government "without concluding the case" if an adulterous lover were killed in a place not far from the adultery spot.[73] These two edicts were later codified into the 1865 *Comprehensive Collection of Dynastic Codes*, which combined them in the following terms: "As for not obtaining evidence of consensual fornication on the spot of adultery, if a place where the man and woman had a meal together is the same as the adultery spot, do not close the case but report to the king in writing" (see table 4.5).[74]

Dealing with numerous adultery-led homicides, King Chŏngjo faithfully followed the two edicts his predecessor had stipulated. When reviewing the brutal murder of a man named Han Ch'unsŏng in 1784 by a male slave named Ch'wisam, Chŏngjo drew attention to the testimony of Ch'wisam's wife, Ms. Kim. In her testimony, Ms. Kim claimed

---

72. *Ilsŏngnok* 446:57–58 [1793/11/25]; *T'ŭkkyo chŏngsik*, 47a–b; *Sugyo chŏngnye*, 46–47.

73. *T'ŭkkyo chŏngsik*, 47b; *Sugyo chŏngnye*, 47.

74. *Taejŏn hoet'ong* 5:43a; Yi Chongil, *Taejŏn hoet'ong yŏn'gu*, 4:195.

that she only had a drink with Ch'unsŏng, though she acknowledged sitting knee to knee, holding hands, and his pulling her skirt. Her husband Ch'wisam, she argued, had mercilessly beat Ch'unsŏng to death without witnessing the adultery scene or presenting evidence. On the one hand, the king regarded Ms. Kim's testimony as valid, but he also found that what she had done was still enough to meet the elements of adultery, so Ch'wisam, despite his grave crime of homicide, received only the reduced punishment of exile. On the other hand, the king lamented that Ms. Kim had accused her husband of being the principal offender. Even though his killing of Ch'unsŏng falsely branded her an adulterous woman, she should have instead sought to save him from punishment. The king judged that Ms. Kim be punished for her unfaithful efforts as a wife who had neglected her spousal duty (to protect her husband from legal penalty) in an effort to avoid her own arraignment.[75] Furthermore, in 1785 Chŏngjo's final verdict on Ch'wisam's case became an official edict on pulling a woman's skirt that appeared in later compilations of royal edicts, with the added specification that, "from now on, the edicts of 1758 and 1773 should be applied to the cases similar to this."[76]

Chŏngjo's commitment to keeping these two edicts effective is also revealed in his criticism of local officers for neglecting to follow them. On the same day he reviewed Ch'wisam's case, he dealt with a total of eight homicides in Yŏngam County of Chŏlla Province that had been reported through the Ministry of Punishment. Among them, Ch'wisam's case, which was the fifth to be examined, was the only one concerning adultery—or a husband's suspicion of his wife's illicit sexual conduct. Wrapping up a long, overall review of all eight cases, however, Chŏngjo somewhat abruptly added his special admonition on the significance of applying the two edicts of 1758 and 1773 in judicial decisions on adultery. He solemnly stated that local and provincial officers in charge of investigations had not honored the two edicts issued by the previous king, Yŏngjo. For the 1773 edict in particular, no open-ended reports had been submitted to the court

75. *Ilsŏngnok* 146:32–33 [1784/3/13]; *Simnirok* 10:137b.
76. *T'ŭkkyo chŏngsik*, 47a–b; *Sugyo chŏngnye*, 47.

inquiring about the course of judgment. Chŏngjo called for collecting all such cases from local offices, whether or not they had been already completed.[77]

The context of issuing and emphasizing these edicts primarily concerned revisiting the punishable range of adultery-led homicide. Under the law on killing adulterous lovers, the offender would be exonerated or punished depending on the two factors of spatiality and temporality: whether the adulterers were caught in flagrante (or "on the spot of adultery") and whether the homicide was committed promptly. These were the two key premises contested during judicial reviews of adultery-related cases in both local and central courts. Under the 1758 and 1773 edicts, however, the state took an even more lenient position toward the husband of an adulteress, disregarding these two premises of adultery-led homicide. Reaching a verdict on Sŏ Tolnam's murder of his wife's adulterous partner in 1787, for instance, the king confirmed that the state should be "generous [toward the accused husband] in dealing with adultery-led homicide caused by [the adulterer's] dubious acts such as pulling a skirt and sitting face to face over a meal."[78] Although, in principle, adultery meant having illicit sexual intercourse by mutual consent, simply pulling a woman's skirt could now constitute the crime of adultery. In treating flirting or suspicious behavior in the same way as adultery, the state redrew the standing definition of adultery as well as its putative boundaries, justifying "the right to kill the adulterous" to reflect the increased anxiety about female chastity in late Chosŏn society.

PUNISHING VIOLATORS OF CHASTITY

This broadened range of adulterous acts signified heightened expectations for women's sexual integrity. The promulgated edicts and expanded codification clearly echoed the state's pledge to punish anyone

---

77. *Ilsŏngnok* 146:37–38 [1784/3/19]. A decade later, in 1794, Chŏngjo criticized local officers for not strictly abiding by the 1785 edict on pulling a woman's skirt but interpreting such a case based on their own interests. Chŏngjo, *Hongjae chŏnsŏ*, 168:26b–27a.

78. *Ch'ugwanji*, 2:263–64. Sŏ Tolnam was released.

engaged in violation of female chastity under the Chosŏn law. We have seen how the Chosŏn court often exonerated a husband from the crime of killing an adulterer by honoring his outrage and resentful feeling upon witnessing his wife's illicit relations with another man. This attitude was not limited to a woman's husband but extended to the two other patriarchs most intimately connected with a woman's life—her father while she was unmarried and her son when widowed.

However, the stricter stance toward crimes against female chastity did not mean exclusive or indiscriminate sympathy toward patriarchs whose female family members were involved in licentious behavior and sexual crimes. A woman who failed to keep her fidelity came under heavy punishment, of course, and so did a man who violated a woman's chastity, for his crime threatened both the moral principle and the socio-familial order. Codification of a statute in the 1785 *Great Code for Ruling the State*, on a father killing his unmarried daughter's aggressor (see the 1785 codification in table 4.5), indicates the state's determination to "officially" punish such offenders. A careful reading of the statute, however, reveals that the father is to be punished for "recklessly killing a man deserving the death penalty," rather than for the crime of homicide itself, which was in fact not questioned. In other words, the aggressor ought to receive an appropriate punishment executed by the government in public, and the father, though his authority over his daughter's chastity was acknowledged, should not have thwarted the proper judicial procedure for punishing the vicious aggressor. While the state honored the enraged father's position and implicitly sanctioned a private way to punish the violator, it also endeavored to prevent people from exploiting this stance.

In addition, despite the state's resolution to properly punish sexual criminals as an imperative aspect of maintaining moral and legal justice, there was a critical fissure in the law on adultery-led homicide with respect to the surviving adulterer's punishment. The law states, "If he [the husband] kills only the adulterous lover, the adulterous wife shall be punished in accordance with the code [on committing fornication] and shall be remarried or sold by her husband" (see table 4.4). Also, a husband who murdered both his adulterous wife and her lover immediately, on the spot of adultery, should be forgiven. Then, what about a case in which a husband kills his adulterous wife, while her adulterous partner manages to escape? In outlining how to handle the adulterous wife, the law was silent about the surviving male adulterer: how and by which statute was the man to be punished?

In the eighth month of 1790, a man named Cho Myŏnggŭn residing in Chungbu stabbed his wife, Sammae, to death. Married for eighteen years, Cho and Sammae had eight children—seven sons and one daughter.[79] The couple was poor and had to live in a small rented room in the house of Yi Sŏnsan, where Sammae worked as a servant. Around this time, Sammae began to have illicit sexual relations with two other men, while treating her husband Cho coldly. According to Cho's testimony, even if their baby cried peevishly, looking for its mother, Sammae indulged in adultery and did not return home until far into the night. Hoping that she would repent her fault, Cho reproached her earnestly several times, but she only confronted Cho with violence, insisting that Cho leave their home. With a dreadful heart, Cho had stabbed Sammae three times, and she eventually died.

The Ministry of Punishment, although seeing Sammae's promiscuous conduct as the cause of this homicide, noted that Cho remained punishable for the crime of murder without "directly seeing the adultery scene." In the meantime, testimonies of people confirmed Sammae's intimate relations with the outside men, indicating that Cho's claims about her adultery were true. When the investigation report was submitted to King Chŏngjo for review, he pointed directly to the 1785 edict on pulling a skirt and having meals together and criticized officials for establishing Cho's incident as a criminal case. What Sammae had done could not be compared to simply pulling her skirt and sharing a table with an outside man. A private slave displaying licentious behavior, Sammae had committed adultery even to the extent of changing partners day and night—a far more serious crime than being discovered at the very spot of adultery, from the king's perspective. Describing Cho as an unnecessarily generous man who had tolerated his wife's lewd actions too long, Chŏngjo ordered special exoneration of Cho. There should be no pity at all for his dead wife. In turn, the king punished one of Sammae's partners in adultery, Chang Taedŭk—whose ignoble life had continued only thanks to the

79. *Ilsŏngnok* 351:60–64 [1790/8/22]; *Simnirok* 21:81a–82a.

oblivious Cho: he was flogged with the heavy stick and was permanently enslaved in Cho's household.[80]

The grave punishment of the adulterer Chang Taedŭk was determined based on the king's own legal reasoning. Even though the law on adultery-led homicide did not specify the punishment of the surviving adulterer, King Chŏngjo determined that it was Sammae's partner Chang who should be severely punished, not her poor husband Cho, whose indignation had finally reached the point of committing murder. Later, revisiting the king's judgment on this case, Chŏng Yagyong lamented that Chosŏn law lacked any account of an official trial of the surviving adulterer in such a case where a husband kills his adulterous wife. Citing the Qing Code, which in such a case condemned a surviving adulterer to strangulation, Chŏng inferred that King Chŏngjo's final verdict had not been as weighty as it should have been—Chang's crime deserved exile to a remote island.[81]

If strictly following the law on adultery that did not lead to homicide, the male adulterer Chang would only have received "eighty strokes of beating with the heavy stick" (see table 4.1). The lack of detailed stipulations about a surviving adulterer in the law on adultery-led homicide could thus generate potential judicial disputes, but at the same time it inadvertently allowed the state to determine an appropriate punishment for his crime instead of simply applying the adultery statute. As this chapter has illustrated, the Chosŏn state, though fully grounded upon the legal underpinning of written laws, always prioritized the specific circumstances (chŏng 情) that led to each crime and did not limit itself to the prescribed range of punishments during the judicial review. Understanding the fury of betrayed husbands, the state certainly supported their patriarchal authority over their wives' sexual integrity. Yet this does not mean that the state simply accepted a husband's anger toward his wife's illicit act, invariably defending his right to kill adulterers. The Chosŏn state was just as keen to properly punish the male partners in adultery-led death cases as it was to punish the female violators of their own chastity—and thus to close the gap left by the statute on killing adulterous lovers (see table 4.4).

80. Ilsŏngnok 351:60–64 [1790/8/22]; Simnirok 21:81a–82a.
81. Chŏng Yagyong, Hŭmhŭm sinsŏ, 3:284–85.

Women at Court: Judging Sexual Crimes
and Honoring Women's Words

As emphasized earlier, the reason for the heated debates to determine
the most precise punishments for adultery was that adultery disrupted
not only the moral vision of the state itself but the domestic order
centered on spousal fidelity in Chosŏn society. Whereas rape was
viewed exclusively as a man's crime against a woman's sexual purity,
mutually consensual acts of adultery indicated that the woman involved prioritized sexual desire over marital stability and female virtue.
This made a huge difference in the severity of the punishments for
women accused of illicit sexual intercourse. Depending on how the
court interpreted the testimonies of each party, a woman was at a
crossroads: she could be deemed an accomplice subject to heavy punishment or she could be judged a victim deserving acquittal. Since
there was often no concrete evidence or witness available (given the
secret nature of the crime), women's testimonies could be critical in
shaping the course of legal decision, as well as the final verdict itself.
How did women accused of illicit conduct speak at the court in cases
where drawing the line between consensual and coercive fornication
would render them either licentious women or chaste victims? Let us
turn to two suspected adultery cases with different results to see how
women's voices were treated in the adjudication of sexual crimes.

In the second month of 1787, a man named Yi Samch'i of Kusŏng
County in P'yŏngan Province was allegedly beaten by Ms. Ch'oe, a
married woman who lived in the same town. After seven days Yi died,
Ms. Ch'oe was put in jail for killing him, and the first trial took place
at the local magistrate's office. Yi's wife, Ms. Yun, asserted that Yi and
Ms. Ch'oe had often quarreled because they shared the same house. On
the eighteenth day of the month, Yi, drunken, had entered Ms. Ch'oe's
room, and Ms. Yun had then heard Yi shout, "Ms. Ch'oe hit my head
with an iron!" Surprised, she ran into the room and found a bloody Yi,
seriously injured. Shortly before he died on the twenty-fourth day, Yi
had said, "I am dying now, but it is all because Ms. Ch'oe beat me."[82]

---

82. *Ilsŏngnok* 239:53–54 [1787/4/16].

Designated as the principal offender, Ms. Ch'oe contradicted Ms. Yun's accusation of her, testifying:

> Yi Samch'i had always lusted after me. Whenever my husband was absent, working as a servant at the station in another area, he entered my room and attempted to rape me. I always scolded him and resisted. In the early evening of the eighteenth day of this month, I was ironing alone in the room. Yi, heavily drunk, entered the room and tried to kiss me, holding my body. My ten-year-old daughter saw this scene and cursed him, so he left, after beating me many times. Around midnight, he entered the room again with a knife, pulling my skirt to rape me again. I barely escaped to hide, but he followed me, stepping on my body countless times. *As a woman with a small body, how could I beat a strong man?* The injury around his right ear must have been made when the drunken Yi fell down. But I was not aware of this.[83]

In her second testimony, Ms. Ch'oe again proclaimed her innocence, stressing Yi's desire to rape her:

> After Yi Samch'i's repeated rape attempts, I wanted to report [this] to the local magistrate's office. But my neighbors discouraged me from doing that. I also thought of telling my husband [about this] but could not, because I was afraid he would become suspicious [that I was indeed having illicit relations with Yi]. I only slapped [Yi Samch'i's face] several times to warn him to desist in his immoral behavior that night.[84]

As Ms. Ch'oe stated, she had been afraid to bring up Yi's sexual aggression for fear that she could be mistakenly accused of consensual relations with him, but now did so to defend herself from the charge of beating him to death. The emphasis in her first testimony is on the violence of Yi's attack—even threatening her with a knife and stepping on her body—not on the sexual nature of his aggression toward her. Ms. Ch'oe underscores her physical weakness as a woman, incapable of confronting a powerful man with a weapon. Despite Yi's continuing

---

83. *Ilsŏngnok* 239:54–55 [1787/4/16].
84. *Ilsŏngnok* 239:55 [1787/4/16].

attempts to rape her, she focuses only on his violent actions on the night in question, implying that no actual sexual intercourse occurred. By doing so, she was able avoid the subtler questions of her own sexual desire and complicity while maintaining her claim of sexual integrity.

Despite Ms. Ch'oe's defense, the Kusŏng County magistrate Yi Chingman, who conducted the first round of postmortem and trial, rendered a judgment different from what Ms. Ch'oe argued. In his concluding statement, the magistrate pointed to a widespread rumor in the town that Ms. Ch'oe had committed adultery with Yi Samch'i while living under the same roof with him. Because her husband's vocation as a servant at local stations required trips to other regions, she and Yi had not only maintained sexual relations secretly but had fostered the love affair for a long time. Realizing that the rumor had already spread to the community, Ms. Ch'oe had tried to conceal the truth by refusing Yi this time. The autopsy of Yi's corpse also indicated her use of a heavy iron tool in beating him to death, not just slapping Yi's face a few times as she had testified. In the eyes of the county magistrate, that was how the fight that ended with Yi's death had started. He determined that Ms. Ch'oe was the principal offender in the case.[85]

The county magistrate's decision was soon challenged. Yi Konsu (1762–1788), a secret inspector dispatched to the northwest region, countered the magistrate's adjudication.[86] In his report to the central government, he stressed that Ms. Ch'oe herself never confessed or confirmed the rumor that she had committed adultery. Yi noted that the way the county magistrate had affirmed the rumor as trustworthy was very strange and that this should not be how a legal decision was made. He further stated:

> There is no doubt that beating caused this death. However, chastity is the foremost element of a woman's conduct, and nothing is more humiliating than being raped by a strong man. If it is impossible to avoid a sudden

85. *Ilsŏngnok* 239:55–56 [1787/4/16].
86. Yi Konsu was a secret inspector to Hwanghae and P'yŏngan provinces at that time. *Chŏngjo sillok* 23:47b [1787/4/16].

assault late at night, the only method [to avert it] is using violence—whether that is by stabbing him with a knife or by beating him with wood or stone is unimportant. If Ms. Ch'oe had articulated the reason behind killing him more succinctly [during the court trial], her determination to keep her chastity would have been better exposed. But this dim-witted woman just mentioned slapping him three or four times.

The first investigator [the Kusŏng County magistrate] was interested only in accentuating some trivial flaws [in Ms. Ch'oe's acts]. As I have argued, his investigation report fails to do justice [to the case]. As a mere commoner woman of the remote countryside, she tried hard to protect her body and avoided losing her sexual integrity. This is something to be honored, not punished. In accord with our policy of encouraging moral conduct, I recommend that Ms. Ch'oe be freed and praised.[87]

The Ministry of Punishment then reviewed the secret inspector's report. It supported his points that an adulterous affair between Ms. Ch'oe's and Yi had not been verified during the trial and that the first investigator's legal reasoning was illogical. Confirming that Ms. Ch'oe's use of force had directly caused Yi's death, however, the Ministry of Punishment judged her an actual murderer, not just someone whose violence later led to Yi's death. Even if Ms. Ch'oe had used violence for the sake of protecting her chastity, she could not be exempted from the crime of causing someone's death. In the meantime, the Ministry of Punishment recommended punishing the first investigator, the Kusŏng County magistrate, for his carelessness in dealing with the legal case by simply making conjectures.[88]

Though her testimony was considered fully, Ms. Ch'oe again faced punishment for causing Yi's death. It was up to the king to accept the Ministry of Punishment's recommendation, or not, since he had the authority to overrule the death penalty. Reviewing Ms. Ch'oe's case, Chŏngjo applauded her upholding chastity at the risk of her life. He compared Ms. Ch'oe's hitting Yi over the head with her iron to the way the Jin state Chinese woman Madam Ko had used a thread-picker to break the teeth of a man who had tried to seduce her when he found

87. *Ilsŏngnok* 239:56–57 [1787/4/16].
88. *Ilsŏngnok* 239:127 [1787/4/20].

her sitting alone at her weaving. The king considered Ms. Ch'oe's effort to keep her chastity truly outstanding and wondered whether it was reasonable to make her case a criminal one. He was torn: the secret inspector had advised excusing Ms. Ch'oe's crime, whereas the Ministry of Punishment opposed exoneration and still proposed punishment for her violence. After deliberation, the king finally decided to release Ms. Ch'oe without any punishment.

Around the same time, a *yangban* woman of P'yŏngsan County, Madam Ch'oe, was punished for committing adultery. The king noted that two women with the same surname (Ch'oe) in the same P'yŏngsan County were involved in similar cases, yet the low-status Ms. Ch'oe had espoused her chastity whereas the *yangban* Madam Ch'oe had not. Agreeing with the secret inspector's opinion that freeing Ms. Ch'oe would magnify the state's agenda of recognizing virtuous conduct and reprimanding evil deeds—the preeminent task of a king— King Chŏngjo concluded that Ms. Ch'oe's case could be used as an example to rectify the declining morality of that time.[89]

Like Chokkŭmaji, whose case was introduced in the outset of this chapter, Ms. Ch'oe was freed despite an allegedly widespread rumor about her misconduct. The adultery of the *yangban* Madam Ch'oe living in the same county must have helped Ms. Ch'oe's situation. But it was her more careful testimonies, in which she described herself as a victim while reiterating Yi's immoral behavior, that must have been seen as expressing her formidable oath to preserve her chastity. Besides, Ms. Ch'oe stressed another condition beyond her personal sense of injustice: the neighbors discouraged her from reporting Yi's repeated sexual assaults to the local office, though she originally had planned to do so. To make her testimonies compelling, she also depicted herself both as a weak woman and as having always resisted Yi, eventually convincing the court that she was the one who had been wronged.

With her words utterly credited, Ms. Ch'oe was not only exonerated but emerged as a paragon of female chastity. Meanwhile, the state punished the first investigator for relying on rumor in dealing with the case. Above all, the series of judgments made by the first investigator,

89. *Ilsŏngnok* 239:129–30 [1787/4/20]; also recoded in *Simnirok* 18:209a–210b.

the secret inspector, the Ministry of Punishment, and, finally, the king indicates the significance of the woman's testimony in judging between consensual and forcible fornication. A woman whose narrative could persuade officials that she had resisted sexual overtures would not be punished.

The court's judgment, however, was not always supportive of an accused woman's testimony, as illustrated in another case of adultery versus rape. In 1828 (or 1888), a commoner named Sin Kaeji informed the local court of his brother's death in Kŏch'ang County of Kyŏng-sang Province.[90] His brother, Sin Ilmun, had gone to a marketplace to purchase a cow with a neighbor man, Kim Ch'isun, but Kim had returned home alone. The body of the missing brother was found about twenty days later, after Sin Kaeji's own tireless but fruitless search. Sin Kaeji was sure that the neighbor had killed his brother. Further, he argued that Kim had had an adulterous relationship with his brother's wife (i.e., his sister-in-law).

In his testimony at the local magistrate's office, Sin Kaeji stated that he had run to his brother's house as soon as he heard his body had been found, but his sister-in-law had already fled with Kim Ch'isun. Kim avoided being arrested, but the runaway wife, Ms. Chŏng, was soon caught and brought to the court. Though admitting her flight with Kim, she asserted that the relationship had begun with Kim's rape of her. According to her, a month before the murder incident, Kim had suddenly entered her room and raped her, knowing that her husband and mother-in-law were absent. Ms. Chŏng testified:

[One day] in the early seventh month of this year, when my mother-in-law and husband together went to the mountain [to gather firewood], Kim Ch'isun opened the bedroom door all of a sudden and entered the room. Because I could not resist the man's physical power, I was forced to have relations [with him]. A couple of days later, Kim returned and greedily told me, "I will get rid of your husband, and you should follow and live with me." I scolded him, asking him not to do so.

90. *Ogan ch'ogae*, 1:19–26. *Ogan ch'ogae*, consisting of two volumes, is a compilation of criminal incidents of the Kyŏngsang area from the *muja* year (either 1828 or 1888) to the *kich'uk* year (either 1829 or 1889).

On the nineteenth of this month, my husband left [home] to sell a
cow at the Chirye market and did not come back even late at night. For
several days, [Kim] Ch'isun did not visit me either. Later I met Kim beside
a well, and he told me, "I already killed your husband with a stone and
took his 26 *yang* [of money]. No one would imagine I have done that."
He [then] had [a neighbor] Kim Musŏng's wife deliver his message [to
me], [instructing] me to put on clothes and leave while my mother-in-law
was away, but I did not follow [his command]. . . . That night he abducted and confined me in the backyard of his house first, then we moved
from place to place to hide.[91]

Although we do not know whether or not Ms. Chŏng had maintained
an illicit relationship with Kim Ch'isun and eventually joined the plot
to kill her husband, it is clear that she based her claim of innocence
on her contention that the illicit sexual intercourse began with an
incident of rape: again, as a weak woman, she could not physically
resist Kim in the end—a defense similar to that used by Ms. Ch'oe in
the previous case. Also, considering Ms. Chŏng's argument that Kim
forcibly took her to another place to continue the adulterous relations,
the case could be viewed as one of seduction-led adultery. Most importantly, since Kim Ch'isun had eluded capture, Ms. Chŏng's testimony was critical to the course of investigation: without Kim, who
might have given conflicting testimony, Ms. Chŏng's account was the
most essential point—whether their intercourse had been consensual
or coercive. How, then, did the court respond to her testimony, and to
what extent did her words affect the judicial decision?

The Hamyang County magistrate who investigated this murder
case (because the position of Kŏch'ang County magistrate was vacant)
determined that Ms. Chŏng was an accomplice (*kanbŏm*) to Kim
Ch'isun, who was designated the principal offender (*chŏngbŏm*) in the
murder of her husband. Kim's crime was doubled as he had fornicated
with a married woman and also murdered her husband to keep having
sexual relations. For Ms. Chŏng, the magistrate made three points in
his postscript to the case: first, as one man's wife, Ms. Chŏng had tainted
the wifely duty of chastity; second, even if Kim had threatened her

91. *Ogan ch'ogae*, 1:21.

at first, she had accepted him without a word of resistance; and third, though she had heard Kim's plan to kill her husband and tried to dissuade him, she had not told anyone about it. Instead, she had joined Kim at last and run away with him, so her crime was just as grave as Kim's.

To ensure the fairness of the trial, the Sanch'ŏng County magistrate was invited to conduct the second round of autopsy proceedings and testimonies. Confirming the results of the previous trial, he emphasized that the murder was done by Kim and that Ms. Chŏng had known of his intention. Concluding that her crime was heavier than simply being an accomplice, he judged the murder to be an adultery-led homicide that should be punished in accord with the statute on killing adulterous lovers, which states, "If the adulterous lover himself kills the husband, the adulterous wife shall be punished by strangulation even if she does not know the circumstances. She is a criminal for violating moral principles" (see table 4.4).[92] Despite Ms. Chŏng's strong assertion that she had been a victim of Kim's coercive sexual violence, she proved unable to depict the case as a rape incident; rather, she was deemed a criminal involved in both adultery and adultery-led homicide.

Why did the court not believe Ms. Chŏng's words when they had believed those of Ms. Ch'oe? Aside from a local rumor, there was no actual "evidence" of sexual intercourse in the case of Ms. Ch'oe, who powerfully articulated how she had repeatedly resisted her assailant's sexual attacks. In contrast, Ms. Chŏng herself acknowledged that, though initially forced, she ended up having intercourse with Kim Ch'isun, and she did not clearly enunciate in her testimony how she had reacted to the initial rape attempt. Moreover, her assertions that she was forced against her will were contradicted by her behavior thereafter, for she had remained completely quiet about Kim's plot to kill her husband (whereas Ms. Ch'oe explained that her neighbors had dissuaded her from reporting Yi's sexual assaults to the local magistrate's office).

Ms. Ch'oe and Ms. Chŏng—two women accused of committing adultery—received completely different verdicts, yet both cases show

92. *Ogan ch'ogae*, 1:25.

how women's words mattered during the trials. They illustrate ordinary women's exertions to effect change on their own behalf by judiciously presenting themselves as victims of the system, while also not promoting their cases too vigorously or strategically. During their testimonies, both women attempted to seize the moral high ground and convince the court that they were the party who had been wronged. Despite the notion that sexual crimes were violent acts against women, and the idea of "the law as an intrinsic and powerful part of patriarchy operated for men against women," women were still brought to testify on sexual crimes in public and the court was receptive to their voices.[93] Especially when sexual integrity and the ideal of chastity were at stake, it was momentous "to speak words of self-exoneration in one's own voice."[94] The rhetoric of telling women's own versions of stories at court, as seen in the testimonies of Ms. Ch'oe and Ms. Chŏng, unveils that women were not only aware of the moral expectations prescribed by the society but had their own understandings of how to employ the existing law to effectively defend their position. Even if women's testimonies were not always credited by the investigators and did not always faithfully represent the truth of a given case, they nevertheless provide crucial insights into women's encounters with the crisis of being charged with sexual misconduct and infidelity.

Shifting Discourses: Performances of Morality and Sexual Crimes

In drawing the legal distinction between adultery and rape, the Chosŏn state counted on the woman's oral testimony as a decisive element in determining the final verdict on a case. Despite the patriarchal institutions that imposed socio-legal limitations on women, accused women proved to be active and persistent participants in their trials. Women's testimonies that were honored at court therefore gave them the chance to carve out their subtle status within the legal context.

93. Bashar, "Rape in England," 34–35, 40–42. Bashar notes that failed or reluctant prosecution of rape cases discouraged victims from filing at the early modern England court. See also Kaiser, "He Said, She Said," 199.

94. Peirce, *Morality Tales*, 194.

Given that legal decisions were made through a combination of debate, contention, complexity, and accommodation that was generated during a series of court testimonies involving people of different socio-familial backgrounds, what other factors influenced judicial decision in defining crimes against female chastity?

As the cases of Ms. Chŏng and Ms. Ch'oe illustrate, a woman's consent to illicit sex was difficult to prove, and it was even more difficult to judge the degree to which a woman had resisted or submitted to sexual assault. The Chosŏn state's general policy—that the intensity of a victim's resistance mattered little in prosecuting the case as long as her *intention* to rebuff a rape attempt was proved (even if only through the oral testimony of the victim herself)—was followed until the end of the dynasty. As the earlier section of this chapter on coercive fornication discusses, however, judicial authorities raised concerns about false accusations. Taking advantage of the law's ambiguity, women who were originally accused of adultery often sought to escape punishment by insisting that they had been forced into the relationship.

Responding to persistent concerns about such strategies, the Chosŏn court began to take into consideration various conditions involving sexual assault, supplementing the existing statutes. Just as the articles on rape under "Offenses of Illicit Sex Statutes" in the Ming Code continued to change with the shifting policies adopted by the new Qing imperial court, so the criteria identifying the crime of rape were gradually transformed in the second part of the Chosŏn dynasty.[95] In China, for example, tangible evidence of violent coercion—such as physical injury, eyewitnesses to a victim's cries, and torn clothing—was required to prove rape in 1646, when the first edition of the Qing Code was compiled.[96] The Qing law also added a specification that "if an offender joins with a woman by coercion, but consummates the act by means of her consent, then it does not count as coercion," which

95. Perhaps the biggest difference in the Qing and Chosŏn laws on sexual crime compared was the male rape law—punishments for sexual assault on males by males. Unlike Qing China, a trial on homosexuality was uncommon (I have not seen one so far), and the issue of homosexuality itself is hard to come by in Chosŏn records.

96. Sommer, *Sex, Law, and Society*, 325 (appendix 2). See also Ng, "Ideology and Sexuality," 57–59.

actually echoes the Chosŏn court's adjudication of Ms. Ch'ŏng's case above.[97] These new sub-statutes affixed to the law manifested the Qing state's strict view in making a final decision on rape.[98]

While evidence that a woman had struggled against an aggressor during an incident of sexual violence continued to help define rape, the Chosŏn court did not specify, as the Qing government did, that detailed criteria of physical evidence be met. Instead, the issue of how a woman reacted *after* the incident emerged as pivotal in late Chosŏn judicial proceedings. In particular, a victim's extreme action after being violated—such as taking her own life—was a key element in judging the level of punishment to be meted out to the offender. In 1737, for example, a seventeen-year-old named Mun Chunggap was hauled into court on charges that he had attempted to rape his third cousin (*p'alch'on*), Mun Okchi of Ch'angnyŏng County. The rape had not been completed, so his crime was subject to the punishment of one hundred blows of the heavy stick followed by exile for life to a distance of 3,000 *li*, as outlined in the law (see table 4.1). King Yŏngjo, however, claimed that this was too light for the seriousness of Mun Chunggap's crime and ordered him banished to a remote unknown island (*tobae*).[99]

Because Mun Chunggap had sexually assaulted a female member of his own kinship circle, the heavier punishment was not questioned. Besides that, there was another important factor behind the king's judgment: the victim, Mun Okchi, had committed suicide by poisoning after Mun Chunggap's sexual aggression. Even though the rape was incomplete, the king ascertained that the attempt itself had humiliated Mun Okchi, who found her integrity, once tainted, impossible to restore. A victim's suicide was taken as evidence of her unwavering determination to embody the morality of the chastity ideal, increasing

97. Sommer, *Sex, Law, and Society*, 325 (appendix 2).

98. Vivien Ng sees the Qing government's stringent definition of rape as motivated less by high numbers of false accusations and more by Qing efforts to "discourage the Chinese from bringing rape charges against Manchu soldiers." Ng, "Ideology and Sexuality," 59.

99. *Sŭngjŏngwŏn ilgi* 857:77a–b [1737/9/23]; *Yŏngjo sillok* 45:25a [1737/9/23]. Mun Okchi's first name is recoded differently as "Ogi" in *Yŏngjo sillok*.

the severity of the offender's punishment. Praising her chaste act, the king awarded Mun Okchi a memorial arch, to be built in her town.[100] Furthermore, he made his adjudication of this incident into a royal edict, stipulating that "for those committing forcible fornication of a third cousin that was unconsummated, if the woman [victim] poisoned herself to death out of humiliation, punishing [the man] under the statute of unconsummated forcible fornication with heavy beating and exile is too light, while it is [also] inappropriate to execute the law of 'using coercion to cause others to die' directly. Considering the situation, punishment shall [thus] be exile to a remote island. For the woman, a memorial arch shall be erected." This 1738 edict was formally included in the 1743 *Newly Supplemented Collected Royal Edicts* (see table 4.3).

The death of a female victim of sexual assault necessarily resulted in more severe penalties for the offender. In addition, the issue of *how* the victim took her own life emerged as a matter of debate during adjudication. In 1779, when handling an attempted rape case of a poor *yangban* woman, Madam Kim, by a commoner man, Kim Ponggi, residing in the same town of Hamp'yŏng, Chŏlla Province, the court had an intense discussion about Madam Kim's delayed suicide.[101] Madam Kim ended up poisoning herself, but did so twenty days after the incident occurred. Knowing that Madam Kim's death would increase his sentence, the accused man, Kim Ponggi, argued that it was his nephew's insult that had directly caused Madam Kim's death, not his own sexual offense. During the first trial at the local level, whether Madam Kim's suicide had occurred twenty days after the attempted rape was not a critical issue. Yet suspicion was indeed raised later, at the court discussion, even though Kim Ponggi could not avoid admitting his crime of attempted rape. The king himself speculated that Madam Kim might not have killed herself had she not been humiliated by Kim's nephew: had she been determined to die because of the attempted rape, she ought to have done so right after

---

100. *Sŭngjŏngwŏn ilgi* 857:77a–b; *Yŏngjo sillok* 45:25a [1737/9/23].

101. *Ch'ugwanji*, 2:252–54. The incident had actually occurred in 1775 but was reinvestigated because Kim Ponggi's son petitioned to claim his father's innocence.

the incident, rather than postponing her suicide. Accepting this point, the court reduced Kim's punishment from the death sentence to exile, though it still honored Madam Kim's chaste act by granting tax exemption to her family.

Also in 1779, in Anju of P'yŏngan Province, Ms. Kim, a commoner wife of Yi Nŭngbaek, committed suicide after being raped by a man named Kim Ch'undong. Kim lived next door and took advantage of Yi's absence to commit the crime. Upon her husband's return, Ms. Kim filed at the court together with her husband, but eventually killed herself by poisoning. In judging this case, the P'yŏngan provincial governor noted a somewhat regrettable aspect of Ms. Kim's death, stating that "having resolved to die, she could have carried out [her death] immediately [after the rape], could have died the next day, could have died on the day her husband returned, or could have died on the day she reported Kim Ch'undong's crime to the court." However, Ms. Kim had killed herself thirty-three days after the incident—prompting him to comment that "she was too tolerant and waited too long."[102]

Similar verdicts based on a female victim's post-violence reaction continue to appear in legal cases. When an unmarried No woman of Chech'ŏn in Ch'ungch'ŏng Province poisoned herself to death in 1784 after being sexually harassed on the street by a *yangban* man, Yi Kit'ae, the Ministry of Punishment again noted her deferred death, expressing that it was pity about her "delayed" decision to clear her tainted integrity via death. Because she had killed herself about a year after the incident, the ministry averred, the No woman's suicide should be regarded differently from suicide carried out "immediately" after the violation. Praising the No woman's chaste spirit and performance, the king nevertheless concurred with the Ministry of Punishment's point: Yi could not avoid being accused of driving the No woman to kill herself, but he was to be released after one round of punishment.[103]

All these cases reveal that, in ruling on sexual offenses, the late Chosŏn court used a female victim's post-violence reaction as a critical yardstick for gauging her moral integrity. In addition, a victim's

102. *Ch'ugwanji*, 2:234–35.
103. *Ilsŏngnok* 152:122–23 [1784/5/29].

sexual history became an important factor in deciding the male violator's punishment, as in the Qing law on rape, which saw the ideal
rape victim as someone who had not previously engaged in illicit
sexual intercourse.[104] During the early Chosŏn, rape was treated
equally, regardless of the victim's previous sexual behavior, even if
she was a female entertainer whose vocation was rather irrelevant to
keeping chastity.[105] Entering the later part of the dynasty, however,
the victim's sexual history mattered importantly in deliberating and
adjudicating sexual crimes. In prosecuting a female entertainer's rape
case in 1748, King Yŏngjo noted that "even if the victim was threatened at first, she would have been unable to keep her chastity to the end
(since she is a female entertainer); thus this case cannot be solely dis
cussed as rape." The king took into consideration her sexual behavior
as a female entertainer, which factored into reducing the offender's
punishment to exile.[106]

The increasing emphasis on these two issues—a victim's reaction
and her prior sexual behavior—reflects the intensification of chastity
discourse, which resulted in stricter moral expectations of women in
the latter part of the dynasty. Even though a female victim's oral testimony had significant bearing on how the crime of sexual violence
was treated at the trial, the society's changing perspective on the chastity ideal required the victim to display greater moral performance
even after the violence took place. To qualify as a victim of sexual
violence, a woman had to meet the standards of sexual integrity prescribed by the society (which in fact echoes the court's decision dis-
qualifying a remarried woman from receiving a chastity reward, as
discussed in chapter 2). The late Chosŏn court continued to follow a
stringent definition of sexual violence against women and punished
male violators severely; at the same time, however, the heightened
attitude toward female chastity during this time burdened female victims with the need to provide further, irrefutable proof of their moral
commitment.

104. Sommer, Sex, Law, and Society, 103–4.
105. Chungjong sillok 47:45a [1523/yun4/6]. Here the rape of a female entertainer
by an official named Kim Ŭnson is dealt with as a typical rape case under the rape law.
106. Yŏngjo sillok 67:23b [1748/3/24].

Rethinking Gender and Social Status
in Chosŏn Sexual Crimes

Chosŏn society was undeniably hierarchical. As revealed in the shifting judicial views over the course of the dynasty on the relevance of a woman's sexual background, gender and sexual crimes could not be separated from the issue of social status. Most postscripts (*palsa* 跋辭) attached to investigation reports place social status at the center, projecting a person's virtue or guilt based on the group to which he or she belonged. In cases where a person's social status and gender conflicted with each other, the distinction between *yangban* and non-*yangban* 班常之分 always preceded the distinction between men and women 男女 之別, highly influencing any judicial decision.[107] This demonstrates the incongruity between the ideal of virtue expected of everyone in society and the attitude of the investigators (local magistrates), whose judgments represent the general view held by the state and the elites.

As much as one's social status affected the ways gender roles were defined, therefore, gender and social status—as the two pillars of one's identity in Chosŏn society—also competed to shape the legal reasoning behind regulating female sexuality in legal processes. Gradual discrimination based on different social status was applied in adjudging sexual crimes as the law was amended and supplemented over the course the dynasty. The reinforcement of elite status was one of the conspicuous aspects of the statutes that were added or revised in the mid- to late Chosŏn. The term *sajok* (distinguished aristocrat family) became legally settled in the early sixteenth century and was defined as referring to those who were either present civil or military officials or descendants of illustrious ancestors up to the fourth generation.[108] Although the Ming penal code incorporated status discrimination by imposing different punishments for the same crime depending on societal status, it did not recognize strict separations in status, such as the Chosŏn distinction of *sajok* from the category of *yangin* (literally,

107. *Ogan ch'ogae*, 2:121.
108. *Kaksa sugyo*, 57a–b; Sim Chaeu, "Chosŏn sidae pŏpchŏn p'yŏnch'an kwa hyŏngsa chŏngch'aek ŭi pyŏnhwa," 252; Han Sanggwŏn, "Chosŏn sidae kyohwa wa hyŏngjŏng," 279.

"good people"), or commoners.[109] In China, the meaning of the legal term 良 (*liang*; Kr. *yang*) changed its earlier emphasis "from free commoner legal status to moral goodness" with Qing emperors' unprecedented promotion of female chastity among the common people.[110] As Matthew Sommer discusses, for Chinese jurists, "morality demonstrated in conduct should determine status before the law," and one's "willed conduct," rather than birth or social status, became the most essential factor in regulating sexuality.[111] In contrast, late Chosŏn statutes drew a clear line, even within the *yangin* group, identifying members of the elite group as *sajok*, *sadaebu* (scholar-official), or *yangban* and providing them with privileged legal treatment in cases involving sexual crimes.[112]

In 1585, a royal edict prescribed that "for women of conscripted soldiers or wives of palace guardsmen committing consensual fornication with a clerk at the station, treat [them] with the law corresponding to punishment of *yangban* (*sajok*)" (see table 4.2). However, in 1677, this prescription was reversed by a new edict, which stated: "In the past, palace guardsmen were generally *yangban* (*sajok*), and many conscripted soldiers came from *yangban* families. However, things have altered remarkably by now and it is impossible to apply under the same statute [as before]. Revise this after having discussions among high officials" (see table 4.2).[113] The 1677 edict denotes the narrower boundary of the elite group redrawn by the state, which had already issued a series of edicts delineating punishments based on the victim's social status.

Heavier punishment for a man who raped a virgin of a *yangban* family was articulated in a 1671 royal edict. Whereas punishment of the male violator of a non-*yangban* woman remained unchanged from

109. In theory, *yangin* included all people except those categorized as *ch'ŏnmin*, and Chosŏn social status was outlined as the *yang-ch'ŏn* system. In practice, however, Chosŏn society was divided into four groups—*yangban* elites, *chungin* (middle-class commoners with technical and administrative skills), commoners, and the debased.

110. Sommer, *Sex, Law, and Society*, 312.

111. Sommer, *Sex, Law, and Society*, 315.

112. Deuchler, *Under the Ancestors' Eyes*, 2–6.

113. For the details on the royal edicts on sexual crimes discussed here, see tables 4.2 and 4.3.

the existing code, this edict emphasized that a man violating a *yang-ban* woman's chastity should be decapitated whether he was a principal offender or an accomplice (see table 4.3). Shortly later, in 1682, another edict specified that a man violating a *yangban* woman be punished by decapitation "without waiting." This discriminative treatment was then extended to rape of the daughter of a *yangban*'s concubine (i.e., an illegitimate daughter). In 1702, royal edicts stipulated that men committing forcible fornication against *yangban* daughters by concubines be penalized under the same statute that punished the rape of *yangban* women (see table 4.3). The violation of their sexual integrity was taken as a threat to the *yangban* patriarchy, and protecting *yangban*'s illegitimate daughters in the face of sexual violence was in line with the tightening of elites' status. In the same year, an additional edict was announced differentiating punishments in unconsummated rape cases of *yangban* daughters and non-*yangban* daughters: for the former, "the male violator shall be decapitated whether consummated or not; for the latter, he shall be punished by exile [to a distance] of 3,000 *li* when unconsummated." All these edicts were codified in the 1746 *Continuation of the Great Code*, stressing greater punishment for anyone involved in sexual violence toward *yangban* women (not only legal wives and daughters but concubines and their daughters) compared with those accused of violence toward non-*yangban* women. In other words, whether an attempted rape was consummated or unconsummated did not affect the punishment for men who assaulted *yangban* women (all decapitation), whereas it yielded different levels of punishment when the victims were women of a non-*yangban* class.

These newly supplemented statutory laws strengthening elites' rights reflect a range of social changes during the late Chosŏn that could not be addressed by the Ming Code. In his 1745 audience with King Yŏngjo to discuss the case of a male slave who had violated the female owner of his slave wife, Prime Minister Kim Chaero (1682–1759) pointed to the absence of a specific statute on this matter in the Ming Code. According to Kim, Chosŏn custom was distinctive in treating a female slave's husband as the slave of the same person who owned the female slave herself (even if the couple belonged to different households), so the sexual offense committed by the female slave's husband against his wife's owner (even if she was a commoner in the countryside, or *yŏhang sŏin*) should be punished much more harshly than otherwise because the female slave's owner could be considered the male slave's owner as well.[114]

The state's conspicuous efforts to articulate each person's social status, in the meantime, did not merely buttress *yangban* power and position in the legal environment but also entailed expectations of higher moral cultivation and performance for members of the elite group. Along with heavier punishments for violators of *yangban* women, *yangban* men who were involved in sexual crimes received stricter verdicts. The 1679 royal edict on men committing adultery with relatives of their wives was expanded and codified in the 1746 *Continuation of the Great Code* by detailing discriminative punishments for *yangban* and non-*yangban* for the same crime. As table 4.2 illustrates, the state penalized a *yangban* man more severely than a non-*yangban* man in prosecuting adultery cases. The same applied to women of *yangban* families: the 1734 royal edict on a *yangban* woman committing adultery, sentenced by the law of corrupting public morality, was codified in the *Continuation of the Great Code* as follows: "Women of *yangban* families (*sajok*) who taint custom and corrupt morality by committing licentious acts shall be punished by strangulation along with male adulterers" (see table 4.2).

The differing moral expectations based on social status were evident in the legal reasoning applied in actual cases. In 1720, a man named T'ak Ch'ŏllip, residing in Yangju, Kyŏnggi Province, murdered his own daughter who was engaged in adultery. T'ak then threw his daughter's body into a river. Troubled in judging whether this crime should be punished as "mercilessly killing one's own children," the provincial governor submitted an investigation report to the Ministry of Punishment for review.[115] In forwarding the case to King Sukchong for a final verdict, the ministry commented:

> T'ak is originally not a *yangban* but an ordinary man of the countryside. Therefore, he could marry his adulterous daughter off to a man living far away, or simply let her remain unmarried, rather than killing her. But

---

114. *Yŏngjo sillok* 62:9a [1745/8/12].
115. Yonglin Jiang, *Great Ming Code*, 174.

because of the humiliation he would face in the community, his cruel crime reached the point of throwing the corpse of his own daughter into a river—a crime that certainly goes against the heavenly principle.[116]

On the surface, T'ak's case illustrates the perplexities of applying legal reasoning in adjudicating crimes that could be viewed as immoral— such as the tragic circumstance of a father killing his own child. Reading the Ministry of Punishment's comments on ways T'ak should have handled his licentious daughter short of killing her, however, reveals the state's tolerant attitude toward non-*yangban* women's immoral behavior: not only could T'ak's daughter still have been married off even after committing adultery, but it was excessive for T'ak, as a mere commoner, to take such extreme measures to uphold the reputation of his family.

As we have seen, the goal of moralizing all levels of Chosŏn society lay at the heart of the state orthodoxy, and the state-reward policy touched people of all social classes. Moreover, the state praised exemplary figures from the bottom of the social hierarchy even more highly than those of higher social status, precisely because of their humble backgrounds. Nevertheless, doubts about their inborn moral capacity seem to have persisted in the minds of the elite officials. In 1763, Yi Sudŭksan, a man residing in Kasan, P'yŏngyan Province, caught his runaway wife, Ms. Sŏ, and took her back home. Wanting to leave her husband forever, Ms. Sŏ asked Yi to abandon her permanently in writing (*susŏyŏnggi*).[117] Infuriated, Yi beat her to death and faced the crime of killing his wife. In judging this case, King Yŏngjo strongly blamed Ms. Sŏ's unfaithful conduct and defiance of her conjugal duty. At the same time, he noted that some people might question "why it is necessary to care about these [lowborn] people's morality." Yet if the state did not make efforts to inspire low-status people with moral principles, the king continued, there would not be a single woman of the lowest status included in moral texts such as the *Illustrated Guide*

116. *Ch'ugwanji*, 2:193. In light of the Ministry of Punishment's recommendation, the king, seeing that it would be precarious to judge T'ak's crime under one definite statute, punished him with exile.

117. *Ch'ugwanji*, 2:241.

to the Three Bonds. He therefore reduced Yi's punishment from the death penalty to lifelong exile.[118]

Yŏngjo's lenient judgment of Yi's crime of killing underlines the prime task of the king and the supreme agenda of the Chosŏn state: the moral transformation of the entire society. A wife's immoral conduct deserved grave punishment, whereas a husband's violence toward a disloyal wife earned compassion. Non-*yangban* ordinary people were no exception to this rule, as Yŏngjo's statement on Yi Sudŭksan's case shows. Yet the question the king raised as to why it is necessary to care about these people's morality echoes the elites' collective doubt about low-status people's capacity for moral cultivation and moral conduct—a view that eventually led to differential sanctions and punishments in Chosŏn law based on social status.

The crucial disparity between *yangban* and non-*yangban* that steadily emerged in the late Chosŏn codification and adjudication of sexual crimes also indicates an integral relationship between gender and social status: a woman's conduct served as a critical marker of her status identity. The state's increasing emphasis on each person's social status was certainly a product of reconfiguring the discourse of chastity in accord with the deepening of Confucian patriarchal structure, which subsequently solidified the lineage system and bolstered the *yangban* obsession with upholding their family positions in the community. This also meant that heightened chastity was demanded of *yangban* women, and that both a female victim's social status and her post-rape reaction were seriously considered in defining sexual crimes. The state's exaltation of extreme reactions particularly burdened *yangban* women as suicide became an approved and preeminent way for a woman to declare her moral integrity and clear the disgrace inflicted on her family.

Transgressing Marginality: Two Women Testifying

As scholars have noted, social hierarchy was an inescapable element in early modern legal culture, and "one's social class affected certain aspects of legal process directly."[119] Leslie Peirce, in her observation

---

118. *Ch'ugwanji,* 2:241.
119. Peirce, *Morality Tales,* 143.

of law and social class in the early modern Ottoman court, asserts that "the formulators and arbiters" of the legal discourse "considered themselves members of an elite."[120] The shifting discourse in late Chosŏn statutes on sexual crimes was, no doubt, a product of the hierarchical vision that was promoted by *yangban* interest in (and anxiety about) augmenting their privileges in the highly stratified Chosŏn society. Nevertheless, legal cases reveal that the boundaries of social status fluctuated and that people were aware of how to situate their position in their conflicts with others. As we have seen, a woman's verbal testimony as to how she had resisted sexual assault was the crucial factor in judging whether the crime committed had been adultery or rape—and also whether she was deemed the accused, the accuser, or the victim; moreover, a woman was often given the opportunity to voice her innocence. Confronting an environment in which she had to deal with unfavorable testimony from her male counterpart as well as from other witnesses—whether these were men or women, *yangban* or non-*yangban*—a woman could restore her moral integrity provided she could convince the investigator who was seeking to reconcile conflicting points, including prevailing gossip in the community, as the case below illustrates.

In the ninth month of 1796, a commoner man, Kim Such'ŏn of P'ungch'ŏn in Hwanghae Province, was found dead.[121] According to the man's mother, Ms. Kim, her son had lived in a rented room in the house of a *yangban* man, Ko Chonghan, where Ko's married sister, Madam Ko, also resided. Kim Such'ŏn and Madam Ko happened to like each other and had committed adultery.[122] When Ko Chonghan had become aware of their illicit relations, he had asked Kim Such'ŏn to leave the house. Kim Such'ŏn's mother Ms. Kim also stated that

120. Peirce, *Morality Tales*, 154.

121. *Pyŏgyŏng surok* 10:1b–18b.

122. The Ko family members indicated their social status as *yangban*. In the original text, however, the *yangban* Ko Chonghan's married sister is noted as *yangnyŏ* and is recorded with *choi*, the colloquial reading of *sosa*, which is the term referring mostly to a commoner woman and which I translate as "Ms." in this book. To differentiate the Ko family's social status from that of the Kim family, I instead use "Madam" to refer to Ko's married sister in this case.

Madam Ko had given her son things such as shoes and clothes, advising him to go away and stay far from the town until the rumor of their affair died down. Kim Such'ŏn therefore left for Kyŏngsŏng (Hanyang) in the middle of the seventh month and came back home after three weeks. Upon returning, he had confronted Ko Chonghan about his relations with Ko's sister Madam Ko, and Ko Chonghan thus informed the local *yangban* association (*yuhyangso*) of Kim's imprudent aggression. After being called to the local *yangban* office and hit with the light stick, Kim Such'ŏn had gotten drunk and returned home, and again had a big fight with Ko Chonghan. Shortly afterward, Kim suffered from severe pain and died. Ms. Kim argued that Ko Chonghan had endlessly persecuted her son to cover up the adulterous relations and that her son's death was entirely due to Ko Chonghan's threatening Kim Such'ŏn and even using the power of the local *yangban* association.[123]

The *yangban* Ko Chonghan testified that Kim Such'ŏn was a man with a bad temper who neglected his duties, such as farming, even though Ko generously provided Kim with a room to stay in. With a good heart, he had tried to chasten Kim several times, but Kim had defied him instead. Abiding by the law, Ko had reported Kim's behavior to the local *yangban* association, where Kim had received punishment the next day.[124] Nevertheless, Kim Such'ŏn had continued to fight Ko Chonghan. It had been while Ko was on his way to the local magistrate's office to formally accuse Kim of his unending violence that Kim had committed suicide. Ko Chonghan also completely denied Kim's mother's claim that his married sister had secretly fornicated with Kim. This was an unmentionable and utterly unjust accusation that she had fabricated. Even if his sister was an ignorant woman, she

123. *Pyŏgyŏng surok* 10:3a–4a; 10:6a–b; 10:10a–b.

124. The head of the local *yangban* association (*chwasu*) testified that they had decided to punish Kim Such'ŏn with thirteen blows with the light stick, and Ko Chonghan also stated the same. *Pyŏgyŏng surok* 10:7a; 10:12a. However, the exact number of blows Kim received is inconsistent in other people's testimonies. For example, Kim Such'ŏn's mother Ms. Kim, his sister, and his brother-in-law claimed that he received seventeen blows. *Pyŏgyŏng surok* 10:10ab; 10:14b. Some other members of the *yangban* association also stated seventeen blows. *Pyŏgyŏng surok* 10:11b.

was a *yangban* who could not even think of engaging in such immoral conduct with a commoner man.[125]

Ko Chonghan's assertion was backed up by the testimony of his accused sister, Madam Ko—a thirty-three-year-old woman who had been married for nine years.[126] She had returned to her natal home because of the extreme poverty of her husband's family. Though illiterate, she asserted that she was still the daughter of a *yangban* family (*p'umgwan chi nyŏ*) and the wife of a *yangban* man (*p'umgwan chi ch'ŏ*), whereas Kim Such'ŏn had been a brute of the lowest status. Given the status difference, she would never have covertly fostered illicit relations with him. If her brother Ko Chonghan had wished to conceal her illicit relations, he should have kicked her out of the house. She confessed that she had indeed offered Kim some clothes and shoes when he went on a trip. However, she argued that if she had felt any affection for Kim, she would have followed him when he left, not merely provided him with those things. The gossip about her adultery circulating in the town was due to her not garnering people's favor and sympathy, she testified. Reaching this point, Madam Ko lamented the difficulty of clearing the false charge against her, expressing no desire for life but only the wish to die soon.[127]

With no one having witnessed the moment Kim Such'ŏn died, it was difficult to clarify whether the case was homicide (as claimed by his mother) or suicide. His corpse carried injuries from beating, though it passed the silver-pin test for poisoning. The magistrate who conducted the first autopsy wrote in his postscript that "only heaven and the gods, not a human being, would know the real cause of Kim's death."[128] Nonetheless, the magistrate viewed the Ko brother and sister as the principal offenders in Kim Such'ŏn's death—Ko Chonghan for his consistent oppression of Kim to cover his married sister's immoral behavior, and Madam Ko for her lewd conduct, a crime as grave as that of her brother: both had driven Kim Such'ŏn to kill himself.[129]

125. *Pyŏgyŏng surok* 10:5ab; 10:6b.
126. *Pyŏgyŏng surok* 10:12b.
127. *Pyŏgyŏng surok* 10:5b–6a; 10:12b–13a.
128. *Pyŏgyŏng surok* 10:8b–9a.
129. Although the investigation required the testimony of a village head (*p'unghŏn*), the magistrate notes that he could not interrogate the head, who was actually the father

Despite the Ko brother and sister's consistent strong denials, townspeople testified to Madam Ko's adultery with Kim Such'ŏn, including Such'ŏn's own brother-in-law, who had shared a room with him.[130] A neighboring magistrate of Changyŏn was invited to conduct the second trial and postmortem, and he decided that the two women most closely involved in Kim Such'ŏn's death—the accused, Madam Ko (Chonghan's sister), and the accuser, Ms. Kim (Such'ŏn's mother)—should go through a cross-examination (*myŏnjil*) to sort out the truth of the adultery rumor. Facing each other, Ms. Kim asked the first question:

MS. KIM SAYS TO MADAM KO: "How come you argued for no adultery between you and my son?"

MADAM KO REPLIES TO MS. KIM: "How come you said I had fornicated with your son?"

MS. KIM SAYS AGAIN: "Now you deny your adulterous relations [with my son]. In the past year of the fourth month, you divided twelve *ch'ŏk* of white cloth dyed jade green and gave [it to my son Kim Such'ŏn] secretly, saying, 'I only wait for you to come back by praying and making offerings to the gods, as a way to cover words and traces.' Didn't you say that?"[131]

MADAM KO REPLIES TO MS. KIM: "How could you create such groundless stories? You are evil!"

MS. KIM ASKS AGAIN: "In the fifth month of this year, you provided [my son Kim Such'ŏn with] new wooden shoes and also gave [him] 6 copper *chŏn* to have [him] equip [himself] with leather shoes. If you were not having illicit relations, why did such events happen [i.e., why would you have offered him those things]?"

---

of the Ko brother and sister. According to the law, a father serving as a witness for a son violates the law. *Pyŏgyŏng surok* 10:9b. A village elder, Hong Yunbok, also testified that he had had to report Kim Such'ŏn's death to the magistrate's office because the village head, Ko Chonghan's father, did not want to do so, even though the village consensus (*tongjung kongŭi*) was that Kim Such'ŏn's death resulted from Ko Chonghan's reproach. *Pyŏgyŏng surok* 10:11b.

130. *Pyŏgyŏng surok* 10:14b.

131. *Ch'ŏk* is a unit of length. Several different *ch'ŏk* (rulers) were used during the Chosŏn dynasty, and the length of these different *ch'ŏk* varied from 20.8 to 46.7 centimeters.

MADAM KO REPLIES: "[I understand] your forlorn heart at your son's death. But why did you fabricate these imprecise stories and drive me to the point of death?"

MS. KIM STATES AGAIN: "My son's death was absolutely caused by your secret fornication. If I had caught you on the day my son died, I would have killed you. [But] you, seizing an opportunity first, hid yourself, so I could not avenge [his death on] you. How are you not my foe?"

MADAM KO REPLIES AGAIN: "Why did I have to flee [to conceal myself,] and why you are uttering absurd words?"[132]

Immediately following the confrontation between the two women, Madam Ko's brother, Ko Chonghan, was given a last chance to testify, in which he again proclaimed his sister's innocence. No such illicit relations would have been possible between a *yangban* woman and a man of lowly status, he stated, and Ms. Kim was only slandering the Ko siblings out of grief over the loss of her son.[133] Ko Chonghan's efforts came to naught, however. Madam Ko's responses to Ms. Kim did nothing to convince the second investigator during the cross-examination, who saw Madam Ko as illogical and babbling. Supporting the people's testimonies that "there was no one in the town who did not know about the secretive illicit relations between Such'ŏn and Madam Ko," he charged Madam Ko, as "a married woman with a husband, not only committing adultery but driving the adulterer to death."[134]

Unlike Chokkŭmaji and Ms. Ch'oe, described earlier, who succeeded in clearing their indictments through their testimonies, Madam Ko could not avoid being charged with having committed adultery. When given a venue to stand up against her accuser, Ms. Kim, and prove her integrity, Madam Ko failed to persuade the investigator. Both Madam Ko and her brother Ko Chonghan relied on the rhetoric of class difference—that is, on the notion that the daughter of a *yangban* family would never dream of having illicit relations with a man of lower status. Madam Ko's real situation was, however, quite far from the privileged lives of *yangban* women who remained secluded

132. *Pyŏgyŏng surok* 10:16a–b.
133. *Pyŏgyŏng surok* 10:16b.
134. *Pyŏgyŏng surok* 10:17a.

from the public. Though employing the elite discourse, she was a married woman whose husband's family was so poor that she had to return to her natal home. In the cross-examination, Madam Ko simply denied everything when faced with the powerful and concrete testimony of Ms. Kim. Despite her lower social standing, it was Ms. Kim—an ignorant, marginalized old woman at the bottom of society—who succeeded in challenging Madam Ko's strategy of insisting on a *yangban* woman's moral integrity.

The legal case of these two women reveals the complex landscape of gender and social status that interacted with the shifting norms of chastity, as well as with the legal boundaries of sexual crimes in late Chosŏn society. The social bias on moral superiority, articulated by the privileged, almost automatically gave the benefit of the doubt to *yangban* women such as Madam Ko, while non-*yangban* were considered less moral. But as such cases illustrate, the Chosŏn court was nonetheless receptive to a wide range of strategies and voices employed by people from all social backgrounds. Women regularly came before the local magistrate, taking on varied roles and demonstrating the ability to give sophisticated testament, as demonstrated in the cogent testimony of the commoner Ms. Kim, who seems perhaps to have fully understood the nature of hierarchy in the morality discourse and used it to carve out a place for her marginalized status at the court.

* * *

With the ideal of chastity established as the foremost female virtue, sexual crimes were considered a serious threat not only to Confucian morality but to the patriarchal system on which the state was founded and operated. The various sexual crimes and violent acts against female chastity examined in this chapter disclose the state's striking complexity and flexibility in handling judicial procedure. Although the Ming penal code remained instrumental throughout the Chosŏn dynasty, the state neither followed that code uncritically nor allowed itself to be bound by any single specific statute when adjudicating such cases. Taking all possible backgrounds into close legal consideration— from motivation for a crime to social status—the state constantly issued new edicts supplementing existing laws, compiling a Chosŏn version of criminal laws on sexual crimes that was aimed at achieving the state's moral vision and legal justice.

At the same time, the intricacy of each sexual crime required a thorough investigation of all parties involved, often leading to leniency in determining punishment while sorting out the contending testimonies that people gave to defend their respective positions. Throughout history, men and women alike have, of course, negotiated the application of law in different ways, depending on their social position or individual circumstances. In their testimonies, late Chosŏn women, too, expressed diverse responses to the challenges and conflicts they faced. In doing so, they used existing laws to defend their morality and innocence, since their *intention* when faced with sexual assault was what defined the nature of the crime.

The legal cases on sexual crimes presented in this chapter therefore complicate the linear picture of the limited choices that Chosŏn women were assumed to have, in terms of both their perception and their performance of the chastity ideal. Although theses legal cases signify a shared notion of female chastity for self-identity and social reputation, they also suggest that there was no unity about the practice of chastity or its implications for women's behavior. In light of the variety of scenarios divulged in these legal cases—scenarios interwoven with human emotions, compromises, and responses to society and social norms—it becomes clear that the choices of women of all statuses vis-à-vis how transgressions of a woman's sexual integrity were presented in court almost always entailed ongoing dialogues of negotiation among those involved in the crimes, their families and communities, and the state.

CHAPTER FIVE

Widows and Sexuality

In the ninth month of 1782, a commoner man named Ch'oe Kwang-yul ran across a *yangban* widow named Madam Cho on a street of Ŭisŏng, Kyŏngsang Province. Ch'oe touched Madam Cho's hand, whereupon Madam Cho, taking this as an outsider man's assault, cut the arm that Ch'oe had touched. Although Ch'oe admitted to briefly holding Madam Cho's hand during his subsequent testimony, he was sentenced to decapitation without delay (*pudae sich'am*)—the gravest punishment pertinent to the crime of forcible fornication with a wife or daughter of a *yangban* as codified in the 1746 *Continuation of the Great Code*.[1] Shortly afterward, the government honored Madam Cho for her pledge to protect her chastity.[2]

Reading this case, one's mind turns to at least three questions: Might the widow's cutting her own arm have been an overreaction to what Ch'oe had done? Was holding a widow's hand tantamount to the crime of coercive fornication, putting Ch'oe at risk of immediate

1. *Sok taejŏn*, 309. The punishment of decapitation without delay was not bound by a timeline. Whereas capital punishment was normally conducted after the autumnal equinox, those who committed the most heinous crimes could be decapitated any time under the rule of *pudae sich'am*.

2. *Simnirok* 9:15b–16a. Like many other cases included in the *Simnirok*, or *Records of Royal Reviews*, Madam Cho's case starts with a series of abbreviated reports from the provincial governor followed by verdicts of the Ministry of Punishment, without providing detailed trial testimonies.

beheading? And lastly, what was the legal reasoning behind the harsh verdict? The provincial governor's report on this incident notes that "the lowly commoner tried to violate the descendant of a *yangban*." This implies that Choe's crime was seen as much graver than a man's usual sexual assault because of his transgression of class boundaries: Ch'oe, a non-*yangban* man, had dared to covet Madam Cho, a *yangban* widow. More importantly, Ch'oe's attempt was met by Madam Cho's violent response of harming her own body. The ways women reacted to sexual assaults ultimately factored into the course of judicial decisions, as examined in chapter 4, including the degree of punishment in the final verdict. Madam Cho's rather extreme bodily self-harming was taken as a clear expression of her commitment to upholding her widow fidelity. The heavy punishment Ch'oe received therefore affirmed the state's stiff attitude toward the social hierarchy and moral expectations—two pivotal dimensions of maintaining the social order that served as the fundamental law and backbone of Chosŏn Korea.

At the same time, this brief legal case captures many facets of the status of widows in Chosŏn society. On the surface, Madam Cho's dramatic reaction can be understood as indicator of women's deepening internalization of the chastity ideal by the eighteenth century—the fruit of the state's unwavering moralization campaign, embarked upon from the very beginning of the dynasty. Official documents such as the *Sillok* contain similar incidents, and we have also seen them in many biographical records of chaste women written by male literati.[3] For example, Madam Chŏng, a wife of Sŏ Munbae, a Confucian scholar residing in Changsu, Chŏlla Province, cut her arm after an outside assailant twisted it while trying to violate her; upon receiving a report on her case, King Yŏngjo ordered that her act be honored. Her story was also circulated widely beyond her own town, to such an extent that Sin Sui (1688–1768), a scholar-official based in

---

3. The scholar Im Hŏnhoe (1811–1876), who drafted a number of records on chaste women, includes an account akin to Madam Cho's—the story of a widow cutting her arm with an ax after being touched by an outside man, then hanging herself. Im Hŏnhoe, "Yi yŏlbu chŏngnyŏgi," *Kosan chip*, 9:29b–31a.

Kyŏngsang Province, composed a biography in Madam Chŏng's honor.[4] Nor was it only *yangban* widows who had extreme responses to various challenges to their vulnerability, as revealed in the case of the commoner widow Ms. O. Faced with her mother-in-law's intention to remarry her, Ms. O rushed to her husband's tomb carrying her baby on her back. Wailing bitterly, she blamed her husband for putting her in a shameful situation by dying early, then ended her life by taking poison. The government recognized Madam Chŏng's and Ms. O's acts of widow fidelity on the same day in 1782.[5]

In the countless tales of chaste women, widows are the female subjects covered most frequently, both in official and local histories and in the biographical accounts written by literati. Despite the conventional view that widows maintained secluded lives, they in fact enjoyed public acclamation in Chosŏn society, as long as they proved to be heroines of marital fidelity. To be clear, as perhaps in other patriarchal societies, loss of a spouse in premodern Korea was presented mostly as a female experience, even though it happened to men as well.[6] The wide circulation of the compound term "chaste widows" (*sujŏl kwabu*) indicates that widows in Korean history were branded with the idea of *sujŏl* (literally, "keeping one's chastity"), or chastity.[7] Today, Koreans use the term *sujŏl* almost interchangeably with the term

4. *Yŏngjo sillok* 102:11b–12a [1763/8/1]. Sin Sui, "Yŏlbu yuin sŏsan Chŏngssi chŏn," *Hwanggo chip*, 6:14b–15a.

5. *Yŏngjo sillok* 102:11b–12a [1763/8/1].

6. There are scarcely any records dedicated to widowers in Chosŏn society. On the terminology of "widower," which derives from the female term "widow," see Cavallo and Warner, *Widowhood in Medieval and Early Modern Europe*, 4–5.

7. Another term frequently used to refer to a widow is *mimangin* (Ch. *wei wang ren*), or "a person who has not yet died." Originating from the ancient Chinese narrative history the *Zuo Tradition* (*Zuo zhuan*), *mimangin* means "'soon-to-perish-widow,' a way for a widow to refer to herself." Durrant, Li, and Schaberg, *Zuo Tradition / Zuozhuan*, 212. Although *mimangin* indicates a wife who regrets remaining alive after her husband's death, it has been generally misused as simply another term for widows in contemporary South Korean society. In 2017, the National Institute of the Korean Language corrected its usage, urging that *mimangin* be employed exclusively by widows themselves, not by others. My quick search of the *Sillok* reveals that *mimangin* referred predominantly to widowed queens or queen dowagers during the Chosŏn dynasty, except for a few cases denoting the way of a widow 未亡人之義 or the status of a widow

kwabu (widow), even though, in a strict sense, it is difficult to assume that every widow who does not remarry remains chaste. Also, upholding chastity can actually be said of any wife who maintains absolute sexual loyalty to her husband (even if she dies earlier than he does). Nevertheless, the notion that chastity is exclusively relevant to widows signifies the general attitude toward chaste widowhood and the ideas about widow sexuality within a society. As discussed in chapter 2, even though moral, familial, and socioeconomic concerns motivated the state's discouragement of widow remarriage, the core goal implanted in the remarriage provision was regulation of widow sexuality. Just as stories of chaste widows such as Madam Cho and Ms. O reflect the state's edifying efforts, so they also reveal another side of the social perception of widowhood—namely, the assumption that widows, regardless of social status, were still sexual beings.

Women's lived experiences as widows in fact encompassed both moral conventions and the discrepancies found in the real world. Although the state ardently promoted widow chastity and urged women to sustain it, institutions such as the state-reward policy served more as a motive for widows to be celibate than as a fundamental way to protect widows of all different socio-economic-familial backgrounds. Non-elite widows in particular often had to venture beyond the cloistered inner quarters where they were supposed to stay; forced to do so in order to eke out a living in public life, they then became subject to extended contact with male outsiders. The position of a widow caught between the ideal of a long, chaste widowhood and the socioeconomic reality of having no husband was therefore extremely precarious. Her options were limited: remarriage or virtuous widowhood. Choosing the former would stigmatize her as a woman of lost sexual integrity and affect the reputation of her family, yet the latter did not guarantee her a life free of vulnerability. A widow with some economic independence often found herself not only a target of sexual transgression but a source of conflict for family members and neighbors. As the literatus Pak Chiwŏn saw it in his biography of the widow Madam Pak, "In the minds of chaste women who were widowed at a young age, it is

---

未亡人之身. For the former example, see *Sŏngjong sillok* 33:18b [1473/8/25]; for the latter, *Yŏnsan'gun ilgi* 28:31b [1497/12/12].

preferable to think of dying sooner rather than remaining alive for a long time, so as to avoid groundless speculation by others."[8]

Pak's view resonates with the range of sexual offenses against widows explicated in numerous legal cases, where they appear as victims of sexual and verbal threats that could be as direct as rape or as indirect as gossip. Rumors (which had a long history of prompting legal cases on various disputes) functioned as a powerful weapon for attacking a widow's sexual integrity. As an eighteenth-century local magistrate notes, "In general, the slander about a young widow who lives alone is [always] that she makes eyes at a man while leaning against the door [of the house]"—a comment that profoundly illuminates the intricate linkage between rumors and widowhood, as well as the general perception about widow sexuality in society.[9]

Bringing widows to the center of the discussion, this chapter continues to explore the dynamic relationship between chastity discourse and actual practice in Chosŏn society. In particular, it focuses on legal cases involving widow sexuality—cases that complicate Chosŏn society's drastically divided yet stereotyped representation of widows as either virtuous or promiscuous. Records of the lives of widows *not* recognized for their chastity are scarce; the only time a widow's voice carried weight was when she made a decision about remarriage that could directly influence the future of her sons. The provision that rendered sons of remarried women ineligible for official positions mainly affected widows of elite families, leaving the lives of the larger number of non-elite children intact. It is thus hardly surprising that the bulk of existing studies on widows during the Chosŏn dynasty have been examined under the framework of the institution of remarriage—or as a mere reflection of the moral models whereby a widow was characterized in prescriptive literature and literati writings.[10]

8. Pak Chiwŏn, "Yŏllyŏ Hamyang Pakssi chŏn," 1:32b–34b.

9. *Osan munch'ŏp*, 444.

10. Although a comprehensive study of widowhood is almost absent in the historiography of the Chosŏn dynasty, some recent studies have shed alternative light on widows by analyzing late Chosŏn household registers. These include Ji Young Jung, "Questions Concerning Widow's Social Status," 109–38; Chŏng Chiyŏng, *Chilsŏ ŭi kuch'uk kwa kyunyŏl*; and Kim Kyŏngnan, "Tansŏng hojŏk e nat'anan yŏsŏng," 94–119. For a study of a widow and honor based on a legal case, see Jungwon Kim, "'You

In contrast, I provide close analyses centered on several legal testimonies featuring widows. Indeed, women's sexuality, especially
widow sexuality, was thrust into the moral discourse in Chosŏn society. Investigating the very experiences of ordinary, non-elite widows
of diverse backgrounds (in terms of age, social status, economic situation) in particular, and the ways they related to both moral conventions and discrepancies in the real world, this chapter offers a social
history of gender relations from below—one that demonstrates not
only how social expectations shaped a widow's options and actions in
gendered ways, but also how widows negotiated the ideals and perceptions associated with their conditions.

Widow Kidnapping and Widow Sexuality

In the seventh month of 1738, a violent attempt to kidnap a widow
named Yŏngdae was reported by her natal mother, Ms. Kim, to the
local magistrate's office in Imch'ŏn, Ch'ungch'ŏng Province.[11] Known
as a beautiful young widow, Yŏngdae was the daughter of a commoner
man named O Kyet'ak. After her husband's unfortunate death, she
continued to reside in her in-law parents' house with her widowed
father-in-law, Kim Ch'ŏnsŏk. A male slave named Pang Chisang had
participated in the kidnapping attempt by hiding along with the horse
that was to carry Yŏngdae away. According to Pang's testimony, it was
a *yangban* widower, Yi Sehak, who made the detailed plans, although
Yi himself did not join in the actual attempt.[12] Moreover, this was not
Yi's first attempt to kidnap Yŏngdae: three months earlier, in the
fourth month of the same year, a group of men had entered Yŏngdae's

---

Must Avenge.'" And Sungyun Lim's recent study, *Rules of the House*, is devoted to
widows in colonial Korea.

    11. *Karim poch'o*, 512–24. Comprising two volumes, *Karim poch'o* covers roughly
three years, from the seventh month of 1738 to the sixth month of 1740. For this case,
I used a reprinted copy included in vol. 3 of *Han'guk chibangsa charyo cho'ongsŏ*.
Trials of this particular case lasted about three months, from the twenty-second day
of the seventh month to the twentieth day of the tenth month in 1738. Page references
are to the modern edition.

    12. *Karim poch'o*, 512–13.

house to abduct her, but had failed because townspeople kicked them out. Yi Sehak had put a second attempt in motion with the help of other men, but it had also failed, while seriously injuring Yŏngdae's father-in-law, Kim Ch'ŏnsŏk, who was stabbed and beaten while blocking the abduction of his widowed daughter-in-law.[13]

Yi Sehak was thus brought to the local magistrate's office. The forty-eight-year-old *yangban* widower, though acknowledging his involvement in the first attempt, denied that he was the main actor behind the second action. Yi testified that he had sent people to the widow Yŏngdae's home after hearing about her intention to remarry, but they had been met with her father-in-law's armed challenge. Yi stated that an illegitimate son named Pak Ch'wisang had later approached him and learned about the incident. Pak had then secretly plotted to kidnap Yŏngdae despite Yi's dissuasion. Yi insisted that Pak had carried out the second attempt alone, against Yi's will.[14]

Though Yi Sehak claimed his noninvolvement in the second event, the local magistrate assumed that he was behind both incidents. Listening to Yi, the magistrate became suspicious because he noticed that in the first kidnapping trial Yi portrayed the initial incident as having been prompted by the rumor of a formal marriage proposal to Yŏngdae, yet he had laid the blame for the second incident on Pak Ch'wisang. Thus, though acknowledging his misbehavior as a *yangban* man, Yi had maintained that Pak committed the second kidnapping by himself, repudiating his own connection with it.[15] Because of his consistent denials, Yi was subjected to a series of beatings with a heavy stick. He eventually confessed to being the principal criminal in both incidents and was sentenced to exile.[16]

13. *Karim poch'o*, 513–14.
14. *Karim poch'o*, 514–16.
15. *Karim poch'o*, 516–17.
16. According to the magistrate's report, Yi Sehak's trial was suspended because of his serious illness, caused by heavy torture, and resumed on the tenth day of the ninth month. Although the magistrate suggested concluding the trial on the excuse of the bitter cold and congestion in jail, the provincial governor, tackling Yi's ambiguous rhetoric in his testimonies, ordered that Yi's trial recommence. *Karim poch'o*, 519–23.

"Widow kidnapping"—the crime with which Yi Sehak was charged—was not an unfamiliar or infrequent act during the Chosŏn dynasty, though the state never authorized the practice. In a society that viewed a widow's remarriage negatively, widow kidnapping was an unofficial, clandestine yet acceptable way for widows to remarry. Often arbitrated between the widow's family and the man who wished to marry her, kidnapping was usually carried out not by the kidnapper alone but with support from other men, as in Yi Sehak's case. As described in earlier chapters, although the Chosŏn statute prohibiting remarriage was never formally codified, a widow's remarriage greatly affected the future standing and economic well-being of *yangban* families, whose social status was sustained primarily by producing officials who had passed the civil service examination. Pitying the fate of a young widow who had not yet borne a child, family members sometimes overlooked her remarrying as long as it would not hurt the family's position in the community, and they used kidnapping to accomplish this. The practice of widow kidnapping thus began as a way to avoid ruining the reputations of both the family of her late husband and her natal family and as a variation on young widows' remarrying secretly. Serving as a kind of tacit acknowledgment of widow remarriage, widow kidnapping involved "negotiation" between the interests of the widow's family and those of the kidnapper (the potential new husband).

Yangban widowers such as Yi Sehak did not simply aim for a one-time illicit affair with a widow and employed kidnapping to devise a quasi-marital relation with her. Ordinary men then emulated widow kidnapping as a practical method for obtaining widows they desired. For non-elites, remarriage did not carry the stigma of their sons' disqualification for officialdom (since these sons, like the illegitimate sons of *yangban* fathers, had no right to take the civil service examination); thus widow kidnapping became a functional way to settle a widow's remarriage among commoners by the late Chosŏn. In addition, the social status of both the widow and the kidnapper mattered in achieving the goal of kidnapping. In the case of Yŏngdae, the *yangban* widower Yi Sehak seems never to have negotiated or made arrangements with her natal and in-law families before taking action. Given his *yangban* status, he may have thought that kidnapping a commoner widow would be easy. Yet Yi encountered unexpected resistance from Yŏngdae's side, and the local magistrate noted in his postscript that, as a *yangban* scholar (*saja*), Yi was subject to receive heavier punishment than non-*yangban* offenders. The provincial governor, in his reply to the magistrate's report, also stresses this point that Yi had failed to meet his moral duty as a *yangban*, despite the fact that kidnapping widows had become a chronic evil custom of the province (*pondo p'yesŭp*).[17]

In light of the way the *yangban* Yi Sehak tried to kidnap a commoner widow, it appears that widow kidnapping was not something shameful but an informal way to accomplish widow remarriage in a society that cherished widow chastity and despised remarriage. Because this practice took the form of "kidnapping," some degree of coercion was unavoidable, often generating various forms of violence—from physical collisions to unexpected death. Conflicts did erupt when different interests clashed, when the widow daringly resisted being kidnapped, or when the offenders overused coercion and neglected negotiation. Conflicts among the men who joined a kidnapping plot were not uncommon, as seen in Yŏngdae's case. The 1780 homicide case of a widower named Ko Chibang was one of many such incidents resulting in a death. Ko was accused of killing his assistant Ch'oe Wŏnse, who had aided Ko in a kidnapping attempt but was blamed by Ko when it failed.[18] Conflicts could also emerge while negotiating the *kwabujŏn*, the money required to formally settle a remarriage among the widow's natal family, a go-between, and the widow's future

17. The provincial governor wrote: "[Yi] Sehak cannot avoid graver penalization because he is different from those of lower class." Just as Yi Sehak was about to go into exile, his eighty-year-old father petitioned for his son's release in consideration of his father's old age. Since a legal statute allowed a criminal son to be freed, in exchange for bail, to serve aging parents, the provincial governor approved this, and Yi Sehak was released. *Karim poch'o*, 523–24.

18. *Ilsŏngnok* 94:145 [1780/12/23]; *Simnirok* 4:157b–160b. Because there was another man who joined this kidnapping and ended up killing Ch'oe, it took about ten years to determine the principal offender and finalize the investigation of Ko's homicide. *Ilsŏngnok* 152:139–41 [1784/5/29]; 330:113–14 [1790/2/15]. The 1795 death case of Kim Chŏnguk is one of many such incidents in which the victim in widow-kidnapping turned out to be someone unrelated to it. Kim was beaten to death by his neighbor, Yi Kyŏngwŏn, who had been fighting with Kim's son, Kim Ponghae, over a widow named Ms. Sin who lived in the town. *Pyŏgyŏng surok* 7:1–32b.

husband. It was the widow's family that covered the expenses of a man taking the widow as his wife (or the fee to the go-between for efforts to find a suitable match), and this was a heavy burden for poor families with widowed daughters. Clashes also erupted when there were misunderstandings among the different parties or when the offenders used force and neglected negotiation.[19]

A later court meeting reveals that widow kidnapping had become rampant in late Chosŏn society and that the state had to deal with constant crime. On the tenth day of the first month in 1805, Minister of Punishment Yi Myŏn'gŭng (1753–1812) made a report to King Sunjo during the morning meeting as follows:

Our country has been referred to as a state of propriety. A proper ritual is required for weddings, even among the ordinary populace. In recent days, however, if there are widows remaining chaste in local towns, vicious men join with hooligans and, taking advantage of the dark of night, attempt rape, then bind and kidnap the widow [thus making her a wife]—this is called *pakch'wi*. It is beyond description how this ultimately disturbs custom and disorders morality. Sometimes it leads to homicide cases, and even goes so far as to affect *yangban* [widows]. Those ignorant people take it as a normal [practice] since there is no law barring it by the government. Indeed, what a pity it is that it has become worse than ever! Thieves climbing over the wall are punished under the robbery law—how much more so for those forming a band, violating [widows], and taking materials. Are [the widow kidnappers] different from robbers holding torches? Without heavy disciplinary measures, the harmful consequences will continue and will be indescribable.[20]

19. The homicide of a man named Kim Ch'angsŏng is a case in point. In his role as a matchmaker, a neighbor man named Chang Ŭngsam asked for 400 *yang* to arrange the remarriage of Kim's widowed daughter. Kim offered 300 *yang* instead, saying 400 was too much. However, Chang happened to overhear a conversation between his wife and Kim's wife, in which he learned that Kim had gathered 400 *yang* but kept 100 *yang* for his own use. A fight broke out between Chang and Kim, and Kim was stabbed by Chang's dagger. "Sŏhŭng-gun yuli-bang ch'angdae-dong."

20. *Sugyo tŭngnok, kon* (vol. 2), 84–86. Also found in *Sugyo chŏngnye*, 87; *Ilsŏng-nok* 130:85–86 [1805/1/10]; *Sŭngjŏngwŏn ilgi* 1889:38a–40b [1805/1/10].

In describing the widow kidnapping practice, the report uses the term *pakch'wi* 縛娶—a compound of the character *pak* 縛 (meaning "binding [a widow] up") and the character *ch'wi* 娶 ("marrying [her]"). The practice was commonly known in colloquial Korea as *possam* ("wrap in a cloth"), and *pakch'wi* does not appear in any document prior to this 1805 report. Though its origin is untraceable, its existence around this time encapsulates the way widow kidnapping had become firmly connected to a road to an informal marriage. As Minister of Punishment Yi Myŏn'gŭng pinpointed, widow kidnapping had long been an unsanctioned practice employed by ordinary people, and there was no law effective in controlling it. In the absence of legal enforcement, Yi proposed applying the statute on regulating thieves (*ch'idoyul*) to the crime of widow kidnapping, by which the kidnappers could be arrested and taken to provincial governors' offices.[21] This would apply to any and all participants in the course of widow kidnapping so that no one would dare assist in the crime. The king accepted Yi's proposal, and a formal royal edict soon declared that the state would "punish those who attempted widow kidnapping under the statute on regulating thieves."[22]

The existing statute on thieves that was used to punish cases of widow kidnapping, instead of creating new legislation, was consistent with the sub-statute (examined in chapter 4) added to the "Theft" section in the *Continuation of the Great Code*: "a man coercively violating a woman is to be treated and punished like someone plundering the marketplace during the daytime."[23] This implies that widow kidnapping was handled almost on the level of forcible fornication—the crime that was conceptualized as the theft of female sexual integrity. To put it the other way around, regulating widow kidnapping under the theft statute confirms the normative expectation imposed on all widows in society—namely, that they uphold their sexual integrity. It is, however, difficult to track how successful the regulation was in monitoring widow kidnapping, which seems to have persisted as a chronic problem to the end of the dynasty. Reports of house break-ins

21. *Sugyo tŭngnok, kon* (vol. 2), 84–86.
22. *Sugyo tŭngnok, kon* (vol. 2), 84–86.
23. *Sok taejŏn*, 285.

to abduct widows did not cease, and numerous deaths resulted from widow kidnapping. Yŏngdae's case in fact reveals that Yi Sehak was not the first man to try to kidnap her. According to the magistrate's reports, a number of *yangban* and non-*yangban* men in the town had targeted the beautiful young widow over the preceding five years—among them, at least ten men who had been punished, either by beating or exile.[24]

Indeed, such conflicts over a widow among male townsmen hint at Chosŏn society's collective perception of a widow's identity and status in local communities. In 1793, when a commoner bachelor named Kim Sunt'ae testified about beating to death a widow named Ms. Han, he confessed that it was the widow's aunt who had suggested that he kidnap Ms. Han, telling Kim: "While I myself cannot decoy her, you may secretly kidnap her in the dark of night if you wish to live with her."[25] Kim was a twenty-two-year-old single man who had been desperately looking for a wife. Knowing that the young widow Ms. Han was staying with her parents, he discussed his situation with her aunt and uncle. It was also Ms. Han's own aunt who informed Kim about the best time to act—when the widow's parents would be out of town. Taking the aunt's words as implicit permission, Kim kidnapped Ms. Han with the help of his father, siblings, and other male relatives. The kidnapping case was brought to the court only because she was eventually beaten to death while resisting Kim. It is noteworthy that male and female family members of both the widow and the kidnapper worked together, tacitly accepting abduction as a way to match a young widow and a bachelor. But none of them cared about the widow Ms. Han's wishes, so it was her resistance to the death that showed that the kidnapping was completely against her will. Even though ideal widowhood was deeply rooted in the notion of chastity in Chosŏn society, the clandestine yet popular practice of widow kidnapping powerfully illustrates that widows in the real world were viewed more as subjects of sexuality than as subjects of morality (fig. 5.1).

24. *Karim poch'o*, 793–94.
25. *Ilsŏngnok*, 461:179–81 [1794/5/26].

5.1. The woman's white mourning attire indicates that she is a widow. Although flowers bloom outside the wall, there is no sign of spring in the courtyard where she sits. In showing her looking at two dogs copulating, the widow's sexual desire is indirectly expressed. *A Widow Enjoying the Springtime* (*Ibu t'amch'un*), by Sin Yunbok (1758–?). Album leaf; ink and color on paper. 28.2 × 35.6 cm. Photograph courtesy of Kansong Art Museum, Seoul.

From a Chaste Widow to a Licentious Woman

Widows' vulnerability to sexual violence is evident in the countless widow-kidnapping events reported in official records. As soon as a husband died, his widow's position became ambiguous within her husband's family (especially for a sonless widow), and also a potential source of scandal in the community. In the seventh month of 1739, a year after Yi Sehak's second attempted kidnapping of the beautiful young widow Yŏngdae, the entire Imch'ŏn region was upset again, this time by rumors of Yŏngdae's shocking affair with her father-in-law, the widower Kim Ch'ŏnsŏk. Reports from the heads of two subdistricts reached the magistrate's office on the same day. A head of Chigok sub-district, in which Yŏngdae's natal home was located, wrote:

> A daughter of O Kyet'ak residing in this subdistrict is the [widowed] daughter-in-law of Kim Ch'ŏnsŏk of Sŏbyŏn subdistrict. Losing her husband at an early age, Yŏngdae remained as a widow, keeping her fidelity, and there was no one who did not praise her chastity. Then, word of Yŏngdae having licentious relations with her [widowed] father-in-law and becoming pregnant was widespread among the townspeople. This is why [I] contact your office. Bring both Kim and Yŏngdae to the court and investigate.[26]

A head of Sŏbyŏn subdistrict, where Yŏngdae lived with her father-in-law, reported:

> Kim Ch'ŏnsŏk's daughter-in-law, Yŏngdae, has lived as a widow for many years. Though never having remarried, she has become pregnant and is [now] parturient. People have been suspicious as to why she was not sent back to her natal home but has remained hidden in the house [of her father-in-law]. [Moreover,] talk is prevalent that what Kim Ch'ŏnsŏk has done deserves a thousandfold beheading and ten-thousandfold ripping [apart of his body]. This evening a stranger from the western direction even appeared, calling himself the husband of Yŏngdae. Another man showed up all of a sudden, insisting that he had made her pregnant. [Their claims] are all groundless. Arrest all of them and punish them according to the law.[27]

Needless to say, a widow becoming pregnant was beyond scandalous in a society where a woman's sexual loyalty to her husband—whether alive or dead—was the utmost norm. Yŏngdae's pregnancy was astounding not only because she was known for her formidable fidelity when faced with a series of kidnapping attempts, but because her partner in adultery was alleged to be her father-in-law, Kim Ch'ŏnsŏk. Adultery was an intolerable sin for a married woman, and

26. *Karim poch'o*, 792.
27. *Karim poch'o*, 792–93.

if a widowed daughter-in-law was found to be pregnant, her in-law family had the right to kick her out on the spot.[28] Yŏngdae's father-in-law, in contrast, continued to cherish her and keep her close in his house. Townspeople therefore speculated that Kim might have fathered her child.

The upsetting rumors described in the two reports brought everyone involved to the magistrate's office for investigation. The magistrate was aware of the multiple attempts to kidnap Yŏngdae in past years, which had resulted in many men receiving severe punishments. This meant that there might well be people who resented Kim Ch'ŏnsŏk's response to the kidnappings and intentionally spread rumors that he had engaged in illicit relations with his widowed daughter in law Yŏngdae. The magistrate was also careful to investigate whether the heads of the two villages had been intimidated by townspeople into making the reports.[29]

At the trial, crowds of bystanders hoping to see Kim Ch'ŏnsŏk and Yŏngdae almost formed a wall surrounding the local magistrate's office. During the testimony, Yŏngdae stated that she had become pregnant after marrying a man named Kim Sunsam. In fact, her father-in-law Kim Ch'ŏnsŏk, upon hearing rumors that Yŏngdae was pregnant, had hurriedly arranged for her to marry Kim Sunsam to conceal his own adulterous relations with her. When the false charge against Kim Sunsam was cleared, Yŏngdae named another man, Kim Mongi, as having forced sexual relations upon her, which had led to her pregnancy. This new claim was also revealed to be false, and it was discovered that her father-in-law, Kim Ch'ŏnsŏk, had tried to buy both these men to exonerate himself. To make matters worse, Yŏngdae had an abortion during her imprisonment. The magistrate assumed that Yŏngdae had deliberately aborted the baby herself, collaborating with her rich mother, who must have bribed the jailers and managed to bury the aborted baby in secret.[30]

---

28. Adultery falls into the category of the Seven Disobediences (ch'ilgŏ) for which a wife could be disowned. The others were being talkative, having an incurable illness, displaying jealousy toward her husband's concubines, not producing a male hair, disobeying her parents-in-law, and stealing.

29. Karim poch'o, 794.

30. Karim poch'o, 794–96.

According to the law, punishment for adultery was to be carried
out immediately. When the accused woman was pregnant, however,
the punishment was to be postponed until after delivery. Also, she was
not to be tortured for confession within a hundred days of childbirth.[31]
Taking the incident to be extremely grave, the magistrate wanted to
push for Yŏngdae's testimony, but the provincial governor ordered that
he wait until she had recovered from childbirth, as prescribed in the
law.[32] In the meantime, Kim Ch'ŏnsŏk underwent severe torture because he continued to deny committing adultery with his widowed
daughter-in-law. After eight months of harsh torture, Kim was on the
brink of dying of malaria on the nineteenth day of the third month in
1740.[33] He died in jail later that day, and a postmortem confirmed
that his death was a result of malaria.[34] Despite undergoing prolonged
trial and torture, Kim Ch'ŏnsŏk died without admitting guilt. The
magistrate decided to continue the testimony of Yŏngdae, but she, too,
contracted malaria and died in jail, in the sixth month of 1740, about
three months after Kim's death.[35] This bizarre case had begun with
attempted kidnappings, proceeded to rumors about illicit relations
between a beautiful young widow and her widowed father-in-law, and
ended with the deaths of the two accused, yet without unwrapping the
truth: neither Yŏngdae nor Kim ever confessed before meeting death.

   In his concluding report to the provincial governor, the magistrate
designates Yŏngdae as the criminal who violated moral principle
(yun'gi), not merely for losing her widow fidelity but for having illicit
relations with her own father-in-law, whereas he identifies Kim
Ch'ŏnsŏk simply as a criminal in a postmortem report on Kim's
death.[36] This case of a young widow, once acclaimed for her chastity
in the region, who eventually became tainted as the most promiscuous

31. *Taejŏn hoet'ong* 5:44a.
32. *Karim poch'o*, 804–5.
33. *Karim poch'o*, 829–30.
34. Though the inquest report states the true cause of Kim Ch'ŏnsŏk's death as
illness, the punitive torture would have contributed to his deteriorating health. The
report states that Kim's right and left shins were heavily injured, with all the bones
exposed. *Karim poch'o*, 830–32.
35. *Karim poch'o*, 842.
36. *Karim poch'o*, 843–44.

of women, typifies the position of widows caught between ideal and reality and how they were susceptible to every conceivable sexual challenge.

What is more illuminating in Yŏngdae's case is the complex matrix of a widow's economic and social status. Because Yŏngdae was a commoner, not only *yangban* widowers such as Yi Sehak but many non-elite men assumed that they could easily take her via kidnapping, as was widely practiced in the society. It seems, however, that both Yŏngdae's natal family and her husband's family were wealthy enough to block such attempts.[37] As a young, rich widow under familial protection, she could still afford her (chaste) widowhood without being compelled to remarry or to engage in economic activities outside the household, as other non-*yangban* widows often had to. Yŏngdae's case therefore complicates the convenient logic about a widow's social status and economic standing. It reveals how critically a widow's economic capacity, regardless of her social class, served as a viable option in sustaining ideal widowhood as she wished.

Widows between Morality and Survival

Yŏngdae's legal case attests in multiple ways to the close linkages between widow sexuality, social status, and economic standing. As seen in the prolonged debates over the abolishment/restoration of the widow lands program (discussed in chapter 2), the Chosŏn state considered widowhood to be a vital point of intersection between property relations and sexual relations. The widow lands program targeted primarily *yangban* widows. With the permanent abolition of the lands program in the fifteenth century and women's gradual loss of inheritance rights in the second half of the dynasty, *yangban* widows encountered increasing hardship in managing their widowhood if they did not have financial support from their families. Moreover, the familial provision securing a *yangban* widow's position depended completely on

37. *Karim poch'o*, 514, 793. Testimonies of people involved in Yŏngdae's kidnapping incident stated that both her natal family and her husband's family were rich.

her chastity, a status that could be damaged by either entering remarriage or having illicit sexual relations.

For non-elite widows without economic means, choices were even more limited. There were some exceptions, like the rich commoner widow Yŏngdae, but most non-*yangban* widows were impoverished and thus were forced to face the reality of unfavorable economic conditions. Sources show that the government was concerned about many widows—both *yangban* and non-*yangban*—lacking financial means. Outlining relief plans for regions hit by a lean year in 1793, King Chŏngjo noted that the names of widows in insolvent *yangban* families were often missing from the relief lists because, out of shame (as *yangban*), they did not want to make their names known.[38] The king also directed local offices to help destitute non-elite widows before they starved to death. While widow chastity served as a status symbol for the elite and as a celebrated act for the non-elite, the same discourse did not always work for poor, ordinary widows whose lives were much more exposed to, and shaped by, the connection between sex and economic condition, as detailed in the case of the widow Ms. Kim, described below.

In the eighth month of 1795, a woman's death was reported to a local office of Paekch'ŏn and Yŏnan counties of Hwanghae Province.[39] The dead woman was a fifty-one- or fifty-two-year-old widow named Ms. Kim who ran a tavern in the marketplace (fig. 5.2). Her forty-two-year-old foster son, Wŏn Chaehan, charged a *yangban* named Yi Pongjin with beating his foster mother to death. According to Wŏn, Ms. Kim had been a widow for about five years, since the fourth month of 1791. Within a month of being widowed, she had begun relations with Yi, who was sixteen years her junior. Although Ms. Kim and Yi did not live in the same house, Yi came in and out of the widow's tavern frequently, treating her as his concubine. Yet Yi stopped visiting her place after Ms. Kim unreasonably insulted Yi's parents in front of people. Wŏn testified that, lamenting Yi's absence, Ms. Kim told him: "I have no children and no place to rely on, so there is no reason I

---

38. *Chŏngjo sillok* 37:14a [1793/2/20].
39. *Pyŏgyŏng surok* 8:1b–21b.

5.2. Painting of a woman running a tavern in a marketplace. *Having a Drinking Party and Holding a Cup* (*Chusa kŏbae*), by Sin Yunbok. Album leaf; ink and color on paper. 28.2 × 35.6 cm. Photograph courtesy of Kansong Art Museum, Seoul.

cannot marry another man."[40] Finding it difficult to manage the tavern without a man, Ms. Kim met a *yangban* widower, Kang Sehyo, through Kang's nephew, and they spent two nights together. However, Yi Pongjin soon discovered the affair. Furious, he ran into Ms. Kim's place and dragged her around by her hair while kicking her mercilessly. Ms. Kim was rescued by her foster son Wŏn and his wife, Ms. Chŏn, but she died a few days later, uttering only, "I am dying because Yi Pongjin beat me. Please take revenge [on] him for me."[41]

Ms. Kim's family members indicated Yi Pongjin as the principal offender who killed her by beating, but Yi denied such a claim. In his

40. *Pyŏgyŏng surok* 8:13a–13b.
41. *Pyŏgyŏng surok* 8:10a.

testimony, Yi asserted that Ms. Chŏn, the (foster) daughter-in-law of Ms. Kim, had clearly mentioned the cause of Ms. Kim's death as poisoning by drinking the bittern stored in the backyard of her house. The severe injuries on Ms. Kim's body had occurred during her fight with Yi—not from his beating her, but from her falling down, Yi maintained. In the meantime, Ms. Chŏn countered that she had never said such a thing and that Yi's account was completely groundless, a fabricated story to avoid admitting his crime of homicide. Faced with conflicting testimonies, the investigators called for a cross-examination between Yi Pongjin and Ms. Chŏn, but both were resolute in their position.[42] In the end, the true cause of Ms. Kim's death was determined to be Yi's beating, as established through the second rounds of the postmortems conducted by two investigators.

After being formally designated the principal offender, Yi Pongjin nevertheless continued to proclaim his innocence. During the second round of testimonies, he stated:

Ms. Kim was a woman of lowest status, selling alcohol in a market-place. She was a wife of Mr. Chang in the morning and became [a wife of] Mr. Lee in the evening. After her so-called husband, Kim Tŏksam, died in 1791, she started relations with me and became my concubine. It has been five years since I [first] visited her place, spending nights there.... Although she tended to get wild when drunken, we maintained deep affection. In the early sixth month of this year, ... I witnessed an incident in which she humiliated my mother in front of crowds. Upset, I stopped going to her place for about ten days but resumed visiting her since I originally had no intention to abandon her. I then heard a rumor that Kang Chŏngyŏl of our village had arranged a match between his [widowed] uncle Kang Sehyo [and Ms. Kim], setting a date to spend a night [at Ms. Kim's place] on the seventeenth day to make her a concubine.

42. This cross-examination between Yi and Ms. Chŏn took place twice, during the first and second investigations and is detailed in colloquial language in the second investigation, as follows: Ms. Chŏn toward Yi Pongjin: "Indeed, you beat my mother-in-law to death, yet claim that that is groundless. [Your] begging for a life in the midst of death is extremely malicious." Yi Pongjin toward Ms. Chŏn: "I was captured by village people while heading to your place. [I] asked how [she] died, and [heard from you] that a bottle filled with bittern in the backyard of your house is completely empty. How can you deny what you said?" *Pyŏgyŏng surok* 8:7a–b; 8:17b.

Therefore, on the nineteenth, I went to the marketplace and indeed saw Kang Sehyo and his nephew staying there. . . . I reproached them for getting together and conspiring between an uncle and a nephew to take a concubine, which should not be a way of *yangban* men. . . . [Then] Ms. Kim, drunken, came to see me, hurling countless insults at me. . . . [But] as a *yangban* man, I could not [confront her] reciprocally, and it was impossible to do [so] in the crowded marketplace. I only scolded [her] with several words. . . .

In the afternoon of the twenty-second day, a group of seven people residing in the market area came to my place and said, "Ms. Kim unfortunately died, thus [we] came to take you." I replied, "I have no idea about her death, and what is the use in seeing [her dead body]?" Unable to resist the seven brutes, I went and entered Ms. Kim's room, asking about how she died. Her daughter-in-law, Ms. Chŏn, said, "The bittern stored in the house is almost empty. [She] must have died by drinking this bittern." Indeed, the seven brutes accompanying me [also] heard this together. When Ms. Kim wildly confronted me, Kang Sehyo saw the scene too. Ms. Kim's family now claiming that her death was by my beating is absolutely ridiculous![43]

In his lengthy testimony, Yi Pongjin emphasized the immoral character of Ms. Kim—a widow of lower class who did not care about her sexual integrity—and also his years of semi-marital relations with Ms. Kim, as a way to save his situation. Did Yi's rhetoric strategy succeed in clearing his criminal charge or reducing his punishment? In postscripts to the investigation report, the county magistrates responsible for adjudicating this case concluded as follows:

Ms. Kim was essentially a woman of humble origins and misconduct. She wanted to be a wife of [Yi] Pongjin because she was aged, without a place to depend upon. For the past five years, Yi Pongjin and Ms. Kim continued intimate relations with affection, yet she betrayed her husband all of a sudden . . . then dared to invite another man, [and] stayed with him for several nights. . . . How evil she was! *It could be human nature that Pongjin became furious, beating [Ms. Kim].* It is obvious that he had no intention of killing [her], but this case was set up because

43. *Pyŏgyŏng surok* 8:10b–11b; emphasis added.

[Ms. Kim] unfortunately died in three days. . . . This death incident was absolutely caused by Yi's severing relations with Ms. Kim. . . . There is no doubt that Ms. Kim was beaten to death, but Yi concocted some elaborate story to save his situation. . . . [Although Yi's crime of killing Ms. Kim is acknowledged,] Ms. Kim's death cannot constitute a homicide case that deserves punishment of the death sentence (*sŏngok sangmyŏng*).[44]

While the investigators all agreed that Yi Pongjin was the principal offender, they sympathized with his frustrated heart (like that of a formal husband) caused by Ms. Kim's illicit relations with another man, rather than criticizing his violent action. What they found Yi guilty of was his fabricated testimony, not his beating of Ms. Kim, which unfortunately led to her death. Most importantly, Ms. Kim's death did not "constitute a homicide case that deserves punishment of the death sentence," precisely because she was already a woman without fidelity. In other words, it was the widow Ms. Kim who had betrayed Yi Pongjin by her licentious behavior: as a woman who had maintained relations with Yi Pongjin for years, her seeking another man was tantamount to committing adultery and subject to heavy punishment.

This verdict indicates that the investigators viewed Ms. Kim and Yi's relations as a conjugal bond, like that between a wife (concubine) and a husband, even though they had never entered any type of a formal marriage. Despite the lack of any legal or ritual enforcement that defined the relationship, the investigators expected Ms. Kim to uphold fidelity to her new partner, Yi Pongjin, even though she had been married before. Postscripts adjudicating legal cases normally conclude with moral statements about family relationships, gender roles, and virtuous conduct, but they also reflect a collective perspective toward non-elite widows such as Ms. Kim. Indeed, it would be interesting to know how the widow Ms. Kim viewed her relationship with Yi Pongjin, since her traces in the testimonies clearly indicate that she used remarriage or changing partners according to her needs. For her,

44. *Pyŏgyŏng surok* 8:18b–21b.

living as a (licentious) widow was not optional, but a desperate survival strategy. Trapped between the practical logic of survival and the priorities of the state's moral vision, widows—especially those who were impoverished non-elites—remained somewhere both within and outside the marriage system, as the most vulnerable, marginalized, and ambiguous subjects in Chosŏn society.

*   *   *

In reviewing the homicide case of a brother drowning his sister in 1790, Chŏng Yagyong states, "On the whole, it is not a mortal crime even if a young widow fails to uphold chastity." The dead woman, Ms. Kyŏn, had been widowed at a young age, yet somehow had remarried three years before her death despite her allegedly lewd conduct. Because of her constant marital conflict with her new husband's family, she was often sent back to her natal home. Her brother, repulsed by his sister's vulgar personality and dissolute behavior, dropped her into a river while they were riding in a boat together. On the brother's crime of killing his own sister, Chŏng Yagyong observes that no one, even parents, has the right to kill a young widow for not keeping her chastity. A widow's lecherous conduct was a sin, but she could not be recklessly punished without adhering to the law.[45]

While concubines and courtesans were female groups that were "legally" marginalized or excluded in Chosŏn society, a widowed woman's familial status and legal condition did not change unless she entered a second marriage within the patriarchal system. Provided they did not remarry and remained faithful to their deceased husbands, widows became celebrated exemplary figures, enjoying long-lasting fame recorded in numerous official, local, and biographical records, as well as in commemorative arches erected in their name. In this sense, chaste widows are the female group that appears most frequently in various records produced in Chosŏn society, where women's invisibility in the public realm was a normative expectation.

45. Chŏng Yagyong, Hŭmhŭm sinsŏ, 9:187.

As the widow cases examined in this chapter show, however, the vulnerability of a widow's position largely depended on her socio-familial-economic position in the society. Widows who either decided not to remarry or could not afford to do so easily became the targets of illicit rumors, which were sometimes purposely mobilized by men who wished to take a widow as their wife.[46] Once a woman's husband died, not only did her position within her husband's family become uncertain but her very existence became a potential source of scandal within the family and community as well. Like the case lamented by Chŏng Yagyong, in a society that cherished chaste widowhood as a moral paragon, the life of a widow was often complex and contradictory.[47] Widows were subjects of the state whose sexuality needed to be "controlled," and monitoring a widow's transgression was a crucial concern for male family members. Widows who selected remarriage had to endure social prejudice regardless of whether they had been forced into it (e.g., via kidnapping) or had no choice but to remarry as a survival strategy. Various incidents revolving around widows' lives therefore suggest the complexity of ideas, values, and anxieties associated with widow sexuality, unveiling not a monolithic picture of celebrated chaste widowhood but diverse views and attitudes on widow identity on the part of the state, male counterparts, and widows themselves. The precarious position of widows in Chosŏn society also illuminates how ideological assumptions crystallized into a number of potent social perceptions and expressions (such as the intimate connection between chastity and widows in the widely used compound *sujŏl kwabu*, or chaste widow), making the experience of women's

46. On the study of widows, gossip, and honor, see Jungwon Kim, "'You Must Avenge.'" For the politics of rumors surrounding women's sexuality, see Yi Sugin, "Somun kwa kwŏllyŏk," 67–107.

47. Incidents of a family member killing a lewd widow are not uncommon in legal cases. In 1787, a widow named Ms. Ku was drowned by her own brother and uncle-in-law. The way they drowned her was extremely brutal—by muzzling her and tying her body to a big stone. Despite the fact that Ms. Ku had already lost her fidelity, delineating the principal offender was therefore an intricate problem; the local investigators, provincial governors, and Ministry of Punishment presented different adjudications with respect to the levels of punishment for her brother and uncle. *Ch'ugwanji*, 1:340–47.

widowhood different from that of men. In turn, these complex lines of cleavage and practical logic ultimately shaped the lives of widows as they faced their own individual familial and economic situations. Concomitantly, the testimonies of widows in legal cases reveal how they constructed widowhood by negotiating the ideals and practices associated with their condition—whether by conforming to or by transgressing the moral boundaries imposed on their lives.

CHAPTER SIX

Between Virtue and Passion

What could be more specifically human than voluntary death?
　　　—Jean Baechler, *Les suicides*

Love to live, hate to die; that is human nature.
　　　—Song Suyŏn, postscript to a 1796 suicide case‡

In a postscript to a suicide case in 1796 of Ms. Kim, a magistrate of Hwangju named Song Suyŏn (1745–?), who conducted the first round of the investigation, wrote the second epigraph above.[1] Having been married for about ten years, Ms. Kim drank bittern after a quarrel with her husband, Kim Sagil, over what was viewed as "a trivial matter" by her family and the investigators. The source of the quarrel was Ms. Kim asking her husband to clean their two-year-old baby girl,

‡ The Jean Baechler epigraph from *Les suicides* (Paris: Calmann-Levy, 1975) is taken from Barry Cooper's English translation (New York: Basic Books, 1979). The Song Suyŏn epigraph, a postscript to Kim Choi's suicide case, reads in Korean "hosaeng osa inji sangjŏng." *Pyŏgyŏng surok* 11:8a.

　　1. The roster of the classic and licentiate examination shows that Song Suyŏn was born in 1745 and passed the exam in 1777. For a digital image of the roster containing Song's information, see http://people.aks.ac.kr/front/imageView/imageViewer.aks?exmId=EXM_SA_6JOc_1777_024940 (NLK, Ko-cho 26-29-60). No details on his career are available, but his tenure as a Haeju County magistrate indicates that he may have been fifty-one or fifty-two years old in 1796, according to *Sunjo sillok* 7:2a [1805/1/7].

who had soiled her pants, when he was just about to go to the riverbank to make a fishing net. Instead of listening to his wife's request, Kim Sagil chastised her by pulling her hair. Upon returning home later that day, he found Ms. Kim nearly dead from drinking the poison.[2] The magistrate Song Suyŏn viewed the main factors leading to Ms. Kim's suicide as the conflict stemming from the husband's oppression and the wife's "narrow mind" (p'yŏnhyŏp) during the quarrel; he consequently saw Ms. Kim's suicide as having been avoidable. Because people's testimonies confirmed that Ms. Kim had maintained good relations with her husband and was loved by her father-in-law, the magistrate wondered what had brought her to take her own life. Echoing Song's remark that it is human to "love to live, hate to die," the second investigator of this incident, the magistrate of the neighboring region of P'ungsan, noted in his postscript, "If one likes life, one would seek a way to live even though it is a must-die situation." By choosing death, the second investigator laments, Ms. Kim had put numerous townspeople in a difficult situation, including her husband, who was designated the accused (p'igo) and received thirty rounds of beating.[3]

Because the dead tell no stories, it is seldom possible to fathom the true motivation for suicide. Unless one speaks of—or leaves a note revealing—one's reason for taking one's own life, the meaning of one's death can only be imagined or interpreted by those who remain alive. In a case such as that of Ms. Kim, the investigator's foremost task was to figure out what had driven her to death, to determine whom to designate as the accused. Chosŏn law prescribed that any death incident be reported to the local magistrate for investigation, and suicide was no exception. Like other criminal cases, investigations of suicides required thorough postmortems and a series of testimonies at the local court—keys to mapping the specific circumstances of the suicide and discovering whether anyone had prompted the person to take their own life. Whereas modern Korean society tends to consider suicide to be an act of self-violence that does not involve other people, the Chosŏn court almost always identified someone as the accused (if not as the principal offender) and punished him or her under "the statute of triggering one's

2. *Pyŏgyŏng surok* 11:2a–3b; 11:6a.
3. *Pyŏgyŏng surok* 11:13a–14b.

death" (*yuajiyul*)—a specific decree that was unique to Chosŏn Korea in its application of the Ming law on "using coercion to cause others to die" (*wip'ipch'isa*), the crime normally related to a person's suicide.[4] This was the legal reasoning behind charging Ms. Kim's husband as the accused (that is, as the person who sparked her suicide), even though he "did not commit the crime by his own hands."[5]

Women's voluntary deaths—including those acclaimed as chaste—are not infrequent in Chosŏn investigation records, which contain a variety of compelling stories of self-killing regardless of gender, age, and socio-economic-marital status. For women's chaste suicide only, perhaps writings of male literati carry the largest number of accounts, though the authors' primary interest tends to be confined to the moral aspect of death, which is invariably linked to the ideal of chastity (as chapter 3 discusses). Glimpsing such texts, we find women who are preoccupied with the ideal of chastity but who are vouchsafed little individual will or choice about their own lives. Given the tension between fulfilling filial piety and wifely fidelity, for instance, we can never know whether or how women may have reconciled these two core values, although we might surmise that those who chose death to idealize their chastity may have wondered whether this act of chaste suicide violated their filial duty.

Moreover, because the large corpus of biographical writings celebrating chaste women was written by men, it is difficult to learn the real motivations of these chaste women, and the same is true in suicide cases such as that of Ms. Kim, who left no word about the feelings or reasoning behind her choice. Nevertheless, it remains imperative to unearth the voices of dead women that we do find inscribed in a variety of sources—whether words brushed by women's own hand or conveyed through the lips of others in legal testimonies—because these voices reveal society's most vital values and shared perspectives. Considering the close linkage between female chastity and female suicide in the later Chosŏn, how might the excessive culture of honoring chaste suicide have endorsed the discursive construction of the gendered notion of

---

4. Han Sanggwŏn, "Taemyŏngnyul wip'ipch'isa ŭi pŏmni wa Chosŏn esŏ ŭi chŏgyong," 27–28.

5. *Pyŏgyŏng surok* 11:13a.

suicide by men and women? In other words, how did the society view women's suicide in general differently from men's? Moreover, once suicide was deemed a manifestation of chastity, might the abstract ideal alone have moved a woman to resolve to end her own life? In this final chapter, I explore these previously unprobed questions. I do so by investigating the general perception of female suicide in Chosŏn society—infiltrated as it was by a dominant chastity paradigm—as well as by inquiring into the extremely complex relationships among Confucian moral codes, women's agency, and the tension between virtue and sentiment found in the act of female chaste suicide.

Moral Strictures on Chaste Suicide

In almost any premodern society with a religious affiliation, whether Christianity, Buddhism, or Islam, suicide was regarded both as a crime and as a moral sin. In Western culture, at least before 1700, suicide was condemned as self-murder and was considered an insult to God.[6] Georges Minois notes that the word "suicide" began to be used only at the end of the seventeenth century, replacing the expression "self-murder."[7] Chosŏn society, like Confucianism in general, viewed self-killing negatively, as an act tantamount to an inhumane action. Not only did suicide defy the Confucian emphasis on the principle of nature (or of heaven; ch'ŏlli; Ch. t'ien-li), but it was an act of the gravest unfiliality to one's parents, disturbing the natural cosmic harmony of ascendants predeceasing their descendants, who were honor bound to fulfill their mortuary and ancestral duties. As I examine in chapter 3, the tensions between virtuous suicide and filiality remained "irresolvable value conflicts" in Confucian thought and dominated debates among scholars throughout the Chosŏn dynasty.

6. Minois, *History of Suicide*, 9. Minois also points out that studying suicide poses a methodological problem because "suicide is significant for philosophic, religious, moral, and cultural reasons rather than demographic ones" (1).

7. For a detailed discussion of the birth of the term "suicide," see Minois, *History of Suicide*, 181–83. See also McGuire, *Dying to Be English*.

Confucianism nonetheless seems to have approved of individuals renouncing life in certain circumstances. In the context of political loyalty, Confucius voted for "killing oneself if doing it would achieve humaneness" (*salsin sŏngin*).[8] Centuries later, Mencius reiterated this idea, emphasizing "abandoning one's life for the sake of righteousness" (*sasaeng ch'wiŭi*).[9] In other words, preserving one's own life but failing to follow supreme virtue is ethically worse than taking one's own life in pursuit of benevolence and righteousness, for such a self-sacrificing act is morally justified and even laudable. Serving as the loci classici of the Confucian perspective on self-killing, these two discourses, signified in the *Analects* and *Mencius* persisted as the backbone for understanding and shaping the meaning of suicide in Chosŏn society—whether it was a man killing himself for loyalty or a woman killing herself for chastity.

Yet not all suicides were considered a monolithic expression of moral integrity, even when done to uphold virtue. We know that scholars invested enormous effort in validating violent acts of self-killing and distinguishing meaningful deaths from those that were not.[10] The scholar-official Hong Ho (1586–1646), for example, saw the act of self-killing as a manifestation of one's subtle state of mind, arguing that it can be ranked according to three levels:

The highest is that [committing suicide would] attain humaneness and righteousness, ultimately fulfilling the way of heaven. This is a truly an incomparable achievement and cannot be contested. Next is sacrificing oneself out of sorrowful indignation. The last is killing oneself knowing of an impossible situation that cannot be avoided.[11]

---

8. Confucius, *Analects*, 15:9.

9. *Mencius* 6A:10.

10. Kim Ho, "Politics and the Discourse," 45–70.

11. *Injo sillok* 46:11a [1645/3/11]. Hong Ho brought up this issue in relation to the suicide of a former official named Pak Sŭngjong (1562–1623), who killed himself during the 1623 Injo Restoration because of his son's involvement with the opposite side. After the Restoration, Pak's entire family was destroyed. Taking Pak's suicide as a righteous act, however, the state later restored his family's reputation, and Hong Ho criticized Pak for killing himself only because his family's situation had been unavoidable, rather than from a righteous heart.

Hong viewed the last motivation, in particular, as capitulation in the face of an inevitable difficulty, and not as noble mastery over one's life. Ranking suicide by one's motivation, Hong advised that self-killing cannot be glorified or justified without deeply deliberating upon the state of mind in which one reaches the decision to die.

Hong's first two motivations resonate with the late Chosŏn male literati's understanding of chaste suicide, which separates suicide committed out of a sincere mind from suicide carried out on an impatient impulse. The idea of female suicide as a moral imperative can be seen as early as the Han dynasty, in Liu Xiang's *Categorized Biographies of Women (Lienü zhuan)*, which includes several cases of women who took their lives to perfect the way of womanhood in a section entitled "Rectitude and Compliance."[12] In addition to Liu's text, the case of a mother-in-law's suicide, recorded in the *History of the Han*, recurs throughout Chosŏn official histories such as the *Sillok* as well as in literati writings on chaste suicide.[13] This particular account, in which a widow takes her own life so that her widowed daughter-in-law can be free of filial burdens and can remarry, served as a conventional trope of, and moral stricture on, virtuous suicide, in terms of judging the level of a woman's moral commitment. Recognizing a widow's suicide in the face of forcible remarriage, for instance, King Yŏngjo cited this Han dynasty mother-in-law when acknowledging the contemporary widow's act to be virtuous and thus worthy to be honored.[14]

Such perceptions of moral imperatives sanctioned the dramatic increase in chaste suicide during the late Chosŏn. At the same time, female suicide at large came to be reckoned differently from male suicide and was frequently connected to women's inborn nature. In criticizing the manner in which the government indiscreetly exalted

12. The female suicides appear in three biographies in Liu Xiang's *Categorized Biographies of Women*: "Bo Ji, Consort of Duke Gong of Song," "The Wife of the Lord of Xi," and "The Wife of Qi Liang of Qi." For English translations, see Kinney, *Exemplary Women of Early China*. For studies of how Liu Xiang's *Categorized Biographies of Women* landed on the intellectual soil of Korea and had an influence on forming the image of virtuous women in Korea, see Yi Hyesun, "Yŏllyŏsang ŭi chŏnt'ong kwa pyŏnmo," 163–83.

13. Ban Gu, *Hanshu*, 2041–42.

14. *Yŏngjo sillok* 81:19b [1754/4/14].

widow suicides, we recall from chapter 3 that Chŏng Yagyong stressed the distinction between truly meaningful suicide and the very opposite. For Chŏng, a widow's self-killing for "not being able to overcome the resentment of a miserable situation, but merely following a woman's narrow-minded personality" should not be accounted the height of moral behavior.[15] Unless widow suicide was proven to be genuinely motivated chaste suicide, Chŏng warns that family members and community scholars are supporting its empty beatification. Here, what Chŏng emphasizes is "women's narrow-minded personality," which he believed mobilized widows to reach the point of meaningless death. In his other writings, too, Chŏng often laments women's inborn tendency to approach death lightly.[16] Interestingly, he was not alone in this stance; there seems to have been a general inclination to frame suicide as a gendered action in Chosŏn society. This stance is echoed in the magistrate's reasoning on Ms. Kim's suicide (introduced at the outset of this chapter) and is examined further in the following case.

Gendered Suicide and "Narrow-Minded" Women

On the fourth day of the eleventh month in 1797, a commoner man named Yi Chŏmson residing in Yŏn'gi, in Ch'ungch'ŏng Province, reported his sixteen-year-old younger sister's death to the local magistrate's office. According to Yi, a *yangban* neighbor man, Pak Tong, had spread a rumor about his secret illicit relations with Yi's sister, circulating it to the community through his mother. Yi's sister was already engaged and waiting for her wedding date, which was scheduled for the twenty-fifth day of the same month. Claiming that his sister had committed suicide because she had been unable to overcome her shame and resentment inflicted by the groundless rumor, Yi requested an investigation to punish Pak according to the law.[17]

15. Chŏng Yagyong, *Kyŏngse yup'yo*, 3:312.

16. Chŏng Yagyong, "Chinju ŭigi sagi," *Tasan simunjip*, 6:114–5.

17. "Yi Ikch'ae nyŏ ogan" (Criminal Investigation Report on a Daughter of Yi Ikch'ae) is included in *Kiyang munjŏk* (Official Documents from Kiyang). Comprising two volumes, *Kiyang munjŏk* covers roughly five years, from 1797 to 1802. I used a reprinted copy included in *Han'guk chibangsa charyo cho'ongsŏ*. Page number citations are for the reprinted edition.

After the first round of the postmortem on the sister's body, the magistrate of Yŏn'gi in charge of this investigation concluded that the true cause of her death was indeed poisoning with bittern, stemming from her resentful humiliation driven by repeated intimidation.[18] During his testimony, Yi Chŏmson described how his sister had bewailed her miserable situation:

> Upon learning what had happened, my sister told me, "I have lived relying on my old father since I lost my mother when young. Now that I think of it, hearing this insulting story suddenly overnight, and causing disgrace to my parents and siblings, I do not want to live even for one day. If there is a law, work off my shameful grudge. Will my taking a life be [that] difficult?!" Considering her *narrow-minded personality*, my family took her words seriously. Fearing what she might intend to do, [we] bottled and sealed the bittern stored in our home and placed it under a big chest in my widowed sister-in-law's place.[19]

Nevertheless, around the second watch of that night (10:00 p.m.), Yi's sister began vomiting and having diarrhea simultaneously, which appeared to have been caused by poisoning. Going through increasingly excruciating pain, she eventually died around dawn. As she approached death, she spoke her final words: "Now I die; my resentment is extreme. Please avenge on my behalf after my death."[20] Her father confirmed in his testimony that before she expired she had told him, "[I am] dying now, [and] my indignation will remain in the other world. Make sure to avenge [my death]."[21]

This suicide case is one of many that combined rumor, defamation, and sexual integrity in Chosŏn society—subjects that chapter 5 closely explores in the case of widows. Based on the testimonies of everyone involved in this case, the Yŏn'gi County magistrate judged that it was the *yangban* Pak Tong's baseless words that had led to Yi's sister's tragic demise. The magistrate therefore arrested and punished the accused Pak

---

18. "Yi Ikch'ae nyŏ ogan," 9–11.
19. "Yi Ikch'ae nyŏ ogan," 15; emphasis added.
20. "Yi Ikch'ae nyŏ ogan," 15.
21. "Yi Ikch'ae nyŏ ogan," 18–19.

under the law of using coercion to cause others to die, and Pak received
one hundred strokes of beating with the heavy stick.[22] In his postscript,
the magistrate sympathizes with Yi's sister, commending her resolution
to vindicate her tainted integrity even to the extent of taking her own
life.[23] Although Ms. Kim (introduced earlier) and Yi's sister both chose
death instead of facing reality and/or filing a complaint directly with
the local court, there was a clear difference: before taking her life, Yi's
sister testified to her innocence by leaving verbal appeals with her family
members, whose lawful actions fulfilled her last wish that her act restore
her sexual integrity and that Pak Tong be punished. Above all, her aggrieved voice in the investigation report, delivered through testimonies
of others, was listened to, weighed, and recorded during the trials.

Interestingly, even though the court viewed Yi's sister's suicide as
a righteous one—that is, as the bodily refutation of a disgraceful rumor attempting to destroy her sexual integrity—she is also described
as a girl with a "narrow mind." In her family's testimony and in the
magistrate's questioning, her narrow-mindedness is singled out as the
driving factor in her suicide, just as it was in the case of Ms. Kim. Both
her brother Yi Chŏmson and her widowed sister-in-law attested to her
inborn intolerant nature.[24] The magistrate was thus cautious, and the
matter of whether or not she had been narrow-minded was factored
into the interrogation. Apart from the official adjudication, which
fulfilled her wish to punish Pak Tong, Yi's sister is consistently depicted
as a woman whose narrow-minded personality led to the extreme act.
Why then was her suicidal motivation ultimately interpreted in such
a conflicting way, showing her to have been a young woman of great
moral integrity rather than one who may have been bigoted?

In Chosŏn legal testimonies, it is not unusual to encounter observations that depict women as narrow-minded and that deem this quality
an impetus for their suicide. Not only magistrates in charge of investigations but those called upon to testify often characterize a woman
as narrow-minded—whether she is the accused, a witness, or a neighbor
in the case under consideration. In a postscript to the suicide case of a

22. "Yi Ikch'ae nyŏ ogan," 96.
23. "Yi Ikch'ae nyŏ ogan," 29–32.
24. "Yi Ikch'ae nyŏ ogan," 19–20.

different Ms. Kim, for example, the magistrate displayed a similar view. Living with a husband who was six years younger than herself, thirty-six-year-old Ms. Kim ran a tavern for a living. The couple had lived together for seven years, maintaining good marital relations. They had never had a formal wedding ritual, according to the husband, echoing ordinary people's marriage practices as revealed in many legal testimonies.[25] One day, Ms. Kim had a dispute with a man named Kim Ch'isŏn who had bought drinks on credit, then visited the tavern again, requesting more drinks without paying his tab. Seeing this fuss, Ms. Kim's husband kicked the man out and chastised his wife for not behaving herself. Shortly thereafter, Ms. Kim poisoned herself and died.[26] The magistrate at first assumed that Ms. Kim's suicide stemmed from spousal conflict, but this theory did not pan out. According to Ms. Kim's mother, who testified at the court, after a fight with her husband, Ms. Kim had expressed no desire to continue living, saying, "I do not mind spousal quarrels, but being humiliated by an outside man is a vexed matter that I cannot get over. I have practically no reason to remain alive."[27] Ms. Kim's statement, conveyed through the lips of her mother, was effective enough to designate the man Kim Ch'isŏn as the accused, whose insult had led Ms. Kim to the point of killing herself.[28]

In his postscript, however, the magistrate, while understanding Ms. Kim's aggravated heart, caused by the accused, lamented her taking her life lightly, just as the magistrate who presided over Yi's sister's suicide case did. To die or to live is the most vital matter for a human being, he stated, yet "women in general tend to have a narrow personality (p'yŏnsŏng)."[29] His point supports the shared perception of female suicide in Chosŏn society at that time, which saw it as fundamental to women's inborn nature. Moreover, the magistrate added

25. "Taegu-bu pokkŏm mun'an." The document includes no year of its production, except for a note of the kyŏngsin year, which could be either 1820 or 1880.

26. It seems that Ms. Kim did not die immediately after taking poison. Her brother brought a medical doctor to Ms. Kim's tavern in an effort to save her. In his testimony, however, the doctor stated that he had only learned from Ms. Kim's husband that she had already died. "Taegu-bu pokkŏm mun'an," 5:7b–8a.

27. "Taegu-bu pokkŏm mun'an," 5:11a–b.

28. "Taegu-bu pokkŏm mun'an," 5:19a–b.

29. "Taegu-bu pokkŏm mun'an," 5:18a.

that "the degree [of women's narrow-mindedness] is even greater for those of the lower class."[30] This jibes with why the Chosŏn state was enthusiastic about recognizing women of low class who upheld their chastity (see chapter 4), while also underlining the society's discriminative view of the extent to which non-elite people were capable of moral cultivation.

In legal testimonies on female suicide, the terms most frequently used to describe women's "narrow" personality are "intolerant" (p'yŏnhyŏp), "eccentric" (p'yŏnbyŏk), "biased" (p'yŏnsŏng), "small-minded" (p'yŏnae), and "ill-tempered" (p'yŏnp'yak). As we have seen, people brought in to testify at court were inclined to point to a woman's so-called narrow-mindedness as the key factor in the violent action of taking her own life, positing its direct link to female suicide. This tendency, recorded in surviving legal documents, shows Chosŏn society's supposition that women were more prone to killing themselves than men. Existing studies examining suicide patterns also reflect such a view, not only contending that there was a higher proportion of female than male suicide in late Chosŏn society but also connecting this to a collective phenomenon intimately related to women's obsession with upholding chastity, as enforced by the state.[31]

Although it is challenging to present comprehensive data for a male/female comparative suicide ratio over the entire dynasty, some late Chosŏn legal documents provide an interesting glimpse into this subject.[32] One major source, analyzed by scholars of Chosŏn suicide patterns, is the late eighteenth-century *Records of Royal Reviews* (*Simnirok*), which carries hundreds of judicial decisions during Chŏng-jo's reign. It contains thirty-two female suicides but only fifteen male suicide cases, and scholars point to sexually related matters as the dominant factors prompting women to kill themselves.[33]

30. "Taegu-bu pokkŏm mun'an," 5:18a.

31. Kim Hyŏnjin, "Simnirok ŭl t'onghae pon 18-segi yŏsŏng," 197–230; Chŏng Ilyŏng, "Chosŏn hugi sŏngbyŏl e ttarŭn chasal ŭi haesŏk," 155–75.

32. An analysis of suicide figures in the *Sillok* finds only 29 female suicides out of 109 suicide cases. But this number cannot offer any generalized picture, given the nature of the *Sillok*. Song Pyŏngu, "Chosŏn sidae kaein ŭi chasal," 115–39.

33. I follow Kim Hyŏnjin's numbers here. Chŏng Ilyŏng's study presents sixty-five female suicide cases from the *Records of Royal Reviews*, but this includes homicides

However, other legal sources produced around the same time vary in the proportions of female versus male suicides they document, complicating this general assumption of a higher female suicide rate in Chosŏn society. The two volumes of inquest reports for Kyŏngsang Province for 1842 (table 6.1), for example, show twenty-four suicide cases out of a total of forty-two death incidents: fifteen by females; nine by males. Women indeed took their lives more often than men in these reports. In contrast, a collection of various administrative and judicial reports compiled by the Hwanghae provincial governor's office (kamyŏng) between 1795 and 1796 reveals far more male suicides than female (table 6.2).[34] Out of eleven suicides recorded in this compilation, nine were of males and only two were of females. Coincidentally or not, the Records of Royal Reviews does not include any cases from Hwanghae Province for these years, although it does thereafter include entries from Hwanghae Province into 1800—the last year covered by the Reviews.[35] In fact, if the 1795–1796 suicide cases from Hwanghae Province judicial reports are combined with the suicide numbers in the Reviews, the ratio is thirty-four female suicides to twenty-four male. Thus, we can see that the gender pattern for suicide varies depending on the sources examined. Even given the fact that the Records of Royal Reviews is not comprehensive, it is problematic to claim that women in Chosŏn society were more disposed to kill themselves than men were.

---

disguised as suicides. For representative Korean scholarship on the Records of Royal Reviews, see Kwŏn Yŏnung, "Simnirok ŭi kich'ojŏk kŏmt'o," 1320–38; Sim Chaeu, "Simnirok ŭl t'onghae pon 18-segi huban sŏul," 58–94; Sim Chaeu, Chosŏn hugi kukka kwŏllyŏk kwa pŏmjoe t'ongje; and Kim Hyŏnjin, "Simnirok ŭl t'onghae pon 18-segi yŏsŏng," 197–230. In English scholarship, William Shaw's pioneering book on Chosŏn legal culture carries a partial translation of the Records of Royal Reviews; see Shaw, Legal Norms in a Confucian State.

34. Entitled Collected Reports from Pyŏgyŏng (Pyŏgyŏng surok), the compilation has thirteen volumes covering from the third month of 1795 to the twelfth month of 1796. The collection has a total of twenty-seven legal cases (twenty-five legal testimonies with postmortem reports and two inferences on petitions).

35. There is only one overlapping death case included in both Records of Royal Reviews and Hwanghae Province judicial reports—that of a man named O Puksul, whose death actually occurred in 1792 and was reinvestigated following his wife's petition in 1795. O's case is under the year 1794 in the former, but under the year 1795 in the latter. See Pyŏgyŏng surok 5; Simnirok 26:1b–3b.

Table 6.1. Suicide Cases in Kyŏngsang Province, 1842

Name	Sex	Age	Region	Social / marital status
Ch'oe Aji*	F	19	Kosŏng	Commoner/unmarried
Ch'oe Choi*	F	32–33	Ch'ŏngdo	Commoner/married
Yi Choi*	F	24	Kimhae	Commoner/widow
Sŏ Choi	F	39	Haman	Commoner/married
Yŏm Choi	F	18–19	Hapch'ŏn	Commoner/married
Sin Choi	F	32–33	Kunŭi	Commoner/married
Chŏng Choi*	F	NA	Sŏnsan	Commoner/married
Pak Yŏa	F	21–22	Ulsan	NA/unmarried
Yi Choi*	F	28–29	Chinhae	Commoner/ remarried
Chŏng Choi	F	67–68	Sach'ŏn	Commoner/widow
Kim Yŏa†	F	4	Ch'ŏngha	Commoner/child
Yi Chosi*	F	41–42	Taegu	Lowborn/ married
Madam Chang	F	NA	Yech'ŏn	*Yangban*/widow
Kim Choi*	F	NA	Miryang	Commoner/married
Hŏ Choi	F	37–38	Kimhae	Commoner/married
Kim Tusul	M	23–24	Sanch'ŏng	Slave/ unmarried
Sŏ Yŏndae	M	32–33	Kunŭi	Commoner/married
Cho Sŏngho	M	43–44	Anŭi	Commoner/married
Hwang Tori	M	28–29	Chain	Commoner/NA
Yi Pongdol	M	54–55	Anŭi	Slave/NA

Primary reason for suicide	Method of suicide
Reprimand by a brother for quarreling with a sister-in-law (偏隘)	Hanging
Conflict with a male neighbor over money (偏狹)	Drowning
Humiliation and beating by a male neighbor (偏隘)	Hanging
Failure to collect money loaned to a male neighbor	Hanging
Marital violence over adultery	Poisoning (after being beaten)
Husband's adultery with a married slave	Poisoning
Conflict with a mother-in-law (偏愎, 偏性)	Drowning
Conflict over marriage arrangement	Poisoning
Conflict with a stepdaughter-in-law and her male relatives (偏狹)	Hanging
Conflict with a female neighbor over son's imprisonment	Drowning
Falling into a well	Drowning
Humiliation at being called a licentious woman (偏隘)	Poisoning
False rumor about lewd conduct spread by a female neighbor	Hanging
Altercation with a female relative about her daughter (偏狹)	Poisoning
Reprimanded by a husband for not purchasing a chicken	Drowning
Humiliated and bound by an owner for cheating about grain	Poisoning
Scolded by father for not being diligent	Drowning
Inability to tolerate severe pain due of illness	Stabbing
Chastened for missing firewood	Stabbing
Altercation with a yangban male neighbor	Drowning

(continued)

Table 6.1. *(continued)*

Name	Sex	Age	Region	Social/marital status
Yi Akchi[‡]	M	NA	Kŭmsan	Lowborn/married
Nam Sŏngjik	M	39	Sangju	Commoner/married
Pak Yunson[*]	M	34–35	Ch'ŏngdo	Commoner/NA
Ch'u Kuksŏn	M	41–42	Sillyŏng	Commoner/married

SOURCE: *Kŏmanch'o*. Madam Chang's and Yi Pongdol's suicides cases are translated in Sun Joo Kim and Jungwon Kim, *Wrongful Deaths*, 55–71.

NOTE: The first fifteen cases listed are of women, while the remaining nine (shaded) are of men. Although no exact year of records is known, it can be assumed, after tracing some investigators' personal backgrounds, that all these suicides took place between the fourth month and the twelfth month of 1842. NA = data not available.

What these sources nevertheless confirm is the shared perception of women's "narrow personality," which was thought to be the major factor leading them to end their lives carelessly. In death reports of female suicide cases, as revealed in tables 6.1 and 6.2, most female victims are characterized by one of the terms denoting "narrow-minded." The only woman commended for realizing the chastity ideal through suicide is the *yangban* widow Madam Chang in table 6.1. Although all the women listed resorted to suicide in response to various inside and outside assaults, ranging from spousal and familial conflicts to sexual insults, both the magistrates making reports on the cases and people testifying at court were inclined to link women's suicidal acts to their "narrow" personalities. There was even a case of homicide disguised as female suicide to avoid heavy punishment, and the rhetoric used to establish it as a suicide case was the victim's "inborn intolerance" (*p'yŏnhyŏp chi ch'ŏnsŏng*).[36] The principal

36. *Kŏmanch'o, kŏn* (vol. 1), 107. I did not include this case in table 6.1 because it was eventually ruled a homicide.

Primary reason for suicide	Method of suicide
Reproached and bound by a yangban neighbor	Poisoning
Threatened for repayment of a loan by neighboring brothers	Poisoning
Pressed for money by a neighbor man (偏狹)	Drowning
Inability to repay money borrowed from three neighbors	Hanging

* Case of suicide, male or female, where "narrow personality" was noted as a driving force in his/her suicide. The terms for "narrow personality," as written in the original texts, are provided in parentheses: "intolerant" (*p'yŏnhyŏp* 偏狹), "biased" (*p'yŏnsŏng* 偏性), "small-minded" (*p'yŏnae* 偏隘), and "ill-tempered" (*p'yŏnp'yak* 偏愎).

† Although this incident of a four-year-old child falling into a well may not be considered a suicide case, I include it in this table because the original document notes the root cause of death as "self-drowning" (*chaik* 自溺).

‡ Because the corpse was already buried and no autopsy was conducted, the report provides no age information.

offender, who was in fact the husband of the female victim, claimed that she had poisoned herself after having a squabble with him and that it was her bad-tempered personality that had prompted the suicidal act. Although the postmortem revealed the husband's beating of her as the true cause of her death and designated him the principal offender, the magistrate still bemoaned the female victim's small-mindedness for not coping with her frustrating situation.[37]

In contrast, people scarcely ever identified male suicide with the man's narrow-mindedness, for there is only one known case that relates a man's suicide to his narrow personality (see Pak Yunson's case in table 6.1). Instead, male suicidal action was mostly thought to

37. The female victim, Ms. Kang, was a sixty-three- or sixty-four-year-old widow who had married a man named Yi Hugap after her first husband's death. The couple lived together for about nineteen years, but Ms. Kang often had conflicts with Yi's children by his former wife. It was Ms. Kang's brother who questioned her suicide and requested a formal investigation of her death by pointing to Yi as a possible principal offender.

Table 6.2. Suicide Cases in Hwanghae Province, 1795–1796

Name	Sex	Age	Region	Social/ marital status
Kim Choi*	F	24–25	Hwangju	Commoner/married
Yi Choi*	F	21–22	Koksan	Commoner/married
Kang Kangdong	M	34–35	Haeju	Commoner/married
Kim Chongdae	M	46–47	Suan	Commoner/ married
Pyŏn Tŏksŭng	M	31–32	Pongsan	Commoner/married
Yi Paekchŭng	M	NA	P'ungch'ŏn	Commoner/NA
Kim Such'ŏn	M	27–28	P'ungch'ŏn	
Yang Sŏnghang†	M	23–24	P'yŏngsan	*Yangban*/unmarried
Yu Sŏngdŭk	M	44–45	Pongsan	Commoner/married
Ch'oe Ch'unsam	M	NA	Chaeryŏng	Commoner/married
Kim Chonghae	M	48–49	Haeju	Commoner/married

SOURCE: *Pyŏgyŏng surok*. Yang Sŏnghang's case appears in "P'yŏngsan Yi Ch'undae kŏman," *Pyŏgyŏng surok* 10:18b–25a.

NOTE: The first two cases listed are of women, while the remaining nine (shaded) are of men. Ages of the dead are only approximate in postmortem reports. For those whose ages are unavailable, it is because the corpse was buried before investigation (Yi Paekchŭng) or a postmortem was not conducted at the request of the dead person's family (Ch'oe Ch'unsam). NA = data not available.

spring from individual reasons, even though some of the underlying situations—such as humiliation, menace, and conflicts with spouses, family members, and neighbors—were shared in common with female suicide. In the case of Kim Chongdae (see table 6.2), who hanged himself after being threatened by *yangban* men for trespassing on a pine forest, the magistrate states, "People in general voluntarily abandon their lives due to extreme anger and resentment. What a pity is that this poor and imprudent man could not overcome his fear and

Primary reason for suicide	Method of suicide
Scolded by a husband for not caring for a baby (偏狹)	Drinking bittern
Spousal conflict and narrow personality (偏性, 偏狹)	Drinking bittern
Fear of being suspected of larceny	Hanging
Threatened by *yangban* men for trespassing on a pine forest	Hanging
Threatened and persecuted by a neighbor man over land	Drinking bittern
Fear of a cousin's critical injury caused by his beating	Stabbing
Threatened by a brother of a *yangban* woman with whom he had committed adultery	Poisoning
Frustration at putting parents in a humiliating situation	Drinking bittern
Intoxication from excessive drinking	Hanging
Humiliated by a nephew after heavy intoxication	Jumping into a well
Falsely charged as a thief	Drinking bittern

* Case where the woman's "narrow personality" was noted as a driving force in her suicide. The terms for "narrow personality," as written in the original texts, are provided in parentheses in the "Primary reason for suicide" column: "intolerant" (*p'yŏnhyŏp* 偏狹) and "biased" (*p'yŏnsŏng* 偏性).

† Although the title of a death report generally begins with the name of the dead person, this particular case is misleading, beginning with the name of the accused, Yi Ch'undae, whereas the person who committed suicide was Yang Sŏnghang. Also, Yang is the only person of *yangban* status in this table.

reached the point of killing himself without thinking of his family."[38] Another magistrate, who adjudicated a similar suicide case, of a male slave who challenged a *yangban* man, also remarked in the same tone, depicting the male victim as "foolish" to end his life by throwing himself to his death.[39] In both cases, the magistrates acknowledged

38. *Pyŏgyŏng surok* 6:31b–32a.
39. *Kŏmanch'o, kŏn* (vol. 1), 29.

overwhelming anguish as a motivation for these men to end their lives, but did not classify it as a shared tendency, as was typically done in cases of female suicide.

Why did a "narrow personality" matter in adjudicating female suicide cases, and on what grounds were women collectively branded in this way?[40] Could the surge of chaste suicide in late Chosŏn society possibly have shaped people's perceptions about gendered suicide? In commemorating the *kisaeng* (female entertainer) Non'gae's righteous death, Chŏng Yagyong offered his reflections on female suicide as follows:

> A woman's disposition takes death lightly. A lowly death is when [a woman] takes her life because she cannot overcome anger, bitterness, and frustration deep inside [her heart]; a lofty death is when [a woman] takes her life because she cannot overcome humiliation after her body has been tainted, and because, by dying, people generally praise [her as] virtuous and chaste. Yet all these [suicidal actions] merely concern her own life, [not others'].[41]

Chŏng wrote this passage in a preface to his poem dedicated to Non'gae, who killed herself, together with a Japanese general, during the Imjin War. Despite her lowborn status as an entertainer, the state

40. In examining female suicide cases from the *Records of Royal Reviews*, Kang Hyejong notes women's "narrow personality" as a common narrative in court cases. Kang does not, however, contextualize why this collective attitude toward female suicide dominated in late Chosŏn legal testimonies or how it may have been affected by the phenomenon of chaste suicides of that time. Kang states that, unlike chaste suicide, which was accepted as an act of moral sentiment, the state did not sympathize with women's narrow personality as a cause for suicidal actions. Kang Hyejong, "Sarin sagŏn ŭl tullŏssan Chosŏn ŭi kamsŏng chŏngch'i," 130–33.

41. Chŏng Yagyong, "Chinju ŭigi sagi," *Tasan simunjip*, 6:114–15. We do not have any documentary evidence from Non'gae's time to prove what she is said to have done—I thank a reviewer for this careful point. For a study of controversies over commemoration of Non'gae, see Ji Young Jung, "War and the Death of a Kisaeng," 157–80. For heroization of Non'gae by local Confucian literati during the late Chosŏn and by the South Korean state in the aftermath of the Korean War (1950–1953), see Pak Noja/ Vladimir Tikhonov, "Ŭigi Non'gae chŏnsŭng," 229–54.

acknowledged Non'gae's suicide as a noble act driven by her "loyal heart" and enshrined her as a righteous female entertainer (*kisaeng*). Chŏng differentiates Non'gae's death from the two types of women's suicide he remarks on, pointing to their egocentric motive (even for the one acclaimed as achieving a chaste death), whereas Non'gae killed herself not for her own moral pursuit or self-interest but for the sake of the state. We know that Chŏng criticized some suicides in the name of chastity as a selfish form of fidelity and strove to define the justifiable boundaries of a meaningful death. Most of all, although Chŏng ranks chaste suicide higher than suicide committed out of emotional intolerance, what he stresses is women's innate nature of taking their lives lightly in both situations. In other words, Chŏng distinguishes women of low virtue who kill themselves out of vile anger from women of high virtue who kill themselves out of the unbearable dishonor of injustice. Ultimately, however, he relates female suicide to women's temperament, joining the dominant view on gendered suicide in Chosŏn society of that time.

As I discuss in chapter 3, with the later Chosŏn witnessing unprecedented numbers of chaste suicides, applauding suicide as the utmost manifestation of female virtue became a pretext for judging the degree to which a given woman had internalized morality. Facing the increasing numbers of chaste suicides, scholars largely engaged in vindicating these violent actions against filiality, while debating *how* one should properly perform a chaste death and which forms of death legitimized the act of suicide. Noting the far higher number of women's chaste suicides than men's suicides committed under the banner of loyalty, some Confucian scholars even lamented that "Heaven bestowed the spirit of righteousness (*yŏl*) on women alone, but not on [contemporary] scholar-officials."[42] While men of that time had lost their morality, merely seeking profit, women were different: it was because of women's chaste spirit that, "suppressing their grief over the deaths of their husbands, successive generations of women have continuously killed themselves to follow their deceased husbands."[43]

42. Kim Yangnyŏn, "Kim yŏllyŏ chŏn," *Tuam chip*, 5:35a–36b.
43. Kim Yangnyŏn, "Kim yŏllyŏ chŏn," *Tuam chip*, 5:35a–36b.

Ironically, such depictions of women's chaste spirit stood in direct contrast to the characterization of women as "narrow-minded" for taking their own lives in Chosŏn society. Celebrating chaste suicide as the utmost indicator of female virtue ultimately germinated a number of discursive contexts in which female suicide was variously perceived: women were susceptible to killing themselves lightly; it was women's "narrow" disposition that drove them to resort to such an extreme action. No matter how profoundly women's suicide was extolled in the countless writings commemorating their virtuous actions, as well as through the court testimonies attesting to their pure motivations for choosing to die by their own hands, female suicide remained bound by dual views of women's moral agency and innate personality traits. Still, what was seen as women's narrow nature in connection to suicide issued not from women themselves but from the minds of others, since their deaths were objectified only in other people's speculative definitions.

In My Voice: Women's Testaments

In 1739, an officer of the Office of the Inspector-General memorialized the throne to request recognition of a commoner widow's virtuous death in Ch'ungch'ŏng Province. The memorial stated that after her husband's death, a grandson from her husband's lineage had pressured her to have licentious relations with him, but she had firmly declined. The grandson then beat her to death and concealed her body. Only about nine months later was her death discovered and reported to the local magistrate's office, which located her corpse. During the postmortem, observers were amazed by her face, which still looked like that of a living person, without a trace of decay, despite her body having endured scorching summer heat. Learning about this bizarre incident, local people assumed that heaven had responded to her ardent chaste spirit and made this miraculous preservation happen. In the meantime, the provincial governor, thinking of the woman's indignant heart, offered a rite on her behalf. Although the area had suffered from a drought for two years, it suddenly rained during the performance of the ritual. People in the region believed that the woman's utmost manifestation of fidelity had brought the precipitation, which they dubbed "chaste-wife rain" (*chŏlbuu*). Reading the memorial, the king was touched, too, and approved the request to commemorate the woman's death.[44]

To what extent and how people connected the auspicious rain to the widow's death is hard to say. As an illiterate commoner, the woman had left no word behind her. In the absence of the woman's own account of her actions, it must have seemed to be her body that, when found, bore powerful witness to her committed fidelity and indignant heart, inscribing the very resistance that had enraged her attacker and deprived her of life. Chapter 2 discusses how essential it was to gather testimonies about a deceased subject who was under consideration for state recognition of her chaste suicide. It is difficult to tell whether such women took their lives of their own free choice or under duress, because all the posthumous writings about them can only conjecture as to exactly why they took the action they did. Unlike a sati widow immolating herself on her husband's public funeral pyre in India, Chosŏn women performed chaste suicide privately and in secret, with no one present to observe their expressions upon death. If a woman left behind a piece of writing disclosing her chaste intent to die, that became the strongest proof that her death was honorable. If not, it was a daunting task to reconstruct her true motive for selecting the extreme path of suicide—a task that could be accomplished only by assessing the testimonies given by those still alive. Given the impossibility of directly accessing the dead woman's voice, statements about her moral upbringing and conduct from members of her family as well as her community served as important narratives during the official reward-selection procedure and were often the only sources the court had to rely on.

In fact, leaving a last will before dying was not an uncommon practice among male literati in Chosŏn Korea, and many such wills were passed down from generation to generation through ardent preservation by families. While carrying traces of personal sentiment, they also often functioned as precepts for family members and disciples on matters such as funeral arrangements, refining ritual practices,

44. *Ch'ugwanji*, 1:250.

and pursuing moral cultivation.[45] Women, too, left testaments. Although we do not know when the practice began or how extensive it was, the earliest extant woman's testament is generally considered to be the one left by Madam Yi of Wansan in 1651 (fig. 6.1).[46] Facing a vigorous conflict over the ritual and succession rights in her family, Madam Yi, who was in her eighties, drafted a testament addressed to her descendants. Writing in Korean script, she expressed her wish that her testament serve as a document for a possible litigation after her death. She ended, "[I desire that] my handwriting in ŏnmun will become evidence for my offspring, so do not treat [this will] lightly and hand it down to posterity."[47]

Existing records include at least forty-four testaments produced by thirty-one women during the Chosŏn dynasty. Rather than each one being preserved as a single, discrete document, these records have largely been found "in passing" in other writings, such as epitaphs and biographies of women included in male literati collections.[48] Four are dated in the seventeenth century, fifteen in the eighteenth, and ten in the nineteenth century. Because the eighteenth and nineteenth centuries saw the largest number of women's testaments, and twenty of them were authored by women whose deaths were designated "chaste suicides," scholars tend to take this as indication of the close connection between the dominance of chastity discourse and the increasing

45. On Chosŏn male literati's testaments, see Yi Hongsik, "Chosŏn sidae sadaebu namsŏng yusŏ," 213–36.

46. Yi Hongsik notes that there is possibly one earlier testament, left by the mother of Kim Kwangwŏn (1478–1550) in the early sixteenth century. Yi Hongsik, "Chosŏn hugi sadaebu yŏsŏng," 100–101.

47. "Hwang ch'amŭi ch'ŏ sukpuin Nisi." Madam Yi was a third wife of the scholar-official Hwang Yŏil (1556–1622), whose first two wives died earlier than Hwang. Hwang had four sons—one from his first wife, and three from Madam Yi. Hwang's first son, Chungyun (1577–?), had only one son from his slave concubine. Hwang was succeeded by Chungyun, but the conflict arose after Chungyun's death, when his slave-born son tried to secure succession and ritual rights. Madam Yi left this will to block such an attempt.

48. Many male authors of women's biographies note that women left letters to their family members (and even to their slave maids sometimes) before committing suicide, but do not mention the actual contents of the letters. See Yi Kwangsa, "Ch'oe yŏlbu ch'an," Wŏn'gyo chip 8:10a–11a; Sin Kwangsu, "Chŏng yŏlbu chŏn," Sŏkpuk chip, 15:19b–21a.

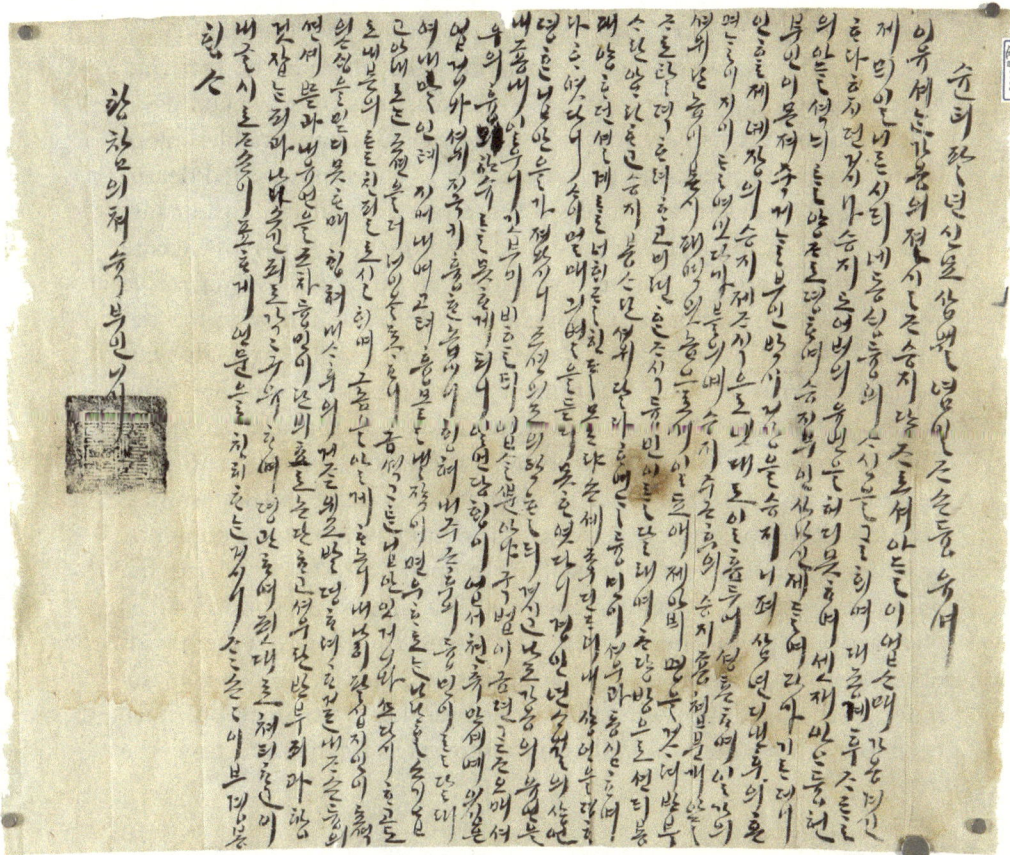

6.1. The 1651 deathbed letter of Madam Yi of Wansan, a wife of Hwang Yŏil, to her children ("Hwang ch'amŭi ch'yŏ syukpuin Nisi"). Photograph courtesy of Korean Studies Advancement Center (entrusted by P'yŏnghae Hwangssi Haewŏl chongt'aek).

production of women's testaments in the late Chosŏn period.[49] In other words, the larger number of women's testaments during this period resulted from women's internalization of the chastity ideal and the excessive mode of honoring it.[50] The assumption of such a linkage

49. Yi Hongsik, "Chosŏn hugi sadaebu yŏsŏng," 98–99; Kim Chŏnggyŏng, "Chosŏn hugi yŏllyŏ ŭi sunjŏl," 9–35.

50. Kim Chŏnggyŏng, *Chosŏn hugi yŏsŏng han'gŭl sanmun yŏn'gu*, 101; Kang Myŏnggwan, *Yŏllyŏ ŭi t'ansaeng*, 548.

seems to be precarious, however: along with the possible ideological or political impetus for women to write wills, there is the fact that Korean script had become available. As was true in other genres of women's letters, this new access to writing would have enabled more women to take up brushes to write a will as they approached death, fulfilling their desire to express a sense of self by leaving their last words.[51] For example, a widow called Madam Yi (1723–1748) wrote a piece of testament in a literary form known as *kasa* (a narrative verse) in Korean script, displaying a wish to be united with her deceased husband. Another widow, Madam Yun (1768–1801), also left a *kasa*, together with nine testaments to members of both her natal and in-law families, before committing suicide on the hundredth day after her husband's death.[52] Moreover, the way women's testaments became available to readers was intimately related to their families' decision either to conserve or to release them based on their contents. Families were, of course, more willing to open the testaments after the widow's death was officially recognized as a chaste one; some families were active in publishing women's testaments by compiling them with other writings, such as their biographies and eulogies.[53] Also, many more (perhaps earlier) wills may have been left by women but have been lost or forgotten, or still await discovery.[54] At the same time, the

51. Haboush, "Versions and Subversions," 289. On the subject of how the Korean script served as a powerful tool in the communicative space on various personal, familial, scholarly, and political matters, and how women benefited most from using Korean script, actively participating in and shaping the written culture, see Haboush, *Epistolary Korea*.

52. Yun Pyŏngyong, "Namwŏn Yunssi ŭi yusŏ," 201–39.

53. Madam Yun's in-law family compiled a volume that included her testaments along with her *kasa* and biography, and her testaments, originally written in Korean script, were translated into literary Chinese. Yun Pyŏngyong, "Namwŏn Yunssi ŭi yusŏ," 202. Such publication activity, especially translating from Korean script into literary Chinese, testifies to how her in-law family considered it an important task for promoting the family's moral reputation. For a similar case, see Jungwon Kim, "Deeper than the Death," 163–82.

54. Although most women left their wills in Korean script, there is a 1715 testament written in literary Chinese by an unmarried woman, which her family published in a compilation of her other writings. For more information on this piece, see Jungwon Kim, "Daughters' Letters of Farewell," 382–90.

handful of extant women's testaments does not silence but only augments their voices embedded in their stories from various sources.

Unlike other types of deaths which could also be accompanied by testaments, written notes left before committing suicide grant us a crucial glimpse into the inner motives behind a voluntary death, since the act of suicide is conspicuously selected by individuals to (unnaturally) end their life. Chapter 3 discusses how male literati's accounts often recount how "persistent" chaste women were in wishing to die (or to follow their deceased husbands into death), attesting to their formidable commitment to pursue the path of chastity once they decided to do so, despite family members' strong opposition to and measures to prevent their suicidal acts. Even though the countless chaste-woman biographies written by male literati do not fully disclose the complex sets of emotions behind these women's extreme choices, women's own testaments could fill this gap. In her 1831 testament addressed to her young daughter, for example, a widow called Madam Yu (1807–1831) states two reasons she plans to kill herself: first, because she is unable to meet the obligation of producing a male heir, thus failing in the Three Followings; and second, because she misses her deceased husband dearly and has no motive to sustain her life in this world.[55]

Madam Yu had married a man who was one year older than she was, but lost him after eight years of marriage, when she was the tender age of twenty-four. Before taking her life, she left several testaments for her family members, including her parents-in-law and her five-year-old daughter—the only child from her short marriage.[56] For her first reason to die, she stressed her inability to produce a son as preventing her from completing the Three Followings—following a father's order before being wed, that of a husband while married, and then that of a son when widowed. Although the Three Followings do not prescribe failing to bear a son as a transgression of a husband's

55. Yussi puin, "Yusŏ." For Madam Yu's two testaments, I used the facsimile version of the original texts included in Han'gŭl p'ilsabon kososŏl charyo ch'ongsŏ, 181–224.

56. Im Ch'igyun notes that Madam Yu also left a letter addressed to her own parents, although it has not yet been found. Im Ch'igyun, "Sŏnyŏng Yussi puin yusŏ yŏn'gu," 47–65.

wish, securing a male heir—a matter necessary for continuing the family line—constituted a critical component of wifely duties, and failing to do so was an enormous burden, especially as a *yangban* wife.

That her husband no longer existed in the same world with her was Madam Yu's second motivation for suicide. This feeling of loss was a very private matter, an "agony reaching the peak of the sky" (*ch'yŏnbong chit'ong*), in Madam Yu's words. In the testament addressed to her daughter, she laments, "Thinking of your deceased father [my dead husband], I weep every second and my heart is choked up. How can I stand up and carry on my life in this world?"[57] Madam Yu devotes most of this testament to describing her marriage and the illustrious path of her husband with utmost pride and affection. She writes, "When we married, your father was an exceptionally talented, virtuous, and beautiful seventeen-year-old man. [After the marriage] he became known for being an exemplary husband and father, and was a beloved son-in-law [in my natal family]. I always feared for his exceeding reputation in the area."[58] According to Madam Yu, shortly after her daughter was born, the couple cherished the joy of her husband passing the civil service examination at the remarkably young age of twenty, which earned people's admiration and honor. But he soon met an illness that eventually led to his death, notwithstanding all possible efforts to save him. Written in an unfathomably aggrieved and grief-stricken tone, emotional terms such as "resentful" and "bitter" dominate her testament.

Madam Yu also explains why she is resorting to suicide in a testament to her parents-in-law. Listing the first reason for committing suicide—the impossibility of realizing the Three Followings—she justifies her plan to honor chastity, the foremost virtue a woman has to uphold, even at the cost of deserting her filial responsibility. In contrast to the personal, emotional voice she uses in her testament to her daughter, Madam Yu appears to be calm and determined in her testament to her parents-in-law: she asks them to take care of her daughter's upbringing and to make sure that her daughter will inherit

57. Yussi puin, "Yusŏ," 193–94.
58. Yussi puin, "Yusŏ," 181–82.

Madam Yu's assets and slaves. In another short note attached to the testament to her parents-in-law, Madam Yu pleads with them to follow what she has requested for her daughter, including that they ensure the family line by adopting an heir.[59]

As revealed in Madam Yu's testaments, women's voices emerge strikingly differently depending on whom they are addressing. Testaments to parents-in-law and other members of a husband's family present a woman's wish to maintain her deep moral rectitude as the primary reason to die. Such testaments often begin by emphasizing the writer's chaste intention, but they also serve as an opportunity to discuss details about the world she is about to leave forever—matters ranging from adoption, childcare, and inheritance to more trivial issues. In her study of the most recently discovered deathbed letter written by a widow to her parents-in-law, Hong Insuk points out the widow's feeling of distress toward her in-law family, hinting at conflict with her parents-in-law over an adoption issue. The widow does not hide her regret at not being fairly treated by her parents-in-law over the issue and claims her role in deciding on a foster son as the logical way to proceed. Hong sees this testament as a concerted attempt not merely to justify the widow's suicide as fulfilling a virtuous path but also to carve out her precarious position and rights in her husband's family.[60]

Deathbed letters therefore served as a critical context in which women navigated the moment when they turned to the final act of suicide. Though it is difficult to generalize about them, most

59. Although not bearing a male heir was considered one of the seven disobediences (see chapter 5, note 28), a sonless wife was still protected by the institution of adoption during the Chosŏn dynasty. Also, there were three instances when a husband could not expel a wife (*sambulgŏ*): "If the family fortune had improved greatly during the marriage, if the wife could not return to her natal family, and if she had performed mourning rituals for either or both parents-in-law." Deuchler, *Confucian Transformation of Korea*, 272.

60. The letters do not reveal the writer's natal family; they only indicate that her husband was a member of the Sin family and that she was thus a daughter-in-law of the Sin family. Hong Insuk, "Chosŏn hugi sunjŏl yŏsŏng Sinssi," 265–85; "Chosŏn hugi yŏsŏng yusŏ yŏn'gu," 247–81.

testaments never fail to frame a widow's action within the normative ideal of following her deceased husband into the ground. In the case of so-called deferred suicide, a widow would use the space to justify why she had not committed suicide immediately after her husband's death and how her survival had enabled her to faithfully serve her deceased husband's patriline. For example, Madam Yi (1716–1784?), who committed suicide on the forty-third anniversary of her husband's death, stresses her lifelong wish to die with her husband to fulfill the wifely way, while explaining the situations and familial duties that prevented her from doing so sooner.[61] In contrast, Madam Yun of Namwŏn (introduced earlier), who took a hundred days to carry out her decision to die, reveals her inner struggles in choosing death and thereby abandoning filiality toward her parents, especially her father. Repeatedly stating that the only reason for delaying her act was to see her father while alive, her testament unveils Madam Yun's strong filial attachment to him.[62] No matter how formidably widows voiced the link between their deaths and their moral duty, the most eloquent and personal words in their testaments are thus often reserved for the emotional torments that underlay their virtuous suicides. Above all, what is clearly missing in the literati's widow biographies is a wife's affection for her deceased husband and absolute despair about living without him, as voiced in Madam Yu's testament quoted above.[63] Madam Kim (1883–1904), who killed herself ninety-three days after her husband died, put it this way:

61. For a study and translation of Madam Yi's testament, see Jungwon Kim, "Madam Yi's Farewell Letter," 375–81.

62. Yun Pyŏngyong, "Namwŏn Yunssi ŭi yusŏ," 212. In her autobiographical writing, Madam Cho of P'ungyang (1772–1815), who lost her husband at the tender age of twenty, explained why she elected to walk a different path from that of other widows who took their lives—namely, to avoid committing unfiliality toward her parents. She states, "Ruminating on my situation, I see there are things that cannot be controlled by human power. Imagining unfiliality and the miserable scene that my suicide would bring to my parents, I could not kill myself." What distinguishes Madam Cho's writing from other widows' testaments is that she decided to survive, not die. P'ungyang Chossi, *Chagirok*, 222.

63. On Madam Kim's testaments, see Jungwon Kim, "Deeper than the Death," 163–82.

For about six years [of marriage], we did not have even one leisure moment to drink together [given his illness]. Because [I believe] my affec-
tionate husband returned to heaven [when he died], I try not to be
contrite. [Yet] if I had known this would happen, I would have done
better. How hard-hearted I was! Now, realizing that I was heartless, my
remorse is eternal and my bitterness is infinite. How resentful and most
regrettable! In this world, whom can I rely on [if I continue to live]?[64]

It has been a month since my husband died. How tiring my inscrutable
life is; two months have passed since my husband left. How tedious the
remainder of my doomed, inscrutable life is; three months have passed
since I was parted forever from my husband. How harsh and lonely the
remainder of my wearisome life is. How ignorant the ghost is [for not
taking me to death sooner].[65]

Although Madam Kim does state that her motive for taking her
own life is to tread the great path of fidelity, as we see in other widows'
testaments, her words convey her conjugal attachment to her dead husband in emotional terms. Even though marriage was established on
economic and social grounds by family members, this did not always
mean that the couple remained distant and without marital affection
throughout their lives. What we can glean about women's choice of death
as voiced in their testaments is, in fact, the inseparability of chastity
and affection, marital obligation and marital intimacy. Careful reading between the lines in widows' testaments—studded as they are with
expressions of moral values, family concerns, and diverse individual,
intimate conjugal feelings—unwraps the multifaceted situations
women lived through, complicating the nature of the conventional
mechanisms thought to govern women's experiences. These women's
voices confirm that they had the ability to choose and that their voluntary deaths do not entirely represent their submission to the normative value of chastity.[66] Rather, their written testimonies reveal

64. *Chongyongnok*, 1:5b.
65. *Chongyongnok*, 1:6a–b.
66. For widows' self-inscriptions and suicide notes, see Fong, "Signifying Bodies,"
105–42.

some of the complex emotions that surrounded this apparently formal acknowledgment of social obligations.

*   *   *

In reviewing the suicide case of a woman called Ms. Hwang, who hanged herself after a man named Pak Sŭngmun attempted to rape her, King Chŏngjo discussed the pervasive socio-familial conditions that drove women to death:

> Generally, in the countryside, ruthless men often violate women of good disposition regardless of their social status—*yangban* or non-*yangban*. If a woman, while gathering wild greens, is taken [by a man] even once, a rumor about her having an adulterous affair fills the air and she suffers disgrace for being a promiscuous woman. Whether she is forcibly violated does not matter: the existence of slander about an illicit relation itself is something [eternally] unremovable and buried in darkness, to the extent that, with a pathetic heart, [she] becomes determined to take her life by hanging. Appealing to her family [about the false charge] upon returning home, some leave [the room], wiping away tears; others just go away, as if seeing a stranger. Humiliation and anger cross, and there is nothing she can do, even if she tries to manage a pitiful life.[67]

The king's postscript presents a situation in which even family members were unwilling to listen to a woman's resentful voice if she had been tainted by or associated with unvirtuous behavior (whether falsely or not). Whether she took her life out of despair or to rectify her lost integrity, her intention was often read as demonstrating her commitment to the chastity ideal, and her suicide was not only sympathized with but highly praised.[68] In the meantime, the increasing emphasis on the performative aspect of female chastity and the surge

67. *Simnirok* 3:93–94.
68. Ms. Hwang is identified as a secondary daughter (*sŏnyŏ*), without a note on her marital status. To honor her chaste spirit, the king offered a tax exemption for her family, in addition to ordering the provincial governor to build a memorial arch in her hometown.

in female suicide in the latter part of the dynasty abruptly generated conflicting views on the practice: chaste death was still glorified, whereas women's tendency to kill themselves became connected to their inborn narrow-mindedness. Rather than being seen as motivated by a women individual backgrounds, suicide was branded as prompted by personality traits of "intolerance" or "narrow-mindedness," which were attributed to women as a group.

As powerfully demonstrated in women's own testaments, however, it was not exclusively the pursuit of morality that prompted them to take the path of suicide. The motives behind the act of suicide were diverse, based on women's own understandings of wifely duty, familial obligations, conjugal love, and filial emotions—whether ingrained within or existing beyond any ideological impetus or parameters. Voices in women's testaments also indicate the difficulty in drawing a clear-cut line between choosing to die solely for the sake of virtue or out of emotional anguish. Women's testaments not only throw into question the notion of any monolithic driving force behind chaste suicide but highlight long-standing questions as to what inspired women to make the extreme choice of suicide and to what extent moral indoctrination influenced their decision—the very questions that have continued to puzzle modern readers of these stories.

Indeed, one criticism of the "old chastity" brought up by early twentieth-century intellectuals and reformers was its lack of passionate love, which was neither expected nor required for spousal relations in the past, according to their observations.[69] Without the emotional component of the conjugal ideal, they argued, chastity can never be a virtue in itself. However, a woman's marital fidelity is most closely related to the human feeling of spousal affection, and chastity is a fluid concept that can be truly achieved only through an active consciousness of the self and genuine feeling toward one's spouse. As we have seen, the voices left by Chosŏn women illuminate their emotional states before they took their own lives, along with the conundrums posed by their ideological commitments. By voluntarily taking their own lives,

69. I use this term "old chastity" as it was originally used in Kim Wŏnju's essay in Hyaeweol Choi, *New Women in Colonial Korea*, 142.

they may have envisioned themselves as attaining the highest mastery over life or as capitulating to the inevitable difficulties of life as a precarious widow. These historical and conceptual differences are crucial to our reconceptualizing of chaste women as neither archetypal victims nor free agents, and to analyzing the interconnections between the normative ideal and a woman's individual deliberations.

EPILOGUE

Female Chastity and
the Unending Question

> Alas! Morality and propriety have disappeared with the
> declining world, where people become beasts. In the past,
> women did not go outside even a single step. These days,
> however, women of all classes gather like a cloud under
> the pretext of women's meeting (*yŏhoe*) and walk in the
> wide street without hesitation, brushing shoulders with
> unrelated men. Benighted men and felonious barbarians
> all praise such a bizarre scene—how terribly stupid of
> these people!
>
> —Yu Insŏk (1842–1915)[‡]

The rich records on chaste women produced during the Chosŏn
dynasty tell us far more complex stories about women's lives than
does a monolithic representation of their moral indoctrination and
virtuous conduct. There is no doubt that female chastity was considered the ethical foundation of the family and of social stability, or that
the state mobilized the ideal of chastity to control women's behavior.
Chastity-centered gender norms permeated the heart of Chosŏn political culture, and we have seen that various factors at both the central

[‡] The epigraph is from Yu Insŏk, "Yuin Changhŭng Imssi chŏn," *Ŭiam chip*,
50:39b–40b.

and local levels—from legislation and reward policy to local *yangban* collectivism—are crucial to understanding the diffusion of the very influential language of chastity in Chosŏn society.

This book addresses the extremely complicated evolution of chastity discourse under shifting historical realities, rather than principles confined to the realm of prescriptive, philosophical ideas. Contextualizing the concept of chastity in these broader historical settings, on multiple levels of people's interactions, this book has presented female chastity as a distinctive cultural phenomenon that extends beyond a gender-specific virtue imposed on female sexuality and the private realm of women's lives. Examining Chosŏn society through the culture of chastity opens an important analytical window onto topics pertinent to gender relations and to the everyday lives of people, within a framework that epitomizes the dynamics of relations among individuals, families, local communities, and the state.

I began this study by asking whether the notion of female chastity was a radical departure from the preexisting cultural underpinnings of the Chosŏn dynasty; how the sociopolitical environment led to a boom in the culture of chastity in the late Chosŏn; and what chastity meant to various groups within that society, from rulers, court officials, and Confucian literati to ordinary people, and especially to women themselves. From the very start of the dynasty, the state's preeminent goal was the moralization of the entire society based on Confucian principles. Despite a trial-and-error approach throughout the dynasty, the ideal of chastity that had been institutionalized, popularized, and fetishized became the supreme norm essential for women. On the one hand, the sociocultural fluorescence of female chastity profoundly implicated interests of the state, elite families, and local politics. On the other hand, chastity was persistently contested by and interwoven with issues of the state's moral agenda, elite priorities, social status, and people's perceptions and values. As the remarkable popularity of chastity in the elite realm gradually trickled down to the ordinary population in the second part of the dynasty, the state's moral vision of chastity was appropriated by men and women of all classes, who adapted it to their lives in their own ways. The diversity and flexibility that culminated in the practice of chastity therefore require a fluid and multifaceted interpretation of the chastity culture in Chosŏn society—a culture best understood not as a unidirectional consequence of Confucianization but as the distinct repository of Chosŏn's own salient historical journey.

Just as I opened this book with an account of extreme wifely devotion in 1921, so I close it with the perennial question of female chastity, one that is still contemplated and disputed in the modern era. In the last phase of the Chosŏn dynasty, the debates on chaste women did not cease, but continued in tandem with the profound societal transformation brought by the opening of the country in 1876—a moment that Korean historiography has seen as a watershed in the modern era.[1] Korea after this point is often imagined as experiencing a sudden influx of foreign, modern ideas, and it is true that the events of that year posed external challenges previously unfamiliar to the Chosŏn state. However, nineteenth-century Korean society had witnessed numerous internal problems, such as peasant uprisings and the rise of new religious movements, even before the arrival of imperial powers from East Asia and the West.[2] Chosŏn society had also already struggled between existing ways and the new ways it might take. Thus, although 1876 has served as a convenient marker for the dawn of modernity, the year hardly revolutionized how people lived all at once. The dynasty lasted for another three decades, until formal annexation by Japan in 1910. This was almost as long as Korea was officially a Japanese colony (1910–1945).

It was during this last, turbulent phase of the dynasty that the discourse on womanhood was most rigorously revisited and impugned, bringing the "woman question" to the table, which then culminated in the image of New Women in the 1920s and 1930s.[3] Intermingled with

1. Chosŏn Korea signed the first modern treaty with Japan in 1876, which scholars see as a conventional marker for dividing premodern and modern Korea.

2. There is rich scholarship on this issue. Representative English scholarship on popular uprisings includes Sun Joo Kim, *Marginality and Subversion in Korea*; Sun Joo Kim, "Taxes, the Local Elite," 993–1027; Karlsson, "Hong Kyŏngnae Rebellion"; Karlsson, "Central Power, Local Society," 207–38; and Kallendar, *Salvation through Dissent*.

3. New Women were generally seen as "challenging tradition and crafting new female identity" under the shifting gender discourses that were constantly interwoven with the discursive forces of nationalism and colonialism. Theodore Jun Yoo, *Politics*

the tensions between existing Confucian norms and new ideals, criticisms of women's status in Korean society gradually surfaced during this period through new media venues and literary genres, targeting Korean women of that time for lacking formal education and opportunities outside the home. Further, in seeing women confined to the inner quarters as "a reflection of national stagnation," this woman question began to occupy the debates over the modern nation-state.[4] Reformers challenged the Confucian precepts as well as the sociocultural setting of Chosŏn Korea that had prevented and discouraged women from engaging in public activity. As such condemnation became more pronounced, what had been acclaimed as exemplary womanhood in the past was denounced as a regressive model that needed to be overcome.

However, new, "progressive" values did not permeate the Korean populace seamlessly, nor did established values encounter challenges from the inside. Though the influx of Western ideas fascinated Korean intellectuals by offering alternative outlooks for correcting social ills of that time, people resisted new and rather "radical" ideas that would undermine the principles appreciated and practiced for several hundred years and threaten the very core of the Chosŏn state. Having long recognized women's bodies and sexual purity as critical to sustaining the dynasty's lineal, social, political, and cosmic stability, the culture of chastity, too, did not dissolve swiftly. The state-reward system honoring chaste women continued to operate, and petitions to commemorate virtuous subjects were submitted through the end of King Kojong's reign.[5] The last such record is found in 1906, when Kojong commemorated a wife who in 1641 had thrown herself into a river to

---

of Gender in Colonial Korea, 13. However, production of the collective ideal of New Women gradually appeared dangerous because women's demands for gender equality could disrupt the ideal womanhood delineated by male intellectuals. Hyaeweol Choi, Gender and Mission Encounters, 147. On the rise and fall of New Women, see Ji-Eun Lee, Women Pre-scripted.

4. Molony, Theiss, and Choi, Gender in Modern East Asia, 154–60.

5. The Sillok does not seem to actively record rewards after about 1883, when the king granted two wives memorial arches for following their deceased husbands. Kojong sillok 20:64a–65b [1883/10/27].

follow her deceased husband into death.[6] More than 250 years later, the state still cherished her death, thereby vindicating the tireless efforts of members of her husband's lineage to receive official acknowledgment of her virtuous commitment.

Literati writings on chaste women also persisted during the last chapter of the dynasty.[7] Out of a sense of urgency that the imperialist barbarians were endangering the country's morals, Neo-Confucian scholars such as Ch'oe Ikhyŏn (1834–1907), like many before him (see chapter 3), extolled women for taking their own lives to maintain their chastity while simultaneously invoking the lost virtue of political loyalty on the part of scholar-officials.[8] Yu Insŏk, one of hundreds of Confucian scholars who opposed the Kanghwa Treaty of 1876 by memorializing the throne, wrote six biographies of chaste women, including one dedicated to a female slave named Yŏndŏk who had killed herself to uphold her wifely fidelity a hundred years before. Commending Yŏndŏk's chaste vow, Yu criticized scholar-officials of the day who joined the interests of barbarians, only contributing to the collapse of the state. Yu closes his biography of Yŏndŏk in grim tones: "I have composed this [biography] to shame those thieves [scholar-officials] for causing the dynasty to perish, and also to astonish all foreign barbarians [with this virtuous story]."[9] Writings on chaste women continued to serve as political indictments of scholar-officials and also to highlight the higher morality of which Chosŏn culture was capable when faced with a series of external threats.

Production of moral handbooks remained active as well, especially at the local level. In 1898, the Confucian scholar No Sangjik (1855–1931) compiled a new abridged version of a didactic text for women. Entitled *Essential Knowledge for Women* (*Yŏsasuji*), No first produced it in literary Chinese, but soon printed it in Korean script for a wider female audience. In 1906, a number of scholar-officials called

6. *Kojong sillok* 45:45a–b [1905/5/1].

7. Kim Kyŏngmi locates about thirty chaste women's biographies produced during the so-called Enlightenment Period (Kaehwagi). Kim Kyŏngmi, "Kaehwagi yŏllyŏjŏn yŏn'gu," 187–211.

8. Ch'oe Ikhyŏn, "Yŏlbu Hassi chŏngnyŏgi," *Myŏnam chip*, 22:31b–32b; and Ch'oe Ikhyŏn, "Yŏlbu Yissi chŏngnyŏgi," *Myŏnam chip*, 20:32a–33b.

9. Yu Insŏk, "Yŏllyŏ sabi Yŏndŏk chŏn," *Ŭiam chip*, 50:35b–36b.

for nominations of virtuous people from local areas to be included in a new compilation of the *Amended Sequel to the Record of the Three Bonds* (*Soksu samgangnok*), aiming to supplement those names left out in earlier versions.[10] In 1907, the *Four Women's Classics, with Annotations in Korean* (*Yŏsasŏ ŏnhae*), first compiled in 1736, was republished through the collective effort of scholars who sought to restore women's virtue as a critical means to reinstate the lost morality of the country. And in 1915, Wang Sŏngsun (1869–1923), a rather unknown local Confucian scholar, completed a three-volume didactic text out of his desire to provide women with "correct education." In his preface, Wang laments that women's proper education had disappeared a long time ago, implicitly defying the modern instruction promoted by reformers of that time. Volume 3 of Wang's text is devoted to the subject of women's fidelity and chastity and opens with the famous dictum from the *Book of Rites* that "a wife cannot change her husband, so she cannot marry even if he dies," followed by sixty-eight accounts of chaste women.[11]

As much as the rise of newspapers such as the *Tongnip sinmun* (Independent) played a pivotal role in inculcating a new vision of gender relations, such new media also provided space for the rekindled discourse of chastity during this period. Although the *Hwangsŏng sinmun* (Capital Gazette) and the *Cheguk sinmun* (Imperial Post) denounced the practices of remarriage, early marriage, and concubinage as inhumane and as oppressive customs to be eradicated from Korean society, they kept printing many stories of virtuous women as miscellaneous reports. Whether conservative (*Hwangsŏng sinmun*) or progressive (*Cheguk sinmun*), these newspapers appeared to laud women's self-sacrifice and suicide for the sake of their husbands or other family members, rather than disparaging such actions as an outmoded, anti-modern legacy of Confucianism.[12] For example, after becoming editor in chief of the *Kyŏngnam ilbo* (Kyŏngnam Daily) in 1909, the renowned enlightenment activist Chang Chiyŏn (1864–1921) published more than twenty chaste-woman stories derived

10. Chŏng Insŏp et al., *Soksu samgangnok*.

11. Wang Sŏngsun, *Kyumun kwebŏm*, 212–71.

12. Kim Kiran, "Kŭndae kyemonggi maech'e," 7–39.

from Chosŏn dynasty gazetteers, despite his two publications on women—the *Story of a Patriotic Woman* (*Aeguk puinjŏn*, 1907) and the *Guidebook for Women* (*Nyŏja tokpon*, 1908)—both of which emphasized women's active participation in the public sphere.[13]

Amid debates over the woman question in the early twentieth century, the renewed discourse of chastity therefore lingered alongside new political and cultural landscapes. Because female chastity had long been considered the counterpart of male political loyalty and a core driving force in the country's moralizing project, the rhetoric of chastity remained deeply imbued with nationalistic concerns, and the subject of chastity was intimately tied to reformers' urgent sense of Korea's struggle for dynastic survival and reform. It was hoped that examples of chaste women's heroic acts could help rescue the declining country on the brink of its collapse, and the discourse of chastity was sustained through the tensions between past and present—that is, between those who strove to defend the old practices and those who wished to adopt the new ideas.

Korea became an official colony of Japan in 1910, which marked the demise of the dynasty as well as the end of the long-standing state-reward system. However, this loss of sovereignty neither blocked people's passion for remembering virtuous subjects of the past and present nor obstructed their enduring activities to recognize them. Although the Japanese colonial government did not offer an equivalent of the reward system that had been appreciated for five hundred years in Korea, petitions requesting that chaste women be honored were still drafted and circulated throughout the colonial period. Local Confucian academies and county schools stepped into the government's position, handling petitions with enthusiastic support from local families to ensure that exemplary candidates were properly commemorated (fig. E.1).

For instance, in 1918, when Ms. Pak, the twenty-three-year-old widow of a man named Yi Wŏnhae, killed herself with poison, a circular elucidating her virtuous action was drafted by the local association (*hyanghoe*) of Taejon, in Ch'ungch'ŏng Province, where the

13. Hong Insuk, *Kŭndae kyemonggi yŏsŏng tamnon*, 63–65.

E.1. A circular issued by a Confucian school of Yŏngch'ŏn, in Kyŏngsang Province, on the fifth day of second month in 1919, addressed to the Oksan Academy in Kyŏngju, calling for a certain Madam Kim, who had followed her husband into death, to be honored. Although she had wished to die right away, she was pregnant when her husband died. At the urging of her parents-in-law, she waited until after she gave birth to a daughter; she then stopped eating and, finally, stabbed herself to death. 53.8 × 94 cm. Photograph courtesy of Oksan Sŏwŏn, Kyŏngju, North Kyŏngsang Province.

couple had resided.[14] Yi was three years younger than Ms. Pak but died from an illness despite her devoted care. When he was about to expire, Ms. Pak threw herself into the cellar of their house, wishing to perish before her husband. After his death, she tried to kill herself again by jumping from a pavilion. Although her parents-in-law saved her, she finally took her life around the first anniversary of her husband's death, leaving two testaments—one for her parents and another for her sister-in-law. Like earlier circulars composed to commemorate chaste women, the 1918 document begins by noting the significance of Ms. Pak's chaste act and the superior criteria for the honor that need be validated through public consensus. Reminding its readers that Chosŏn used to have a law formally distinguishing chaste women, the circular asserts that no one is better qualified for official recognition than Ms. Pak and proposes following the old policy of erecting a memorial arch at the entrance of her town.

The circular is addressed to the Oksan Academy (Oksan Sŏwŏn), located in Kyŏngju, in Kyŏngsang Province, where the original document is now preserved. About a week later, the Oksan Confucian Academy received a second circular requesting that Ms. Pak be commemorated, issued by the Tosan Academy (Tosan Sŏwŏn) in Andong. The Tosan circular describes Ms. Pak's unwavering determination to die for the ideal of chastity and emphasizes that her husband, Yi Wŏnhae, was a descendant of the prominent Neo-Confucian scholar Yi Hwang, who had been enshrined and ritualized at the Tosan Academy.[15] In fact, the Oksan Academy holds a number of circulars produced during the colonial era that sought the public commemoration of virtuous subjects (see fig. E.1.). These circulars reveal that Confucian academies represented the collective opinions of local Confucian scholars under the colonial government and played a much-needed role in upholding the "old practices" that had served as a powerful symbol of the country's moral character and reputation for hundreds of years.[16]

14. "1918 Taejŏn hyanghoe hoejung t'ongmun."

15. "1918 Tosan Sŏwŏn t'ongmun." One reason the Tosan Academy sent out the circular on behalf of Ms. Pak's death in Ch'ungch'ŏng Province may have been its link to her husband's family.

16. Ch'oe Insuk, "19-segi Tosan Sŏwŏn ŭi sahoe insik kwa sot'ong pangsik," 119–63. Also see Hwisang Cho, "Circular Letters in Chosŏn Society," 100–120. Cho

E.2. A special flower trolley (*kkot chŏnch'a*) adorned with the words "Long live President Rhee. Happy eighty-first birthday." 1956. CET0056892. Photograph courtesy of National Archives of Korea.

Although the practice of honoring chaste women continued at the local level during the colonial era, official recognition of chaste wives resumed after the Korean War (1950–1953), when the first president of the Republic of Korea, Syngman Rhee (1875–1965), revived the system of government rewards. Often held in conjunction with celebrations of President Rhee's birthday (*t'ansinil*), an annual ceremony of the award took place in Seoul, along with other public events (fig. E.2). Before the president's eightieth birthday in 1955, the government asked each region to select and nominate three candidates for filiality and chastity, and twenty-seven people received commendations before the musical concert for Seoul citizens began in Ch'anggyŏng Garden.[17] Although

introduces a circular from Tosan Academy, issued in 1920, commemorating Madam Yi's chastity.

17. *Tonga ilbo*, "Yi taet'ongnyŏng 80-hoe t'ansinil," March 14, 1955, 2.

the forms of reward were different (no memorial arches, exemption from taxes, or changes in social class), the ceremony nevertheless recalled the state-reward system of the Chosŏn dynasty. The award event was held in Seoul each year on the president's birthday, and in 1958 the selected awardees were recognized at each district's office.[18]

With the onset of modernity, chaste women certainly lost their traditional status and symbolic significance, even though new perceptions of women's position did not suddenly overturn the long-standing value of chastity practice in Korean society. Embracing the new does not always mean complete desertion of the old. Perhaps what survived the early twentieth-century competition between the old and the new was precisely the zeal to maintain the old. Although our view of women after the arrival of the so-called modern era has been heavily influenced by the late nineteenth-century narrative and construction of New Women—the most visible and avid discourse upheld by a new wave of intellects of that time—the issue of women's chastity continued to have an enduring impact on Korean society even a century later, in the early twenty-first century.

18. *Chosŏn ilbo*, "Kyŏngch'uksik ŭn sŏul undongjang sŏ," March 26, 1958, 3.

Glossary

Personal Names

An Chŏngbok 安鼎福
An Po 安輔
Chang Chiyŏn 張志淵
Chang Yu 張維
Cheng Yi (Ch.) 程頤
Cho Ch'anhan 趙纘韓
Cho Hyŏnmyŏng 趙顯命
Cho Kusang 趙龜祥
Cho Kyŏngnam 趙慶男
Cho Yuhyŏng 趙有亨
Ch'oe Ch'ung 崔冲
Ch'oe Ikhyŏn 崔益鉉
Ch'oe Malli 崔萬理
Ch'oe Myŏnggil 崔鳴吉
Ch'oe Nubaek 崔婁伯
Ch'oe Yong 崔湧
Ch'oe Yunŭi 崔允儀
Chŏng Ch'angson 鄭昌孫
Chŏng Sihan 丁時翰
Chŏng Yagyong 丁若鏞
Chŏng Yu 鄭裕
Chu Sebung 周世鵬
Feng Menglong (Ch.) 馮夢龍
Gongbo (Ch.) 共伯
Ha Hakho 河學浩
Hong Ho 洪鎬
Hong Uryong 洪遇龍
Hwang Sau 黃士祐
Hwang Yŏil 黃汝一

Hyangnang 香娘
Im Hŏnhoe 任憲晦
Im Kyŏngju 任敬周
Im Tŏkchung 林德重
Iryŏn 一然
Kil Chae 吉再 (pen name Yaŭn 冶隱)
Kim Anguk 金安國
Kim Chaero 金在魯
Kim Ch'ŏnsŏk 金天石
Kim Chosun 金祖淳
Kim Hansin 金漢藎
Kim Idan 金已丹
Kim Koengp'il 金宏弼
Kim Kukpo 金國輔
Kim Kwangwŏn 金光遠
Kim Pusik 金富軾
Kim Pyŏnghak 金炳學
Kim Sohaeng 金紹行
Kim Sŭnggyŏng 金升卿
Kim T'aehyŏn 金台鉉
Kim Tŏgwŏn 金德遠
Kim Yŏngbu 金永夫
Kim Yunson 金胤孫
Kim Yusin 金庾信
King Kongmin 恭愍王
King Kongyang 恭讓王
King U 禑王
Ko Ŭmdŏk 古音德

Kwŏn Sangha 權尙夏
Kwŏn Si 權諰
Kwŏn Tugyŏng 權斗經
Lady Cho 曺氏
Lady Chŏng 靖嬪
Lady Gongjiang (Ch.) 共姜
Liu Xiang (Ch.) 劉向
Lu Yongqing (Ch.) 魯永清
Min Ch'ihŏn 閔致憲
Min Chinwŏn 閔鎭遠
Min Chonghyŏn 閔鐘顯
Mun Chunggap 文仲甲
Mun Okchi (or Ogi) 文玉只
　(or 玉伊)
Mundŏk Wanghu Yussi
　文德王侯 劉氏
Myoch'ŏng 妙淸
Nam Hyoon 南孝溫
Nam Yuyong 南有容
No Sangjik 盧相稷
O Kyet'ak 吳戒卓
Ŏ Sukkwŏn 魚叔權
Okkŭm 玉今
Pak Chiwŏn 朴趾源
Pak Chŏnji 朴全之
Pak Munsu 朴文秀
Pak Sungjil 朴崇質
Pak Sŭngjong 朴承宗
Pak Yunwŏn 朴胤源
Princess Hwasun (Hwansun
　ongju) 和順翁主
Queen Chŏngsun (Chŏngsun
　wanghu) 貞純王后
Queen Dowager Chŏnghŭi
　(Chŏnghŭi wanghu)
　貞熹王后
Queen Inhyŏn (Inhyŏn wanghu)
　仁顯王后
Queen Sohye (Sohye wanghu)
　昭惠王后
Rhee Syngman 李承晩

Sima Qian 司馬遷
Sim Chaedŏk 沈載德
Sim Chŏng 沈貞
Sim Naksu 沈樂洙
Sin Sui 愼守彝
Sin T'ongnye 申通禮
Sin Yunbok 申潤福
Sŏk Uro 昔于老
Sŏlssinyŏ 薛氏女
Song Hŏndong 宋獻仝
Song Hwan'gi 宋煥箕
Songja 宋子 Master Song
Sŏng Sammun 成三問
Song Siyŏl 宋時烈
Song Suyŏn 宋守淵
Sŏng Taejung 成大中
Sukch'ang Wŏnbi Kimssi
　淑昌院妃金氏
Sunbi Hŏssi 順妃許氏
Sun'gŭm 順今
Tomi 都彌
Wang Minhao (Ch.) 王民皞
Wang Sŏngsun 王性淳
Wang Xiuchu (Ch.) 王秀楚
Wi Paekkyu 魏伯珪
Wŏn Ch'ŏnsŏk 元天錫
Wŏn Kyŏngha 元景夏
Xu Jing (Ch.) 徐兢
Yang Sabo 楊思輔
Yang Sŏnghang 梁成恒
Yang Susaeng 楊首生
Yi An 李晏
Yi Chae 李栽 (1657-1730)
Yi Chae 李縡 (1680-1746)
Yi Ch'angbŏm 李昌範
Yi Chehyŏn 李齊賢
Yi Chokkŭmaji 李足今阿只
Yi Chŏng 李定
Yi Chŏngdŏk 李鼎德
Yi Chosŭng 李祖承
Yi Ch'undae 李春大

Yi Hwang 李滉 (pen name
  T'oegye 退溪)
Yi I 李珥 (pen name
  Yulgok 栗谷)
Yi Ik 李瀷
Yi Imyŏng 李頤命
Yi Kok 李穀
Yi Konsu 李崑秀
Yi Kŭkki 李克基
Yi Kwangjŏng 李光庭
Yi Kwangsa 李匡師
Yi Kyŏngse 李經世
Yi Maktong 李萬同
Yi Myŏn'gŭng 李勉兢
Yi Ok 李鈺
Yi P'aengnyŏng 李彭齡
Yi P'ilhwa 李苾和
Yi Pongjin 李奉辰

Yi Sehak 李世學
Yi Sihang 李時恒
Yi Sisŏn 李時善
Yi Sŏ 李曙
Yi Sungin 李崇仁
Yi Sŭngjang 李勝章
Yi Tŏngmu 李德懋
Yi Tŭkp'yo 李得表
Yi Ŭngwŏn 李應元
Yi Yŏ 李畬
Yŏm Kyŏngae 廉瓊愛
Yŏngdae 永代
Yu Hŭich'un 柳希春
Yu Insŏk 柳麟錫
Yu Sudol 柳守乭
Yu Sun 柳洵
Yun Sŏndo 尹善道
Zhu Xi (Ch.) 朱熹

General Terms

Aeguk puinjŏn 愛國夫人傳 *Story of a Patriotic Woman*
aguk kŭm chaega 我國禁改嫁 our country prohibits remarriage
chaega kŭmjipŏp 再嫁禁止法 the law prohibiting remarriage
chaenyŏ 才女 talented woman
chaik 自溺 self-drowning
chaksŏl 綽楔 elongated wooden lintel of a door
chaksŏl chi chŏn 綽楔之典 the law granting a memorial arch
ch'albang 察訪 station officer
"Changgwŏn" 獎勸 "Encouragement," a section in the *Kyŏngguk taejŏn*
Chanyŏ an 恣女案 *Register of Licentious Women*
ch'idoyul 治盜律 the statute on regulating thieves
chikchŏnbŏp 職田法 office land system
chikhae 直解 direct explanation
ch'ilgŏ 七去 the Seven Disobediences
chinsa 進士 literary licentiate
Chiphyŏnjŏn 集賢殿 Hall of Worthies
cho 刁 pulling, gong
chogan 刁姦 seduction-led fornication
choi 조이 (or *sosa* 召史) Ms., or title for a commoner woman

ch'ŏk 尺 unit of length

chŏl 節 principledness

chŏlbu 節婦 principled wife

chŏlbuu 節婦雨 chaste-wife rain

ch'ŏlli / t'ien-li (Ch.) 天理 principle of nature, or of heaven

ch'ŏlli injŏng 天理人情 heavenly principle and human nature

chŏlyŏl 節烈 fidelity and chastity

chŏn 典 permanent laws

chŏn 錢 monetary unit, 10 *chŏn* = 1 yang

chŏng 貞 chastity

chŏng 情 emotion, feeling, affection, or one's heart; also specific circumstances

chŏng 正 right [path]

chŏngbŏm 正犯 principal offender

chŏngbyŏng 正兵 conscripted soldiers

chŏnggyŏl 貞潔 a wife's chastity

chŏngjŏl 貞節 [women's] chastity

chŏngmi 丁未 name of a year in the sixty-year cycle

chŏngmun 旌門 memorial arch

chŏngnyŏ 貞女 faithful maiden; faithful woman

chŏngnyŏ / jingbiao (Ch.) 旌閭 the state-reward system for moral subjects; erection of a memorial arch or a tombstone

chŏngnyŏ yenapchŏn 旌閭例納錢 payment required to receive the reward

chŏngp'yo 旌表 the state-reward system

chŏngyŏl 貞烈 ardent spirit

ch'ŏnmin 賤民 the debased

chonsein hasein 存世人下世人 living or dead

chŏrŭi 節義 chastity and righteousness

chŏrŭi chi to 節義之道 the way of fidelity and righteousness

Chosŏn chunghwa 朝鮮中華 Chosŏn-centered ideology

Chosŏn hyŏngsaryŏng / Chōsen keijirei (J.) 朝鮮刑事令 Chosŏn Penal Order

Chungbu 中部 a region name

chungin 中人 middle-class commoners with technical and administrative skills

ch'ungsin 忠臣 loyal subject

Chusa kŏbae 酒肆擧盃 *Having a Drinking Party and Holding a Cup*

chwasu 座首 head of local *yangban* association

Chwaŭijŏng 左議政 Left State Counselor

ch'wi 娶 marrying [her]

ch'yŏnbong chit'ong 천봉지통 agony reaching the peak of the sky

diaojian (Ch.) 刁姦 seduction-led fornication

Gaoli tujing (Ch.) 高麗圖經 *Illustrated Account of Koryŏ*

Gujin lienü zhaun 古今列女傳 *Biographies of Exemplary Women of the Past and Present*

Haejo 該曹 Ministry of Rites

haengno chi sojŏm 行露之所沾 wet with street dew

Haengsilto sipkok pyŏngp'ung 行實圖十曲屏風 Ten-Panel Folding Screen with Paintings on the *Illustrated Guide* [*to the Five Relations*]

Han'guk kubi munhak taegye 韓國口碑文學大系 *Compilation of Korean Oral Literature*

Hanshu 漢書 *History of the Han*

"Hassinyŏ chŏn" 何氏女傳 "The Biography of Madam Ha"

Hojo 戶曹 Ministry of Taxation

hŏmun 虛門 a (false) gate

Honam 湖南 Southwestern Region

hongmun 紅門 red gate

Hongmungwan 弘文館 Office of the Special Counselors

"Hong yŏlbu chŏn" 洪烈婦傳 "The Biography of Chaste Wife Madam Hong"

hosaeng osa inji sangjŏng 好生惡死人之常情 love to live, hate to die; that is human nature

hwagan / *hejian* (Ch.) 和姦 consensual fornication

hwanhyang-nyŏ 還鄉女 "brought-back women"; women who were taken [to China] as prisoners of war and later returned [to Chosŏn]

Hwasun ongju chi mun 和順翁主之門 Memorial gate for Princess Hwasun

hyanggyo 鄉校 county schools

hyanghoe 鄉會 local association

Hyangnang t'ugang susa 香娘投江水死 Hyangnang jumps into the water and dies

Hyangnang yŏ ch'onyŏ ŏ 香娘與樵女語 Hyangnang speaks to a girl woodcutter

hyoja 孝子 filial children

hyŏn 縣 county

Hyŏngpŏp taejŏn 刑法大全 *Comprehensive Collection of Penal Codes*

Hyŏngjo 刑曹 Ministry of Punishment

"Hyŏngjŏn" 刑典 "Laws on Penal Affairs," a chapter in the *Kyŏngguk taejŏn hyŏnmo* 賢母 wise mother

hyŏnnyŏ 賢女 wise daughter; virtuous woman

Hyonyŏ Chiŭn 孝女知恩 the filial daughter Chiŭn

"Hyosŏn" 孝善 "Filiality and Goodness," a section in the *Samguk yusa*

hyoyang-bang 孝養坊 a village fostering filiality

hyoyang-ri 孝養里 a village nurturing filiality

hyuryangjŏn 恤養田 land to safeguard upbringing

Ibu t'amch'un 嫠婦耽春 *Widow Enjoying the Springtime*

idu 吏讀 clerk's readings

Ilsŏn ŭiyŏlto 一善義烈圖 *Illustrations of the Righteousness and Chastity of Sŏnsan*

Imo Incident 壬午禍變 the death of the Crown Prince Sado

in / ren (Ch.) 仁 humane mind; supreme virtue

injŏng 人情 one's [sincere] heart

jiefu (Ch.) 節婦 chaste widow

Kaehwagi 開化期 Enlightenment Period

Kaesŏng 開城 Koryŏ capital

kajang 家長 household head

kamyŏng 監營 provincial governor's office

kanbŏm 干犯 accomplice

kanggan / qiangjian (Ch.) 強姦 forcible fornication, rape

kangsang 綱常 fundamental Confucian norms

katcha yŏllyŏ 가짜 열녀 fake chaste women

kich'uk 己丑 name of a year in the sexagenary cycle

"Kii" 紀異 "Unfamiliar Stories," section in the *Samguk yusa*

kisaeng 妓生 female entertainer

kkot chŏnch'a 꽃전차 flower trolley

kogong 雇工 hired labor

kojŏl 苦節 painful fidelity

kongnon 公論 public consensus

kongŭi 公議 collective agreement

kŏpkan 劫姦 violating a woman's body

kŏpt'al 劫奪 taking things by force

Koryŏsa 高麗史 *History of Koryŏ*

kubunjŏn 口分田 land provided for the family of a deceased or retired soldier

kun 郡 prefecture

kunja 君子 person of high virtue

kwabu 寡婦 widow

kwabujŏn 寡婦錢 money required to settle a widow's remarriage

kwajŏnpŏp 科田法 rank-land system

kwanbi 官婢 government slave
kwich'ŏn 貴賤 high or low
kyohwa 敎化 moralization
kyŏkchaeng 擊錚 oral petition
Kyŏngguk taejŏn 經國大典 *Great Code of Administration*
Kyŏngje yukchŏn 經濟六典 *Six Codes of Administration*
kyŏngjŏk sambuja 更適三夫者 [re]married more than three men
Kyŏngse yup'yo 經世遺表 *Treatise on Government*
kyŏngsin 庚申 name of a year in the sexagenary cycle
Kyŏngsŏng 京城 Hanyang (capital of the Chosŏn dynasty)
Kyosŏgwan 校書館 Office of Editorial Review
Kyumun suji yŏhaeng chi to 閨門須知女行之圖 *Illustration of Women's Essential Knowledge and Conduct in the Inner Quarters*
li 里 unit of distance, equal to 2,100 *ch'ŏk* (from 430.08 to 453.6 meters, according to the late Chosŏn Zhou ruler)
liefu (Ch.) 烈婦 chaste wife
lienü (Ch.) 烈女 chaste woman
Lienü zhuan (Ch.) 列女傳 *Categorized Biographies of Women*
Lüshi xiangyue 呂氏鄉約 Lü Family Community Compact
Luxue jieyi (Ch.) 律學解頤 *Clear Elaboration on the Great Ming Code*
mansang taeban 挽裳對飯 pulling a skirt and sitting face to face over a meal
"*Mich'ŏ haedo*" 彌妻偕逃 "Tomi's Wife Running Away Together [with Her Husband]"
"*Mich'ŏ tamch'o*" 彌妻啖草 "Tomi's Wife Eating Grass"
mimangin / wei wang ren (Ch.) 未亡人 widow
Mongmin simsŏ 牧民心書 *Admonitions on Governing the People*
muja 戊子 name of a year in the sexagenary cycle
mullon 勿論 not questioning the guilt
munjip 文集 individual collections of male literati
myojimyŏng / muzhiming (Ch.) 墓誌銘 epitaph
myŏnch'ŏn 免賤 release from the lowest status of one's social class and making them commoners
myŏnjil 面質 a cross-examination
naegŭmwi 內禁衛 palace guardsmen
Naehun 內訓 *Inner Instruction*
namnye 納禮 (or *napch'ae* 納采) a preliminary part of the wedding ritual
Nyŏja tokpon 女子讀本 *Guidebook for Women*
nyŏn 年 "years in age," or years old
nyŏnse kugŭn 年歲久近 old or young

Oksan Sŏwŏn 玉山書院 Oksan Academy
ŏnmun 諺文 Korean script
Oryun haengsilto 五倫行實圖 *Illustrated Guide to the Five Relations*
"Paekchu" 柏舟 "Cypress Boat"
pak 縛 binding [a widow] up
pakch'wi 縛娶 widow kidnapping
p'alch'on 八寸 third cousin
P'algwanhoe 八關會 Assembly of the Eight Prohibitions
p'alcho 八條 Eight Regulations
palsa 跋辭 a postscript
p'igo 被告 the accused
p'iro chi nyŏ 被虜之女 (or sokwhan p'iro punyŏ 贖還被虜婦女)
   hwanhyang-nyŏ (see "hwanhyang-nyŏ" entry above)
pokho 復戶 exemption of the household from miscellaneous duties
"Pŏmgan" 犯姦 "Committing Fornication"
pondo p'yesŭp 本道弊習 chronic evil custom of the province
pŏbŭi 法意 spirit of the law
possam 보쌈 "wrap in a cloth," a colloquial term for widow
   kidnapping
pu 府 special city
pudae sich'am 不待時斬 decapitation without delay
Pujehak 副提學 First Counselor of the Office of the Special
   Counselors
p'umgwan chi ch'ŏ 品官之妻 wife of a *yangban* man
p'umgwan chi nyŏ 品官之女 daughter of a *yangban* family
p'unghŏn 風憲 village head
pusa 府使 county magistrate
Puyŏ / Fuyu (Ch.) 夫餘 Puyŏ state
Pyŏgyŏng surok 碧營隨錄 *Collected Reports from Pyŏgyŏng*
pyŏn 變 anomaly
Pyŏngjo 兵曹 Ministry of War
p'yŏnae 偏隘 small-minded
p'yŏnbyŏk 偏僻 eccentric
Pyŏngsul taejon 丙戌大典 *Great Code of Pyŏngsul*
p'yŏnhyŏp 偏狹 narrow mind; intolerant
p'yŏnhyŏp chi ch'ŏnsŏng 偏狹之天性 inborn intolerance
p'yŏnp'yak 偏愎 ill-tempered
p'yŏnsŏng 偏性 narrow personality; biased
sadaebu 士大夫 scholar-official
"Saeng yollyŏjŏn" 生烈女傳 "Tale of a Living Chaste Woman"
saengwŏn 生員 classics licentiate

Saganwŏn 司諫院 Office of the Censor-General
Sahŏnbu 司憲府 Office of the Inspector-General
saja 士子 *yangban* scholar
sajok 士族 distinguished aristocrat families
salsin sŏngin 殺身成仁 killing oneself if it would achieve
  humaneness
samasi 司馬試 lesser examination
sambulgŏ 三不去 three instances when a husband could not expel
  a wife
samgang 三綱 Three Bonds
Samgang haengsilto 三綱行實圖 *Illustrated Guide to the Three
  Bonds*
Samgang haengsil yŏllyŏdo 三綱行實烈女圖 *Illustrated Guide to
  the Three Bonds and Chaste Women*
Samguk sagi 三國史記 *Historical Records of the Three Kingdoms*
Samguk yusa 三國遺史 *Memorabilia of the Three Kingdoms*
Samhan sŭbyu 三韓拾遺 *An Addendum to Korea*
samjong 三從 Three Followings
sangjik 賞職 (or *sŏyong* 敍用 or *kaja* 加資) awarding or upgrading
  official positions for the sons of virtuous people
sangmin 常民 commoners, or ordinary people
sangmul 賞物 award of rice, cloth, land, and houses
"*Sangnang chŏn*" 尙娘傳 "Tale of Sangnang"
sang yŏmch'i 尙廉恥 commemorate one's sense of honor
sangŏn 上言 written petition
sanjŏngbon 刪定本 abridged vernacular edition
sasaeng ch'wiŭi 捨生取義 abandoning one's life for the sake of
  righteousness
sasajŏn 寺社田 Buddhist temple lands
shanshu (Ch.) 善書 books to promote good deeds
Shiji (Ch.) 史記 *Records of the Grand Historian*
Shijing (Ch.) 詩經 *Book of Poetry*
Sinju Muwŏllok 新註無冤錄 *Newly Supplemented Coroner's Manual
  for the Elimination of Grievances*
silchŏl 失節 woman without fidelity
Simnirok 審理錄 *Records of Royal Reviews*
Sinbo sugyo chimnok 新補受敎輯錄 *Newly Supplemented Collected
  Royal Edicts*
sinch'ung 宸衷 king's inner mind, king's agony
sirhaeng 失行 misconduct
sirhak 實學 practical learning

sobyŏng 素屛 blank screen
sogakpu 俗樂府 collection of folk poetry
Sŏgyŏng 西京 Western capital
Sohak / Xiao xue (Ch.) 小學 *Elementary Learning*
Sok taejŏn 續大典 *Continuation of the Great Code*
Soksu samgangnok 續修三綱錄 *Amended Sequel to the Record of the Three Bonds*
sŏmin 庶民 commoners
Sŏngho sasŏl 星湖僿說 *Sŏngho's Discourses on the Minute*
sŏngok sangmyŏng 成獄償命 homicide deserving punishment of the death sentence
sŏnyŏ 徐女 secondary daughters
sŏŏl 庶孽 illegitimate son of *yangban*
sŏŏl t'ongch'ŏng 庶孽通淸 hiring talented illegitimate sons
sŏwŏn 書院 Confucian academies
ssi 氏 Madam, or title for a *yangban* woman
"*Such'ik chŏn*" 守則傳 "Tale of Such'ik"
sugyo 受敎 received instructions
Sugyo chimnok 受敎輯錄 *Collected Royal Edicts*
sujŏl 守節 sexual integrity, keeping one's chastity
sujŏl kwabu 守節寡婦 chaste widows
Sŭngjŏngwŏn 承政院 Royal Secretariat
sung chŏrŭi 崇節義 respect one's fidelity
sunjŏl 殉節 chaste suicide
susin 守信 maintain permanent fidelity
susinjŏn 守信田 widow lands program
susŏyŏnggi 手誓永棄 abandon her permanently in writing
suyuk 熟肉 boiled meat slices
Taejŏn hoet'ong 大典會通 *Comprehensive Collection of Dynastic Codes*
Taejŏn husongnok 大典後續綠 *Continued Supplementary Great Code*
Taejŏn songnok 大典續錄 *Supplementary Great Code*
Taejŏn t'ongp'yŏn 大典通編 *Great Code for Ruling the State*
Taemyŏngnyul / Da Ming lü (Ch.) 大明律 *Great Ming Code*
Taemyŏngnyul chikhae 大明律直解 *Direct Explanation of the Great Ming Code*
T'aengniji 擇里志 *Classic for Choosing Settlement*
Taesagan 大司諫 Censor-General
Taesahŏn 大司憲 Inspector-General
t'aksŏl 棹楔 wooden arch

tan'ch'ŏng 丹靑 cinnabar and blue-green

t'ansinil 誕辰日 birthday

to 道 way

tobae 島配 banishing to a remote unknown island

tobaek 道伯 provincial governor

Todang 都堂 Privy Council

t'onggan 通姦 or 通奸 fornication

Tongguk sinsok samgang haengsilto 東國新續三綱行實圖 *New Expanded Illustrated Guide to the Three Bonds of the Eastern State*

Tongguk sok samgang haengsil yŏllyŏdo 東國續三綱行實烈女圖 *Revised Illustrated Guide to the Three Bonds and Chaste Women of the Eastern State*

Tongjisa 冬至使 Winter Solstice Envoy to China

"T'ongjŏngdaebu Ko Chŏngŏn ch'unghyoyŏl Changssi ryŏ" 通政大夫高廷彦 忠孝烈張氏之閭 "Memorial arch of Madam Chang, the loyal, filial, and chaste wife of the scholar-official Ko Chŏngŏn"

tongjung kongŭi 洞中公儀 village consensus

tongsa / tongshi (Ch.) 彤史 a female teacher

Tosan Sŏwŏn 陶山書院 Tosan Academy

Tosŭngji 都承旨 First Royal Secretary

tŭngnok 謄錄 collected royal edicts

ŭi 義 righteousness

ŭibu 義夫 righteous husbands

Ŭijŏngbu 議政府 State Council

"Ŭiudo" 義牛圖 "Illustrated Account of a Righteous Cow"

ŭiyŏl 義烈 righteousness and chastity

ŭmjik 蔭職 protection privilege

ŭmnyŏ 淫女 licentious woman

Ŭnggyo 應敎 Fourth Counselor of the Office of the Special Counselors

ŭpchi 邑誌 local gazetteers

Wae 倭 (J. Wa) Wae kingdom, Wae raiders

wip'ipch'isa 威逼致死 using coercion to cause others to die

yang 兩 monetary unit; 1 *yang* = 10 *chŏn*

yangban 兩班 ruling aristocrats

yangin 良人 commoners or good people

yangnyŏ 良女 commoner woman

Yaŭn Sŏwŏn 冶隱書院 Confucian Academy built to worship Kil Chae

Yegi / Liji (Ch.) 禮記 *Book of Rites*

"Yejŏn 禮典" "Laws on Ritual Affairs," a chapter in the *Kyŏngguk taejŏn*

"Yi yŏlbu chŏn" 李烈婦傳 "Tale of Chaste Wife Madam Yi"
Yŏch'ik 女則 *Regulations for Women*
Yŏgye 女誡 *Instructions for Women*
yŏhang sŏin 閭巷庶人 commoner in the countryside
yŏhoe 女會 women's meeting
yŏl 烈 chastity; also righteousness
yŏlbu 烈婦 chaste wife
"Yŏlbu ipkang" 烈婦入江 "A Chaste Wife Entering the River"
"Yŏlburon" 烈婦論 "Discussion on Chaste Wives"
"Yŏlchŏn" 列傳 "Biographies," chapter in *Samguk sagi*
yŏllyŏ 烈女 chaste women
yŏllyŏdo 烈女圖 illustrations of chaste women
"Yollyŏ Hongssi chŏn" 烈女洪氏傳 "Biography of Madam Hong"
Yŏllyŏjŏn 烈女傳 *Biographies of Chaste Women*
yŏllyŏmun 烈女門 chastity gate
yŏllyŏ tamnon 烈女談論 discourse of chaste women
Yŏndŭnghoe 燃燈會 Lantern Festival
Yŏngŭijŏng 領議政 Chief State Counselor
Yŏrha / Rehe (Ch.) 熱河 region where the Qing emperors' summer
    residence was located; present-day Chengde in China
Yŏsasŏ 女四書 *Four Women's Classics*
Yŏsasŏ ŏnhae 女四書諺解 *Four Women's Classics, with Annotations
    in Korean*
Yŏsasuji 女士須知 *Essential Knowledge for Women*
youjian futao (Ch.) 誘姦婦逃 fornication through seduction and flight
    with the woman
yu 唯 even though
yuajiyul 由我之律 the statute of triggering one's death
yuhyangso 留鄉所 local *yangban* association
yuin 孺人 an honorific title for the deceased wife of a Confucian
    scholar without a governmental position
Yukcho 六曹 Six Ministries
"Yuksinjŏn" 六臣傳 "Biographies of Six Officials"
Yullye yoram 律例要覽 *Conspectus of Laws and Precedents*
yun'gi 倫紀 moral principle
"Zhen shun" (Ch.) 貞順 "Rectitude and Compliance"; a section in
    Lienü zhuan
zhennu (Ch.) 貞女 faithful maiden
Zhinang (Ch.) 智囊 *Sack of Wisdom*
Zuo zhuan (Ch.) 左傳 *Zuo Tradition*

Bibliography

Abbreviations

CSG: Changsŏgak Archive (Han'gukhak Chungang Yŏn'guwŏn)
HMC: *Han'guk munjip ch'onggan*
KYU: Kyujanggak Institute for Korean Studies (Kyujanggak Han'guhak Yŏn'guwŏn)
NLK: National Library of Korea (Kungnip Chungang Tosŏgwan)
Sillok: Chosŏn wangjo sillok

Primary Sources

"1918 Taejŏn Hyanghoe hoejung t'ongmun" 1918 大全鄉會 會中 通文 [1918 circular of the Taejŏn Local Association]. Oksan Sŏwŏn, Kyŏngju, North Kyŏngsang Province.

"1918 Tosan Sŏwŏn t'ongmun" 1918 陶山書院 通文 [1918 circular of the Tosan Confucian Academy]. Oksan Sŏwŏn, Kyŏngju, North Kyŏngsang Province.

The Academy of Korean Studies. Han'guk yŏktae inmul chonghap chŏngbo sistem. http://people.aks.ac.kr/index.aks.

An Chŏngbok 安鼎福. "Che yŏllyŏ Yŏhŭng Yissi haengnok hu" 題烈女驪興 李氏行錄後 [A postscript to a biography of chaste woman Madam Yi of Yŏhŭng]. *Sunam chip* 順菴集 [Collected Works of Sunam]. 15 vols. 1900. NLK, Ko 3468-45-21. 19:9b–11b. HMC 230:182–83.

———. "Yŏllyŏ sugin Chossi chŏngmun kimyo taein chak" 烈女淑人趙氏 呈文 己卯 代人作 [A report on the chaste woman Madam Cho written on behalf of someone in the *kimyo* year]. *Sunam chip*, 17:34a–35b. HMC 230:154c–55b.

Ban Gu 班固. *Hanshu* 漢書 [History of the Han]. Seoul: Kyŏngin Munhwasa, 1975.

Cheng, Hao 程顥. *Er Cheng yishu* 二程遺書 [Surviving works of the two Chengs]. 7 vols. 1498. CSG, K3-115.

Cho Ch'anhan 趙纘韓. "Ŭiudo" 義牛圖 [An illustrated account of a righteous cow]. *Ilsŏn ŭiyŏlto* 一善義烈圖 [Illustrations of the righteousness and chastity of Sŏnsan]. 1703. KYU, Karam ko 398.4-Il9. 3a–8b.

Cho Hyŏnmyŏng 趙顯命. "Yŏllyŏ pyŏngsŏ" 烈女屏序 [Preface to virtuous women folding screen]. *Kwirok chip* 歸鹿集 [Collected Works of Kwirok]. 20 vols. n.d. KYU, Kyu 3471-v.1-20. 18:1a–3a. *HMC* 213:1283–85.

Cho Kusang 趙龜祥. "Yŏllyŏ Hyangnangdo ki" 烈女香娘圖記 [An account of chaste woman Hyangnang attached to illustrations]. *Yuhyŏn chip* 猶賢集 [Collected works of Yuhyŏn]. Reprinted in *Han'guk yŏktae munjip ch'ongsŏ* [Comprehensive compilation of Korean literary collections], edited by Cho Pyŏnghŭi, 455–60. Seoul: Kyŏngin Munhwasa, 1999.

Cho Kyŏngnam 趙慶男. *Nanjung chamnok* 亂中雜錄 [A miscellaneous record written during the war]. Seoul: Minjok Munhwa Ch'ujin Wiwŏnhoe, 1977.

Ch'oe Ikhyŏn 崔益鉉. "Yŏlbu Hassi chŏngnyŏgi" 烈夫河氏旌閭記 [On honoring chaste wife Madam Ha]. *Myŏnam chip* 勉菴集 [Collected works of Myŏnam]. 24 vols. 1909. Koryŏ Taehakkyo Chungang tosŏgwan, D1-A76. 22:31b–32b. *HMC* 325:527b.

———. "Yŏlbu Yissi chŏngnyŏgi" 烈夫李氏旌閭記 [On honoring chaste wife Madam Yi]. *Myŏnam chip.* 20:32a–33b. *HMC* 325:490a–d.

Chŏng Pŏmjo 丁範祖. "Sŏ Yissi chŏngyŏ sasil" 書李氏旌閭事實 [Record the event of erecting a memorial arch for Madam Yi]. *Haejwa chip* 海左集 [Collected works of Haejwa]. 39 vols. 1876. KYU, Kyu 4195. 38:24b–25a. *HMC* 240:193a–b.

Chŏng Yagyong 丁若鏞. "Chinju ŭigi sagi" 晋州義技詞記 [Record of the righteous courtesan of Chinju]. *Kugyŏk Tasan simunjip* 國譯 茶山詩文集 [Poetry and literary collection of Tasan, Korean translation]. 10 vols. Edited by Minjok Munhwa Ch'ujinhoe. Seoul: Sol Ch'ulp'ansa, 1996. 6:114–15.

———. "Chŏlbu Ch'oessi myojimyŏng" 節婦崔氏 墓誌銘 [Epitaph written for Madam Ch'oe]. *Kugyŏk Tasan simunjip.* 7:203–4.

———. *Hŭmhŭm sinsŏ* 欽欽新書 [New treatise on the legal system]. 4 vols. Translated by Pak Sŏngmu and Yi Kanguk. Seoul: Hanguk Inmun Kojŏn Yŏn'guso, 2019.

———. *Kyŏngse yup'yo* 經世遺表 [Treaties on government]. 4 vols. Seoul: Minjok Munhwa Ch'ujin Wiwŏnhoe, 1985.

———. *Mongmin simsŏ* 牧民心書 [Admonitions on governing the people]. 6 vols. Translated by Tasan Yŏn'guhoe. Seoul: Ch'angbi, 1988.

———. "Yŏlburon" 烈婦論 [Discussion on chaste wives]. *Kugyŏk Tasan simunjip.* 5:151–54.

Chŏngjo 正朝. *Hongjae chŏnsŏ* 弘齋全書 [Complete works of Hongjae]. 100 vols. 1814. KYU, Kyu 572-v.1-100.

Chongyongnok. 從容錄 [A record of following the path]. 3 vols. Edited by Sim Hakhwan. Kangnŭng: Naksan Chŏngsa, 1909. KYU, Ko 4655-94.

Chosŏn ilbo 朝鮮日報. "Kyŏngch'uksik ŭn sŏul undongjang sŏ" 慶祝式은 서울 運動場서 [The celebration to be held in Seoul stadium]. March 26, 1958.

Chosŏn wangjo sillok 朝鮮王朝實錄 [Veritable records of the kings of the Chosŏn dynasty]. 48 vols. Seoul: Kuksa P'yŏnch'an Wiwŏnhoe, 1970.

Ch'ugwanji 秋官志 [Records of the Ministry of Punishment]. Compiled by Pak Irwŏn 朴一源 in 1791. Reprint in 4 vols. Seoul: Pŏpchech'ŏ, 1975. Page references are to the modern edition.

Chŭngsu Muwŏllok ŏnhae 增修無冤錄諺解 [Amplified and corrected *Coroner's Manual for the Elimination of Grievances* in vernacular Korean]. 2 vols. Originally compiled by Wang Yü 王與. Edited by Ku T'aekkyu 具宅奎. Translated by Sŏ Yurin 徐有隣. 1792. CSG, K2-3454.

Confucius. *The Analects of Confucius.* Translated by Burton Watson. New York: Columbia University Press, 2017.

Feng Menglong 馮夢龍. *Zhinang* 智囊 [Sack of wisdom]. 3 vols. Translated by Yi Wŏngil. Seoul: Sinwŏn Munhwasa, 2004.

Han'guk chibangsa charyo cho'ongsŏ 韓國地方史 資料叢書 [Comprehensive compilation of sources on Korean local history]. 19 vols. Seoul: Yŏgang Ch'ulp'ansa, 1987.

Han'guk kubi munhak taegye 韓國口碑文學大系 [Compilation of Korean oral literature]. 85 vols. Edited by Han'guk Chŏngsin Munhwa Yŏn'guwŏn. Sŏngnam: Han'gukhak Chungang Yŏn'guwŏn, 2002. http://yoksa.aks. ac.kr/jsp/ur/Directory.jsp?gb=3.

Han'guk munjip ch'onggan 韓國文集叢刊 [Comprehensive publication of Korean literary collections]. 500 vols. Edited by Han'guk Kojŏn Pŏnyŏgwŏn. Seoul: Minjok Munhwa Ch'ujin Wiwŏnhoe, 1988–2013. http://www.krpia.co.kr/product/main?plctId=PLCT00005160#none.

"Hwang ch'amŭi ch'ŏ sukpuin Nisi" 황참의쳐 슉부인 니시 [Madam Yi, a wife of Hwang, third minister of the Six Ministries]. 1651. Han'guk Kukhak Chinhŭngwŏn.

Ilsŏngnok 日省錄 [The record of daily reflections]. 2,329 vols. 1760–1910. Edited by Kyujanggak Institute of Seoul National University. Seoul: Sŏul Taehakkyo Kyujanggak, 1982–1996. https://kyudb.snu.ac.kr/series/main .do?item_cd=ILS.

Im Hŏnhoe 任憲晦. "Yi yŏlbu chŏngnyŏgi" 李烈夫旌閭記 [A record dedicated to the chaste Widow Yi's memorial arch]. *Kosan chip* 鼓山集 [Collected works of Kosan]. 10 vols. 1876. KYU, Kyu 11474-v.1-10. 9:29b–31a. *HMC* 314:215d–216c.

Im Kyŏngju 任敬周. "Hassinyŏ chŏn" 何氏女傳 [The biography of Madam Ha]. *Ch'ŏngch'ŏnja ko* 靑川子稿 [Manuscripts of Ch'ŏngch'ŏnja]. 1794. KYU, Kyu 5855. 3:24a–25b.

Iryŏn 一然. *Samguk yusa* 三國遺事 [Memorabilia of the Three Kingdoms]. Translated and edited by Yi Pyŏngdo. Seoul: Tongguk Munhwasa, 1956.

Jiang, Yonglin, trans. *The Great Ming Code*. Seattle: University of Washington Press, 2005.

Kaksa sugyo 各司受敎 [Received royal edicts from each ministry]. 1554. KYU, Kyu 7901.

Karim poch'o 嘉林報草 [Official reports from Karim]. 2 vols. 1724–1776. KYU, Kyu 12352-v.1-2. Reprinted in *Han'guk chibangsa charyo cho'ongsŏ*, vol. 3. Page references are to the modern edition.

Kim Chingyu 金鎭圭. "Ae Oyang yŏlbu sa" 哀烏壤烈婦辭 [Eulogy to a chaste woman of Oyang Station]. *Chukch'ŏn chip* 竹泉集 [Collected works of Chukch'ŏn]. 12 vols. 1773. KYU, Kyu 4111. 6:10b–12a. *HMC* 174:86.

———. "Ch'ŏng Yu yŏlbu chŏngp'o myŏnju" 請柳烈婦旌褒面奏 [A report to request honoring chaste wife Madam Yu]. *Chukch'ŏn chip*. 7:20b–23b. *HMC* 174:103d–105b.

Kim Chip 金集. "Sŏnjobi chŭng chŏnggyŏng puin Yangch'ŏn Hŏssi myogal" 先祖妣 贈貞敬夫人陽川許氏墓碣 [Epitaph of Madam Yangch'ŏn Hŏ, the consort of a minister]. *Sindokchae yugo* 愼獨齋遺稿 [Posthumous works of Sindokchae]. 7 vols. n.d. NLK, Hankojo 46-Ka 89. 8:1a–2b. *HMC* 82:349c–350b.

Kim Pusik 金富軾. *Samguk sagi* 三國史記 [Historical records of the Three Kingdoms]. 2 vols. Translated and edited by Yi Pyŏngdo. Seoul: Ŭryu Munhwasa, 1977.

Kim Yangnyŏn 金若鍊. "Kim yŏllyŏ chŏn" 金烈女傳 [Biography of the chaste woman Kim]. *Tuam chip* 斗庵集 [Collected works of Tuam]. 5 vols. 1836. Koryŏ taehakkyo chungang tosŏgwan, D1-A2381. 5:35a–36b. *HMC* 91:597c–98b.

Kim Yongsŏn, ed. *Yŏkchu Koryŏ myojimyŏng chipsŏng* [Collected epitaphs of the Koryŏ dynasty, translated and annotated]. 2 vols. Ch'unch'ŏn: Hallim Taehakkyo Ch'ulp'anbu, 2006.

Kŏmanch'o 檢案抄 [Selected inquest reports]. 2 vols. (*kŏn* 乾; *kon* 坤). n.d. NLK, Hankojo 34–37.

Koryŏsa. 高麗史 [History of Koryŏ]. Edited by Chŏng Inji 鄭麟趾 et al. 3 vols. Seoul: Asea Munhwasa, 1972.

Kugyŏk Ch'ilgok chi 國譯 漆谷誌 [Ch'ilgok prefectural gazetteer, Korean translation], vol. 4. Translated by Kwŏn Oung. Seoul: Ch'ilgok Munhwawŏn, 2002.

Kwŏn Si 權諰. *T'anong sŏnsaeng chip* 炭翁先生集 [Collected works of Master T'anong]. 7 vols. 1738. KYU, Kyu 3004-v.1-7.

Kwŏn Tugyŏng 權斗經. "Yi yŏlbu Kimssi chŏngmun myŏng pyŏngsŏ" 李烈婦 金氏旌門銘 并序 [Preface to epitaph written for the memorial arch dedicated to chaste wife Madam Kim of Yi family]. *Ch'angsŏlchae chip* 蒼雪齋 先生文集 [Collected works of Master Ch'angsŏlchae]. 9 vols. n.d. NLK, Ko 3468-Mun 07-76. 15:31a–33b. *HMC* 169:287b–88b.

Kyŏngguk taejŏn 經國大典 [Great code of administration]. Compiled in 1485. Keijō: Chōsen Sōtokufu, Chūsū-in, 1934.

Liji 禮記 [Book of rites]. Translated by Yi Sangok. Seoul: Myŏngmundang, 2003.

Liu Xiang 劉向. *Lienü zhuan* 列女傳 [Categorized biographies of women]. Translated by Yi Sugin. Seoul: Kŭl Hangari, 2013.

Mencius. Translated by D. C. Lau. London: Penguin, 2004.

Miryang Hyanggyo 密陽鄉校. "Ipŭi" 立議 [Discussion]. In "Injo muja chŏlmok" 仁祖戊子節目 [Articles from the muja year of Injo's reign]. 1648. *Miryang Hyanggyo chungsurok pyŏlp'yŏn* 密陽鄉校重修錄別篇 [Supplementary record of the Miryang Confucian local school renovation]. Edited by Miryang Hyanggyo. Miryang: Miryang Hyanggyo, 1960.

Nam Yuyong 南有容. "Yŏlbu Kimyuin aesa" 烈婦金孺人哀辭 [Eulogy for the chaste wife Madam Kim]. *Noeyŏn chip* 雷淵集 [Collected works of Noeyŏn]. 15 vols. 1783. KYU, kyu 2900-v.1-15. 18:38a–39b. *HMC* 217:399–400.

Nonŏ chipchu 論語集註 [The analects: A variorum edition]. Translated by Sŏng Paekhyo. Seoul: Han'guk Chŏnt'ongmunhwa Yŏn'guhoe, 1990.

Ŏ Sukkwŏn 魚叔權. *P'aegwan chapki* 稗官雜記 [Records of miscellaneous writings]. 2 vols. Keijō: Chōsen Kosho Kankōkai, 1909.

Ogan ch'ogae 獄案抄概 [Summary of inquest records]. 2 vols. n.d. NLK, Hankojo 34–39.

Oryun haengsilto 五倫行實圖 [Illustrated guide to the Five Relations]. 4 vols. 1797. KYU, Karam ko 170-Y510-v.1-4.

Osan munch'ŏp 烏山文牒 [Collected reports from Osan]. 2 vols. 1758–1763. CSG, K2-3364. Reprinted in *Han'guk chibangsa charyo cho'ongsŏ*, vol. 4. Seoul: Yŏgang Ch'ulp'ansa, 1987.

Pak Chiwŏn 朴趾源. "Pak yŏlbu sajang" 朴烈婦事狀 [Record of chaste wife Madam Pak]. *Yŏnam chip* 燕巖集 [Collected works of Yŏnam]. 17 vols. Kyŏngsŏng, 1932. 10:8b–10a.

———. "Yŏllyŏ Hamyang Pakssi chŏn pyŏngsŏ" 烈女咸陽朴氏傳 幷序 [Preface to biography of the chaste wife Pak of Hamyang]. *Yŏnam chip*. 1:32b–34b.

———. *Yŏrha ilgi* 熱河日記 [Diary of a trip to Yŏrha]. Translated by Yi Kawŏn. 3 vols. Seoul: Taeyang Sŏjŏk, 1966.

Pak Yunwŏn 朴胤源. "P'alcho yŏgye sŏ chongjabu Yissi ch'imbyŏng" 八條女誡 書從子婦李氏寢屏 [Writing eight passages on women's conduct on the bedroom folding screen of a niece-in-law, Madam Yi]. *Kŭnjae chip* 謹齋集 [Collected works of Kŭnjae]. 16 vols. n.d. KYU, Kyu 4425-v.1-16. 13:8b–10b.

P'ungyang Chossi 豊壤 趙氏. *Chagirok: Yŏja kŭllo marhada* [Record of myself: A woman speaks through her writing]. Translated by Kim Kyŏngmi. Seoul: Naŭ Sigan, 2014.

Pyŏgyŏng surok 碧營隨錄 [Collected reports from Pyŏgyŏng]. Edited by Hwanghae Kamyŏng. 13 vols. 1796. KYU, Kyu 5936-v.1-13.

Samgang haengsilto 三綱行實圖 [Illustrated guide to the Three Bonds]. n.d. KYU, Kyu 138.

Simnirok 審理錄 [Records of royal reviews]. 16 vols. 1801. KYU, Kyu 1770-v.1-16.

Sin Kwangsu 申光洙. "Chŏng yŏlbu chŏn" 鄭烈娘傳 [Biography of chaste wife Madam Chŏng]. *Sŏkpuk chip* 石北集 [Collected works of Sŏkpuk]. 8 vols. 1906. NLK, Ilsan ko 3648-Mun 40-18. 15:19b–21a. *HMC* 231:491b.

Sin Sui 慎守彝. "Yŏlbu yuin sŏsan Chŏngssi chŏn" 烈夫孺人瑞山鄭氏傳 [Biography of chaste wife Madam Chŏng of Sŏsan]. *Hwanggo chip* 黃皐集 [Collected works of Hwanggo]. 3 vols. 1845. KYU, Kyu 4754-v.1-3. 6:14b–15a. *HMC* 69:342–43.

Sinbo sugyo chimnok 新補受敎輯錄 [Newly supplemented collected royal edicts]. 2 vols. 1743. KYU, Kyu 1158-v.1-2.

"Sŏhŭng-gun yuli-bang ch'angdae-dong ch'isa namin Kim Ch'angsŏng munan: Ch'ogŏm, pokkŏm" 瑞興郡栗里坊創岱洞 致死男人金昌成文案 [First and second postmortem records of a dead male, Kim Ch'angsŏng of Sŏhŭng District]. 1904. KYU, Kyu 21328.

Sok taejŏn 續大典 [Continuation of the *Great Code*]. 5 vols. Compiled in 1746. KYU. Kyu 1926-v.1-5.

Soksu samgangnok 續修三綱錄 [Amended sequel to the *Record of the Three Bonds*]. Edited by Chŏng Insŏp 鄭寅燮 et al. 1906. KYU, Kyu 5523.

Song Hwangi 宋換箕. "Yŏlbu Yunssi chŏn" 烈夫尹氏傳 [Biography of the chaste wife Madam Yun]. *Sŏngdam chip* 性潭集 [Collected works of Sŏngdam]. 16 vols. 1891. NLK, Han 46-Ka 1078. 30:41b–43b. *HMC* 245:170b–171b.

Song Siyŏl 宋時烈. "Tap Kwŏn Sasŏng kihae p'arwŏl sibiil" 答權思誠 己亥八月十二日 [In response to Kwŏn Sasŏng on the twentieth day of the eighth month in the kihae year]. *Songja taejŏn* 宋子大全 [Complete works of Songja]. 91 vols. KYU, Kyu 3543. 39:28b–30b. *HMC* 109:264d–65d.

Sŏng Taejung 成大中. *Ch'ŏngsŏng chapki* 青城雜記 [Miscellaneous records by Ch'ŏngsŏng]. Translated by Kim Chongtae et al. Reprint. Seoul: Minjok Munhwa Ch'ujin Wiwŏnhoe, 2006.

Sugyo chimnok 受教輯錄 [Collected royal edicts]. 2 vols. (*sang* 上; *ha* 下). 1698. NLK, Hankojo 33–37.

Sugyo chŏngnye 受教定例 [Received edicts on deciding regulations]. n.d. NLK, Ko 6607–3.

Sugyo tŭngnok 受教謄錄 [Compilation of received edicts]. 2 vols. (*kŏn* 乾; *kon* 坤). n.d. NLK, Ko 6022–77.

Sŭngjŏngwŏn ilgi [Records of the Royal Secretariat]. 3,045 vols. 1623–1894. KYU, Kyu 12788-v.1-3047. https://kyudb.snu.ac.kr/series/main.do?item_cd=SJW#none.

"Taegu-bu pokkŏm munan" 大邱府覆檢文案 [Second postmortem report of Taegu County]. KYU, Ko 5125–73.

Taejŏn hoet'ong 大典會通 [Comprehensive collection of dynastic codes]. 5 vols. Compiled in 1865. KYU, Kyu 1302-v.1-5.

Taejŏn husongnok 大典後續綠 [Continued supplementary great code]. 1543. Reprinted in 1613. KYU, Kyu 1939.

Taejŏn songnok 大典續錄 [Supplementary great code]. Compiled in 1492. Reprinted in 1613. NLK, Ko 6025–43.

Taejŏn t'ongp'yŏn 大典通編 [Great code for ruling the state]. 5 vols. Compiled in 1784. KYU, Kyu 201-v.1-5.

Taemyŏngnyul chikhae 大明律直解 [Direct explanation of the *Great Ming Code*]. Reprint, Seoul: Sŏul Taehakkyo Kyujanggak, 2001.

Tonga ilbo. "Yi taet'ongnyŏng 80-hoe t'ansinil" 李大統領80回誕辰日 [President Rhee's 80th birthday]. March 14, 1955.

T'ŭkkyo chŏngsik 特教定式 [Special edicts deciding legal codes]. 1794. KYU, Kyu, Ko 951.009-T296.

"Ŭiyŏlsa t'ongmun" 義烈祠通文 [A circular for a righteous and chaste man]. *Komunsŏ chipsŏng 9: Ch'angwŏn Hwangssi p'yŏn* [Collection of old documents 9: Ch'angwŏn Hwang family], 626–34. Sŏngnam: Han'guk Chŏngsin Munhwa Yŏn'guwŏn, 1990.

Wang Sŏngsun 王性淳. *Kyumun kwebŏm* 閨門軌範 [Rules of the inner quarters]. Andong: Han'guk Kukhak Chinhŭngwŏn, 2005.

Wang Xiuchu 王秀楚. "Yangzhou shiri ji" 揚州十日記 [Account of ten days in Yangzhou]. Beijing: Beijing Ai ru sheng shu zi hua ji shu yan jiu zhong xin, 2009. Electronic copy through Zhongguo ji ben gu ji ku.

Weishu 魏書 [History of Wei]. Edited by Chen Shou 陳壽. In *Sanguozhi* 三國志 [History of the Three Kingdoms]. 8 vols. 1887. KYU, Karam ko 952.01-J563s-v.1-8.

Wi Paekkyu 魏伯珪. "Ch'ŏngp'o yŏlbu Ossijang tae" 請襃烈婦吳氏狀 代 [Petition written on behalf of the chaste wife Madam O]. *Chonjae chip* 存齋集 [Collected works of Chonjae]. 12 vols. 1869. NLK, Hankojo 46-Ka 436. 4:3b–7a. *HMC* 243:62b–64a.

———. "Ch'ŏngp'o yŏllyŏ Ch'oessijang tae" 請襃烈女崔氏狀 代 [Petition written on behalf of the chaste woman Madam Ch'oe]. *Chonjae chip*. 4:7a–9a. *HMC* 243:64a–65a.

———. "Yŏllyŏ Kimssi chŏngmun Okkwa ki" 烈女金氏旌門 玉果 記 [Record of the chaste woman Madam Kim's memorial arch built in Okkwa District]. *Chonjae chip*. 21:16a–18a. *HMC* 243:454c–55c.

Wŏn Ch'ŏnsŏk 元天錫. *Un'gok haengnok* 耘谷行錄 [Biographical record of Un'gok]. 3 vols. 1858. NLK, Hankojo 45-Ka 462.

Yi Chae 李栽 (1657–1730). "Hong yŏlbu chŏn" 洪烈婦傳 [The biography of chaste wife Madam Hong]. *Miram chip* 密菴集 [Collected works of Miram]. 15 vols. n.d. NLK, Han 46-Ka 2250. 16:1a–6b. *HMC* 173:314–16.

Yi Chae 李縡 (1680–1746). "Yŏlbu Yissi chŏn" 烈婦李氏傳 [Record of chaste woman Madam Yi]. *Toam chip* 陶庵集 [Collected works of Toam]. 25 vols. 1776–1800. KYU, Ko 3428-27-v.1-25. 25:12a–14a. *HMC* 194:534a–35a.

Yi Chunghwan 李重煥. "Kyŏngsangdo." *T'aengniji* 擇里志 [Classic for choosing settlement]. 1753. KYU, Kyu, Ko 4790–55.

Yi Ik 李瀷. *Sŏngho sasŏl* 星湖僿說 [Sŏngho's discourses on the minute], vol. 6. Seoul: Minjok Munhwa Ch'ujin Wiwŏnhoe, 1978.

"Yi Ikch'ae nyŏ ogan" 李益采女獄案 [Criminal investigation report on a daughter of Yi Ikch'ae]. *Kiyang munjŏk* [Official documents from Kiyang], vol. 1 (*kŏn*). KYU, Kyŏnggo 365-G449-v.1. Reprinted in *Han'guk chibangsa charyo cho'ongsŏ*, vol. 6. Page references are to the modern edition.

Yi Imyŏng 李頤命. "Yuin Yussi myop'yo" 孺人柳氏墓表 [Tomb inscription for Madam Yu]. *Sojae chip* 疎齋集 [Collected works of Sojae]. 10 vols. 1759. KYU, Ko 3428-163-v.1-10. 40:10b–13a. *HMC* 172:350d–52a.

Yi Kok 李穀. "Chŏlbu Chossi chŏn" 節婦曹氏傳 [Record of chaste woman Madam Cho]. *Kajŏng chip* 稼亭集 [Collected works of Kajŏng] 1:8b–10a.

Yi Kwangjŏng 李光庭. "Hyo yŏlbu Yigongin myojimyŏng" 孝烈婦李恭人墓誌銘 [Epitaph written for filial and faithful wife Madam Yi]. *Nurŭn chip* 訥隱集 [Collected works of Nurŭn]. 11 vols. 1808. KYU, Kyu 12497-v.1-11.14:13b–15b. *HMC* 187:390b–91b.

Yi Kwangsa 李匡師. "Ch'oe yŏlbu ch'an" 崔烈婦贊 [Eulogy for the chaste wife Ch'oe]. *Wŏn'gyo chip* 圓嶠集 [Collected works of Wŏn'gyo]. 4 vols. n.d. KYU, Kyu 15551-v.1-4. 8:10a–11a. *HMC* 221:539c–40a.

Yi Ok 李鈺. "Saeng yŏllyŏ chŏn" 生烈女傳 [Tale of a living chaste woman]. *Yŏkchu Yi Ok chŏnjip* 譯註 李鈺全集 [Complete works of Yi Ok]. 3 vols. Seoul: Somyŏng Ch'ulp'ansa, 2001. 2:217–18.

———. "Such'ik chŏn" 守則傳 [Tale of Such'ik]. *Yŏkchu Yi Ok chŏnjip*. 2:212–16.

———. "Yŏllyŏ Yissi chŏn" 烈女李氏傳 [Tale of chaste wife Madam Yi]. *Yŏkchu Yi Ok chŏnjip*. 2:210–11.

Yi Sisŏn 李時善. "Yŏllyŏ Hongssi chŏn" 烈女洪氏傳 [The biography of Madam Hong]. *Songwŏlchae chip* 松月齋集 [Collected works of Songwŏlchae]. 3 vols. 1763. KYU, Kyu 4772-v.1-3. 3:39b–47a. *HMC* 37:535–39.

Yi Sungin 李崇仁. "Pae yŏlbu chŏn" 裵烈婦傳 [Record of chaste woman Pae]. *Toŭn chip* 陶隱集 [Collected works of Toŭn]. 2 vols. n.d. Koryŏ taehakkyo chungang tosŏgwan, Mansonggwi 265. 5:3a–4b. *HMC* 34:605c–6b.

Yi Tŏngmu 李德懋. *Sasojŏl* 士小節 [Small matters for scholars]. Translated by Kim Chonggwŏn. Seoul: Yanghyŏngak, 1983.

Yi Yuwŏn 李裕元. *Imha p'ilgi* 林下筆記 [Jottings in retirement]. 33 vols. n.d. KYU, Kyu 4916-v.1-33. 16:69a–b.

Yŏngjo 英祖. "Yŏngjo ŏje Hwasun ongju yujemun" 英祖御製 和順翁主諭祭文 [King Yŏngjo's royal composition of funeral ode to Princess Hwasun]. *Yŏngjo chason charyojip* 英祖子孫資料集 [Sourcebook of King Yŏngjo's descendants]. Edited by Changsŏgak. 5 vols. Sŏngnam: Han'gukhak Chungang Yŏn'guwŏn Ch'ulp'anbu, 2013.

Yu Insŏk 柳麟錫. "Yŏlbu yuin Yissi chŏn" 烈婦孺人李氏傳 [The biography of chaste wife Madam Yi]. *Ŭiam chip* 毅菴集 [Collected works of Ŭiam]. 2 vols. Reprinted in 2009. Chech'ŏn: Chech'ŏn Munhwawŏn. 50:19a–20b. *HMC* 339:334a–d.

———. "Yŏllyŏ sabi Yŏndŏk chŏn" 烈女私婢緣德傳 [Biography of a chaste woman, female slave Yŏndŏk]. *Ŭiam chip*. 50:35b–36b. *HMC* 339:341d–42b.

———. "Yuin Changhŭng Imssi chŏn" 孺人長興任氏傳 [Biography of Madam Im of Changhŭng]. *Ŭiam chip.* 50:39b–40b. *HMC* 339:343d–44b.

Yu Ŏnho 俞彦鎬. "Cheju o chŏllyŏ chŏn kyŏngsul" 濟州五節女傳 庚戌 [Biography of five virtuous women of Cheju composed in the *kyŏngsul* year]. *Yŏnsŏk* 燕石 [Stone from Yŏn Mountain]. 13 vols. 1777–1796. CSG, K4-6275. 13:9b–12b. *HMC* 247:266c–68a.

Yullye yoram 律例要覽 [Conspectus of laws and precedents]. Seoul: Pŏpchech'ŏ, 1970.

Yussi puin. "Yusŏ" 遺書 [Testaments]. *Han'gŭl p'ilsabon kososŏl charyo ch'ongsŏ* [Comprehensive sources on facsimile editions of Korean vernacular old fictions], vol. 30, edited by Wŏlch'on Munhŏn Yŏn'guso, 181–224. Seoul: Osŏngsa, 1986.

Zhu Xi 朱熹. *Xiao xue* 小學 [Elementary learning]. Translated by Yun Hoch'ang. Seoul: Hongik Ch'ulp'ansa, 2005.

———. *Zhuzi jiali* 朱子家禮 [Zhu Xi's family rituals]. Translated by Im Minhyŏk. Seoul: Yemun Sŏwŏn, 1999.

Secondary Sources

Ahn, Juhn Y. *Buddhas and Ancestors: Religion and Wealth in Fourteenth-Century Korea.* Seattle: University of Washington Press, 2018.

Baechler, Jean. *Les suicides.* Paris: Calmann-Levy, 1975. Translated by Barry Cooper. New York: Basic Books, 1979.

Baker, Donald L. "The Use and Abuse of the Sirhak Label: A New Look at Sin Hu-dam and His Sohak Pyon." *Kyohoesa yŏn'gu* 3 (1981): 183–254.

———. "Writing History in Premodern Korea." In *The Oxford History of Historical Writing*, vol. 2, edited by Sarah Foot and Chase F. Robinson, 125–31. Oxford: Oxford University Press, 2012.

Bashar, Nazife. "Rape in England between 1550 and 1700." In *The Sexual Dynamics of History: Men's Power, Women's Resistance*, edited by London Feminist History Group, 28–42. London: Pluto Press, 1983.

Binhammer, Katherine. *The Seduction Narrative in Britain, 1747–1800.* Cambridge: Cambridge University Press, 2009.

Bohnet, Adam. "Subversive Ming Loyalist Narratives in Late Chosŏn Korea." *Seoul Journal of Korean Studies* 25, no. 1 (2012): 1–29.

Bossler, Beverly. *Courtesans, Concubines, and the Cult of Wifely Fidelity: Gender and Social Change in China, 1000–1400.* Cambridge, MA: Harvard University Press, 2013.

———, ed. *Gender and Chinese History: Transformative Encounters.* Seattle: University of Washington Press, 2017.

Bourgon, Jérôme, and Pierre-Emmanuel Roux. "The Chosŏn Law Codes in an East Asian Perspective." In *The Spirit of Korean Law*, edited by Marie Seong-hak Kim, 19–51. Leiden: Brill, 2016.

Bray, Francesca. *Technology and Gender: Fabrics of Power in Late Imperial China.* Berkeley: University of California Press, 1997.

Breuker, Remco. *Establishing a Pluralist Society in Medieval Korea, 918– 1170.* Leiden: Brill, 2010.

Breuker, Remco, Grace Koh, and James B. Lewis. "The Tradition of Historical Writing in Korea." In *The Oxford History of Historical Writing*, vol. 2, edited by Sarah Foot and Chase F. Robinson, 119–37. Oxford: Oxford University Press, 2012.

Brownell, Susan, and Jeffrey N. Wasserstrom. "Gender and the Law (Qing Dynasty)." In *Chinese Femininities/Chinese Masculinities: A Reader*, edited by Susan Brownell and Jeffrey N. Wasserstrom, 43–46. Berkeley: University of California Press, 2002.

Brownmiller, Susan. *Against Our Will: Men, Women and Rape.* New York: Simon and Schuster, 1975.

Carlitz, Katherine. "Desire, Danger, and the Body: Stories of Women's Virtue in Late Ming China." In *Engendering China: Women, Culture, and the State*, edited by Christina K. Gilmartin, Gail Hershatter, Lisa Rofel, and Tyrene White, 101–24. Cambridge, MA: Harvard University Press, 1994.

———. "Shrines, Governing-Class Identity, and the Cult of Widow-Fidelity in Mid-Ming Jiangnan." *Journal of Asian Studies* 56, no. 3 (1997): 612–40.

———. "The Social Uses of Female Virtue in Late Ming Editions of the *Lienü zhuan.*" *Late Imperial China* 12, no. 2 (1991): 117–48.

Cavallo, Sandra, and Lyndan Warner. *Widowhood in Medieval and Early Modern Europe.* Harlow, UK: Longman, 1999.

Cha, Joohang. "The Civilizing Project in Medieval Korea: Neo-Classicism, Nativism, and Figurations of Power." PhD diss., Harvard University, 2014.

Chang Pyŏngin. *Chosŏn chŏn'gi honinje wa sŏngch'abyŏl* [Marriage law regulation and sexual discrimination in the early Chosŏn]. Seoul: Ilchisa, 1997.

———. "Chosŏn sidae sŏngbŏmjoe e taehan kukka kyuje ŭi kanghwa" [Intensification of the state's control over sexual crimes in the Chosŏn dynasty]. *Yŏksa pip'yŏng* 56 (2001): 228–50.

———. *Pŏp kwa p'ungsok ŭro pon Chosŏn yŏsŏng ŭi sam* [Chosŏn women's lives through law and custom]. Seoul: Hyumŏnisŭt'ŭ, 2018.

Chaudhuri, Nupur, Sherry J. Katz, and Mary Elizabeth Perry. *Contesting Archives: Finding Women in the Sources*. Urbana: University of Illinois Press, 2010.

Cho, Hwisang. "Circular Letters in Chosŏn Society." In Haboush, *Epistolary Korea*, 100–120.

———. "Feeling Power in Early Chosŏn Korea: Popular Grievances, Royal Rage, and the Problem of Human Sentiments." *Journal of Korean Studies* 20, no. 1 (2015): 7–32.

Cho Namuk. "Yuga hyoron kwa yuksin hyohaeng ŭi munje" [A study on the theory of confucian filial piety and the problem of filial acts of self-harming]. *Yugyo sasang yŏn'gu* 37 (2009): 123–45.

Cho Yunsŏn. *Chosŏn hugi sosong yŏn'gu* [A study of late Chosŏn litigation]. Seoul: Kukhak Charyowŏn, 2002.

Ch'oe Insuk. "19-segi Tosan Sŏwŏn ŭi sahoe insik kwa sot'ong pangsik" [Social consciousness and communication by Tosan Confucian Academy in the nineteenth century]. In *Tosan Sŏwŏn ŭl t'onghae pon Chosŏn hugi sahoesa*, edited by Han'guk Kukhak Chinhŭngwŏn, 119–63. Seoul: Saemyulkyŏl, 2014.

Choi, Hyaeweol. *Gender and Mission Encounters in Korea: New Women, Old Ways*. Berkeley: University of California Press, 2009.

———, ed. *New Women in Colonial Korea: A Sourcebook*. Abingdon, UK: Routledge, 2013.

Chŏng Chaesŏ, ed. *Tongasia yŏsŏng ŭi kiwŏn: Yŏllyŏjŏn e taehan yŏsŏnghakchŏk t'amgu* [Origin of women in East Asia: Studies on *Yŏllyŏjŏn* from the perspective of women's studies]. Seoul: Ewha Yŏja Taehakkyo Ch'ulp'an Munhwawŏn, 2009.

Chŏng Ch'anggwŏn. *Hyangnang, sanyuhwa ro chida* [Hyangnang, falling like a flower petal]. Seoul: P'ulpit, 2004.

Chŏng Chiyŏng. *Chilsŏ ŭi kuch'uk kwa kyunyŏl: Chosŏn hugi hojŏk kwa yŏsŏngdŭl* [Order and fissure: Women in late Chosŏn household registers]. Seoul: Sŏgang University Press, 2015.

——— (Jung, Ji Young). "Questions Concerning Widow's Social Status and Remarriage in Late Chosŏn." In *Women and Confucianism in Chosŏn Korea: New Perspectives*, edited by Youngmin Kim and Michael J. Pettid, 109–38. Albany: State University of New York, 2011.

——— (Jung, Ji Young). "War and the Death of a Kisaeng: The Construction of the Collective Memory of the 'Righteous Kisaeng Non'gae' in Late Chosŏn." *Seoul Journal of Korean Studies* 22, no. 2 (2009): 157–80.

———. "Yŏllyŏ mandŭlgi ŭi yŏksa." [History of the making of *yŏllyŏ*]. *Yŏsŏnghak nonjip* 20 (2003): 133–53.

Chŏng Haeŭn. "Chosŏn sidae yŏsŏngsa yŏn'gu, ŏdiro kago innŭn'ga" [What is the direction of scholarship on Chosŏn women?]. *Yŏksa wa hyŏnsil* 91 (2014): 317–38.

Chŏng Iryŏng. "Chosŏn hugi sŏngbyŏl e ttarŭn chasal ŭi haesŏk" [Interpretation of suicide by gender in the late Chosŏn dynasty]. *Ŭisahak* 17 (2008): 155–75.

Chŏng Kŭngsik. "Chungguk yullyŏng ŭi suyong kwa han'guk chŏnt'ong sahoe" [The reception of Chinese laws and traditional Korean society]. *Justice* 158, no. 2 (2017): 142–66.

———. "Uri nara kant'ongjoe ŭi pŏpchesajŏk koch'al" [Study of adultery in Korea from the perspective of legal history]. In *Hyŏngpŏp kaejŏng kwa kwallyŏn hayŏ pon nakt'aejoe mit kant'ongjoe e kwanhan yŏn'gu* [Study of illegal abortion and adultery relevant to revision of criminal law], edited by Han'guk Hyŏngsa Chŏngch'aek Yŏn'guwŏn, 211–42. Seoul: Han'guk Hyŏngsa Chŏngch'aek Yŏn'guwŏn, 1991.

Chŏng Kŭngsik and Cho Chiman. "Chosŏn chŏn'gi Taemyŏngnyul ŭi suyong kwa pyŏnyong" [The reception and transformation of the *Great Ming Code* in the early Chosŏn period]. *Chindan hakpo* 96 (2003): 205–41.

Chŏng Okcha. *Chosŏn hugi Chosŏn chunghwa sasang yŏn'gu* [A study of Chosŏn-centered ideology in the late Chosŏn]. Seoul: Ilchisa, 1998.

Chŏn Kyŏngmok. *Komunsŏ, Chosŏn ŭi yŏksa rŭl marhada* [Old documents tell the history of Chosŏn]. Seoul: Hyumŏnisŭt'ŭ, 2013.

Clark, Elizabeth A. *History, Theory, Text: Historians and the Linguistic Turn.* Cambridge, MA: Harvard University Press, 2004.

Davis, Natalie. *Fiction in the Archives: Pardon Tales and Their Tellers in Sixteenth-Century France.* Stanford, CA: Stanford University Press, 1987.

Deuchler, Martina. *The Confucian Transformation of Korea.* Cambridge, MA: Harvard University Press, 1992.

———. "The Practice of Confucianism: Ritual and Order in Chosŏn Dynasty Korea." In *Rethinking Confucianism: Past and Present in China, Japan, Korea, and Vietnam,* edited by Benjamin A. Elman, John B. Duncan, and Herman Ooms, 292–336. Los Angeles: UCLA Asian Pacific Series, 2002.

———. "Propagating Female Virtues in Chosŏn Korea." In Ko, Kim, and Piggott, *Women and Confucian Cultures,* 142–69.

———. *Under the Ancestors' Eyes: Kinship, Status, and Locality in Premodern Korea.* Cambridge, MA: Harvard University, 2015.

Du Fangqin and Susan Mann. "Competing Claims on Womanly Virtue in Late Imperial China." In Ko, Kim, and Piggott, *Women and Confucian Cultures,* 219–50.

Duncan, John. "The *Naehun* and the Politics of Gender in Fifteenth-Century Korea." In *Creative Women of Korea: The Fifteenth through the Twentieth Centuries*, edited by Young-Key Kim-Renaud, 26–57. Armonk, NY: M. E. Sharpe, 2004.

———. *The Origins of the Chosŏn Dynasty*. Seattle: University of Washington Press, 2000.

Dunn, Caroline. *Stolen Women in Medieval England: Rape, Abduction, and Adultery, 1100–1500*. Cambridge: Cambridge University Press, 2012.

Durrant, Stephen, Wai-yee Li, and David Schaberg, trans. *Zuo Tradition / Zuozhuan: Commentary on the "Spring and Autumn Annals."* Seattle: University of Washington Press, 2016.

Ebrey, Patricia Buckley. *The Inner Quarters: Marriage and the Lives of Chinese Women in the Sung Period*. Berkeley: University of California Press, 1993.

Elliott, Mark C. "Manchu Widows and Ethnicity in Qing China." *Comparative Studies in Society and History* 41, no. 1 (1999): 33–71.

Elvin, Mark. "Female Virtue and the State in China." *Past and Present* 104 (1984): 112–52.

Fei, Siyen. "Virtue, Talent and Her-Story: Towards a New Paradigm of Chinese Women's History." *Social History* 35, no. 2 (2000): 458–67.

———. "Writing for Justice: An Activist Beginning of the Cult of Female Chastity in Late Imperial China." *Journal of Asian Studies* 71, no. 4 (2012): 991–1102.

Fong, Grace S. "Signifying Bodies: The Cultural Significance of Suicide Writings by Women in Ming-Qing China." *Nan Nü* 3, no. 1 (2001): 105–42.

Gammon, Julie. "Researching Sexual Violence, 1660–1800: A Critical Analysis." In *Interpreting Sexual Violence, 1660–1800*, edited by Anne Greenfield, 13–22. London: Pickering and Chatto, 2013.

Greenfield, Anne, ed. *Interpreting Sexual Violence, 1660–1800*. London: Pickering and Chatto, 2013.

Haboush, JaHyun Kim. "Constructing the Center: The Ritual Controversy and the Search for a New Identity in Seventeenth-Century Korea." In JaHyun Kim Haboush and Martina Deuchler, *Culture and the State in Late Chosŏn Korea*, 46–90. Cambridge, MA: Harvard University Asia Center, 1999.

———. "Dead Bodies in the Postwar Discourse of Identity in Seventeenth Century Korea: Subversion and Literary Production in the Private Sector." *Journal of Asian Studies* 62, no. 2 (May 2003): 415–42.

————, ed. *Epistolary Korea: Letters in the Communicative Space of the Chosŏn, 1392–1910*. New York: Columbia University Press, 2009.

————. "Filial Emotions and Filial Values: Changing Patterns in the Discourse of Filiality in Late Chosŏn Korea." *Harvard Journal of Asiatic Studies* 55, no. 1 (June 1995): 129–77.

————. "Gender and the Politics of Language in Chosŏn Korea." In *Rethinking Confucianism: Past and Present in China, Japan, Korea, and Vietnam*, edited by Benjamin A. Elman, John B. Duncan, and Herman Ooms, 220–57. Los Angeles: UCLA Asian Pacific Monograph Series, 2002.

————. *The Great East Asian War and the Birth of the Korean Nation*. New York: Columbia University Press, 2016.

————. "Versions and Subversions: Patriarchy and Polygamy in the Vernacular Narratives of Chosŏn Korea." In Ko, Kim, and Piggott, *Women and Confucian Cultures*, 279–312.

Haboush, JaHyun Kim, and Martina Deuchler, eds. *Culture and the State in Late Chosŏn Korea*. Cambridge, MA: Harvard University Asia Center, 1999.

Han, Christina. "A Scholar-Soldier in Mourning Robes: The Politics of Remembering Imjin War Hero No In (1566–1622)." *Sungkyun Journal of East Asian Studies* 17, no. 1 (2017): 61–92.

Han Sanggwŏn. *Chosŏn hugi sahoe wa sowŏn chedo* [The petition system and society in the late Chosŏn]. Seoul: Ilchogak, 1996.

————. "Chosŏn sidae kyohwa wa hyŏngjŏng" [Moralization and penal administration during the Chosŏn dynasty]. *Yŏksa wa hyŏnsil* 79 (2011): 271–303.

————. "Taemyŏngnyul wip'ipch'isa ŭi pŏmni wa Chosŏn esŏ ŭi chŏgyong" [Legal principles of the statute on "using coercion to cause others to die" in the *Great Ming Code* and its application in Chosŏn]. *Pŏp sahak yŏn'gu* 50 (2014): 27–28.

Han'guk Kojŏn Yŏsŏng Munhakhoe, ed. *Chosŏn sidae yŏllyŏ tamnon* [Discourse on chaste women in the Chosŏn era]. Seoul: Wŏrin, 2002.

Hŏ Hŭngsik. "Koryŏ yŏsŏng ŭi chiwi wa yŏkhal" [Positions and duties of Koryŏ women]. *Han'guksa simin kangjwa* 15 (1994): 64–83.

Hŏ Namlin (Hur, Nam-lin). "Yŏllyŏ tamnon kwa Imjin waeran" [Chaste women discourse and the Imjin War]. In *Tu Chosŏn ŭi yŏsŏng: Sinch'e, ŏnŏ, simsŏng* [Women of two Chosŏns: Body, language, and minds], edited by Kim Hyŏnju, 183–210. Seoul: Hyean, 2016.

Hong Insuk. "17-segi yŏllyŏjŏn yŏn'gu" [A study of the biographies of chaste women in the seventeenth century]. *Han'guk kojŏn yŏn'gu* 7 (2001): 95–117.

———. "Chosŏn hugi sunjŏl yŏsŏng Sinssi pu han'gŭl yusŏ chaeron" [A review of a testament written in Korean script by a chaste daughter-in-law of the Sin family]. *Komunsŏ yŏn'gu* 54 (2019): 265–85.

———. "Chosŏn hugi yŏsŏng yusŏ yŏn'gu: Sunjŏl yŏsŏng Sinssi ŭi han'gŭl yusŏ rŭl chungsim ŭro" [Study of a woman's testament of the late Chosŏn: Focus on a Korean testament written by a daughter-in-law of the Sin family]. *Onjinonch'ong* 56 (2018): 247–81.

———. *Kŭndae kyemonggi yŏsŏng tamnon* [The discourse on women during the early modern Enlightenment era]. Seoul: Hyean, 2009.

———. *Yŏllyŏ* 列女 X *Yŏllyŏ* 烈女: *Yŏja nŭn ŏttŏke yŏllyŏga toeŏnna* [*Yŏllyŏ* 列女 x *Yŏllyŏ* 烈女: How a woman became a chaste woman]. Seoul: Sŏhae Munjip, 2019.

Hong Yanghŭi. "'Sŏllyanghan p'ungsok' ŭl wihayŏ; Singminji sigi 'kant'ongjoe' wa sŏng (Sexuality) t'ongje" [Toward good custom: Adultery and sexuality in colonial Korea]. *Pŏp kwa sahoe* 51 (2016): 317–41.

Im Ch'igyun. "Sŏnyŏng Yussi puin yusŏ yŏn'gu" [On Madam Yu of Sŏnyŏng's testaments]. *Komunsŏ yŏn'gu* 15 (1999): 47–65.

Im Yugyŏng. "Yi Ok ŭi *Yŏllyŏjŏn* sŏsul pangsik kwa yŏl kwannyŏm" [A way of narrating *Yŏllyŏjŏn* by Yi Ok and his perception of chastity]. *Ŏ Munhak* 56 (1995): 397–418.

Ing, Michael D. K. *The Vulnerability of Integrity in Early Confucian Thought.* Oxford: Oxford University Press, 2017.

Judge, Joan. *The Precious Raft of History.* Stanford, CA: Stanford University Press, 2008.

Judge, Joan, and Hu Ying, eds. *Beyond Exemplar Tales: Women's Biography in Chinese History.* Berkeley: University of California Press, 2011.

Jung, Ji Young. *See under* Chŏng Chiyŏng.

Kaiser, Daniel H. "'He Said, She Said': Rape and Gender Discourse in Early Modern Russia." *Kritika: Exploration in Russian and Eurasian History* 3, no. 2 (2002): 197–216.

Kallendar, George. *Salvation through Dissent: Tonghak Heterodoxy and Early Modern Korea.* Honolulu: University of Hawai'i Press, 2013.

Kang Hyejong. "Sarin sagŏn ŭl tullŏssan Chosŏn ŭi kamsŏng chŏngch'i" [The politics of emotion in homicide cases in Chosŏn]. In *Kamsŏng sahoe,* edited by Ch'oe Kisuk, 109–34. Seoul: Kŭl Hangari, 2014.

Kang Myŏnggwan. *Yŏllyŏ ŭi t'ansaeng: Kabujangje wa Chosŏn yŏsŏng ŭi chanhokhan yŏksa* [The birth of the chaste woman: Patriarchy and the brutal history of Chosŏn women]. Seoul: Tolbegae, 2009.

Karasawa, Yasuhiko. "From Oral Testimony to Written Records in Qing Legal Cases." In *Thinking with Cases: Specialist Knowledge in Chinese Cultural History*, edited by Charlotte Furth, Judith T. Zeitlin, and Ping-chen Hsiung, 89–118. Honolulu: University of Hawai'i Press, 2007.

Karlsson, Anders. "Central Power, Local Society, and Rural Unrest in Nineteenth-Century Korea: An Attempt at Comparative Local History." *Sungkyun Journal of East Asian Studies* 6, no. 2 (2006): 207–38.

———. "The Hong Kyŏngnae Rebellion 1811–1812: Conflict Between Central Power and Local Society in 19th-Century Korea." PhD diss., Stockholm University, 2000.

———. "'Must We Really Cut People's Toes Off to Uphold the Law?': Confucian Statecraft, Punishment and the Body in Chosŏn Korea." *Tasanhak* 24 (2014): 107–47.

———. "Royal Compassion and Disaster Relief in Chosŏn Korea." *Seoul Journal of Korean Studies* 20, no. 1 (2007): 71–98.

Kawashima, Fujiya. "A Study of the Hyangan: Kin Groups and Aristocratic Localism in the Seventeenth- and Eighteenth-Century Korean Countryside." *Journal of Korea Studies* 5 (1984): 3–38.

Kendall, Laurel, and Mark Peterson, eds. *Korean Women: View from the Inner Room*. New Haven, CT: East Rock Press, 1983.

Kim Ch'anghyŏn. "Koryŏ sidae kant'ong kwa kŭ sŏnggyŏk" [Adultery and its characteristics in the Koryŏ dynasty]. *Yŏsŏng kwa yŏksa* 28 (2018): 77–124.

———. *Koryŏ ŭi yŏsŏng kwa munhwa* [Women and culture of the Koryŏ dynasty]. Seoul: Sinsŏwŏn, 2007.

Kim, Charles R., Jungwon Kim, Hwasook B. Nam, and Serk-Bae Suh, eds. *Beyond Death: The Politics of Suicide and Martyrdom in Korea*. Seattle: University of Washington Press, 2019.

Kim Chŏnggyŏng. "Chosŏn hugi yŏllyŏ ŭi sunjŏl ŭi ŭimihwa pangsik yŏn'gu" [Study of the meaning of chaste martyrs in the late Chosŏn]. *Kukche ŏmun* 53 (2012): 9–35.

———. *Chosŏn hugi yŏsŏng han'gŭl sanmun yŏn'gu* [Study of women's prose in the late Chosŏn]. Seoul: Sŏgang Taehakkyo Ch'ulp'anbu, 2016.

Kim Ho. *Paengnyŏn chŏn sarin sagŏn: Kŏman ŭl t'onghaesŏ pon Chosŏn ŭi ilsangsa* [Homicide cases from a hundred years ago: Chosŏn everyday life seen from inquest reports]. Seoul: Hyumŏnisŭt'ŭ, 2019.

———. "Politics and the Discourse of 'Virtuous Sacrifice' in the Late Chosŏn: Chŏng Yagyong's Discussion of 'Righteous Killing.'" In Charles R. Kim et al., *Beyond Death*, 45–70.

Kim Hyŏnjin. "*Simnirok* ŭl t'onghae pon 18-segi yŏsŏng ŭi chasal silt'ae wa kŭ sahoejŏk hamŭi" [Female suicide in the eighteenth century and its social implications reflected in the *Records of Royal Reviews*]. *Chosŏn sidaesa hakpo* 52 (2010): 197–230.

Kim, Jisoo M. *The Emotions of Justice: Gender, Status, and Legal Performance in Chosŏn Korea*. Seattle: University of Washington Press, 2015.

———. "From Jealousy to Violence: Marriage, Family, and Confucian Patriarchy in Fifteenth-Century Korea," *Acta Koreana* 20, no. 1 (2017): 91–100.

Kim, Jungwon. "Between Morality and Crime: Filial Daughters and Vengeful Violence in Eighteenth Century Korea." *Acta Koreana* 21, no. 2 (2018): 481–502.

———. "Daughters' Letters of Farewell to Their Fathers." In Haboush, *Epistolary Korea*, 382–90.

———. "Deeper than the Death: Chaste Suicide, Emotions, and the Politics of Honour in Nineteenth-Century Korea." In *Honour, Violence, and Emotions in History*, edited by Carolyn Strange, Christopher Forth, and Robert Cribb, 163–82. London: Bloomsbury, 2014.

———. "Finding Korean Women's Voices in Legal Archives." *Journal of Women's History* 22, no. 2 (2010): 149–52.

———. "Inscribing Grievances: Litigation and Local Community in Eighteenth-Century Korea." *Journal of Asian Studies* 81, no. 2 (2022): 289–303.

———. "Madam Yi's Farewell Letter to Her Son." In Haboush, *Epistolary Korea*, 375–81.

———. "Pungmi esŏ ŭi Chosŏn yŏsŏngsa yŏn'gu tonghyang" (Historical studies on Chosŏn women in North America). *Yŏksa wa hyŏnsil* 91 (2014): 339–56.

———. "Yŏl (烈): Chaste Martyrdom and Literati Writing in Late Chosŏn Korea (1392–1910)." In Charles R. Kim et al., *Beyond Death*, 25–44. Seattle: University of Washington Press, 2019.

———. "'You Must Avenge on My Behalf': Widows and Honour in Nineteenth-Century Korea." *Gender and History* 26, no. 1 (2014): 128–46.

Kim Kiran. "Kŭndae kyemonggi maech'e ŭi k'odŭhwa kwajŏng ŭl t'onghan yŏsŏng insik ŭi kaeyŏnhwa kwajŏng koch'al" [A study on the process of probabilistic understanding of women through the process of coding in a medium in the 1900s]. *Yŏsŏng munhak yŏn'gu* 26 (2011): 7–39.

Kim Kyŏngmi. "Kaehwagi yŏllyŏjŏn yŏn'gu" [Study of chaste women's biographies during the Enlightenment era]. *Kuggŏ kungmunhak* 132 (2002): 187–211.

Kim Kyŏngnan. "Tansŏng hojŏk e nat'anan yŏsŏng hoju ŭi kijaesilt'ae wa sŏnggyŏk" [The practice and nature of recording female household heads in the Tansŏng household register]. *Yŏksa wa hyŏnsil* 41 (2001): 94–119.

Kim Kyŏngsuk. "Chosŏn hugi kyŏlsongiban kwa yŏsŏng sosong ŭi chuch'e" [Certificates of adjudications and women's legal subjectivity in the late Chosŏn]. *Hanguk saron* 64 (2018): 325–57.

———. "Chosŏn hugi sansong kwa sangŏn kyŏkchaeng yŏn'gu: No Sangch'u ka wa Pak Ch'unno ka ŭi sosong ŭl chungsim ŭro" [A study of gravesite litigation and the practice of written and oral petitions in the late Chosŏn: The lawsuit case of the No Sangch'u and Pak Ch'unno families]. *Komunsŏ yŏn'gu* 33 (2008): 253–80.

———. "Chosŏn hugi yŏsŏng ŭi chŏngso hwaltong" [Women's petitioning activity in the late Chosŏn]. *Han'guk munhwa* 36 (2005): 89–123.

Kim Ponggyun. *Yech'ŏn ŭi hyoyŏl* [Filality and chastity of Yech'ŏn]. Yech'ŏn: Yech'ŏn Munhwawŏn, 2016.

Kim Sŏnggap, ed. *Sosong kwa punjaeng ŭro ponŭn Chosŏn sahoe* [Chosŏn society seen from lawsuits and disputes]. Sŏngnam: Han'gukhak Chung-gang Yŏn'guwŏn, 2017.

Kim Sŏn'gyŏng. "Chosŏn hugi yŏsŏng ŭi sŏng, kamsi wa ch'ŏbŏl" [Women's sexuality in the late Chosŏn, surveillance and punishment]. *Yŏksa yŏn'gu* 8 (2000): 57–100.

Kim, Sun Joo. "Culture of Remembrance in Late Chosŏn Korea: Bringing an Unknown War Hero Back into History." *Journal of Social History* 44, no. 2 (2010): 563–85.

———. *Marginality and Subversion in Korea: The Hong Kyŏngnae Rebellion of 1812.* Seattle: University of Washington Press, 2007.

———. "Taxes, the Local Elite, and the Rural Populace in the Chinju Uprising of 1862." *Journal of Asian Studies* 64, no. 4 (2007): 993–1027.

———. *Voice from the North: Resurrecting Regional Identity through the Life and Work of Yi Shihang (1672–1736).* Stanford, CA: Stanford University Press, 2013.

Kim, Sun Joo, and Jungwon Kim, trans. and eds. *Wrongful Deaths: Selected Inquest Records from Nineteenth-Century Korea.* Seattle: University of Washington Press, 2014.

Kim Tuhŏn. *Han'guk kajok chedo yŏn'gu* [A study of Korean family structure]. Seoul: Sŏul Taehakkyo Ch'ulp'anbu, 1969.

Kim, Youngmin, and Michael J. Pettid, eds. *Women and Confucianism in Chosŏn Korea.* Albany: State University of New York Press, 2011.

Kim Yunsŏp. "Koryŏ malgi yuga sadaebu chisigindŭl ŭi pulgyojŏk naemyŏn ŭisik e kwanhan yŏn'gu" [A study on the Buddhist inner consciousness of the Confucian intellectuals of the Koryŏ period]. *Han'guk ŏmunhak kukche haksul p'orŏm* 38 (2017): 181–212.

Kim-Renaud, Young-Key, ed. *Creative Women of Korea: The Fifteenth through the Twentieth Centuries.* Armonk, NY: M. E. Sharpe, 2004.

————, ed. *The Korean Alphabet: Its History and Structure*. Honolulu: University of Hawai'i Press, 1997.

Kinney, Anne Behnke, trans. *Exemplary Women of Early China: The "Lienü zhuan" of Liu Xiang*. New York: Columbia University Press, 2014.

Ko, Dorothy. *Teachers of the Inner Chambers: Women and Culture in Seventeenth-Century China*. Stanford, CA: Stanford University Press, 1994.

Ko, Dorothy, JaHyun Kim Haboush, and Joan R. Piggott, eds. *Women and Confucian Cultures in Premodern China, Korea, and Japan*. Berkeley: University of California Press, 2003.

Ko Yŏnhŭi. "Chosŏn sidae yŏllyŏdo koch'al" [Examination of chaste women illustrations of the Chosŏn]. *Han'guk kojŏn yŏsŏng munhak yŏn'gu* 2 (2001): 189–225.

Kwŏn Sunhyŏng. "Koryŏ mal yŏllyŏ sarye yŏn'gu: Yang Susaeng ch'ŏ yŏlbu Yissi" [A case study of late Koryŏ chaste women: On Madam Yi, the faithful wife of Yang Susaeng]. *Yŏsŏng kwa yŏksa* 22 (2015): 29–62.

————. "Koryŏ sidae chŏlbu e taehan koch'al" [A study of faithful wives in the Koryŏ dynasty]. *Yŏsŏng kwa yŏksa* 27 (2017): 167–91.

————. "Koryŏ sidae ŭi sujŏl ŭisik kwa yŏllyŏ" [The idea of fidelity and chaste women in Koryŏ]. In *Yŏsŏng, yŏksa wa hyŏnjae* [Women, history and present], edited by Pak Yongok, 53–92. Seoul: Kukhak Charyowŏn, 2001.

————. *Koryŏ ŭi honinje wa yŏsŏng ŭi sam* [The marriage system and women's lives in the Koryŏ dynasty]. Seoul: Haean, 2006.

Kwŏn Yŏnung. "*Simnirok* ŭi kich'ojŏk kŏmt'o: Chŏngjo tae ŭi sajoe p'an'gyŏl" [Basic studies of the *Records of Royal Reviews*: Judgment for capital crimes in Chŏngjo's reign]. In *Yi Kibaek sŏnsaeng kohŭi kinyŏm Han'guk sahak nonch'ong* [Collection of writings on Korean history in commemoration of Professor Yi Kibaek's seventieth birthday], vol. 2, edited by *Han'guk sahak* Noch'ong Kanhaeng Wiwŏnhoe, 1320–38. Seoul: Ilchogak, 1994.

Lee Hai-soon. *See under* Yi Hyesun.

Lee, Ji-Eun. *Women Pre-scripted: Forging Modern Roles through Korean Print*. Honolulu: University of Hawai'i Press, 2015.

Lee Sook-in. *See under* Yi Sukin.

Legge, James, trans. *Li Chi, Book of Rites*. New Hyde Park, NY: University Books, 1967.

Leung, Angela K. "To Chasten Society: The Development of Widow Homes." *Late Imperial China* 14, no. 2 (1993): 1–32.

Lim, Sungyun. *Rules of the House: Family Law and Domestic Disputes in Colonial Korea*. Oakland: University of California Press, 2019.

Lo, Yuet Keung. "Conversion to Chastity: A Buddhist Catalyst in Early Imperial China." *Nan Nü* 10 (2008): 22–56.

Lu, Weijing. "Faithful Maiden Biographies: A Forum for Ritual Debate, Moral Critique, and Personal Reflection." In *Beyond Exemplar Tales: Women's Biography in Chinese History*, edited by Joan Judge and Hu Ying, 88–103. Berkeley: University of California Press, 2011.

———. *True to Her Word: The Faithful Maiden Cult in Late Imperial China.* Stanford, CA: Stanford University Press, 2008.

Mann, Susan. *Precious Records: Women in China's Long Eighteenth Century.* Stanford, CA: Stanford University Press, 1997.

———. "Widows in the Kinship, Class, and Community Structure of Qing Dynasty China." *Journal of Asian Studies* 46, no. 1 (1987): 37–56.

Mattielli, Sandra, ed. *Virtues in Conflict: Tradition and Korean Women Today.* Seoul: Royal Asiatic Society, Korea Branch, 1977.

McBride, Richard D. "Is the *Samguk yusa* Reliable? Case Studies from Chinese and Korean Sources." *Journal of Korean Studies* 11, no. 1 (2006): 163–89.

———. "Preserving the Lore of Korean Antiquity: An Introduction to Native and Local Sources in Iryŏn's *Samguk yusa*." *Acta Koreana* 10, no. 2 (2007): 1–38.

McGuire, Kelley. *Dying to Be English: Suicide Narrative and National Identity, 1721–1814.* London: Pickering and Chatto, 2012.

Meyer-Fong, Tobie. *What Remains: Coming to Terms with Civil War in 19th Century China.* Stanford, CA: Stanford University Press, 2013.

Minois, Georges. *History of Suicide: Voluntary Death in Western Culture.* Translated by Lydia G. Cochrane. Baltimore: The Johns Hopkins University Press, 1999.

Molony, Barbara, Janet Theiss, and Hyaeweol Choi, eds. *Gender in Modern East Asia: An Integrated History.* Boulder, CO: Westview Press, 2016.

Morioka Yasu. "Shokukan hiryo fujin no rii mondai ni tsuite" [On divorce action from brought-back women]. *Chōsen gakuhō* 26 (1963): 56–93.

Mun Hyŏngjin. "Taemyŏngnyul kwa Kyŏngguk taejŏn p'yŏnch'an ŭi pŏpchesajŏk ŭiŭi" [The *Great Ming Code* and compilation of the *Great Code of Administration*: Its significance in legal history]. *Chungguk yŏn'gu* 34 (2004): 199–213.

Ng, Vivien W. "Ideology and Sexuality: Rape Laws in Qing China." *Journal of Asian Studies* 46, no. 1 (1987): 57–70.

No Kwanbŏm, "Kŭndae ch'ogi sirhak ŭi chonjaeron" [Ontology of Korean *sirhak* in the early twentieth century]. *Yŏksa pip'yŏng* 122 (2018): 447–73.

O Hwanil. "Chosŏn sidae chaega kŭmjipŏp yŏn'gu" [A study of the law prohibiting remarriage during the Chosŏn dynasty]. *Han'guk yŏsŏng kyoyang
hakhoeji* 1, no. 1 (1994): 121–44.

Oh, Young Kyun. *Engraving Virtue: The Printing History of a Premodern
Korean Moral Primer* Leiden: Brill, 2013.

Pae Usŏng. *Chosŏn hugi kukt'ogwan kwa ch'ŏnhagwan ŭi pyŏnhwa*
[Changes in views on Chosŏn and the world in the late Chosŏn]. Seoul:
Ilchisa, 1998.

Paek Minjŏng. "Hŭmhŭm sinsŏ ŭi yŏsŏng kwallyŏn pŏmjoe punsŏk ŭl t'ong-
hae pon Chŏng Yagyong ŭi yŏsŏng insik kwa sidaejŏk ŭimi" [Chŏng
Yagyong's view of women in his analyses of crimes involving women in
Hŭmhŭm sinsŏ]. *Tongbang hakchi* 173 (2016): 161–200.

Paek Okkyŏng. "Chosŏn sidae ŭi yŏsŏng p'ongnyŏk kwa pŏp" [The violence
against women and law in the Chosŏn period]. *Han'guk kojŏn yŏsŏng
munhak yŏn'gu* 19 (2009): 93–126.

Pak Chu. *Chosŏn sidae ŭi chŏngp'yo chŏngch'aek* [The state-reward system
during the Chosŏn dynasty]. Seoul: Ilchogak, 1990.

———. *Chosŏn sidae ŭi hyo wa yŏsŏng* [Filial piety and women during the
Chosŏn dynasty]. Seoul: Han'guk Charyowŏn, 2000.

———. *Chosŏn sidae ŭi yŏsŏng kwa yugyo munhwa* [Women and Confucian
culture during the Chosŏn dynasty]. Seoul: Kukhak Charyowŏn, 2008.

Pak Chunho. "Chosŏn hugi p'yŏngmin yŏsŏng ŭi han'gŭl soji kŭlssŭgi" [A
commoner woman's writing a petition in Korean script in late Chosŏn].
Kukhak yŏn'gu 36: 427–28.

Pak Noja/Vladimir Tikhonov. "Ŭigi Non'gae chŏnsŭng: Chŏnjaeng, todŏk,
yŏsŏng" [The Hideyoshi invasion and the "Righteous Kisaeng" legends:
War, morals, women]. *Yŏlsang kojŏn yŏn'gu* 25 (2007): 229–54.

Pak Sohyŏn. "Chosŏn hugi sŏngbŏmjoe ŭi kyuje wa ch'ŏbŏl: Taemyŏngnyul
pŏmganp'yŏn kwa Hŭmhŭm sinsŏ rŭl chungsim ŭro" [Sexual crimes and
punishments in the late Chosŏn: On the *Great Ming Code* and the *Hŭmhŭm sinsŏ*]. *Inmun kwahak* 89 (2023): 185–225.

Pak Ŭngyŏng. "Koryŏ sidae chaega e taehan kŏmt'o: Yugyo sasang kwaŭi
kwallyŏn ŭl chungsim ŭro" [A review of remarriage in the Koryŏ period:
On the basis of relations with Confucianism]. *Yŏsŏng kwa yŏksa* 26
(2017): 111–39.

Palais, James B. *Confucian Statecraft and Korean Institutions: Yu
Hyŏngwŏn and the Late Chosŏn Dynasty.* Seattle: University of Washington Press, 1996.

Park, Saeyoung. "The Expansion of Ideal Subjecthood in Chosŏn Korea:
Remembering the Monk Yujŏng." *Korean Studies* 39, no. 1 (2015): 45–74.

Peirce, Leslie. *Morality Tales: Law and Gender in the Ottoman Court of Aintab*. Berkeley: University of California Press, 2003.

Peterson, Mark. *Korean Adoption and Inheritance: Case Studies in the Creation of a Classic Confucian Society*. Ithaca, NY: Cornell University East Asian Series, 1996.

Pettid, Michael J. "Fashioning Womanly Confucian Virtue." In *The East Asian War, 1592–1598: International Relations, Violence, and Memory*, edited by James B. Lewis, 357–77. New York: Routledge, 2015.

Prusek, Jaroslav. "History and Epics in China and in the West." In *Chinese History and Literature, Collection of Studies*, edited by Jaroslav Prusek, 17–34. Dordrecht, Holland: D. Reidel, 1970.

Raphals, Lisa. *Sharing the Light: Representations of Women and Virtue in Early China*. Albany: State University of New York Press, 1998.

Ropp, Paul S. "Passionate Women: Female Suicide in Late Imperial China—Introduction." In *Passionate Women: Female Suicide in Late Imperial China*, edited by Paul S. Ropp, Paola Zamperini, and Harriet T. Zurndorfer, 3–21. Leiden: Brill, 2001.

Ropp, Paul S., Paola Zamperini, and Harriet T. Zurndorfer, eds. *Passionate Women: Female Suicide in Late Imperial China*. Leiden: Brill, 2001.

Sakai Tadao. "Yi Yulgok and the Community Compact." In *The Rise of Neo-Confucianism in Korea*, edited by William Theodore de Bary and JaHyun Kim Haboush, 323–48. New York: Columbia University Press, 1985.

Scott, Joan W. *Gender and Politics of History*. New York: Columbia University Press, 1988.

Shaw, William. *Legal Norms in a Confucian State*. Berkeley: University of California Press, 1981.

———. "Traditional Korean Law and Its Relation to China." In *Essays in China's Legal Tradition*, edited by Jerome A. Cohen et al., 302–26. Princeton, NJ: Princeton University Press, 1980.

Sim Chaeu. *Chosŏn hugi kukka kwŏllyŏk kwa pŏmjoe t'ongje: Simnirok yŏn'gu* [State authority and crime management in the late Chosŏn from examination of the *Records of Royal Reviews*]. Seoul: T'aehaksa, 2009.

———. "Chosŏn malgi hyŏngsapŏp ch'egye wa Taemyŏngnyul ŭi wisang" [The structure of the penal code and the *Great Ming Code* in the last years of Chosŏn]. *Yŏksa wa hyŏnsil* 65 (2007): 121–53.

———. "Chosŏn sidae pŏpchŏn p'yŏnch'an kwa hyŏngsa chŏngch'aek ŭi pyŏnhwa" [The codification of laws and transformation of criminal policy during the Chosŏn dynasty]. *Chindan hakpo* 96 (2003): 254–56.

———, ed. *Kŏman kwa kŭndae hanguk sahoe* [Inquest documents and early modern Korean society]. Sŏngnam: Han'gukhak Chungang Yŏn'guwŏn Ch'ulp'anbu, 2018.

———. "*Simnirok* ŭl t'onghae pon 18-segi huban sŏul ŭi pŏmjoe yangsang [The state of crime in late eighteenth-century Seoul from the *Records of Royal Reviews*]. *Sŏulhak yŏn'gu* 17 (2001): 58–94.

Sin Sugyŏng. "Yŏllyŏjŏn kwa yŏllyŏdo ŭi imiji yŏn'gu" [Study of images from chaste-woman biographies and illustrations]. *Misulsa nondan* 12 (2005): 171–200.

Sŏ Sinhye, trans. *Yŏllyŏ Hyangnang ŭl marhada* [On the chaste woman Hyangnang]. Seoul: Pogosa, 2004.

Sommer, Matthew. *Polyandry and Wife-Selling in Qing Dynasty China: Survival Strategies and Judicial Interventions.* Berkeley: University of California Press, 2015.

———. *Sex, Law, and Society in Late Imperial China.* Stanford, CA: Stanford University Press, 2000.

———. "The Uses of Chastity: Sex, Law, and the Property of Widows in Qing China." *Late Imperial China* 17, no. 2 (1996): 77–130.

Song Pyŏngu. "Chosŏn sidae kaein ŭi chasal, sahoejŏk t'asal" [Individual suicide and social homicide during the Chosŏn dynasty]. *Tongyang hanmunhak yŏn'gu* 40 (2015): 115–39.

Sŏul Yŏksa Pangmulgwan, ed. *Chosŏn yŏin ŭi sam kwa munhwa* [Life and culture of Chosŏn women]. Seoul: Sŏul Yŏksa Pangmulgwan 2002.

Spiegel, Gabrielle. *Romancing the Past: The Rise of Vernacular Prose Historiography in Thirteenth-Century France.* Berkeley: University of California Press, 1993.

Stanley, Amy. "Adultery, Punishment, and Reconciliation in Tokugawa Japan." *Journal of Japanese Studies* 33, no. 2 (2007): 309–35.

Tao, Chia-Lin Pao. "Chaste Widows and Institutions to Support Them in Late-Ch'ing China." *Asia Major* 46 (1991): 101–19.

Theiss, Janet M. *Disgraceful Matters: The Politics of Chastity in Eighteenth-Century China.* Berkeley: University of California Press, 2004.

T'ien, Ju-K'ang. *Male Anxiety and Female Chastity: A Comparative Study of Chinese Ethical Values in Ming-Ch'ing Times.* Leiden: Brill, 1988.

Vermeersch, Sem. *A Chinese Traveler in Medieval Korea: Xu Jing's Illustrated Account of the Xuanhe Embassy to Koryŏ.* Honolulu: University of Hawai'i Press, 2016.

———. *The Power of the Buddhas: The Politics of Buddhism during the Koryŏ Dynasty (918–1392)*. Cambridge, MA: Harvard University Press, 2008.

Wagner, Edward. "The Civil Examination Process as Social Leaven: The Case of the Northern Provinces in the Yi Dynasty." *Korea Journal* 17, no. 1 (1977): 22–27.

Walker, Garthine. "Rereading Rape and Sexual Violence in Early Modern England." *Gender and History* 10, no. 1 (1998): 1–25.

———. "Sexual Violence and Rape in Europe, 1500–1750." In *The Routledge History of Sex and the Body, 1500 to the Present*, edited by Sarah Toulalan and Kate Fisher, 429–43. London: Routledge, 2013.

Walkowitz, Judith R. *City of Dreadful Delight: Narratives of Sexual Danger in Late-Victorian London*. Chicago: University of Chicago Press, 1992.

Wang, Hwa Yeong. "Against the Ban on Women's Remarriage: Gendering ui 義 in Song Siyeol's Philosophy." *Asian Philosophy* 30, no. 3 (2020): 242–57.

———. "Chastity as a Virtue." *Religions* 11, no. 5 (2020): 259 (13 pages).

Wang, Sixiang. "Filial Daughter of Kwaksan: Finger Severing, Confucian Virtues, and Envoy Poetry in Early Chosŏn." *Seoul Journal of Korean Studies* 25, no. 2 (2012): 175–212.

Wu, Yulian. "Let People See and Be Moved: Stone Arches and the Chastity Cult in Huizhou during the High Qing Era." *Nan Nü* 17 (2015): 111–63.

Yi Chongil, ed. *Taejŏn hoet'ong yŏn'gu* [A study of the *Comprehensive Collection of Dynastic Code*], vol. 4. Han'guk Pŏpche Yŏn'guwŏn, 1996.

Yi Chŏngnan. "Koryŏ sidae honin hyŏngt'ae e taehan chaegŏmt'o" [Reexamination of the marriage patterns of the Koryŏ]. *Sach'ong* 57 (2003): 5–26.

Yi Hongsik. "Chosŏn hugi sadaebu yŏsŏng ŭi yusŏ ch'angjak yangsang yŏn'gu" [A study of *yangban* women's writing wills in the late Chosŏn]. *Hanguk kojŏn yŏsŏng munhak yŏn'gu* 29 (2014): 100–101.

———. "Chosŏn sidae sadaebu namsŏng yusŏ ŭi sahoe munhwa chŏk kinŭng kwa ŭimi t'amseak" [On the sociocultural function and meaning of male literati's wills during the Chosŏn era]. *Hanmunhak nonjip* 47 (2017): 213–36.

Yi Hŭihwan. "Chosŏn malgi ŭi chŏngnyŏ wa kamun sungsang ŭi p'ungjo" [Trends of erecting memorial gates and lineage worship in the last years of the Chosŏn dynasty]. *Chosŏn sidae hakpo* 17 (2001): 141–70.

Yi Hyesun. "Chosŏnjo yŏllyŏjŏn yŏn'gu" [A study of biographies of chaste women in the Chosŏn dynasty]. *Sŏnggok nonch'ong* 30, no. 1 (1999): 95–152.

———. *Koryŏ chŏn'gi hanmunhaksa* [Literary history of the early Koryŏ]. Seoul: Ihwa Yŏja Taehakkyo Ch'ulp'an Munhwawŏn, 2004.

——— (Lee Hai-soon). "Representation of Females in Twelfth-Century Korean Historiography." In Ko, Kim, and Piggott, *Women and Confucian Cultures*, 75–96.

———. "Yŏllyŏsang ŭi chŏnt'ong kwa pyŏnmo: *Samgang haengsilto* esŏ Chosŏn hugi yŏllyŏjŏn kkaji" [Tradition and transformation in the images of chaste women: From *Samgang haengsilto* to late Chosŏn women's biographies]. *Chindan hakpo* 85 (1998): 163–83.

Yi Hyŏngu. "*Samguk sagi* yŏlchŏn ŭl t'onghae pon Silla ŭi yŏsŏng" [Women of Silla examined through the "Biographies" section of the *Historical Records of the Three Kingdoms*]. *Silla munhwaje haksul nonmunjip* 25, no. 2 (2004): 97–127.

Yi In'gyŏng. *Yŏllyŏ sŏrhwa ŭi chaehaesŏk* [Reinterpretation of chaste-woman stories]. Seoul: Wŏrin, 2006.

Yi Sangbaek. "Chaega kŭmji sŭpsok ŭi yurae e taehan yŏn'gu" [A study of the origin of the custom of prohibiting remarriage]. *Chosŏn munhwasa yŏn'gu ko*. Seoul: Ŭryu Munhwasa, 1948.

Yi Sugin. *Chŏngjŏl ŭi yŏksa* [History of chastity]. Seoul: P'urŭn Yŏksa, 2012.

——— (Lee Sook-in). "The Imjin War and the Official Discourse of Chastity." *Seoul Journal of Korean Studies* 22, no. 2 (2009): 137–56.

———. "Somun kwa kwŏllyŏk: 16-segi han sajok puin ŭi ŭmhaeng somun chaegusŏng" [Rumor and power: Restructuring rumors of a *yangban* woman's licentious behavior in the sixteenth century]. *Ch'ŏlhak sasang* 40 (2011): 67–107.

Yoo Mirim. "King Sejong's Leadership and the Politics of Inventing the Korean Alphabet." *Review of Korean Studies* 9, no. 3 (2006): 7–38.

Yoo, Theodore Jun. *The Politics of Gender in Colonial Korea*. Berkeley: University of California Press, 2008.

Yu, Jimmy. *Sanctity and Self-Inflicted Violence in Chinese Religions, 1500–1700*. New York: Oxford University Press, 2012.

Yun Pyŏngyong. "Namwŏn Yunssi ŭi yusŏ wa 'myŏngdo chat'ansa' yŏn'gu" [Study of Madam Yun of Namwŏn's testaments and "myŏngdo chat'ansa"]. *Hanguk kojŏn yŏsŏng munhak yŏn'gu* 40 (2020): 201–39.

Index

Harvard East Asian Monographs
(most recent titles)